BUTTERFLIES
THROUGH
BINOCULARS

THE WEST

Glassberg Field Guide Series
edited by Jeffrey Glassberg

*Butterflies through Binoculars: A Field and Finding Guide to
Butterflies of the Boston-New York-Washington Region*
by Jeffrey Glassberg

*Butterflies through Binoculars: A Field Guide to Butterflies
of Eastern North America*
by Jeffrey Glassberg

*Butterflies through Binoculars: A Field, Finding, and
Gardening Guide to Butterflies of Florida*
by Jeffrey Glassberg, Marc C. Minno, and John V. Calhoun

*Dragonflies through Binoculars: A Field Guide to Dragonflies
of North America*
by Sidney W. Dunkle

*Butterflies through Binoculars: A Field Guide to Butterflies of
Western North America*
by Jeffrey Glassberg

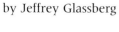

BUTTERFLIES
THROUGH
BINOCULARS

THE WEST

A FIELD GUIDE TO
THE BUTTERFLIES OF
WESTERN NORTH AMERICA

Jeffrey Glassberg

OXFORD
UNIVERSITY PRESS
2001

OXFORD
UNIVERSITY PRESS

Oxford   New York
Athens   Auckland   Bangkok   Bogotá   Buenos Aires
Calcutta   Cape Town   Chennai   Dar es Salaam   Delhi
Florence   Hong Kong   Istanbul   Karachi   Kuala Lumpur
Madrid   Melbourne   Mexico City   Mumbai   Nairobi   Paris
São Paulo   Singapore   Taipei   Tokyo   Toronto   Warsaw

and associated companies in
Berlin   Ibadan

Copyright © 2001 by Jeffrey Glassberg

Published by Oxford University Press, Inc.
198 Madison Avenue, New York, New York 10016

Oxford is a registered trademark of Oxford University Press

Library of Congress Cataloging-in-Publication Data
Glassberg, Jeffrey.
Butterflies through binoculars : the West :
a field guide to the butterflies of western
North America / by Jeffrey Glassberg.
p. cm. — (Field guide series)
ISBN-13: 978-0-19-510669-5
ISBN 0–19–510669–5 (pbk.)
1. Butterflies—West (U.S.)—Identification.
2. Butterfly watching—West (U.S.)
I. Title.   II. Series : Butterflies [and others]
through binoculars field guide series
QL551.W3 G63   2001   595.78'9'0978—dc21   00–055059

9 8 7 6 5 4 3 2

Printed in China
on acid-free paper

Contents

Acknowledgments

THIS BOOK COMPLETES THE MASSIVE PROJECT I BEGAN TEN YEARS AGO, to develop a series of field guides that would, for the first time, allow people to identify most individual butterflies they see in the field. Obtaining the photographs needed for these guides required a tremendous amount of time in the field. The effort and dedication needed to undertake and follow through with this project would not have been possible without the support and belief in me, and in the value of this work, of my wife, Jane Vicroy Scott. I can only hope that Jane's love, support, and personal sacrifice are repaid by this book's leading to an increase in butterfly appreciation and conservation that makes our future world just a little better, and more colorful, than it would have been otherwise.

Without the help of my son, Matt Scott, this book would probably have never been completed. In addition to setting up computer hardware and installing software, he patiently taught me how to use the software required to do the plate layouts and create the maps.

Although many other people have contributed directly to the creation of this guide, two individuals have made especially extensive and critical contributions. Jim Brock and Andy Warren provided help in almost all areas needed to produce this book. Jim's special interest is caterpillars and their foodplants. (For quite a few southeastern Arizona species, their caterpillar foodplant is published here for the first time, based upon as yet unpublished information discovered by Jim Brock. He will expand upon this in a forthcoming caterpillar field guide.) Andy's focus is the systematics of neotropical skippers. In addition to their specialties, both Jim and Andy are exceptionally knowledgeable about almost all aspects of western butterflies. A deep bow of respect and my continuing gratitude to you both.

The following individuals kindly provided information about butterflies and localities so that I could obtain photographs for this book: Norbert

Kondla for Alberta; Richard Bailowitz, Jim Brock, and Harry Zirlin for Arizona; Ray Coyle, Wanda Dameron, Greg de Nevers, John Emmel, Ken Hansen, Fred Heath, Bob Langston, Jack Levy, Rudy Mattoni, Jim Mori, Dave Powell, Ralph Wells, and Harry Zirlin for California; Paul Opler and Andy Warren for Colorado; Steve Kohler for Montana; Steve Cary for New Mexico; George Austin for Nevada; H. A. Freeman and Ro Wauer for Texas; Todd Stout for Utah; Bob Pyle for Washington; Ernest Williams and Andy Warren for Wyoming.

John Acorn accompanied me to windswept Plateau Mountain in Alberta, where we chased green-tinted Labrador Sulphurs over eerily beautiful high tundra, but, alas, Alberta or Astarte Fritillaries we did not see; a film crew from an Oklahoma TV station trailed Jim Brock and me down California Gulch in Arizona on a successful quest for Cestus Skipper, nabbing excellent video footage of this rare species; Aaron Ellingson and I watched hundreds of Purplish Fritillaries glisten in the sun as they spread their dew-covered wings to dry and awaken, high above treeline on Mount Uncompahgre in the San Juan Mountains of southern Colorado; Eric Finkelstein and David Larson of the Amistad National Recreation area in Del Rio, Texas joined us for an exciting hunt among the lecheguilla for Mary's Giant-Skipper—Coahuila Giant-Skipper still beckons; Fred Heath proved an excellent shepherd, as he herded Jane and me through Sentenac Canyon, showing us our first 'Dammers' Dotted Blue and California Giant-Skippers on our first visit to Anza-Borrego State Park in California; docent Jim Mori at Big Trees State Park in California wowed us with the attractive pull of pussypaws; I was led on a brisk five-mile walk up to 13,000 feet on Red Cloud Mountain—no mean feat for a fifty-year-old flatlander from New Jersey—by the irrepressible Amy Seidl, who has been studying the federally endangered 'Uncompahgre' Dingy Fritillaries that live there; meeting at Rabbit Ears Pass in northwestern Colorado, Andy Warren and I had a fritillary fest, photographing most of the ten species found there. Thank you all for your willingness to help. I hope that all of you had as much fun as I did on those field trips and that you approve of the results.

Others whose help is greatly appreciated include: Bruce Blanthorn, who provided horses and expert trail knowledge in the Wind River Mountains of Wyoming and whose indefatigable border collie, Misty, was one of the most amazing dogs I've ever seen; my exploration of Mesa Verde

National Park was greatly facilitated by Marilyn Colyer of the U.S. Parks Service who was instrumental in my obtaining a permit on very, very short notice; our visit to Plateau Mountain was made possible by Dave Heatherington and the Alberta Land and Forest Service, who provided us with permits and keys; special thanks to Officer Dave Lankford of the Wyoming State Police for stopping my wife and me for speeding just outside of Pinedale, Wyoming. The spot where he pulled us over was alive with Ruddy Coppers and Sonoran Skippers, and photos 3 and 4 on page 81, and photo 5 and the inset to photo 4 on page 265 resulted. Officer Lankford did seem slightly mystified by my apparent greater interest in the grassy area across the road (I kept wandering over there) than in the speeding issue at hand; a very large and warm thank-you to Pilar and Andres Sada of Monterrey, Mexico, for their gracious hospitality and friendship, on multiple occasions allowing me to stay at Rancho Picachos, where a number of the photographs that appear in this guide were taken. Thanks also to Kirk Jensen and Helen Mules of Oxford University Press for their careful help in producing the previous books in this series.

In preparing this work, there were many occasions when I examined museum specimens for identification features and for geographical and temporal distributions. I thank Jim Miller, Eric Quinter, and Cal Snyder at the American Museum of Natural History, New York, and John Burns and Bob Robbins at the United States National Museum, Smithsonian Institution, Washington, D.C., for allowing me to examine specimens under their care. Paul Hammond of Oregon State University and Don Harvey and Bob Robbins at the Smithsonian Institution helped me pursue the systematic position of the White Mountains populations of Atlantis Fritillary by dissecting specimens—and determining that they did indeed belong to the Atlantis group despite having different eye color.

A critical feature of this book is the photographs. Although I have traveled extensively in the West for years, searching for and photographing butterflies, still, in the end, there were some 54 of the 1,136 photographs needed for this book that I did not have. The following individuals generously provided their own photographs to fill the gaps (see Photo Dates, Localities and Credits section for credits for specific photographs): Dave Ahrenholz, Ahmet Baytas, Rob Boender, Jim Brock, Priscilla Brodkin, Steve Cary, Rick Cech, John Emmel, Chris Guppy, John Hafernik, Steve Kohler, Jack Levy, Bill Mull, S. Mark Nelson, Phil Nordin, Dave Nunnallee, Paul Opler, Steve Prchal, Ed Ross, Jane Ruffin, Jeff Slotten, Bob Stewart, and Ann Swengel.

An important feature of this guide are the range maps. After constructing a preliminary set of maps, using all published and much unpublished information, I sent these maps to active field workers throughout the West for review. The following reviewers, arranged by state or province of residence, greatly increased the accuracy of the maps. Many of the reviewers were knowledgeable about whole regions. I am indebted to them for taking the considerable time required to closely inspect the almost 500 maps and suggest detailed changes, based upon their firsthand knowledge (individuals in the states of North Dakota, South Dakota, Nebraska, and Kansas are included because of their review of the range maps during the preparation of *BTB: The East*): **Alberta**, Norbert Kondla; **Arizona**, Richard Bailowitz, Jim Brock; **British Columbia**, Jon Shepard; **California**, John Emmel, Ken Hansen, Jack Levy, Jim Mori, Art Shapiro; **Colorado**, Ray Stanford, Andy Warren; **Idaho**, George Stephens; **Kansas**, Marvin Schwilling; **Nebraska**, Neil Dankert, Jim Reiser, Steve Spomer; **New Mexico**, Steve Cary, Richard Holland; **Nevada**, George Austin; **North Dakota**, Ronald Royer; **Oklahoma**, Pat Bergey, John Nelson; **Oregon**, Susan Anderson, Paul Hammond; **South Dakota**, Gary Marrone; **Texas**, Charles Bordelon, Chuck Sexton, Ro Wauer; **Utah**, John Richards, Steve Sommerfeld, Todd Stout.

In addition, most of these correspondents provided information about nectar sources in their areas that was used to compile the list of important nectar sources that appears on page 8.

George Austin and Andy Warren kindly provided supplementary information about the identification of greater fritillaries that should increase your chance of successful identification.

A draft of this manuscript was reviewed by Jim Brock, Jim Mori, Jane V. Scott, and Andy Warren, each of whom made many corrections and provided many suggestions that greatly improved the final product. The time, effort, and knowledge that they brought to this project are greatly appreciated.

Lastly, I would like to thank you, the reader, for using this book, a step that links you to the growing butterflying community. Join with us on an exciting lifetime adventure that is earth-friendly and good for you— butterflying is fat-free and yet still full of flavor!

INTRODUCTION

WARNING: THIS BOOK IS AN EXPRESS VEHICLE TO BUTTERFLYING HEAVEN. If this destination is not in your plans for this lifetime, you may want to turn back now, before it is too late!

Why take up butterflying? Well, perhaps because of the benefits to your health and beauty—and that of the planet's. Butterflying will increase the time you spend in beautiful mountain meadows filled with flowers and encourage you to hike in breathtaking desert canyons in the springtime, following floating patches of turquoise-blue confections as they drift across the flowered landscape. You'll look down to see a metalmark, glinting in the sun, only to find an iridescent tiger beetle at your feet. You'll look up as the nectaring black and white Pine White you startled springs heavenward, just in time to see the multicolored dragonfly that is chasing the same butterfly as you! As you look for butterflies you will learn the plants whose flowers are important nectar sources and you will learn some of the major caterpillar foodplants, as an aid to locating the adult butterflies. In short, you'll be well on your way to being a compleat naturalist.

Besides being just plain fun, butterflying is rewarding and important in many ways. Since so much remains to be learned about these wonderful animals, your knowledge of the butterflies of your area may make a contribution to science—it's possible that you could even find a new species. For example, the stunning Sandia Hairstreak was discovered only in 1960, despite being fairly common in Big Bend National Park and in the hills just outside of Albuquerque, New Mexico. Also, butterflying allows one to monitor the local environment. Knowledge of the stability, or decline or increase, of local butterfly populations is an important tool in environmental protection. On a more personal level, butterflying serves as a stimulus to go outdoors and engage in healthy physical activity. Paradoxically, butterflying has the power to intensely excite and relax you at the same time. Actually, prolonged field-time with butterflies will result in increased mental health, better physical fitness, and a more satisfying sex life—but these subjects are beyond the scope of this book.

The purpose of this book is to enable you to find and identify the adult butterflies that occur in the western United States and southwestern Canada. The area covered by this guide is the western United States and the southern part of western Canada (north to roughly latitude 51) east to include all of Saskatchewan and the United States east to an imaginary line (see range maps) running diagonally from the southeastern corner of Saskatchewan southeastward to just south of Houston, except for the extreme southern part of Texas, south of the southern edge of the imaginary line. This book treats all species regularly found within this area and also those that have strayed into the area. Almost all regularly found species are illustrated (except for a few essentially eastern species that barely enter the West, and that are illustrated in *Butterflies through Binoculars: The East*; and one species of limited range that is superficially indistinguishable from a much more common and widespread species, i.e., Scarce Streaky-Skipper), as are many of the strays. The world of butterflies is multifaceted, and as you learn to identify butterflies you will almost certainly become interested in many other aspects of their world. However, in this guide many interesting topics related to butterfly study are either not treated in depth or are not included, because inclusion of this material would create a bulkier, less portable book — a book that would work less well as a field guide. If you are interested in learning more about butterfly natural history, systematics, ecology, or gardening, please refer to the bibliography, where many fine books covering these and related subjects are listed.

Binoculars

I strongly urge you to get a pair of close-focusing binoculars— that is, binoculars that will present a sharp image when the butterfly you are viewing is less than 6 feet away. Butterflies are mainly small, and it is difficult to see them well with the naked eye. With good **close-focusing** binoculars, the butterfly will fill your field of vision, giving you a new view of the world. Although you'll be able to identify many butterflies without binoculars, you won't see much of the incredible detail and shimmering colors that makes butterflying so rewarding. And those difficult-to-identify skippers and hairstreaks may well be hopeless. If you use standard-issue binoculars, you will need to be constantly backing up, making the butterfly appear smaller and defeating the purpose for which you brought along the binoculars in the first place.

Other factors to consider in buying a pair of binoculars are power, size, weight, field of view, clarity, and brightness. Two numbers (for example 8×42) describe some basic features of binoculars. The first number is the "power." Eight-power binoculars will make an object 8 feet away appear as large as if it were 1 foot away. The second number is the diameter of the objective lens (in millimeters). In general, the larger this number the brighter the image will be.

Because butterflying is so new, you may have to search for binoculars that have the close-focusing feature that is a requisite for butterflying. Ask your butterflying friends what binoculars they are using, or visit the North American Butterfly Association's Web site at www.naba.org for the latest information. Test the binoculars you intend to buy for close-focusing, and to ensure that they feel comfortable for you. Which pair is "best" is a matter of personal preference.

Netting

Historically, people approached butterflies with nets, because a close examination of the butterfly in the hand was the only way to determine the type of butterfly present. But with the advent of close-focusing binoculars, butterfly nets have become an impediment to finding, viewing, and identifying butterflies in North America, where our knowledge has reached a critical mass. It is extremely cumbersome and time-consuming to have to approach and net each butterfly to identify it. In addition, a small percentage of butterflies that are netted are injured. You will find that learning to use close-focusing binoculars will greatly increase your efficiency at finding and identifying butterflies, especially since you can use them to scan fields for butterfly activity and decide at a distance whether a particular butterfly is worth a closer look. Using close-focusing binoculars will encourage you to actually watch the butterfly in its environment—what it's doing, where it's going, how it moves—while watching a butterfly wriggle around in a net or sit in a jar is completely artificial and hardly qualifies as butterflying at all, just as most people wouldn't consider a day spent examining birds caught in a mist net to be a day spent birding. Many old-time lepidopterists bemoan the switch from netting and collection to binoculars and sight records. "Where," they say, "will the new generation of lepidopterists (or, more broadly, entomologists) come from if kids don't run after butterflies with a net?" But, if they are scientists, perhaps they should consider the available data. Generations of children running around with nets has not produced a bumper crop of lepidopterists. The number of people with a serious interest in butterflies was negligible (at any one time, there have been no more than about 100 very active butterfly field people in North America) before the publication of the first *Butterflies through Binoculars* in 1993. In contrast, birding, which switched from shotguns to binoculars from the 1920s to the 1940s, now involves an estimated 20–60 *million* Americans. Very serious birders clearly number in the hundreds of thousands of people. The popularity of birding has directly led to an astounding increase in our knowledge of birds, and in support for ornithologists and the conservation of birds. And although essentially all current ornithologists became interested in birding through binoculars, this has not impeded them, when appropriate, from using mist nets or from collecting specimens of species for scientific study.

How to Identify Butterflies

If you are just beginning to butterfly, the first step is to learn to recognize the six families of butterflies found in the West—swallowtails, whites & yellows, gossamer-wings, metalmarks, brushfoots, and skippers. This shouldn't be too difficult, because, in general, butterflies belonging to these different families have different wing shapes, different sizes, different colors, and different behaviors. Some of the subfamilies are also easy to recognize—for example, hairstreaks and blues among the gossamer-wings, and spread-wing skippers and grass-skippers among the skippers. Once you know what family or subfamily the butterfly belongs to, go to the appropriate page(s) and see if you recognize the butterfly you have found. For many species groups, all closely similar species are shown on the same two-page spread. For example, all tiger swallowtails are on pages 50–51 and all orangetips are on pages 58–59. Other groups have similar species treated on two or three two-page spreads.

With butterflies, you can make identification much simpler by asking your-self, Where am I? What time of the year is it? What habitat is this? Is this but-terfly closely associating with a particular plant? Many species are only found in certain parts of the West. Some fly only in the early spring; oth-ers are most common late in the year. Most species are found in certain habitats and not others, while different species often use different cater-pillar foodplants. Imagine that you are in the Sandia Mountains outside of Albuquerque, New Mexico, observing a bright green hairstreak. There are seven species of green-colored hairstreaks in the West, all illustrated on pages 93–95. Looking at the range maps, you can see that only two species are found in the Sandia Mountains—Juniper Hairstreak and Sandia Hair-streak. If your imaginary hairstreak is perching inside the blades of a bear-grass, then there is a very good chance it's a Sandia Hairstreak. Conversely, if it is sitting 10 feet up in a juniper, it's probably a Juniper Hairstreak! *Prob-able* (but not certain) identification by habitat and foodplant association works well for butterflies, much better than it does for birds.

Sometimes it is useful to know the sex of a butterfly to aid in identifica-tion. For species in which males and females look quite different, both sexes are illustrated. Even for species in which males and females look similar, one can often guess the sex of an individual by the size and shape of the abdomen. Males usually have narrow abdomens, while females often have large and wide abdomens, because they are filled with eggs.

If you are seriously motivated to learn butterfly identification, probably the best approach is to look at the plates in this book whenever possible. This way you can burn the images of the different species into your brain so that when you encounter a species in the field that you have never seen before, it will still look familiar to you. You should also read the species accounts, which often include identification information that is not obvious from an inspection of the photographs.

Remember that **the appearance of a species of butterfly can vary greatly from individual to individual** and that the appearance of the same individ-ual can vary with the quality and quantity of light. So the individual you see in the field may not exactly match the individual illustrated on the plate. Additionally, the appearance of the same individual butterfly will change over time. When it first emerges from its chrysalis it will be very bright and in pristine condition. Often its wings will have a beautiful sheen. As the adult butterfly ages, scales will be lost and wings will become frayed and torn. Its color may fade. Distinguishing very worn duskywings can be a real challenge! Sometimes identifying an individual butterfly is too great a challenge for anyone and it should be left as "unidentified." This might be because the butterfly was too worn, not seen well enough, or was too easy to confuse with similar species. As you gain experience, you will begin to identify an ever-greater percentage of the butterflies you encounter. I strongly recommend that you **don't use a single field mark to identify a butterfly that is unusual for the location, habitat, or season in which you find it**. It is possible to find aberrant individuals that lack a certain spot, or have an extra line, or have a different color. For real rarities, it is best to rely on a combination of marks.

How to Find Butterflies

Location, location, location. Butterflies are found throughout the West, and once you begin looking, you'll see butterflies everywhere. But some areas are a tad more productive than others. The most productive habitats for butterflies, those that have the greatest diversity of species and the largest numbers of individuals, are open areas with natural vegetation. Butterflies are more common in open areas because, as with people, most butterflies like sunshine. They are more common in areas with native plants because, for the most part, these are the plants that caterpillars require as foodplants. So, for example, you will find very few species of butterflies on large manicured lawns—these are essentially biological deserts.

Look for areas with a great variety of vegetation—butterfly diversity will usually be correlated with the complexity of the landscape. Some specialized and geographically limited habitats harbor some special butterfly species. Boundaries between two different types of habitats will usually have more butterflies than either habitat by itself. Thus, butterflying an open meadow adjacent to a woodland will be more productive than searching either in a woodland or in a meadow that is distant from a woodland.

How do you find these butterfly habitats? One way is by looking at a map for, and then visiting, the local, county, state, or national parks near where you live. These parks will often have good habitats for butterflies. Check out the nature preserves in your area—the Nature Conservancy, for example, has important preserves in many parts of the West (see page 346 for the address). A second method is to search for power line cuts or railroad rights-of-way and walk along these corridors. These narrow corridors often slice through a variety of habitats and may provide excellent habitat themselves. Another approach is to randomly drive along roads, searching interesting-appearing and accessible habitats. If you drive along dirt roads, a bonus is that the dirt roads themselves are often a good place to find butterflies. Lastly, for many species, the location at which the photograph of the butterfly was taken may be a good area to find the butterfly (this information is given on pages 314–342).

Timing is important. Although many of the West's butterflies fly throughout the warmer months, some species are much more seasonal. Elfins and orangetips generally fly only in the early spring (which can be in July in the high mountains), while Soapberry Hairstreaks are best found in May and June. Other species, while occurring throughout much of the year, have population peaks in the fall. Because behavioral patterns differ among species, you will find the most butterflies by searching at different times of the day. Some butterflies become active at dawn; however, luckily for people who prefer a leisurely breakfast, the peak of butterfly activity is probably from around 10:30 A.M. to about 3:00 P.M.

Friends are important too. Unless you teach third grade, you don't have eyes in the back of your head. Butterflying with a small group of friends allows each of you to spot some butterflies that the others would have missed.

Butterfly Concentrators

Having found likely-looking habitat for butterflies, you now will want to search for the butterflies themselves. Sometimes butterflies are everywhere, by the thousands. But many times, the numbers of butterflies are much smaller. When this is the case, your search for butterflies can be helped by finding certain environmental features that concentrate butterflies.

Flowers. The great majority of adult butterflies feed by nectaring at flowers. Almost all flowers are used at some time by some butterflies, but some flowers are much more attractive to butterflies than others. Some of the top, widespread, wild nectar sources for spring, summer, and fall are listed below. Others may be important in your area. Locating stands of attractive

Some Important Natural Nectar Sources

SPRING
Ceanothus *Ceanothus* (shrubs)
Wild cherries and plums *Prunus* (small trees)
Dandelions *Taraxacum*
Fiddleneck *Amsincki intermedia*
Penstemons *Penstemon*
Pussypaws *Calyptridium umbellatum*
Yarrow *Achillea*
Gumweeds *Grindelia*
Lomatiums *Lomatium*
New Mexican locust *Robinia neomexicana* (small tree) (Arizona-New Mexico)
California buckeye *Aesculus californica* (tree) (California)
Yerba santas *Eriodictyon* (California)

SUMMER
Buckwheats *Eriogonum*
Dogbanes *Apocynum*
Milkweeds *Asclepias*
Thistles *Cirsium*
Balms *Monarda* & *Monardella*
Fleabanes *Erigeron*
Ragworts *Senecio*
Other yellow composites
Giant hyssop *Agastache urticifolia*
Lantana *Lantana* (southern edge)

FALL
Rabbitbrush *Chrysothamnus nauseosus* (shrub)
Blazing stars *Liatris*
Asters *Aster*
Thistles *Cirsium*
Sunflowers *Helianthus*
Cone flowers *Echinacea*
Goldenrods *Solidago*
Goldenweeds *Haplopappus*
Alfalfa *Medicago sativa*
Mints *Mentha*
Mistflowers *Eupatorium* (Texas)

flowers is the easiest way to find many butterfly species. If you are not familiar with these plants, you will probably want to consult a wildflower guide.

Hilltops. A surprisingly high percentage of butterflies congregate on the tops of hills. For many rare and uncommon species, hilltops offer by far the best chance of seeing the species. What you need is a hilltop that is higher than anything else in the immediate vicinity, that is relatively open at the top, and that is accessible. The definition of accessible will vary greatly according to the butterflier's physical condition and depth of desire. See the behavior section, below, for more about hilltopping.

Canyons and gullies. A fair number of butterfly species use the upside-down version of hilltops—the lowest point around—to search for mates.

Mud puddles. A wide variety of species will congregate at damp sand or gravel.

Trails and dirt roads. Not only are butterflies easier to see along a trail, but the trail itself serves to concentrate some of them. Believe it or not, many butterflies, such as buckeyes, prefer trails to undisturbed vegetation. If the trail is through a woodland, it needs to be wide enough to allow in sunshine to be a useful butterfly concentrator.

Caterpillar foodplants. Many species of butterflies have caterpillars that will use only a few, or even just one, plant species as a foodplant. These special plants act to concentrate the adult butterflies as well, since females will come to these plants to lay their eggs. So look for naked buckwheats to find Dotted Blues, and for yuccas to find Yucca Giant-Skippers. Each species account includes a section on caterpillar foodplants.

Search Image

As you spend more time searching for butterflies, an unconscious "search image" of a butterfly will form in your brain. Without thinking you will brake for "butterfly bumps" on roads and on leaves. Certain spots of color on flowers will scream "look at me," and you will. There haven't been any studies about this, but you may be able to speed up the process by consciously playing a butterfly bump recognition game.

What Is a Butterfly?

Butterflies are a group of evolutionarily related animals. They are grouped as part of the class Insecta, and together with the moths constitute the order Lepidoptera. This word derives from the Greek words for scale (=lepid) and wing (=ptera). True butterflies (superfamily Papilionoidea) and skippers (superfamily Hesperioidea) are usually considered together as "butterflies," and separately from moths. It is generally easy to distinguish butterflies and moths.

Almost all our butterflies are active exclusively during the day, while the great majority of moths are active only at night. Some moths are active during the day, but these can usually be identified by their flight, which is characteristically stiff and very erratic. In part, this is because most moths have structures, called a frenulum and a retinaculum, that hook the forewing to the hindwing. Butterflies lack these structures and thus, in general, fly much more gracefully than most moths. When seen well, our butterflies and moths almost always can be distinguished by the shape of their antennas. Butterflies and skippers have a club (a swelling) at the end of their antennas, while almost all moths do not (see figure on page 41).

Butterfly Biology
Life Cycle

Each butterfly goes through four distinct stages in its life: egg, caterpillar, pupa (chrysalis), and adult. The change from caterpillar to pupa to adult butterfly involves major changes in appearance. This process of great physical change, or "metamorphosis," has captured the imagination of peoples throughout the world. Many native peoples in the Americas, including the Papagos and the Aztecs, have myths and gods based upon these butterfly transformations.

EGG

An adult female that has mated has the capacity to lay fertilized eggs. A considerable part of her day is spent searching for appropriate plants on which to lay her eggs. The butterfly usually recognizes the right plant by a combination of sight and smell. Butterflies have a very acute sense of smell. They have chemoreceptors (cells that respond to "tastes" and "smells") both on their antennas and on the bottom ends of their legs. Most species lay their eggs on a plant that the newly hatched caterpillar will eat. Most species lay only one, or a few, eggs per plant. Others place a mass of eggs together. Some species lay their eggs mainly on flower buds; others place them on the undersides of leaves; still others lay their eggs at the base of a tree. How many eggs a particular female lays varies greatly from species to species. Over the course of their lives some butterflies lay only a few dozen eggs, but most probably lay a few hundred, while some, such as Regal Fritillaries, lay a few thousand. The eggs themselves are quite interesting, with the eggs of each butterfly family having a different architecture.

CATERPILLAR

When the egg hatches, usually after less than a week, a tiny caterpillar emerges. This voracious eating machine spends almost all its time eating and growing. As it rapidly increases in size, it outgrows its outer skin, or exoskeleton. The old skin splits and is shed, revealing a new, larger, and baggier skin below. This process happens a number of times (usually three or four) over the course of about two or three weeks. The great majority of caterpillars do not successfully become butterflies. Most are either eaten by predators, especially wasps and birds, or they are parasitized, usually by one of many species of parasitic wasps or flies, or they become infected by disease-causing fungi or viruses. The world of caterpillars is a fascinating one, with varied shapes and colors and a lot of interesting behavior—much of it used to avoid predators. However, identifying caterpillars is a vast subject—requiring its own book.

PUPA

When the caterpillar has grown to full size, it attaches itself to a support and becomes a pupa. Sometimes this happens on the caterpillar foodplant itself, but more often the caterpillar wanders away from the foodplant and attaches itself to a twig or a blade of grass. The moulted caterpillar, now encased in a hard outer shell (chrysalis), becomes a pupa—seemingly lifeless and inert. But inside this shell, an amazing transformation is taking place. The tissues and structures of the caterpillar are being broken down and replaced with the tissues and structures of the adult butterfly. If development is proceeding without impediment, this process usually takes one to two weeks. If not, the pupa may enter a resting state for a few months, or overwinter.

ADULT

Eventually the adult inside the chrysalis is fully formed, the chrysalis splits open, and the adult butterfly emerges. Often this happens very early in the morning. In the chrysalis, the wings are wrapped tightly around the butterfly's body. After the adult emerges, its wings unfurl as fluid pumps through the wing veins. This is a very vulnerable time in a butterfly's life, as it basks in the sunshine to warm itself and to harden and set its wings. Once the adult butterfly emerges from the chrysalis, it grows no larger. So if you see a small butterfly, it is not a baby butterfly—it is a fully formed adult.

LIFESPAN

Most adult butterflies live for a relatively brief time. Some small blues may live only a few weeks, while large brush-footed butterflies, such as Mourning Cloaks and Monarchs, may live up to about eight months. Most adult butterflies can live about two to four weeks if they are not eaten by predators, such as spiders, dragonflies, birds, and lizards.

BROODS

The adults of some species of butterflies fly only at a particular time of the year. Adults of single-brooded species all emerge from their chrysalids at roughly the same time—over a period of a few weeks or, less commonly, a few months. For example, Brown Elfins fly only in the early spring—the adults then mate and the females lay eggs. The caterpillars that soon hatch feed on flowers and young fruit for about three weeks and then pupate. The pupas enter a resting period (diapause) during the summer, fall, and winter and new adults emerge the following spring. So Brown Elfins are single-brooded.

Some species have two or more broods each year. Adult Juniper Hairstreaks, closely related to Brown Elfins, also fly in the spring. But when the caterpillars grow up, many of the resulting pupas, rather than overwintering as do Brown Elfins, develop quickly into adult butterflies and these then fly in mid to late summer—a second brood. The offspring of this second brood then overwinter as pupas and the resulting adults fly the next spring. Often, the adults of an early brood will have subtle differences in appearance from those of a later brood.

In the north, many species have but one or two broods per year, while in the south most species have three or more broods per year. Even those species that perhaps only have two broods in southern regions may have asynchronous emergences of adults, leading to very long flight periods. Let's go back to the basic concept of broods. When we say that Brown Elfins fly only in the early spring, is this absolutely true? Probably not. Although I know of no reports of Brown Elfins flying in the summer or fall (notwithstanding mountain populations where it's springtime in July), I am sure that, occasionally, a Brown Elfin adult will emerge at an "inappropriate" time of the year. Nature is not absolute. Variation and flexibility lead to new avenues for a species to explore. Sometime, somewhere, a Brown Elfin will either be subjected to unusual environmental conditions, or it will carry a mutation that will cause it to emerge in July, or August, or September! But these events are certainly very rare, and if they have occurred they have probably gone unnoticed because there have been so few butterfliers. I predict that eventually many species of butterflies will be found to fly (very, very rarely) way outside their usual flight times.

In a similar vein, we know that most single-brooded butterflies take one year to complete their life cycle and that some butterflies, mainly those that live in the far north, may require two years to complete theirs. We are now discovering that even in the temperate zone, especially in arid areas, some individual pupas of certain species may remain dormant for two, three, or even four years. Because a local population may be wiped out by drought, or flood, or disease, it makes sense to have a small percentage of a population remain dormant for a number of years. It may be that most butterfly species have this capability.

In addition to helping you know when to search for a butterfly, knowledge of broods is helpful in understanding butterfly ecology and evolution. Often, where a species is single-brooded, the farther south one goes the larger will be the individuals of that species. Then, when one reaches the area where the species becomes two-brooded, individuals are often smaller. This transition zone between single and double-brooded populations of the same species is one of tension. The shift from one to two broods may create something of a barrier to the free flow of genetic material between the populations, because the adults may not fly at the same time of year.

Because different plants may be available south or north of the transition zone, the two populations may become ecologically segregated as well. It may be that this one-brood/two-brood shift sometimes plays a role in speciation events.

Behavior

Because so little is known about butterfly behavior, this is an area where patient observation can increase our knowledge. Here are a few types of behaviors to look for when you are watching butterflies.

BASKING

Butterflies are cold-blooded—their body temperature largely depends on the ambient temperature. Thus when it is cold outside, butterflies want to warm up, and they employ two different basking strategies to do so. Some butterflies sit in the sunshine in an exposed spot (or, even better, on a warm rock) and open their wings. This allows the sun's rays to warm them. Other butterflies engage in lateral basking. These butterflies sit in the sunshine with their wings closed. They then tilt their bodies so that the plane of their wings is perpendicular to the sun's rays, thus most efficiently capturing the warming energy of the sun.

HILLTOPPING

Many humans go to singles bars because prospective mates may be concentrated at these locations. Hilltops are the butterfly equivalent of singles bars. Males of many butterfly species may be most easily found by climbing to the top of the highest hill in the vicinity, especially if the top of the hill is open and if at least some of the slopes are quite steep. Here the males patrol the area looking for females, or they select a favored perch and wait. Unmated females also fly up here (otherwise the system wouldn't work), but already mated females spend more time elsewhere, looking for hostplants and nectar.

GULLY BOTTOMING

Just as there are different types of singles bars that attract participants with different mating predilections, some butterfly species shun hilltops and instead meet at the bottoms of gullies and canyons. Some species seem to prefer the centers of gullies and washes; others appear to hang out closer to the edges. Exploring different zones of canyons and other interesting topological features may yield different butterfly species.

MUDPUDDLING

Many butterflies, especially males, congregate at damp sand or soil. Here they imbibe salts along with the water. The salts are passed along to the female at mating and contribute to the nourishment of the eggs. Seeing a large mudpuddle party with many species of swallowtails and other butterflies is a thrilling experience.

COURTSHIP

We don't really have detailed knowledge about most butterflies' courtship patterns. Males of many species stake out "territories." They then police these, either by flying back and forth, or by occasionally sallying forth from a favored perch, making sure that they're the only male around when a female saunters into the territory. Although the main objective would seem to be to drive away other males of the same species, some aggressive males try to drive off everything that moves, including birds and sometimes humans! Some butterflies have almost no courtship displays. The males simply fly up to a landed female, and if she is receptive, mate immediately.

Other butterflies behave differently. Most male hairstreaks set up territories, then fly up to greet a female flying through their territory. He flies with her until she lands, then lands next to her, usually facing her, and fans his wings. This disperses the "mating perfume" (pheromone) that most male hairstreaks have in special patches of scales on the upper side of their FWs. Many other butterflies are also territorial, while another group of males, taking the initiative, uses patrolling behavior to locate females— they just keep flying till they find them. Male Barred Yellows land alongside a female and flick open their FW that is closest to the female. They place their FW right in front of the female, touching her antennas, to dazzle her with their great-looking and -smelling (because of a mating perfume) bar! Most males of a given species will generally engage in either patrolling or territorial behavior, but not both. But males can sometimes switch between perching and patrolling, and this may be related to population density.

Migration

Perhaps surprisingly, many butterfly species undertake migrations. We know very little about these movements. Here again is an area where careful observation by the increasing number of butterfliers will provide important new information.

While all butterflies move around, most don't "migrate" in the traditional sense. What they do is to disperse in a random direction from the site where they emerge from the chrysalis. Some adults immediately fly away from their emergence site, others stay around for most of their lives, then wander off as they get older, while some never leave. If none of the population ever left the original site, butterflies would never be able to colonize new, suitable sites. Since many butterfly species live in habitats that disappear over time (open meadows being replaced by forests, etc.), this dispersal is critical to the survival of butterfly species. So a stray butterfly could appear almost anywhere.

Many butterflies that spend the summer in the north cannot survive northern winters. Each year, as the weather becomes warmer, butterflies from Mexico fly north to repopulate these regions. Species that move northward each year include Cloudless Sulphur, Little Yellow, Gulf Fritillary, Variegated Fritillary, Painted Lady, Red Admiral, Common Buckeye, Monarch, Fiery Skipper, and Sachem. For most species these northward dispersals are gradual, but in especially good years, one can see Painted Ladies streaming northward.

Monarchs are the most well-known of migratory butterflies. In North America there are two major overwintering areas. The first, and by far the largest, is in central Mexico. Here the millions of Monarchs that emerge as adults in the fall from across the vast expanse of North America, from southeastern Canada west to Alberta and south through the eastern two-thirds of the United States, spend the winter high in the fir-clad mountains. How the Monarchs manage to navigate to these very limited overwintering sites is a complete mystery.

A much lesser, but still impressive, number of Monarchs spend the winter along the central California coast, most of these having been born in the region west of the Continental Divide.

Butterfly Gardening

If you have a garden, even a small one, the chances are good that you can enjoy butterflies right at home. Many common garden flowers, such as zinnias and marigolds, are attractive to butterflies. If you plant special plants such as butterfly bush (*Buddleia*) and orange milkweed (*Asclepias tuberosa*) (called butterflyweed in the horticultural trade), you will attract many of the butterflies in your neighborhood to your garden while these plants are in bloom. Although perhaps more difficult to obtain and maintain than common garden flowers, I encourage you to try some of the native wildflowers that are excellent nectar sources for butterflies (see list on page 8). One advantage of this approach is that the butterflies in your neighborhood may already be familiar with these plants, and thus have learned to come to them for nectar. Of course, which species of butterflies you attract will depend on which species are present in your vicinity. If you live close to woodlands and meadows, you will attract many more species than if you live in a suburban development. But even flower gardens in Los Angeles can attract a fair number of species.

An important point to keep in mind when planning a butterfly garden is that you must have caterpillars before you can have adult butterflies. The best butterfly gardens include many caterpillar foodplants (see Table 1) so the butterfly garden will "grow" butterflies, not just waylay some of the adults that happen to be in the neighborhood. If you are interested in a specific butterfly species, look up the account for that species and note its caterpillar foodplant. Don't overlook the butterfly gardening possibilities of trees and shrubs, such as shrubby willows. If you live within the range of the butterfly, and if there are natural populations close by, planting the indicated foodplant will give you a chance to enjoy this butterfly right in your garden. Unlike many moth caterpillars, most butterfly caterpillars will not destroy the plants they are eating (well, sometimes they do become overexuberant). In addition, because they eat only very specific plants, you do not need to worry about them "spreading" to your roses or your rhododendrons. They will not eat these plants, or the vast majority of others that happen to be in your garden.

Your butterfly garden is likely to be more successful if you plant sizable groupings of the same type of plant, rather than using a single plant or two. Butterflies learn what nectar sources are available in their area and they greatly prefer to go from flower to flower of the same type than to switch in midmeal! The same goes for caterpillar foodplants—a cluster is much more likely to attract attention than is a single plant.

The more complex your garden becomes, the more attractive it is likely to be to butterflies. If you have room, try using many kinds of caterpillar foodplants and different nectar sources. Because butterflies fly from early spring to late fall, your garden should contain a procession of flowers through the seasons. In addition, many butterfly species feed on small, inconspicuous plants that most gardeners would regard as "weeds." If possible, allow a few areas of your garden, perhaps areas that are not easily seen, to become weedy. You'll be amazed by the beautiful butterflies that these areas will export to your more formal garden!

Besides plants, you should consider a few other features for your butterfly garden. As we saw in the behavior section, butterflies like to bask in the sun, and they like to sip moisture at damp sand or gravel. You can provide a basking area by placing some flat stones in a sheltered but sunny location. If you don't have an area that is naturally damp, try burying a bucket or container filled with sand, adding water as necessary.

Butterfly Photography for Nonphotographers

Butterflies are often very approachable. This approachability makes butterflies easy to photograph. With a little patience, a little experience, and most important of all, the right equipment, anybody, even the photographically inept, like me, can take great photographs of butterflies *while still enjoying the butterflies themselves.*

In contrast, birds and flowers, for different reasons, are difficult to photograph, and, at least for birds, the photographer needs to focus single-mindedly on photography at the expense of seeing many birds. While a professional photographer will also take this approach with butterflies—spending the whole day hoping for one great picture—you needn't.

Table 1 Some Caterpillar Foodplants
(Suitable for the Garden) of Widespread Butterflies

PLANT NAME	FOODPLANT FOR THESE CATERPILLAR SPECIES
Asters *Aster*	Northern Crescent, Pearl Crescent, Field Crescent,
Buckwheats *Eriogonum*	Square-spotted Blue, Dotted Blue, Mormon Metalmark
Cassias *Cassia*	Little Yellow, Sleepy Orange, Cloudless Sulphur
Ceanothus *Ceanothus*	California Tortoiseshell, Pacuvius Duskywing
Citrus *Citrus*	Giant Swallowtail
Deerweed *Lotus scoparius*	Orange Sulphur, Bramble Hairstreak, Marine Blue
False Nettle *Boehmeria cylindrica*	Red Admiral
Fennel *Foeniculum vulgare*	Anise Swallowtail, Black Swallowtail
Hackberries *Celtis*	American Snout, Hackberry Emperor, Tawny Emperor
Lupines *Lupinus*	Boisduval's Blue, Melissa Blue, Silvery Blue
Mallows *Malva, Sida*	Gray Hairstreak, Common Checkered-Skipper
Milkweeds *Asclepias*	Monarch, Queen
Pipevines *Aristolochia*	Pipevine Swallowtail
Rock-cresses *Arabis*	Marbles and orangetips
Snapdragon *Antirrhinum major*	Common Buckeye
Sunflowers *Helianthus*	Bordered Patch, Gorgone Checkerspot
Violets *Viola*	Greater fritillaries
Willows *Salix*	Mourning Cloak, Sylvan Hairstreak, Viceroy, Lorquin's Admiral

Why Take Photographs?

You can certainly enjoy butterflies without photographing them, and photography does take some time away from observation and can cost quite a bit. Why do it? Well, for one thing it's the easiest way to share your butterflying experiences with others. You can describe your experiences to others with words, but you need to be a talented speaker or author to do justice to the beauty of butterflies and the thrills of butterflying. But, with modern photographic equipment, you don't need to be a talented photographer to let people see the actual butterfly that you saw, or the field of flowers in which it flew—you just need to push the button.

Another reason to take photographs is that you can document the species that you see. You know, when you see some strange species and describe it to others, they may say, "That can't occur around here, you must have misidentified it." When a Mexican butterfly, the 'Cream-banded' Dusky Emperor, appeared for the second time in the United States, photographers were able to document its occurrence so that there was no question of the validity of the report.

Photographs also allow you to hone your identification skills. By looking carefully at series of photographs that you have taken, you will be able to notice small identification points not mentioned elsewhere.

In the rest of this section I try to provide information that will allow you to obtain clear, in-focus, well-lit photographs of a large percentage of the butterflies that you see and that can be used for identification and illustration purposes. If you are interested in obtaining a much smaller number of spectacular photographs that you can sell to national magazines, your approach may well be different.

Equipment

CAMERA BODY

Most people will find that a 35 mm single-lens reflex camera gives them the best results. I suggest buying a "good" camera body, but not the most expensive top-of-the-line camera body that has all the bells and whistles. This is because in just a few years these camera bodies will be replaced by digital cameras (but the lens and flash that you buy will be transferrable to the appropriate digital cameras). I strongly recommend using a model that has autofocusing and automatic setting programs. Minolta autofocusing has always worked for butterflies. Although the older Canon and Nikon autofocusing models did not work well for butterflies, the newer models are greatly improved. The advantage of autofocusing is that, first, it's probably more accurate than most people, and two, it frees up one of your hands to do other things. If one wants to get close to the ground to approach a butterfly, you can put one hand down to help balance yourself, then lean forward and shoot the scene using only your other hand. Or, if there's a butterfly over your head, you can lift the camera over your head and just point it; the camera will do the rest. With manual focus the requirement that your hand turns the barrel of the camera to focus it increases the chances of the butterfly detecting this movement and flying off.

LENS

Although it is possible to obtain passable photographs using a standard 50mm lens, to take consistently good shots you should use a 100 mm macro lens. Make sure that you are getting a true macro lens, one that at closest focus results in a life-size image on the film. Many lenses listed as "macro" lenses, including all of those that are also zoom lenses, do not have this feature. Without the 100 mm macro lens the butterflies will generally look small in your pictures, while with such a lens, the butterflies will fill the frame.

FLASH

Some photographers like to shoot all their pictures using natural light. They feel that the resulting photos look more natural. This puzzled me for a long time, because while one can certainly obtain some great photographs using natural light, my own experience is that, for the type of pictures most people take, the butterflies in the photographs taken using natural light often look highly unnatural! I now believe that what they mean is that the background is not darkened relative to the butterfly, and so the *background* looks more natural. By and large, with flash the *butterflies* look more natural (that is, more like they appear to your eyes in the field), and so if you are interested in showing people how butterflies appear in the field, flash is extremely useful. In addition, the less light one has available, the longer one must expose the film (slower shutter speed) to obtain the same brightness. Since butterflies often move and your hands move also, using slow shutter speeds is not often an option—unless you've stuck a frozen butterfly on a flower (see below). Also, at closest focus, a 100 mm macro lens has a very shallow depth of field, so with available light one is not likely to get the entire butterfly in focus, let alone parts of the foreground and background. All of this argues for the use of a flash to provide extra light.

For the nonphotographer photographer there are really two choices for flash arrangements. The first is the standard flash mounted on the top of the camera. This can work fairly well. An advantage to these flashes over ring flashes is that they have much more power, allowing good illumination of butterflies that are quite distant. One drawback, however, is that the angle of the flash may not be entirely suitable for illuminating butterflies at the closest focusing distance, leading to unwanted shadows. Also, using a flash mounted on the camera body, you will have only a fixed, point source of light and sometimes it is advantageous to illuminate the butterfly from an angle, or with light from more than one angle.

The second type of flash is a ring flash. Rather than sit on the top of the camera body, the ring flash fits around the end of the macro lens. An advantage of this system is that the flash is always aimed properly, yielding a very high percentage of eminently usable photos. Another advantage is that with multiple lights in the ring, you can vary the angle of light if you want to. A disadvantage of this system is that most ring flashes are underpowered (they are intended for very close macrophotography), making it difficult to properly illuminate targets at a distance, such as swallowtails. Another disadvantage, for some purposes, is that although the butterfly will be sharp and well-illuminated, this system tends to produce a higher percentage of photographs in which the background is black than does a camera-mounted flash. Black backgrounds result when the available light on the butterfly is much greater than the available light on the background. On many camera settings, the flash will overpower any natural light, and because the light from the flash drops off as the square of the distance from the flash, only objects very close to the focal plane of the butterfly will be properly illuminated. (The same effect happens with all flashes, but because the ring flash is closer to the butterfly, the effect is accentuated with a ring flash.) For the purposes of showing other people just how the butterfly looks, black backgrounds may be a plus, because one's attention is focused on the butterfly. However, in terms of a beautiful photograph, some people find a black background objectionable (except for Elvis pictures). Since most of the photographs in this book were taken using the ring flash system, you can judge for yourself if this system might be suitable for you.

FILM

The performance of digital cameras has now approached that of traditional cameras, and in the future, film will be used for special purposes. But as of this writing (spring 2000), I still recommend a traditional camera. This is because (1) high-end digital cameras are still very expense and (2) there are major storage issues with digital photography. When I'm photographing butterflies I typically shoot about 100 photographs a day. Many serious photographers easily shoot about 400 photographs a day. High-quality images use roughly 5 megs of storage space. That means one is generating 500-2000 megs of data a day. Even given that many of these images will be discarded, this still leaves you with a huge, very expensive, and difficult-to-work-with demand for storage. As the cost of storage and ease of manipulation of large files continues to rapidly improve, digital photography, even at the high end of quality, will replace traditional film. With traditional film the basic choice is between print and slide film. An advantage to prints is that you can easily view them yourself or with a small group of people. However, compared to slide film, there are many disadvantages: you can't use them for talks to groups of people, they are bulkier to store, and their resolution is not as good. Since only slide film was used for the photographs shown here, I can't really make a recommendation about which print film to use. Sharper pictures are possible when you use film with lower ASA numbers. ASA 25 film will yield much sharper pictures that can be greatly enlarged than will ASA 200 film, while the ASA 200 film can be used under much lower light conditions. If you are photographing without a flash, you will want to use ASA 200 film or higher. With a flash, you can use ASA 25 or 64 film. I use Kodachrome 64 film; I believe that, overall, its color veracity is the best. This film also has a reputation for long-term color stability.

ACCESSORIES

For most butterfly photographs it is a good idea to keep a UV filter over your lens. You'll want a strap for your camera. A good wide one will do less damage to your shoulder than a narrow one. You'll probably also want to take extra batteries and film with you on hikes. A small pouch that fits around your waist is useful for carrying extra rolls of film and extra sets of batteries for your flash and a battery for the camera itself.

Taking the Photo

APPROACHING THE BUTTERFLY

When you see a butterfly you want to photograph, you naturally want to rush right up to it and grab its picture. Unfortunately, butterflies are pretty good motion detectors. So you need to slow down. And be more graceful. The more slowly and gracefully you move, the less likely it is you will frighten the butterfly. But let's get real. If you move slowly enough, the butterfly is guaranteed to have flown before you get in place for your photograph. So you need to strike a balance. Just where that balance lies is best learned by experience. It will also vary from butterfly species to species, and from butterfly individual to individual. Some butterflies that are nectaring, or that are mudpuddling, will sit still forever. Others almost never stop. If you have a choice, find one that stops. If you are trying to photograph a Small Wood-Nymph and there are a number of them present, watch for one that is landing more frequently and for longer periods of time than others. It will probably continue to do so as you try to photograph it. The same type of advice applies to those times when you especially want the upperside of the butterfly, or alternatively, the underside. Whatever you want, the butterflies will be doing the opposite. The few that occasionally open their wings may well continue to do so. Focus on them.

If you have a choice, it is best to approach the butterfly from a low position, rather than from over its head. This way you'll be less likely to startle it. For the same reason, you will want to avoid having your shadow pass over the butterfly.

FRAMING THE BUTTERFLY

Proper framing is important for both aesthetically desirable results and easy identification of the butterflies in your photos. To clearly see your butterfly, you should strive to have the butterfly's wings parallel to the plane of the film in your camera. Many times you will need to be on one knee, or on your belly, and/or with your body contorted into ludicrous positions to effectively accomplish proper framing. If the angle of the butterfly is off just a little, this will distort the perspective and make it more difficult to examine spot shapes and patterns that are important for identification. Of course, if you want just an interesting angle, that is a different story. Another decision you will make is what to include in the frame along with the butterfly. This is an aesthetic decision that depends upon your "eye"— what looks good to you. Like anything else in this world, some people are better than others in creating pleasing photographic compositions. However, unless you want to sell your photos to mass-circulation magazines, this may not matter to you.

Photo Etiquette

Photo etiquette requires consideration for other people, for the butterfly, and for the environment. As more and more people take up butterflying and butterfly photography, this will become more important.

If you are with other people, you should consider their needs. A record shot from a distance, without a flash, is OK, but going right up to a butterfly to photograph it, or using a flash, carries the risk of frightening the butterfly away. When I lead groups of people on butterflying trips, I ask photographers to wait until everyone has had a careful look at the butterfly and is satisfied. Of course, some people probably think that I'm not so good at policing myself! If there is more than one photographer present, you might try a system of alternating who photographs first, although some butterflies are very cooperative and allow more than one person to photograph them at the same time. If a butterfly is sitting on the ground with its wings closed, but is occasionally opening them, there can be a photographer on each side of the butterfly, each photographing its underside, while another photographer is behind the butterfly, waiting for its wings to open to photograph its upperside. Believe it or not, this has worked on a surprising number of occasions.

You should also consider the butterfly. Some photographers will do almost anything to obtain a photograph. They will capture a butterfly, place it in an ice chest to cool it, then pose the almost frozen butterfly on some colorful flower or background so they can photograph it to their heart's content. Putting aside the fact that there are times when butterflies are injured just by capturing them (and any injury to a butterfly is probably fatal), my opinion is that while photographers may believe that photographs obtained in this way are OK, if they don't inform readers that this is how the photographs were obtained then they are inadvertently deceiving the public. People looking at these photographs will believe that these artificial poses and situations can normally be found in nature. They cannot.

Last, but not least, you should consider the environment. When you walk up to butterflies for your photograph, do not trample flowers and other plants along the way. Any human actions cause environmental problems, especially when repeated by large numbers of people. Although it's probably impossible to avoid accidents, you can minimize the damage your activities cause by being aware of potential trampling problems and exercising care when you photograph.

Care of Your Photographs

RECORD KEEPING

More than just being pretty pictures, your photographs can be important records of what kinds of butterflies were in what locations at what times. I urge you to label your photographs—not with some type of arcane code, but with the date the photograph was taken and the locality where it was taken written directly on the slide holder, or on the back of the print. A code is close to useless. Sure *you* know the code, you've even written it down in a notebook. But as the years go by you'll forget the code or lose the notebook. And, I won't be the first to tell you, you will die. Invariably, eventually your photographs will become separated from your code. Ask any museum curator, and they will tell you that butterfly specimens that do not have date and locality data, written on a label that is on the same pin as the specimen, have almost no value.

In order to write this information on your photographs, you will need to have recorded it when you took the pictures. Relying on your memory is a bad idea and will eventually lead to mistakes that are misleading to others and embarrassing to yourself. Carry a small notebook with you. Number each roll of film you shoot, by year and sequence—for example 98-40 would be the 40th roll of film in 1998. Then, in your field notebook, after the heading 98-40, a handwritten entry might read "13. Sandia Hairstreak, 5/10/98 Juan Tabo Rec. Area, Sandia Mtns., Bernallilo Co. NM. " When your slides from roll 40 come back developed, refer to your field notebook and write the information on the slide. If you have taken more than one photograph of what you *are sure* is the same individual butterfly (the butterfly has never left your sight), then indicate that in your notebook, and cross-label all the slides of the same individual with something like "see 13-25F," writing that same instruction on all 13 slides of the Sandia Hairstreak. This is especially important when you want to study the upperside and underside of the same butterfly, either for ID or to see if certain upperside characteristics are associated with certain underside characteristics.

STORAGE AND PHOTOGRAPH RETRIEVAL

You should protect your photographs from excessive heat, high humidity, dust, and light. Prints can be stored in photo albums, or just in envelopes. Some people store their slides in carousels, others store them in the boxes in which the developed slides are returned, while others use special enamel slide cabinets. I store my slides in clear plastic pages with compartments for individual slides. Use only plastic pages that are labeled as "archival" for slides; others contain polyvinyl chloride, which can destroy your photos over time. These clear plastic pages, generally of polyethylene or of polyester polypropylene, fit into three-ring binders.

Some photographers store their photographs by trip or by time period. I store my butterfly slides in taxonomic sequence. This makes it very easy to find slides of particular butterfly species to illustrate articles or talks.

VIEWING YOUR PHOTOGRAPHS

If you want to share your photos with groups of people, you need to project them onto a screen or a white wall using a slide projector. For viewing yourself, it is best to use a loupe, a type of magnifying glass especially made for viewing slides. Although you can just hold the slides up to a light and look through the loupe, most people probably would prefer placing the slides on a light box. Loupes and light boxes are available from camera supply stores.

Conservation

This is the raison d'être of this book. I want to show you the beauty and thrills to be found in the world of butterflies so that you become passionate about butterflies; so that butterflies become an important part of your life; so that when a government agency sprays the forest with butterfly-killing, anti–gypsy moth spray you will feel their pain; so that when developers intentionally destroy all remnants of native life to create a sterile environment for unknowing new homeowners, you will develop the political will and skills to stop them.

There are still plenty of butterflies to be found in the West. But unless you take action, there won't be in the future. Eventually, *every piece of non-public land that can be developed, will be developed.* The wonderful meadow you visit will become a shopping center. The wooded slopes of the Sierra Nevadas will give way to wooden structures housing people. The prairies will be restricted to scenes in old movies. While working on this book, I watched in horror as developers on the high prairie east of Denver literally scraped all life and topsoil from the housing sites they were building. That this type of planetary rape is legal speaks volumes about human greed and shortsightedness.

What can be done? First and foremost, we need to restrain the growth of the human population and to set a realistic upper limit to the number of people that can inhabit an area. Second, we need to set aside even more land as preserves. Third, we need to enact a policy whereby whenever land is "developed," a healthy percentage of it, perhaps 40%, stays undeveloped. And last, we need to change the aesthetics of homeowners and corporations, encouraging them to re-create natural landscapes rather than using exotic plants (that might as well be artificial Christmas trees as far as most butterflies are concerned) and installing "lawns" of non-native, water-hogging, fertilizer-needing and polluting grasses that are essentially biological deserts.

The good news is that, with proper planning, human and butterfly habitations are compatible. Because most butterfly populations do not need very large expanses of habitat, preservation of most species is feasible by creating an interconnecting network of small protected habitat units along with a few larger units. Small habitat units, perhaps as small as the yards of a few concerned neighbors, are sufficient to support small populations of many species, especially if these small units are connected to other small units. But butterfly populations are commonly subject to very large fluctuations in numbers. In particularly bad years for a particular species of butterfly, perhaps due to a drought or to a disease epidemic, the small units, with their small populations, will probably not survive. However, larger preserves probably will have large and varied populations and habitats that will ensure that some individuals survive a calamity. Then, when the population rebounds, the larger preserves will serve as reservoirs and overflow individuals will repopulate the small units.

A second factor reducing butterfly populations is pollution of the environment, especially pollution with pesticides. The past use of DDT greatly reduced many of our native butterfly populations. Although DDT is now banned, the use of other pesticides is widespread. These pesticides are employed for mass sprayings against gypsy moth infestations and other forest "pests," for agricultural use, and also by private homeowners. In most cases, the harm caused by these pesticides outweighs any possible usefulness.

A third activity capable of harming butterfly populations is the continued killing of rare and local butterfly species by some immoral collectors. Although these collectors claim that colonies of rare insects, including butterflies, cannot be extirpated by collecting, reason and experience argue otherwise. Imagine a greenhouse that you have converted into a butterfly zoo, placing some milkweed plants in the greenhouse and some Monarchs. The Monarchs will breed and establish a small "colony." Now imagine going into your greenhouse every day and killing every adult Monarch you see. Your colony of Monarchs will clearly not survive for very long. Obviously, "collecting" can destroy a butterfly colony; the only question is how small does a colony need to be before a particular level of collection pressure destroys it? In the real world, whenever a heavily collected butterfly population disappears or is diminished, collectors invariably try to place the blame elsewhere—a drought perhaps, or, absurdly, ptarmigans.

But there are two cases in the United States (more in Europe) where it is clear that collecting wiped out a colonial butterfly. In the late 1960s, F. Martin Brown, co-author of *Butterflies of the Rocky Mountain States*, conducted an experiment with a population of Ridings' Satyr. This butterfly lives in colonies, often smaller than an acre, and in many areas these colonies are not very far apart. Brown selected a specific colony near Colorado Springs and deliberately extirpated it by repeated daily collecting on all-inclusive crisscross transects. Although Brown's objective was to determine how quickly the area from which the colony was extirpated would be re-colonized (it wasn't for years afterward), his experiment clearly shows that a colony can be eliminated by collecting.

The second, particularly tragic case is Mitchell's Satyr. In the northeastern United States this butterfly was limited to a few fens in northern New Jersey, but has now been extirpated by relentless collection pressure. One major colony was wiped out almost singlehandedly in the late 1970s by an individual who returned to the fen daily during successive seasons and each day killed every Mitchell's Satyr he saw. At the last colony, toward the end, even chain link fences, guard dogs, and a security man could not keep the collectors out.

Even when collection pressure does not result outright in the demise of a rare colonial butterfly, each individual killed results in the depletion of the gene pool, and this loss of genetic diversity becomes more important as the colony becomes smaller. Each individual killed might have been the individual that contained a mutation that would have allowed the colony to survive the inevitable drought or epidemic that it will face.

Some people might ask: Why save butterfly species? Are they of any value? An extensive consideration of this question is outside the scope of this book, but I would like to put forward a few short answers. In many areas, butterflies play an important role in the pollination of flowers. In addition, each species may possess unique properties useful to humans that will be irretrievably lost should it become extinct. The recent discovery of a potent anticancer drug, taxol, in a species of yew that had been considered a "trash species" highlights this possibility. Because ecological systems are interrelated in complicated ways, the removal of a single species can have a much greater adverse effect than might have been anticipated. In many cases, the extinction of but a single species will result in the removal of a number of other species that are, in some way, dependent on the first species. Often, the fact that a species of butterfly is close to extinction can be seen as a symptom that an entire unique habitat is about to be destroyed. The collapse of many of the earth's ecosystems may result in a world hostile, at best, to humans.

In addition to these other such "practical" arguments for the preservation of butterflies, there are clearly aesthetic and moral reasons to insist that butterflies survive. Only recently have human beings seen peoples from other "tribes" as similar to themselves and thus "real human beings" worthy of protection. As people become ever more conscious of their environment, they may come to see that all biological entities have intrinsic value and are worthy of protection. Many years ago, the Greeks equated butterflies with the souls of people, using the Greek word psyche for both. One does not have to believe in Greek mythology to know that in a world without butterflies, the souls of all people would be greatly diminished.

Commercially Raised Butterflies

A growing fad has been the release of commercially raised butterflies at weddings and other special events. Naive and unsuspecting brides think "what a beautiful idea." Unfortunately, releasing commercially raised butterflies into the environment can only harm wild populations—potentially spreading diseases, inappropriately mixing genetically distinct populations, and disrupting migratory pathways—and terribly disrupts the work of scientists trying to track butterfly movements. Every major scientist working with butterflies is opposed to this practice, as is the North American Butterfly Association, the Lepidopterists' Society, and the Audubon Society. Whenever you learn of someone considering the release of commercially raised butterflies, please let them know about how harmful this can be. Certainly, in my experience, the actual butterflies that are released are harmed, often arriving dead or dying and released into a hostile environment. Also, you should know that releasing these commercially raised butterflies does not, and cannot, increase the population of butterflies. The size of butterfly populations are determined by the carrying capacity of the land—how much suitable habitat is there, and by the prevalence of butterfly predators and diseases. Since releasing commercially raised butterflies does not increase the amount of habitat, but may increase the amount of disease, this practice can only reduce populations of wild butterflies. This is just as true of the release of Painted Ladies that are used in schools throughout the country. If a teacher insists on having children "learn" that butterflies are items to be bought from a store and then raised on artificial glop, they should at least require that the butterflies be kept indoors after emerging. (We don't encourage children to release exotic birds and other animals into the environment.) Besides, much more would be learned if the children were taken on a field trip, to see real butterflies in a real meadow, on real flowers. Finding a caterpillar or two, they could take it back to the classroom, rear it, then release the resulting adult back at the same spot where they found the caterpillar. The commercial interests behind the environmental pollution called "releasing" butterflies say, "No one has ever proved that releasing our commercially-raised butterflies harms the environment." Where have you heard this type of statement before? From the manufacturers of cigarettes, who said for years, "No one has proved that cigarettes hurt people." Well, in the 1890s, people thought "wouldn't it be wonderful to have all the birds mentioned by Shakespeare, right here in North America." So they released European Starlings into Central Park, New York. These birds have caused billions of dollars in damage to crops and have had serious negative impacts on native songbirds. Yet if you had said, in 1890, "Where's your proof that this will damage the environment," one could not provide that proof. **The proof can come only when it is too late and the environment has been severely damaged.**

About the Species Accounts

The order in which species are treated more or less follows the taxonomic order of the North American Butterfly Association's (NABA) *Checklist and English Names of North American Butterflies*. Occasionally a slightly different order is followed to group similar-appearing species or to facilitate a smooth and pleasing layout. The accounts of the species occurring in the West are organized as follows:

Name

English and scientific names follow the North American Butterfly Association's (NABA) *Checklist and English Names of North American Butterflies*. Until recently, each author of a book about butterflies used whatever set of names struck his or her fancy. The result has been a confusing plethora of names that has bewildered the uninitiated and made it more difficult for the public to become involved with butterflies. With the publication of NABA's list in 1995 we are now on the road toward standardization, although this process will take years to be completed. As this book goes to press, the NABA Names Committee is in the process of formulating a second edition to the NABA *Checklist*. In a few cases where the full committee already is in complete agreement on a name change (for example, changing the name of Caicus Skipper to Gold-costa Skipper), I have adopted that change in this work. Because the work of the committee is still in progress as this goes to press, there will almost certainly be cases where the second edition of the NABA *Checklist* has a different name or status for a taxon than that used here. For some names that have been used in other publications, I have included that name in the index.

Identification

Each species section begins with an account of how to identify that species. The most important identification clues are presented in boldface type, the thought being that if you are trying to identify a butterfly in the field you can quickly scan this information first, later reading the entire account if time permits.

Before the *Butterflies through Binoculars* series, butterfly guides were written by collectors for collectors. The approach they took to identification was very different than that used here. One very important difference is that because collectors are looking at a dead butterfly on a pin, they can pick up the pin and look at either the topside or underside of the butterfly. So if separating species A from species B is easy looking at the uppersides but difficult looking at the undersides, books written for collectors might show the uppersides of species A and B, but only the underside of species A, and tell you to separate the species from above but not from below. But in the field, when you tell the butterfly to turn over, it often ignores you! So, ideally one would like to be able to identify each species when seeing only its topside, or only its underside. I have tried to provide the information to allow you to do this. Given the present state of our knowledge and the complexity of western butterflies, this has not been possible in every case. For example, I show upper surfaces of most species of grass-skippers, but for many of them I do not provide identification information about these upper surfaces. The main reason for this is that for many species—for example, many of the *Hesperia* skippers—we do not know how to identify an individual to species by viewing only the upper surface. I have shown the upper surfaces because although it will rarely allow you to definitely establish a species' identity by itself, it will sometimes allow you to eliminate a number of species from consideration.

The size of a butterfly can be a useful clue to its identification but can be difficult to determine in the field—is the length of the forewing (FW) 9/16 in. or is it 11/16 in.? It is much easier to relate the size of a butterfly to other butterflies that one is familiar with. Because similar species are grouped on the same page or nearby pages and are shown at the same magnification (given at the top of each right-hand page), one can easily see how the size of an unknown species relates to the size of a species that one is familiar with. If one wants to know the absolute size of a species, this can be easily calculated by measuring the FW length of the photographic image, then dividing by the magnification given.

When considering size, remember that the size of different individuals of the same species can vary dramatically. Occasionally a "runt" individual will be drastically smaller than is normal for the species. And, although many species have both sexes a similar size, as a general rule, females are larger than males.

Habitat

This section describes the types of areas where this butterfly might normally be found.

Abundance

I try to give information that will allow you to know when to search for a particular species and how likely you might be to find it. Please note that, unless otherwise indicated, abundance information relates only to the area covered in this guide. (So, for example, status of Mimosa Yellow, given as R immigrant, applies to southeastern Arizona and West Texas, not to its status in the Lower Rio Grande Valley of Texas, where it is a common resident.) If the abundance is markedly different in different portions of the species' range in the West, then I often try to provide information for various subregions. **I cannot emphasize enough that this section is intended as a rough guide**, mainly as an aid to identification. If you are seeing many individuals at many sites of a species I list as R, you probably will want to double-check your identification. Keep in mind that butterfly abundance can, and usually does, vary dramatically from year to year and from locality to locality. One of the pleasures of butterflying is that each year is certain to bring its quota of surprises. Flight dates can also vary tremendously, depending upon the weather pattern of the year. Finding a species at a particular time in a particular year may depend on the vagaries of that year's brood sequence and abundance level. In desert areas especially, timing of rains may dramatically affect flight times and abundance. Although flight time may be given as, for example, May–July, in most cases this will refer to much of the range of the butterfly. You've probably noticed that much of the West is quite hilly. If you missed seeing that butterfly in May and now it's June, just go higher up the hill! At any one spot the flight time will generally be shorter than the flight period given, and the exact flight time will vary between localities depending largely, but not entirely, upon the latitude and the elevation of the locality. At any one spot, average flight time for most single-brooded species is probably about 1 month. Some species—for example, Frigga Fritillary—have much shorter flight periods, while others—for example, Coronis Fritillary—have much longer flight periods, even at a single locality.

Again, please note that abundance and flight times relate *only* to the portion of a species' range covered by this guide. The abundance and flight times is probably different in Florida, southern Texas, or northern Mexico.

Food

Listed as an aid to finding the adult butterflies are the **major** plant(s) or group of plants that are eaten by the caterpillars. For many uncommon butterflies the easiest way to locate colonies is to search for sites where the foodplant is common.

Comments

Here I include assorted information and/or thoughts that didn't easily fit into one of the above-listed categories.

About the Maps

The range maps tell you where a species is *normally* found. If an area is colored on a particular map, this means that I believe there are resident populations of the species in this area, or, if the species is an immigrant, that an active field observer is likely to see the species in this area at least once every two to three years. However, if the area that includes your home is shown as part of a butterfly's range, this does not mean that the butterfly will be flying down your street. For most butterflies, one needs to find appropriate habitat for that species to have a reasonable chance of finding the butterfly.

The black diagonal line running from the intersection of North Dakota, Manitoba, and Saskatchewan south to just southwest of Houston, Texas, is, together with the Manitoba–Saskatchewan border, the eastern boundary of the area treated in this book. The complete outline of states, intersected by the line, is shown to facilitate your recognition of map location, but east of the line there will be an increasing number of species that are not treated in this book. The southern end of the black diagonal line also marks the *southern* limit of the area treated in this book. South of Kinney and Bexar Counties in Texas, there will be an increasing number of species that are not treated in this book. Generally, range maps are provided for all species illustrated, even if that species is a stray. So some species will be shown with ranges that fall entirely outside the area treated in this book. Range maps are also provided for a few species that are not illustrated.

The Mexican portions of the range maps are, in many cases, little more than educated (sometimes uneducated) guesses. Although knowledge of butterflies north of the Mexican border is in its infancy, south of the border it is gestational (but developing rapidly).

Remember that butterflies have wings and will wander outside their normal range, occasionally for a great distance. Just because your location is not included in the normal range of a species doesn't mean it is impossible to see that species where you live, just that it becomes increasingly unlikely the farther from the normal range you go. Under the abundance sections I have included information about rare events where a species has strayed far beyond its normal range. It is likely that the increasing number of butterfliers will intercept a higher proportion of these strays.

In addition to showing the ranges of butterflies, to my knowledge, these maps are the first to provide information about butterfly broods (see the discussion of broods on page 12). The different colors on the map indicate the number of broods a species normally has in each portion of its range. Yellow indicates one brood, green indicates two broods, and blue indicates three or more broods. In general, you will need to search for a single-brooded species at a particular time of the year, while three-brooded species may be present during most of the warm season. Because there is so little information about brood sequences in most localities, many of the lines dividing numbers of broods are only my best guess. Often, it is surprisingly difficult to be sure of the number of broods at a particular locality. If fresh adults appear over a period of a few months, are the later-appearing individuals offspring of the earlier-appearing individuals or is there one asynchronous brood? One of the purposes of this part of the maps is to stimulate you to find where they are wrong. Hopefully this will lead to greater knowledge for the entire butterflying community. As I briefly discuss in the butterfly biology section dealing with broods, knowledge of brood transitions may be important to our understanding of butterfly ecology and evolution.

About the Photographs

The 1136 photographs (1082 by Jeffrey Glassberg) arranged on 127 pages represent a first. The *Through Binoculars* books are the first field guides to any group of organisms that use photographs in a true field guide format. Unlike other books that use photographs, the species in the photographs in this book are presented in the **correct size relationships** to the other species on the plate—the photographs having been carefully enlarged or reduced to provide this relationship. On the top left of each photograph page you learn the magnification or reduction from life size of the photographs on that page. If the size is indicated as shown 2× life size, this means that the length of the FWs in the photographs are about twice as long as on a live butterfly of that species (remember that individuals of the same species may vary greatly in size). Also keep in mind that a 2× increase in *length* leads to a 4× increase in *area*, and so the amount of space that the image of the butterfly in the photograph occupies is actually 4× the visual space occupied by a live butterfly at the same distance. On some plates small photographs are inset into larger photographs to show you a different view of the same species. These inset photographs are not to scale.

When males and females differ greatly in their appearance, both sexes are shown. In general, if the illustration is unlabeled as to sex, it can be assumed that both sexes are quite similar (although experienced butterfliers can probably discern the sex of most individuals by subtle differences).

Photographs were chosen and arranged so that similar species are shown in similar poses, making comparisons for identification easier. In general there is a visual consistency to the photographs, making them easily comparable to each other, because almost all of the photographs were taken using the same camera equipment and film. Other factors influencing the choice of photographs to illustrate each species were quality of the photograph, and condition and typicality of the butterfly illustrated. Of course, in some cases there was little choice—for example, the photographs of Cyna Blue and Outis Skipper show the only individuals of these species I have ever seen and I know of no other photographs of these species. To a large extent, I have used photographs of butterflies photographed in the West. Photos taken outside of the West show individuals that are substantially identical to those of the same species that occur in the West.

Unless indicated otherwise, all photographs by the author were taken in the wild, of unrestrained, unmanipulated butterflies (thirteen photo-

STATE ABBREVIATIONS

AZ	Arizona	**MT**	Montana	**OK**	Oklahoma
CA	California	**NC**	North Carolina	**OR**	Oregon
CO	Colorado	**ND**	North Dakota	**PA**	Pennsylvania
FL	Florida	**NV**	Nevada	**SD**	South Dakota
IA	Iowa	**NH**	New Hampshire	**TX**	Texas
MA	Massachusetts	**NJ**	New Jersey	**WA**	Washington
MN	Minnesota	**NM**	New Mexico	**WY**	Wyoming
MO	Missouri	**NY**	New York		

ABBREVIATIONS

A	abundant, likely to encounter more than 20 individuals per field trip to the right locality at the right time.
AMNH	American Museum of Natural History, New York
C	common, likely to encounter between 4 and 20 individuals per field trip to the right locality at the right time.
Co.	county
FW	forewing
HW	hindwing
L	local, not generally distributed, even within the range shown, absent from many areas with seemingly suitable habitat
NF	national forest
NP	national park
NWR	national wildlife refuge
R	rare, rarely seen even at the right place at the right time
S	stray, not part of the region's normal fauna and not seen most years
SF	state forest
SP	state park
U	uncommon, likely to see 0–3 individuals per field trip to the right place at the right time
WMA	wildlife management area
♂	male
♀	female

graphs, for which no photographs of wild butterflies were available, are of museum specimens).

The black and white lines that appear on some of the photographs have been placed over the photographs to draw your eye to field marks whose positions are difficult to explain in words.

Recognizing which wing of a grass-skipper one is viewing may require some practice. Remember that grass-skippers hold their HWs flat but their

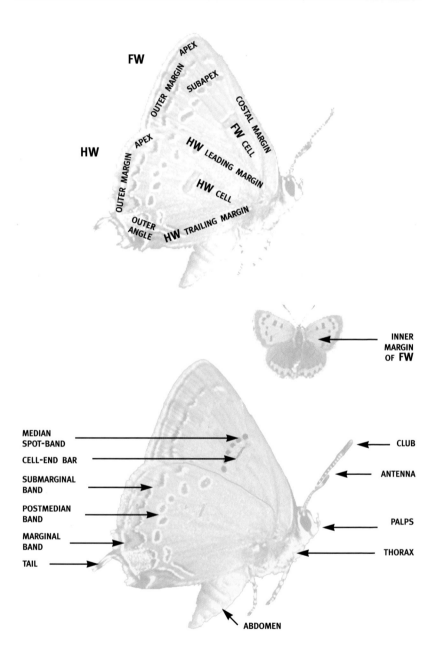

FW

APEX

OUTER MARGIN

SUBAPEX

COSTAL MARGIN

FW CELL

HW

OUTER MARGIN APEX

HW LEADING MARGIN

HW CELL

OUTER ANGLE

HW TRAILING MARGIN

INNER MARGIN OF FW

MEDIAN SPOT-BAND

CELL-END BAR

SUBMARGINAL BAND

POSTMEDIAN BAND

MARGINAL BAND

TAIL

CLUB

ANTENNA

PALPS

THORAX

ABDOMEN

FWs are held at an angle. So, depending upon one's angle of view, one may see the right FW on the right side and the left HW on the left side. For example, photograph 8, on page 263, is of a male Whirlabout. On the right side of the skipper one sees a wing with a black diagonal band. This is the right FW. On the left side one sees a wing that is orange in the middle with a black border—this is the left HW. The left FW is not readily visible; it is angled edge on toward the viewer. The right HW is partially visible as a crescent "northeast" of the right FW. Most of the photos of the upper surfaces of grass-skippers follow this pattern.

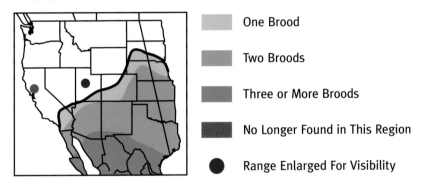

RANGE MAP COLORS AND INFORMATION

One Brood

Two Broods

Three or More Broods

No Longer Found in This Region

Range Enlarged For Visibility

If an area is colored on a particular map, this means that I believe there are **resident populations** of the species in the area, or, if the species is an immigrant, that an active field observer is likely to see the species in this area at least once every two to three years. A purple dot indicates that the species' range in this area is much smaller than the actual area covered by the purple dot.

The black diagonal line running from the intersection of North Dakota, Manitoba, and Saskatchewan south to just southwest of Houston, Texas, is, together with the Manitoba-Saskatchewan border, the eastern boundary of the area treated in this book.

See the introductory text for more information about the maps.

Swallowtails (family Papilionidae)

Because swallowtails are our largest butterflies, they are often seen and appreciated even by those who are not butterfly enthusiasts. Many of the spectacular species live in the tropics, but our tiger swallowtails are no slouches! Most species have long tails (but not the parnassians) making them easy to recognize as swallowtails.

Parnassians (subfamily Parnassiinae)

This distinctive group of swallowtails is restricted to northern climes. Two species are found in the area treated in this book (another, Eversmann's Parnassian, occurs in Alaska and northwestern Canada). After mating, males place a waxy cap, called a sphragis, over the females' abdomen to prevent other males from mating. In Europe, this group is called apollos. Most of the approximately 35 species are Eurasian, and since almost every mountain range has populations that look slightly different from the next mountain range, European and Japanese collectors have gone berserk in their pursuit of each variety, reportedly threatening the existence of some of them.

Clodius Parnassian *Parnassius clodius*

Its large size, white ground color and red spots tell you this is a parnassian. The FWs, especially the margins, are translucent. Note the **black antennas** and strong black FW border. The black bar within the FW cell usually crosses the entire cell and is rectangular. The sphragis is white. Phoebus Parnassian has white and black antennas and lacks a strong black FW border. *Habitat:* Mountain meadows and moist, open mountain woodland down to sea level in the Northwest. *Abundance:* C-A. May–mid Sept., mainly June–Aug. *Food:* Bleeding-hearts. *Comments:* Flight is slow and floating with wings held in a shallow V. Clodius Parnassian often flies higher above the ground than does Phoebus Parnassian.

Phoebus Parnassian *Parnassius phoebus*

Its large size, white ground color, and red spots tell you this is a parnassian. Individuals in some populations have extensive sooty over-scaling. Note the **white and black antennas**. The black bar within the FW cell usually doesn't reach the bottom of the cell and is rounded. The sphragis is dark. Populations in the California Sierra Nevadas sometimes have pale orange-yellow spots rather than red spots. *Habitat:* Open montane habitats, from about 4500 ft. to alpine. In the California Sierra Nevadas, restricted to alpine areas, especially rocky summits. *Abundance:* C, Rocky Mountains. Late May–Aug.; R, Sierra Nevadas. July; R, Siskiyous. Mainly July–Aug. *Food:* Stonecrops. *Comments:* Usually flies within one or two ft. of the ground. Some now treat California Sierra Nevada (*P. p. behri*) and Rocky Mountain (*P. p. smintheus*) populations (including the populations on Vancouver and the Olympic Peninsula) as separate species from (primarily) Old World *phoebus* and from each other, aligning the isolated population in the Siskiyou Mountains of northern California and southern Oregon with the Rocky Mountain populations.

1 Clodius Parnassian

2 Clodius Parnassian ♂

3 Clodius Parnassian ♀

4 Phoebus Parnassian ♂ (low elevation)

5 Phoebus Parnassian

6 Phoebus Parnassian ♂ (high elevation)

7 Phoebus ♂ (Cal. Sierra Nevadas) not to scale

8 Phoebus Parnassian ♀ (low elevation)

True Swallowtails (subfamily Papilioninae)

About 500 species worldwide; 12 species in the West (plus some strays).

Pipevine Swallowtail *Battus philenor*

A very dark swallowtail above with a strongly iridescent blue HW. When worn, outer portions of the FWs can appear quite whitish. Below, note the large **single orange spotband on iridescent blue**. "Black" swallowtails (pg. 46) have blue that is not iridescent and have two orange spotbands. Red-spotted Purple (pg. 194) lacks tails. *Habitat:* Gardens, woodland edges, open thorn scrub; northern California population more restricted to riparian habitats. *Abundance:* C, central to West Texas; otherwise mainly U-LC. Feb.–Oct.; March/April–Sept./Nov. in northern California. Strays to all of southern California and north to northern Colorado. *Food:* Pipevines, both native and cultivated. *Comments:* As butterfly gardeners plant more pipevines, the range of this species will probably expand.

Polydamas Swallowtail *Battus polydamas*

Note the absence of tails (but, of course, other swallowtails sometimes lose theirs). Above with a wide dirty-yellow postmedian band. Below, note the **dull red marginal spots** on the HW and **red spots on the body**. *Habitat:* Gardens and edges of woodlands. *Abundance:* Extremely rare stray (or human-assisted introduction) to southern California, southern Arizona and southern New Mexico (once each). *Food:* Pipevines. *Comments:* The rapidly flying Polydamas Swallowtail is easy enough to identify when one gets a good look at it—something that is not so easy to do!

Ornythion Swallowtail *Papilio ornythion*

Males somewhat smaller and duller than Giant Swallowtail, often detectable in flight. Above, note that the **FW submarginal and median bands do not meet** (in Giant Swallowtail they form an X). Lacks yellow in tail, which Giant usually has. Male Broad-banded Swallowtail (RS to southeastern Arizona) has a yellow spot in FW cell. Below, note the complete red postmedian HW band. Females are black with red, blue, and cream HW median & postmedian bands. *Habitat:* Woodlands, gardens and cultivated citrus groves. *Abundance:* RS to Austin area, West Texas, extreme southeastern New Mexico. *Food:* Citrus.

Giant Swallowtail *Papilio cresphontes*

At a distance, note the contrast between the dark wings above and the pale wings below. Above, the wings are dark brown (almost black) with prominent yellow bands. Note the "Xs" these bands form near the apexes of the FWs. Below, note the **striking cream-colored body and cream-colored wings** with HW blue median spotband. *Habitat:* Woodlands, gardens, and cultivated citrus groves. *Abundance:* R-U. March–Oct. RS north to Nevada, northern New Mexico and North Dakota. *Food:* Citrus, *Zanthoxylum* and *Amyris*. *Comments:* Giant Swallowtails have followed cultivated citrus (on which they are sometimes a pest) into southern California, expanding their range over the past 40 years. Still expanding, the species invaded the Los Angeles area in 1998.

1 Pipevine Swallowtail

2 Pipevine Swallowtail

3 Polydamas Swallowtail

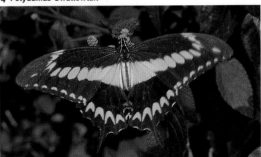

4 Polydamas Swallowtail

5 Ornythion Swallowtail ♀ (inset ♂)

6 Ornythion Swallowtail ♂

7 Giant Swallowtail

8 Giant Swallowtail

"Black" Swallowtails

Four species in the "black" swallowtail group are found in the West—Black Swallowtail, Old World Swallowtail, Anise Swallowtail, and Indra Swallowtail—and they can be extremely difficult to separate, even when seen well. The width of the yellow postmedian band varies on all four species, varying from very narrow to very wide (see page 48).

Black Swallowtail *Papilio polyxenes*

Abdomen has two or three rows of yellow spots with some visible from the top. Black spot at the HW outer angle either small and centered or reaching the inner margin of the HW. **FW marginal yellow spots tend to be rounded** (flattened distally in other species). Above, FW median spots are fairly "clean" basally (fuzzy in Baird's and Anise due to encroaching black scales). Below, the postmedian spotband has at least some orange. Thorax "shoulders" usually black. See pg. 48 for 'Desert' Black Swallowtail. *Habitat:* Widely distributed in open habitats and gardens. *Abundance:* U-C. West Texas west to southern California—Feb.–Oct.; Northward—mainly May–Sept. *Food:* Parsley family and less frequently citrus family. *Comments:* Hilltops.

Old World Swallowtail *Papilio machaon*

Abdomen has two or three rows of yellow spots, some visible from the top. Black spot at HW outer angle reaching the inner margin of HW. Below, postmedian spotband yellow. Thorax "shoulders" usually yellow. "Black" form individuals of 'Baird's' Old World Swallowtail predominate south of central Utah-Colorado. See pg. 48 for yellow forms. *Habitat:* Arid and semi-arid hills—prairie to open woodland. *Abundance:* R-U. Mainly May–June, mid July–Sept. *Food:* Wild tarragon. *Comments:* Hilltops. Isolated population in San Bernardino Mtns. of southern California.

Anise Swallowtail (black form) *Papilio zelicaon*

Abdomen with a single row of yellow spots down the side. Black spot at the HW outer angle small and centered. Thorax "shoulders" either black or yellow. See pg. 48 for the usual yellow form of Anise Swallowtail. *Habitat:* Open areas, including roadsides and disturbed habitats, from sea level to above treeline. *Abundance:* R-U (this color form). One brood. May–July. Mainly occurs along the eastern edge of Rocky Mountains, south through Colorado. *Food:* Parsley family. *Comments:* Hilltops.

Indra Swallowtail *Papilio indra*

Short-tailed forms (most of range) are distinctive. Tails are longer from southwestern Col. south and southwestward through southern Cal.— note the **mainly black abdomen**, except for a short yellow spot or stripe toward the rear. *Habitat:* Dry, rocky slopes and hilltops. *Abundance:* LR-LU. One brood + partial 2nd for desert populations in wet years. March–July (mainly March/April–May in southern and Pacific lowlands, mainly June–early July farther north and in mountains). *Food:* Parsley family, especially lomatiums. *Comments:* Hilltops *just below* the tops of hills and usually lands flat on the ground, not on vegetation.

Spicebush Swallowtail *Papilio troilus*

Male HW with greenish "cloud." See *BTB: East* for illustration.

1 Black Swallowtail

2 Black Swallowtail ♀

3 'Baird's' Old World Swallowtail

4 Black Swallowtail ♂

5 Anise Swallowtail, black form

6 'Baird's' Old World Swallowtail

7 Indra Swallowtail (Colorado)

8 Indra Swallowtail (Southern Sierra Nevadas)

Yellow-form "Black" Swallowtails

Three of the four western "black" swallowtails occur sometimes or predominantly as yellow-forms, with wide yellow bands. Like black-form "black" swallowtails, yellow-form "black" swallowtails are often difficult to distinguish from one another.

Old World Swallowtail *Papilio machaon*

Black with broad yellow bands. **Black spot at HW outer angle is bold and reaches HW inner margin.** 'Oregon' Old World Swallowtail has its thorax and abdomen yellow with black stripe. FW yellow marginal spots tend to be flattened distally. *Habitat:* Arid and semi-arid hills— prairie, sagebrush steppes, to open woodland *Abundance:* R-U. Mainly May–June, mid July–Sept. *Food:* Wild tarragon. *Range:* 'Oregon' Old World Swallowtail is found from British Columbia southeast to southeastern Oregon, western Montana and western Idaho. 'Baird's' Old World Swallowtail occupies the remainder of the range shown (with yellow form individuals predominating north of central Utah-Colorado, except that another subspecies occurs in southern Alberta and Saskatchewan. Old World Swallowtail also ranges widely in Eurasia. *Comments:* Hilltops. Until recently Baird's, Oregon, and Old World Swallowtails were considered to be separate species. Recent DNA analysis by Felix Sperling indicates that they are best considered a single species—Old World Swallowtail. 'Oregon' Swallowtail is the state insect of Oregon.

Anise Swallowtail *Papilio zelicaon*

Black with broad yellow bands. **Black spot at HW outer angle is small and centered** (see inset to photo 6). FW yellow marginal spots tend to be flattened distally. Occurs with 'Desert' Black Swallowtail only along the western edge of the Mojave Desert. *Habitat:* Generally distributed in open areas, including roadsides and disturbed habitats, from sea level to alpine; generally absent from deserts. *Abundance:* U-C. One brood in most of the range—April–early Aug. (with main flight period of less than a month at any locality). Two or three broods in Pacific lowlands. All year in the extreme south, mainly March–Sept farther north. *Food:* Originally used native plants in the parsley family, such as wild parsnip; now increasingly using introduced anise. *Comments:* Hilltops. Over most of the West, this is the most common "black" swallowtail.

'Desert' Black Swallowtail *Papilio polyxenes coloro*

Black with broad yellow bands. Black spot at HW outer angle can be small and centered or can reach HW inner margin. **FW yellow marginal spots are rounded.** Although populations in the southwestern deserts are primarily yellow-form, black-form individuals occur here as well. *Habitat:* Desert. *Abundance:* U-C. Two or three broods. Feb.–Oct. *Food:* Turpentine-broom. *Comments:* Occurs west of central Arizona, as indicated by black line on map. This butterfly is much addicted to the red flowers of chuparosa.

1 'Oregon' Old World Swallowtail

2 'Oregon' Old World Swallowtail

3 'Baird's' Old World Swallowtail

4 'Baird's' Old World Swallowtail

5 Anise Swallowtail

6 Anise Swallowtail (inset: outer angle close-up)

7 'Desert' Black Swallowtail

8 'Desert' Black Swallowtail

Tiger Swallowtails

The boldly patterned tiger swallowtails are some of our most spectacular and familiar butterflies. Five species are found in the West. Western, Eastern, and Canadian are very similar, replace each other geographically, and (along with Mexican Tiger Swallowtail) could easily be considered a single species. Hybrids occur where the populations meet. Males are shown. Above, females are very similar but have more blue in the HW black border.

Western Tiger Swallowtail *Papilio rutulus*
The **top spot of the HW submarginal spotband is yellow.** Below, the FW **marginal band is more or less continuous** and the **black stripe along the HW trailing margin is wide.** *Habitat:* Widely distributed in woodlands, including suburban areas, especially near watercourses. *Abundance:* Mainly C. Mainly June–July; but March/April–Sept./Oct. in Pacific lowlands. *Food:* Willows, aspens and many other trees.

Eastern Tiger Swallowtail *Papilio glaucus*
The **top spot of the HW submarginal spotband is orange.** Below, the FW **marginal band is broken into spots** and the **black stripe along the HW trailing margin is narrow.** Some females, especially southward, are black, rather than yellow. Below these lack the HW median orange spotband of other "black" swallowtails. They usually retain a shadow of the "tiger" pattern. *Habitat:* Deciduous woodland, especially woodland edges and wooded watercourses. *Abundance:* C. March/April–Sept./Oct. *Food:* Cherries, tulip tree, and others.

Canadian Tiger Swallowtail *Papilio canadensis*
The **top spot of the submarginal spotband is orange.** Below, the FW **marginal band is more or less continuous** and the **black stripe along the HW trailing margin is wide.** *Habitat:* Deciduous and deciduous-coniferous woodlands and edges, including suburban areas. *Abundance:* C-A. Mainly late May–mid July. *Food:* Birches, aspens, and others. *Comments:* An avid mudpuddler.

Pale Swallowtail *Papilio eurymedon*
Very similar to Western Tiger Swallowtail, but paler. The ground color is off-white to rich ochre. Also, above, the **black bar in the FW cell is wide.** *Habitat:* Deciduous woodlands and chaparral in hilly or mountainous areas, usually in moist canyons with permanent water. *Abundance:* Generally U-C, but R Dakotas and southern Canada. Mostly May–July, but April–Sept. in Pacific lowlands. *Food: Rhamnus, Ceanothus,* and other Rosaceae. *Comments:* Hilltops more than other tigers.

Two-tailed Swallowtail *Papilio multicaudata*
Averages larger than Western Tiger. Its flight is more powerful, often gliding with wings in a V. The **narrower black bars on the FW above** can often be seen even in flight. When seen well, note the second, albeit smaller, tail. *Habitat:* Wooded areas, especially canyons and ravines near watercourses, but also towns and parks. *Abundance:* C southward, R-U northward. Mainly April/May–Aug./Sept. but as early as March in southeastern Arizona. *Food:* Cherries, ashes and others.

1 Western Tiger Swallowtail

2 Western Tiger Swallowtail

3 Eastern Tiger Swallowtail

4 Eastern Tiger Swallowtail

5 Canadian Tiger Swallowtail

6 Pale Swallowtail

7 Two-tailed Swallowtail

8 Two-tailed Swallowtail

Whites & Yellows (family Pieridae)

These small to large butterflies are usually white or yellow.

Checkered Whites (genus *Pontia*)

These are medium-sized whites with many black spots. They are widely distributed and generally encountered.

Checkered White *Pontia protodice*

Below HW varies from largely unmarked (some males—see photo 1 inset) to strongly veined with brown (or yellowish-brown, sometimes greenish-brown) with females more strongly marked than males. See other checkered whites for separation from them. *Habitat:* Widespread in open habitats, including arid regions, agricultural lands, weedy fields, and suburbs. Most frequently encountered in the lowlands, but can be found on high peaks. *Abundance:* C (but U in Canada and R in northwest). Mainly Feb./March–Oct./Nov. Late summer immigrant to Canada and the Pacific Northwest, mainly July–Aug. *Food:* Crucifers.

Western White *Pontia occidentalis*

Very difficult to distinguish from Checkered White. Usually, Westerns have more, and blacker, dark spots than do checkered whites and are a little larger. On the FW marginal black spotband, **Western males have a set of five or six spots**, while Checkered males almost always lack spots 3 and 5 (counting down from the FW apex). Western females generally have dark gray markings, while Checkered females tend toward brown. Although, in general, Western Whites are found at higher altitudes than are Checkered Whites, Western Whites will move lower in the fall. *Habitat:* Open areas, both natural and disturbed, including woodland openings, mountain meadows, and areas above treeline. *Abundance:* U-C. Mainly two broods, April–Sept., but one brood at high elevations, June–Aug. *Food:* Crucifers.

Spring White *Pontia sisymbrii*

If the butterfly stays still long enough (ha!), note the narrow **FW cell-end bar**—characteristically **notched** in the center. Above, the FW has a series of marginal black spots. Below the HW postmedian area has a **whitish interruption of the dark veining**. *Habitat:* Deserts, sagebrush, dry rocky areas and coniferous woodlands. *Abundance:* U-C. Feb.–April in southwestern deserts to April–June in Oregon, British Columbia, Colorado and South Dakota, into Aug. at high elevations in the north. *Food:* Rock cresses and many other crucifers. *Comments:* Hilltops are the best place to find this butterfly.

Becker's White *Pontia beckerii*

Below, this is a gorgeous white, with bold, bright green HW markings. Note the very large **black "box" at the end of the FW cell** and the yellow veining below. Checkered and Western whites have brown or gray (sometimes green-gray) markings below, lack the bold black "box," and lack yellow veins. *Habitat:* Desert, juniper hills, sagebrush steppes and other arid regions. *Abundance:* Mainly U-C, R in Sierra Nevada. Mainly May–June, Aug. (March–Aug. in SW deserts). *Food:* Crucifers.

SHOWN LIFE SIZE

1 Checkered White

2 Checkered White ♂

3 Checkered White ♀

4 Western White

5 Western White ♂

6 Western White ♀

7 Spring White

8 Spring White ♂

9 Spring White ♀

10 Becker's White

11 Becker's White ♀

Cabbage White *Pieris rapae*

Note the one (male) or two (female) black spots on the middle FW and the **horizontal black spot at the FW apex**. Below, the HW is uniformly white with a yellowish cast. *Habitat:* Gardens, roadsides, and other open disturbed areas. *Abundance:* Mainly U-C, but R at southern edge of range. Continuously brooded from early spring to killing frost. *Food:* Crucifers. *Comments:* This European species, introduced into Canada in the 19th century, is now perhaps the most ubiquitous butterfly in North America, and one of the very few that causes some damage to agricultural crops. Although many people disparage this species, because it is so common and not native, close observation reveals it to be one of the most graceful inhabitants of the air. Four species of large white butterflies are rare strays to the West. See pg. 297 for more information about them.

Mustard White *Pieris napi*

Below, **HW veins are usually outlined with gray scaling**. 2nd generation individuals are much paler, often almost completely white. Above, populations can be immaculate white or have black spots on the FW (male 1, female 2). Cabbage White is not "veined" below and above its FW apex has a horizontal gray/black spot. *Habitat:* Openings in moist forests, usually coniferous. *Abundance:* U-C. Mainly June–mid Aug. in most of range; in Pacific lowlands, mainly May–July (but as early as mid Feb. southward) and in central Arizona and New Mexico, April–Aug. *Food:* Rock cresses, toothworts, and other crucifers. *Comments:* Some treat Eastern populations (*P.n. oleracea*) (which reach the West in Rocky Mountain foothills of southern Alberta) as a separate species from western populations (*P.n. marginalis*) and both distinct from Old World *P. napi*. More study is needed.

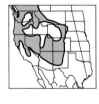

Pine White *Neophasia menapia*

Flight is slow and floating. Both above and below, the **black FW costa curves around to form a black cell-end bar**. *Habitat:* Pine forests. *Abundance:* C-A. July–Aug./early Sept. *Food:* Ponderosa pines and other Pinaceae. *Comments:* Usually seen high in the pines, Pine Whites have perhaps the most graceful, floating flight of any butterfly.

Chiricahua White *Neophasia terlootii*

Found only in southeastern Arizona. Males resemble Pine Whites but the **entire FW cell is black**. Females have a similar pattern but are orange. In flight females resemble ladies, but their floating flight will tell you they are not. *Habitat:* Pine forest. **Range** Extreme southeastern Arizona (Mt. Lemmon and Mt. Graham southward) and possibly adjacent New Mexico, south into Mexico. *Abundance:* C-A. Mid June–early Nov. First brood peaking late June–early July, second in Oct. *Food:* Ponderosa pine and Englemann's spruce. *Comments:* The behavior of Chiricahua Whites is quite strange. One week they'll be high in the pines, then next week they'll all be at ground level. Floating down from the pines they sometimes smash into objects in their way and when landed they sometimes fall over! There's gotta be a fermentation source here somewhere!

SHOWN LIFE SIZE

1 Cabbage White

2 Cabbage White ♂

3 Cabbage White ♀

4 Mustard White

5 Mustard White ♂

6 Mustard White ♀

7 Pine White

8 Pine White

9 Chiricahua White ♀

10 Chiricahua White ♂

11 Chiricahua White ♂

12 Chiricahua White ♀

Marbles & Orangetips
(genera *Euchloe* & *Anthocharis*)

Below, both groups have arresting green, yellowish, or gray marbling. Orangetips, with their giddy orange-tipped flight, are a prime reason to look forward to springtime. Marbles usually perch and nectar with wings closed; orangetips more frequently open their wings.

Large Marble *Euchloe ausonides*

Antennas checked with some black. Above, **FW cell-end bar is narrow** and FW costa usually only lightly checked. Below, marbling is extensive, usually with **veins noticeably yellower than green marbling.** Ground color often buffy off-white. *Habitat:* A wide variety of open habitats, including meadows, roadsides, farmland, and forest openings. *Abundance:* C-A. Mainly May–Aug., depending upon elevation and year. As early as mid March in California (where there may be two broods) and in the Great Basin. *Food:* Rock-cresses and other crucifers.

'California' Pearly

'Desert' Pearly

Pearly Marble *Euchloe hyantis*

Averages slightly smaller than Large Marble. Above with FW costa usually well-checked. **Below, HW veins not usually noticeably yellower than green marbling.** Ground color is white. Above, 'Desert' Pearly Marble (*lotta*) has wide black cell-end bar, 'California' Pearly Marble (*hyantis*) narrower. *Habitat:* 'Desert' Marble in open arid regions including desert, juniper-pinyon pine, and sagebrush. 'California' Marble in forests and chaparral. *Abundance:* U-LC. March–April in southern deserts, April–June farther north, and as late as June–July at higher elevations. *Food:* Crucifers. *Comments:* 'Desert' Marble is a strong hilltopper, 'California' Marble less so. Some consider *lotta* and *hyantis* to be separate species but, where they meet in southern California, extensive hybridization reportedly occurs.

Northern Marble *Euchloe creusa*

See photo 1 inset. HW below **heavily mottled with closely alternating white and green areas producing a striated effect,** often visible from above. *Habitat:* Openings in subalpine coniferous forest. *Abundance:* R. Mainly June–July. *Food:* Rock cresses and *Draba*. *Comments:* Barely enters the U.S. in Glacier National Park.

Olympia Marble *Euchloe olympia*

Antennas are white. Below, with marbling less extensive and **without marbling at the HW outer angle** and, when fresh, has a beautiful rosy flush on the wing bases. *Habitat:* Prairies and grassy hillsides. *Abundance:* U. Mainly April–June. *Food:* Rock-cresses and other crucifers. *Comments:* Hilltops.

Gray Marble *Anthocharis lanceolata*

Below, note the **all-over brownish-gray flocking** with a white "thumb" at the center of leading margin. Above, FW with a small black cell-end bar and very little black markings near the apex. *Habitat:* Rocky slopes and road-cuts in woodlands, from near sea level to about 7500 ft. *Abundance:* LC northern California and San Bernardinos, mainly R-U elsewhere in central and southern California. Late Feb.–May in southern California lowlands, May–June/July at high elevations and in the north. *Food:* Rock-cresses and other crucifers.

1 Large Marble (inset Northern Marble)

2 Large Marble

3 'Desert' Pearly Marble

4 'Desert' Pearly Marble

5 'California' Pearly Marble

6 'California' Pearly Marble

7 Olympia Marble

8 Olympia Marble

9 Gray Marble

10 Gray Marble

Sara Orangetip *Anthocharis sara*

Bright orange wingtips are unique in most of range (but see Desert Orangetip, below). Females are white or yellow, with the percentage yellow females varying from population to population, sometimes over small distances. A **suggestion of a white ray on the HW** is usually present. *Habitat:* A wide variety, from desert hills, to coniferous forests. Subspecies *sara* in desert edge to woodland; *stella* in woodland and sagebrush flats; *thoosa* mainly in pinyon-juniper woodland; *julia* in ponderosa/lodgepole pine forest. *Abundance:* C. Mainly one brood. Southern lowlands. Feb.–early April; Northwest Coast and Cascade ranges. March–mid July; high mountain meadows. Mid July–mid Aug.; Central Colorado. May–July. A partial second brood along the southern California coast. *Food:* Crucifers. *Comments:* Not a hilltopper. This species complex is composed of many populations throughout the West, with at least nine named "subspecies." Recently, some have suggested that there are a number of species in the complex—*A. sara, A. stella, A. thoosa,* and *A. julia. Thoosa* and *julia* are usually darker green below. Although *sara* and *stella* have an elevational disjunction between them in the Sierra Nevadas, they appear to intergrade broadly in the Pacific Northwest. The other "species" also appear to intergrade. Pending more clear-cut evidence, it is best to view this complex as a single species. Even if more than one species is involved, it may be that the above splits are not the most accurate representation of reality.

Desert Orangetip *Anthocharis cethura*

Above, note the **wide white border around the FW apex.** Below, marbling is more coalesced into bands than on Sara Orangetip and lacks the white central gap of most Sara populations. Ground color of both males and females varies from white to yellow-flushed to bright yellow ('Pima' Desert Orangetip). Females of 'Morrisons' Desert Orangetip, found at the southern end of the California Central Valley, have heavier green marbling on the HW below and most lack orange wingtips. They are easily mistaken for marbles but have blue-gray eyes (marbles' eyes are bright green). *Habitat:* Desert hills. *Abundance:* C. Mainly Feb.–April in southern California and southeastern Arizona, to mid April–mid May at the northern edge of its range. *Food:* Crucifers. *Comments:* Often flies with Sara Orangetips. Desert is **a strong hilltopper** (not so Sara), flies with faster wingbeats than does Sara, and averages smaller. Pima Orangetip is included here. Although sometimes treated as a separate species, it completely intergrades with Desert Orangetip in western Arizona and southern Nevada—the two are best considered as one species.

Falcate Orangetip *Anthocharis midea*

The bright orange wingtips of males are unique in its range; females lack the orange wingtips. Note the **hooked FW apex.** Flight is fairly weak and close to the ground. *Habitat:* Open woodlands with small crucifers. *Abundance:* LR-LU. Feb.–April. *Food:* Crucifers. *Comments:* Females usually appear a week or so later than the males.

1 **Sara Orangetip** *(sara)*

2 **Sara Orangetip** *(sara)* ♂

3 **Sara Orangetip** *(sara)* ♀

4 **Sara Orangetip** *(stella)*

5 **Sara Orangetip** *(stella)* ♂

6 **Sara Orangetip** *(stella)* ♀

7 **Sara Orangetip** *(julia)*

8 **Sara Orangetip** (New Mexico) ♀

9 **Sara Orangetip** *(thoosa)* ♀

10 **Desert Orangetip**

11 **Desert Orangetip** ♂

12 **Desert Orangetip** ♀

13 **Falcate Orangetip**

14 **Falcate Orangetip** ♂

15 **'Pima' Desert Orangetip**

Colias Sulphurs (genus *Colias*)

This group is not completely sorted out. There is much disagreement about the number of species in western North America and about which species to assign some populations, especially in the Pacific Northwest. For example, some believe that individuals in a population in the Ochoco Mountains of Oregon are Giant Sulphurs, while others believe that they are Western Sulphurs, or Queen Alexandra's Sulphurs! The relationships among Queen Alexandra's Sulphur, Christina's Sulphur, Western Sulphur and populations referred to as *columbiensis, krauthii,* and others, are remarkably unclear. However, in most locations the situation is much more straightforward. The *Colias* sulphurs almost never open their wings while landed (the exception being females rejecting males).

Orange Sulphur *Colias eurytheme*

The **most common, widespread orange sulphur**. The orange topside can be seen in flight, but look carefully because some individuals have only a small orange patch. Below, the **HW usually has a double cell-spot**, a dark smudge near the center of the leading margin, and at least a few dark postmedian spots. FW has an orange flush and also often has a few dark postmedian spots. Normally with little or no dark overscaling on the HW below. Females have pale spots included in the black FW border and are sometimes off-white (see photo 1 inset). *Habitat:* Very widespread in open habitats, including deserts, prairies, agricultural lands, suburbs, and tundra. *Abundance:* C-A. Mainly early spring–fall, but June–Sept. in the northern portion of its range where it is probably an immigrant. *Food:* Alfalfa and other legumes. *Comments:* Seems to hybridize with Clouded Sulphur in certain areas.

Clouded Sulphur *Colias philodice*

The **most common, widespread yellow sulphur**. The lemon-yellow upperside can be seen in flight. Lacks any orange above, although northern females often have an orange flush to the FW below. Below, the **HW often has a double cell-spot**, a dark smudge near the center of the leading margin, and at least a few dark postmedian spots. FW also often has a few dark postmedian spots. The inside edge of males FW black border (often visible through the wing) is normally slightly scalloped, not straight. Normally with little or no dark overscaling on the HW below, except on northern females. Females have pale spots included in the black FW border and are sometimes off-white. *Habitat:* Open areas, including prairies, agricultural lands, roadsides, and alpine meadows. *Abundance:* Mainly C, but U in southern lowlands. Spring to fall. *Food:* Clovers and other legumes.

Harford's Sulphur *Colias alexandra harfordii*

Yellow above. The only yellow sulphur in most of its range (Clouded Sulphur barely overlaps and is rare where it does). Resembles Clouded Sulphur but **black borders, especially on the male HW, are very narrow**. Flight is generally slower and higher than Clouded Sulphur. Female is paler yellow and lacks included pale spots in narrow black FW border. *Habitat:* Arid hills and canyons. *Abundance:* March/April–May, mid June–Aug. *Food:* Rattleweeds. *Comments:* Separated by quite a distance from other populations of Queen Alexandra's Sulphur and considered to be a full species by some.

1 Orange Sulphur ♀ (inset: white form)

2 Orange Sulphur ♂ (road-killed)

3 Orange Sulphur ♂

4 Clouded Sulphur ♂ (in flight)

5 Clouded Sulphur ♂

6 Clouded Sulphur ♀

7 Harford's Sulphur ♂

8 Harford's Sulphur ♀

Western Sulphur *Colias occidentalis*

Pale- to golden-yellow, above. Below, **HW cell-spot is rimmed with dark red**, darker and seemingly "rawer" than on Clouded or Orange Sulphurs. Black borders on males of the California subspecies, *chrysomelas* (photo 1), are usually wider and straighter than on Clouded Sulphurs. Black borders on more northern males are narrower. **FW black cell-spot is often faint.** HW with light but extensive black over-scaling. On the HW a dark smudge near the leading margin, and/or a few dark postmedian spots, may or may not be present. **Females have indistinct black borders**, are usually paler and occasionally are white. *Habitat:* Coniferous forest and included meadows. *Abundance:* LU-C. May–Sept., mainly June–July. *Food:* Legumes, especially *Lathyrus*. *Comments:* One of the only sulphurs comfortable flying *within* the forest. See page 303 for more information about this species.

Queen Alexandra's Sulphur *Colias alexandra*

Above, males are yellow, females yellow or white, depending upon population. Below, **HW is a pleasing, uniform, soft green**. Most populations have the **HW cell spot pale and with only a faint or no red rim** but populations in southern BC and northwestern Washington to western Montana (*columbiensis*) have a thin pink rim (some place these populations with Western Sulphur). **Christina's Sulphurs** (*C. alexandra christina*) **have varying amounts of orange above** with yellow wing bases. Below, HW is dull green-yellow with the cell-spot red-rimmed. Some place these populations as subspecies of Western Sulphur or consider these a separate species. *Habitat:* Prairies, foothill grasslands, clearings, and wet meadows in woodland; *columbiensis* in open coniferous forest. *Abundance:* U-C. May–Aug. *Food:* Rattleweeds and other legumes. *Comments:* See page 304 for more information about this species.

Christina's

Labrador Sulphur *Colias nastes*

Greenish above, visible in flight. Dull olive green below with bright pink fringe. Note the small white **HW cell-spot with a pink border that is strongly pointed distally**. *Habitat:* Windswept ridges and hilltops, and dry alpine slopes, all above treeline. *Abundance:* R-U. Mainly mid July–early Aug. *Food:* Legumes.

Sierra Sulphur *Colias behrii*

Strongly greenish, both above and below. Note the **green crown** and small **white HW cell-spot without a pink border** on the underwing. *Habitat:* High elevation moist, subalpine meadows. *Abundance:* LC. Mainly mid July–mid Aug. *Food:* Dwarf bilberry. *Comments:* Usually easy to find in the vicinity of Tioga Pass.

Mead's Sulphur *Colias meadii*

The **striking burnt-orange topside** is visible in flight. Below, the **green-tinged HW contrasts with orange FW disk** and the **HW border is pale**. Christina's Sulphur is not so green and doesn't have a pale HW border. *Habitat:* Alpine and subalpine meadows. *Abundance:* LC-LA. Mainly Mid July–mid Aug. *Food:* Rattleweeds, clovers and other legumes. *Comments:* White females are rare in most populations, common in others.

1 Western Sulphur ♂

2 Western Sulphur ♀

3 Queen Alexandra's Sulphur ♂

4 Queen Alexandra's Sulphur ♀

5 Christina's Sulphur

6 Labrador Sulphur

7 Sierra Sulphur

8 Mead's Sulphur

Pink-edged Sulphur *Colias interior*

Above, males are bright yellow with the **black FW border curved and narrow** (often visible from below, through the FW). Females are either yellow or white, with reduced black borders. Below, FW cell-end bar is usually open, HW cell-spot is usually round. No postmedian spots. Black overscaling is not pronounced and is lacking on FW disk. *Habitat:* Blueberry-rich openings, often moist, in coniferous forest. *Abundance:* U-C. Mainly late June–Aug. *Food:* Blueberries.

Pelidne Sulphur *Colias pelidne*

Above, males are yellow with the **black FW border curved and narrow** (often visible from below, through the FW). Females are usually white (predominates northward) or pale yellow (more common southward) with reduced black borders. Below, **FW disk with black overscaling** and HW also usually with pronounced black overscaling. **HW cell-spot often higher than wide**. *Habitat:* Openings (roads, meadows, shrubby areas, etc.) in subalpine forest and open heaths. *Abundance:* R-U. July–August. *Food:* Blueberries and wintergreens. *Comments:* This species and Pink-edged Sulphur are very closely related.

Giant Sulphur *Colias gigantea*

Usually somewhat **larger than other sulphurs** in range. Above, males are yellow with black borders that are usually fairly straight and wide. **Females are pale yellow** (usually) or white, **with much reduced black borders or none at all**. Below, **HW cell-spot is large and often elliptical** (wider than high), often with a small satellite spot above it. *Habitat:* **Willow bogs** in boreal and mixed forests. *Abundance:* R-U. Mainly July–mid Aug. *Food:* Willows.

Scudder's Sulphur *Colias scudderi*

Above, males are yellow, while females are normally white, rarely yellow. Below, female HW is pale- to moss green, with distal 1/4 of wing somewhat paler. Male has fairly uniform gray-green overscaling. Below, HW cell-spot often has a trace of a satellite spot above it and is sometimes elliptical (wider than high). Best separated from Giant Sulphur by range. *Habitat:* **Alpine willow bogs, from 9–12,000 ft.** *Abundance:* R-U. July–Aug. *Food:* Willows. *Comments:* Although there are subtle differences in habitat preference, average size, and wing shape, this species and Giant Sulphur are very closely related and possibly should be treated as one species.

1 Pink-edged Sulphur ♂

2 Pink-edged Sulphur ♀

3 Pelidne Sulphur ♂

4 Pelidne Sulphur ♀

5 Giant Sulphur ♂

6 Giant Sulphur ♀

7 Scudder's Sulphur ♂

8 Scudder's Sulphur ♀

Southern Dogface *Colias (Zerene) cesonia*

A large, bright yellow sulphur with **pointed FWs** and a **bold black outline of a dog's head** above, also visible below. **The distance from the FW outer margin to the "muzzle" of the dog's-head is less than 1/4 of the wing width.** The fall form often has the HW below suffused with pink. Females are occasionally white and their markings are less bold. *Habitat:* Open areas, usually dry, including thorn scrub and agricultural lands. *Abundance:* C-A in three + brood areas, all year; R-U in southern California, April–Oct.; R northward west of the front ranges of the Rockies. R-U summer immigrant to the northern plains, mainly June–Aug. *Food:* False indigo, *Dalea,* and other legumes. *Comments:* So distinctive that it is identifiable from a car traveling at high speed.

California Dogface *Colias (Zerene) eurydice*

Above, males are bright golden yellow with a violet sheen and a **bold black outline of a dog's head**, also visible from below. The **distance from the FW outer margin to the "muzzle" of the dog's-head is more than 1/4 of the wing width.** Females usually lack black borders and resemble Cloudless Sulphurs, especially in flight. Below note the **pointed FW apex** and the **pink ray at the base of the HW**. *Habitat:* Foothill and mountain canyons and meadows. *Abundance:* LU-LC. Mainly April–May, late July–Sept. *Food:* False indigo.

Lyside Sulphur *Kricogonia lyside*

Extremely variable in both size and appearance. Above, varies from yellow to white with yellow patches, to white. Below, **often distinctively green with a prominently whitened vein running through the HW** and a yellow flush to the FW disk, but can be pale yellowish to almost white without the whitened vein. *Habitat:* Tropical and subtropical scrub. *Abundance:* C. South-central Texas to West Texas, all year, mainly April–Nov.; U-C immigrant to southeastern Arizona mid July–Nov. *Food:* Lignum vitae. *Comments:* Often pitches under leaves, landing upside down.

White Angled-Sulphur *Anteos clorinde*

Very large with a powerful flight. Note the reticulated greenish-white underside with prominent veining and **curved wing shape** that distinguishes angled-sulphurs from phoebis. Above, white with a bright yellow patch on the FW. *Habitat:* Open areas. *Abundance:* R-U. Irregular immigrant to southeastern Arizona, mainly Aug.–Sept. Strays to Edwards' Plateau and West Texas. RS north to Nebraska, Colorado and Utah. *Food:* Cassias.

Yellow Angled-Sulphur *Anteos maerula*

Very large with a powerful flight. Similar to White Angled-Sulphur but **yellow above**. *Habitat:* Open areas. *Abundance:* RS, mainly in late summer, to southeastern Arizona; RS to San Antonio area. *Food:* Cassias.

1 Southern Dogface

2 Southern Dogface (captured by spider)

3 California Dogface ♂

4 California Dogface ♂ (inset: in flight)

5 California Dogface ♀

6 Lyside Sulphur (inset: held by ambush bug)

7 White Angled-Sulphur

8 Yellow Angled-Sulphur

Phoebis (genus *Phoebis*)

Sometimes called giant-sulphurs, size alone will usually suffice to distinguish phoebis from other sulphurs. Like most pierids, these butterflies almost never open their wings while landed—you'll need to glimpse their topsides in flight.

Cloudless Sulphur *Phoebis sennae*

This is by far the most common and widespread phoebis. It has a high, directional, sailing flight with characteristic deep, powerful wingbeats. This species can usually be separated on the wing from its congeners by its **solid yellow topside** (see photo 1 inset). Males are pale yellow above; females vary from orange-yellow to off-white. Yellow-green to warm yellow below, males have few markings while females' more extensive markings include a **broken FW postmedian line.** *Habitat:* A wide variety of open situations, including gardens, tropical woodland, and thorn scrub. *Abundance:* R-U southern California; C-A from southeastern Arizona to central Texas. Mainly April–Oct. Decreasing immigrant northward, usually reaching Colorado by June. Has strayed north to Oregon (once), Montana (once), and North Dakota (once). *Food:* Cassias. *Comments:* A strong migrant, in big flight years this species could turn up almost anywhere.

Orange-barred Sulphur *Phoebis philea*

Above, males are yellow with orange patches on both the FWs and HWs. Females range from yellow to white above, lack the FW orange patches, usually have rich reddish HW borders above, and often have rich reddish suffusions below. Below, the **FW postmedian line is broken** as in Cloudless Sulphur. Cloudless Sulphurs are generally all yellow, but some females do have an orange tinge to the HW borders above. Female Orange-barred Sulphurs usually are more richly suffused with pink below, especially along the outer margins, have a clear area just above the HW cell end spots, usually have the FW cell-end spots smaller and less open, and usually have the FW line less disjunct than do female Cloudless Sulphurs. Large Orange Sulphurs are all orange and have a straight FW postmedian line below. *Habitat:* Tropical and subtropical scrub. *Abundance:* R immigrant to west Texas, RS to southeastern Arizona. Mainly Aug.–Nov. Has strayed to Nebraska, Colorado, Nevada, and California. *Food:* Cassias.

Large Orange Sulphur *Phoebis agarithe*

A very large sulphur whose **males are bright orange above**. Females are either orange or off-white both above and below (see inset to photo 6). Below, note the **diagonal, straight line on the FW** (although males can be almost unmarked). Orange-barred Sulphurs are yellow with orange patches above and have a broken postmedian line on the FW below. *Habitat:* General in open tropical and subtropical situations, including gardens and woodland edges. *Abundance:* R-U immigrant. June–Nov. Has strayed to Nebraska, Colorado, Nevada, and southern California. *Food:* Legumes.

1 Cloudless Sulphur ♂ (inset: road-killed)

2 Cloudless Sulphur ♀

3 Orange-barred Sulphur ♂ (inset: in flight)

4 Orange-barred Sulphur ♀

5 Large Orange Sulphur ♂

6 Large Orange Sulphur ♀ (inset: white form)

Yellows (genus *Eurema*)

This worldwide group of small to medium-sized butterflies is most diverse in the tropics. The caterpillars of most species feed on legumes. Adults often choose yellow leaves instead of green ones for overnight roosting.

Mexican Yellow *Eurema mexicana*

Note the **angled HW with small tail**. Above, the ground color is pale yellow to white with a **dramatic dog's head pattern**. Clouded Sulphur and Little Yellow lack angled HWs. Other sulphurs with angled HWs are orange or bright yellow above. *Habitat:* Many types of open habitats. *Abundance:* C-A, in areas of three or more broods, all year. Immigrant northward, U-C in areas of two broods; R-U in areas of one brood. Everywhere most common in the fall. RS north to Wyoming, North Dakota, and Saskatchewan. *Food:* Legumes, including *Acacia*.

Boisduval's Yellow *Eurema boisduvaliana*

Note the **angled HW. Very bright yellow above**, **yellow below**. Males have a weak dog's head pattern; females have FW black border similar to Little Yellow. Sleepy Orange has at least an orange flush on the FW below. Little Yellow is smaller and lacks angled HW and, below, HW diagonal line. Mexican Yellow is pale yellow to white above, has a more angular "dog's head" on the FW above, and has a more pronounced "tail." *Habitat:* Tropical forest and scrub, preferring shady situations. *Abundance:* R immigrant, April–Nov. RS to central and west Texas. Has strayed to New Mexico, Nevada, and California. *Food:* Cassias.

Little Yellow *Eurema lisa*

Small and **bright yellow above** (see photo 3 inset), with variable, scattered, smudged dark markings on the HW below. Note the **two small black spots at the base of the HW**. Most individuals have a pink spot at the HW apex, although this spot is often diminished or absent in males. Some females have yellow replaced by white (see photo 4 inset). *Habitat:* Dry open areas; strongly partial to sunny situations. *Abundance:* C-A central Texas, R West Texas, March–Nov. A strong immigrant northward in late summer. RS north to California and Colorado. *Food:* Cassias.

Mimosa Yellow *Eurema nise*

A small yellow, very bright yellow above, that usually **flies within the edges of woodlands**. Black border at the FW apex is narrower than on Little Yellow. Note the **absence of black spots at the base of the HW**. *Habitat:* Woodland edge. *Abundance:* R immigrant? Mainly mid April–mid Nov. RS north to Kansas, Colorado and southern California. *Food:* *Mimosa*.

Barred Yellow *Eurema daira*

Small and weak-flying. Above, yellow or white. Males have a black bar along FW inner margin—sometimes visible in flight. HW apex is usually vaguely darker. Base of FW costa is white or tan, Little Yellow is pure yellow here. *Habitat:* Open areas, often disturbed. *Abundance:* R immigrant, Aug.–Oct. *Food:* Legumes.

1 Mexican Yellow

2 Boisduval's Yellow

3 Little Yellow ♂ (inset: caught by spider)

4 Little Yellow ♀ (inset: white form)

5 Mimosa Yellow ♂

6 Mimosa Yellow ♀

7 Barred Yellow (summer) (inset: ♂ courting)

8 Barred Yellow (winter form)

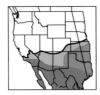

Sleepy Orange *Eurema nicippe*

This butterfly is bright to dull orange above with black borders (see inset to photo 2, caught by a robberfly). It flies closer to the ground than does Orange Sulphur, with weaker wingbeats and is darker orange above. Variable below, note the **characteristic diagonal brown markings on the HW** and the orange flush on the FW. This species has two seasonal forms and the HW ground color below can be either orange-yellow or a dull reddish color. *Habitat:* A wide variety of open areas. *Abundance:* Central Texas west to southeastern Arizona. C-A, all year; Southern California. U-C. March–Sept.; one brood areas. R-U immigrant, mainly June–July. RS to South Dakota, Wyoming and northern Nevada. *Food:* Cassias. *Comments:* The name "sleepy" does not refer to this species' flight—which is quite perky. Rather, the cell-end spots on the FW above look like closed eyes.

Tailed Orange *Eurema proterpia*

Very deep orange above (see photo 4, upperside visible through tear in the HW). Two forms, one tailed and highly reticulated with brown below (winter-dry season); the other with HW sharply angled, but not tailed, and unmarked orange below. Both lack a FW cell-end bar. Sleepy Orange has less angled HW and has a black spot at the end of the FW cell. *Habitat:* Tropical woodlands and thorn scrub. *Abundance:* C-A late summer immigrant (influx varies yearly). RS north to Kansas, northern New Mexico and northern Arizona. *Food:* Cassias. *Comments:* The two seasonal forms are so different that, at one time, they were thought to be two species.

Dina Yellow *Eurema dina*

Dina Yellows are larger and more orange-flushed than are Little Yellows. Males are bright orange-yellow with a very narrow black FW border. Females are yellow with an orange flush. Below, note the **pinkish-brown FW apex** and the **dark spot within the HW cell**. Little Yellow lacks a pinkish patch on the FW apex and the dark spot in the HW cell. *Habitat:* Brushy woods and thorn scrub, preferring shady situations. *Abundance:* R immigrant, mainly mid Aug.–mid Sept. *Food:* Simaroubaceae.

Dainty Sulphur *Nathalis iole*

A tiny sulphur, more greenish-yellow above than Little Yellow, with flight very low to the ground. Below, note the dark **greenish HW** and the **black spots on the FW** submarginal area. *Habitat:* A wide variety of open habitats, from desert to prairie to open woodland. *Abundance:* U-A, mainly C eastward and southward (areas shown as three broods). Decreasing immigrant (mainly late summer and fall) northward and westward. Has strayed to Saskatchewan (one record), Montana, Idaho, and Washington. *Food:* Aster family.

1 Sleepy Orange

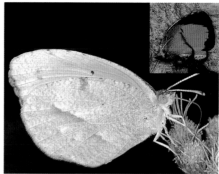

2 Sleepy Orange (winter)

3 Sleepy Orange

4 Tailed Orange (summer form)

5 Tailed Orange (winter form)

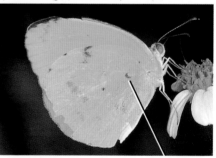

6 Dina Yellow ♂

7 Dina Yellow ♀

8 Dainty Sulphur (inset: male courting)

Gossamer-wings (family Lycaenidae)

This is a very large worldwide family of butterflies consisting, in the West, of coppers, hairstreaks, and blues. Most species are quite small, although a few tropical hairstreaks are larger than an American Lady. Many gossamer-wings are myrmecophilous (ant-loving). The caterpillars secrete a "honey-dew" from special glands that attracts certain species of ants. These ants then "tend" the caterpillars to obtain the "honey-dew," helping to protect them from predator species. The caterpillars of many gossamer-wings feed on flower parts.

Coppers (subfamily Lycaeninae)

The 16 North American species are a treasure to be mined—this group is a favorite of many butterfly enthusiasts. The vicinity of Tioga Pass in, and just east of, Yosemite National Park is a great place to find coppers. This region boasts of possibly the greatest diversity of coppers of any site in the world—with exceptional good fortune it might be possible to find 10 species in a single day (I've seen seven species here in a single day).

Gray Copper *Lycaena dione*

A very large copper. Below, gray with black spots and a **prominent, wide red-orange HW marginal band**. Bronze Copper (pg. 79) has an orange FW disk. Acadian Hairstreak (pg. 89 lacks black spots on HW base and is much smaller. Above, gray. *Habitat:* Areas with an abundance of dock, including moist meadows, fields and grasslands, roadside ditches, edges of ponds and streams. *Abundance:* U-LC. Mid June–July north to the Dakotas, July–mid Aug. in Saskatchewan and Alberta. *Food:* Broad dock, and other docks.

Edith's Copper *Lycaena editha*

Smaller than Great or Gray Coppers. Below, gray **HW with large irregularly-shaped brownish blotches** usually outlined by black. HW without a short tail. Females above are very similar to female Great Coppers. Edith's usually have more orange than female Great Coppers, have FW fringes checkered (Great Coppers usually unchecked), and lack a "tail." *Habitat:* Varied, including moist mountain meadows, openings in coniferous woodland, and moist areas in sagebrush steppes. *Abundance:* C-A. June–Aug. *Food:* Docks and horkelias have been reported.

Great Copper *Lycaena xanthoides*

A very large copper. Below, gray HW with darker gray to black spots. **HW usually with a small "tail."** Gorgon Copper (pg. 79) has a HW submarginal band of red-orange spots. *Habitat:* Chaparral, dry grasslands, grassy hillsides and open fields. *Abundance:* LU-C. Mainly May–June in the California coastal lowlands (but as early as late April), mainly June–July at higher elevations, and into early Aug. in Oregon. *Food:* Docks. *Comments:* Distribution very spotty within range shown.

1 Gray Copper

2 Gray Copper ♂ (inset: ♀)

3 Edith's Copper

4 Edith's Copper ♂

5 Great Copper

6 Great Copper ♂

7 Edith's Copper ♀

8 Great Copper ♀

American Copper *Lycaena phlaeas*

Below, FW is orange with bold black spots; HW is gray with smaller black spots. Red-orange submarginal line usually bordered inwardly by a pale pink aurora. Lacks black spots at HW apex that Lustrous Copper has. Above, FW greasy yellow-orange (Alberta–Montana) to red-orange, HW with wide marginal red-orange band. Female Bronze Copper (pg. 79) is much larger and has an extra black spot at FW base. *Habitat:* High meadows, trails and rocky areas above or near treeline. *Abundance:* LR. July–early Sept. Also, individuals of the Eastern lowland population have been reported from western Nebraska, eastern Colorado, and western South Dakota. *Food:* Docks and sorrels. *Comments:* A few people state, *as fact*, that eastern populations are non-native. This is misleading, at best, because there is almost no information in support of this conjecture.

Lustrous Copper *Lycaena cupreus*

Below, **FW is orange with bold black spots; HW is gray with bold black spots**. Note the two black spots at the HW apex. Only American and Bronze Coppers (see pg. 79) also have a combination of orange FW and gray HW with black spots. Bronze Coppers have a different range, are much larger, and have a wide red-orange HW submarginal band. Above, **fiery red-orange male with black borders is unique**. Female is similar but duller with bolder black spots. Similar female Ruddy (pg. 81), Lilac-bordered Coppers (pg. 82) and some Purplish Coppers (pg.83) have a black spot above the FW inner margin that female Lustrous Coppers lack. *Habitat:* Mainly moderate to high elevation forest openings and meadows in California and western Oregon, mainly rockslides and high mountain meadows elsewhere. *Abundance:* C, California Sierra Nevadas; R-U elsewhere. Mainly July–Aug but also June in California and lower elevations in Oregon. *Food:* Docks and sorrels. *Comments:* While traveling on horseback in the high Wind River Mountains of Wyoming, I espied a male in a small meadow of perhaps half an acre. On my return back through the meadow, the gleam of a perching male again caught my eye. Thinking that the meadow must be full of Lustrous Coppers, I dismounted to photograph them. A thorough search revealed that there was but a single individual in the entire meadow. Lustrous Coppers certainly are standouts!

Tailed Copper *Lycaena arota*

Tailed. Above, males vary from brown to weakly iridescent purple. Females have a dark triangular patch in the middle of the FW. *Habitat:* Most frequently encountered along streamsides and other watercourses through foothill woodlands, but also in chaparral and oak openings, sagebrush steppes, and high mountain meadows. *Abundance:* Mainly U-C, occasionally A. Mainly May–June in lowland California; July–Sept. at higher elevations. *Food:* Gooseberries. *Comments:* Males, which emerge before females, perch higher, from about two feet to 12 feet, than do other coppers.

1 American Copper

2 American Copper

3 Lustrous Copper

4 Lustrous Copper ♂

5 Tailed Copper

6 Lustrous Copper ♀

7 Tailed Copper ♂

8 Tailed Copper ♀

Gorgon Copper *Lycaena gorgon*

A large copper. In flight, the dark upperside strongly contrasts with the pale gray underside. Below, the prominent **HW submarginal red-orange band of separated spots** is characteristic. Male above is dull iridescent purple, with no black spotting or FW cell-end bars. Tailed Copper (pg. 77) is dull iridescent purple but has tails. Other male coppers with purple have black FW cell-end bars. *Habitat:* Many dry open situations, mainly in foothills, including canyons through chaparral, grassy hillsides, and rocky outcrops. *Abundance:* U-C. Mainly May–June; as early as April in San Diego Co., California; June–mid July/early Aug. in the mountains and in Oregon. *Food:* Naked buckwheat and elongate buckwheat.

Bronze Copper *Lycaena hyllus*

A large, floppy-flying copper. Although in a picture it closely resembles an American Copper (below and female above, pg. 77), when encountered in the field there is no doubt about its identity. The logical flip side of this is that if you are in doubt of a butterfly's identity, it is not this species. Below, note the pale, almost white ground color, the **orange FW disk**, and the **broad marginal HW orange band**. Above, males are purple with orange tints, while females have their ground color paler yellowish-orange. Gray Coppers (pg. 75) are gray above and lack the orange FW disk below. *Habitat:* Low wet meadows/marshes, especially in river flood plains. *Abundance:* LR-LU. Mostly June–early July, Aug.–early Sept. In Kansas and parts of Nebraska, mid May–Sept. Possibly only one brood in the Cypress Hills of Saskatchewan, early July–early Aug. Brood emergences appear to be more erratic than most butterflies. *Food:* Water dock and curled dock. *Comments:* Only recently found in northeastern New Mexico.

Hermes Copper *Lycaena hermes*

Rare and local. Note the **FW with extensive yellow** contrasting with the dull **HW with small tails**. Males and females are similar, but females are not quite as bright. The **bright yellow underside** is unique. Female Tailed Coppers (pg. 77) have a dark triangle in the middle of the FW above and have orange on the HW. Some female Gorgon Coppers (much larger than Hermes Coppers) have orange on the FW and none on the HW but the orange patch on the FW is not cohesive, as in Hermes Copper, and there are no tails. *Habitat:* Scrub and chaparral. *Abundance:* LR. One brood, mid May–mid July, usually with a peak around the third week of June. *Food:* Redberry. *Comments:* Extremely restricted geographically, this species appears to be in a serious decline. In the United States it is found only in San Diego Co. California, north to Fallbrook and east to Descanso. In adjacent Baja California it is found south to Santo Tomas. This butterfly needs the help of friends.

1 Gorgon Copper

2 Gorgon Copper ♂

3 Bronze Copper

4 Gorgon Copper ♀

5 Hermes Copper

6 Bronze Copper ♂

7 Hermes Copper

8 Bronze Copper ♀

Ruddy Copper *Lycaena rubidus*

Below, off-white with very limited markings on the HW and an orange flush on FW disk. Males above, with their all-over bright orange with purple highlights, are an easy call. Most females are orange as shown, but some are a dull gray-brown. Note the unchecked, bright white fringes and narrow black marginal border of females. Other similar females lack this combination, except perhaps the smaller female Lustrous Copper, which lacks a black spot at the FW base near the inner margin that this species has. *Habitat:* Moist meadows, streamsides, and other open moist areas in arid country. *Abundance:* LC-A over most of range, LR at the eastern and northern edges. Mid May–Aug. Mainly June at low to moderate elevations. Mainly July–Aug. at higher elevations and from Montana north into Alberta and Saskatchewan. *Food:* Docks. *Comments:* Males often perch in depressions or ditches. An isolated population, 'Ferris' Ruddy Copper, inhabits the White Mountains of Arizona. Some consider this population to be a distinct species. To my eyes these coppers look very similar to Ruddy Coppers found elsewhere and they occur in exactly the same type of habitat, wet meadows, favored by other populations of Ruddy Coppers.

Blue Copper *Lycaena heteronea*

Below, ground color is nearly white with HW spotting varying from essentially absent to more strongly black-marked than the individual in photo 7. Boisduval's Blues overlap in size and can appear very similar (see inset photo 7 and pg. 121). Most are grayer below, with white rings around the HW black spots, and with a pronounced submarginal spotband that Blue Coppers lack. Blue Coppers have a black spot within the FW cell (often obscured by the HW—as in the individual in photo 7) that Boisduval's Blues lack. Females almost always have noticeable blue at the base of the HWs, with the ground color varying from tawnier than shown, to as shown, to a dull blue. Above, **males usually with marked black veining** on bright blue wings. *Habitat:* Sagebrush steppes, dry hillsides, barren rock outcrops, and mountain meadows. *Abundance:* Mainly C-A, LR in southern California. June–early Sept.; June–July in lowlands, mainly July–Aug. at higher elevations and farther north. *Food:* Buckwheats. *Comments:* Males will often return to the same perch after being disturbed, with a flight that is faster and more powerful than a blue's. Ruddy and Blue Coppers are closely related.

1 Ruddy Copper (AZ White Mtns.)

2 Ruddy Copper ♂

3 Ruddy Copper

4 Ruddy Copper ♀

5 Blue Copper

6 Blue Copper ♀

7 Blue Copper (inset: Boisduval's Blue)

8 Blue Copper ♂

Purplish Copper *Lycaena helloides*

Below, with light gray-lavender HW, whose black spotting is weak and with a thin, red-orange zigzag marginal line. Above, females with very variable amount of orange, from almost none to extensive, and with HW submarginal orange line sometimes much more developed than on individual shown. Lilac-bordered Copper is two-toned, below. American Copper (pg. 77, rare in West) has a bright orange FW disk, below. *Habitat:* A great variety of open moist situations, often disturbed, from sea level to high elevations. *Abundance:* C. Two–three broods most locations. April/May–Sept./Oct.; One brood high elevations. June–Aug. *Food:* Docks and knotweeds. *Comments:* Some high-elevation populations in the Rocky Mountains have males with greatly reduced HW red-orange bands and very wide black FW borders. The correct treatment of these populations is uncertain. Individuals in these populations closely resemble Dorcas Coppers, a species found mainly north and east of the area covered in this guide, and some people treat these populations as Dorcas Coppers.

Lilac-bordered Copper *Lycaena nivalis*

Below, **HW with a two-toned appearance**, yellow inwardly, lilac/pink outwardly, that is less pronounced in some populations than on the individual in photo 3. Above, females vary from as shown to quite dark. Above, males are dull to brilliant iridescent purple, depending upon population, one's viewing angle, and the degree of wear of the individual. *Habitat:* Mountain meadows, openings in ponderosa pine and Douglas fir forest, sagebrush steppes. *Abundance:* C-A. As early as late May at low elevations in Oregon and Washington, into Aug. and early Sept. at high elevations. *Food:* Knotweeds. *Comments:* The beauty of fresh Lilac-bordered Coppers is so stunning that anyone viewing a fresh individual through good binoculars is sure to become a butterflier for life! Worn individuals quickly fade.

Mariposa Copper *Lycaena mariposa*

Below, **ash gray**, heavily marked with black spots, including a **HW submarginal band of inwardly directed black chevrons**. FW disk orange flushed. **Fringes with strong black checks**. Above, note the strongly checked fringes. Tailed Copper (pg. 77) has a tail and a red-orange submarginal line at the HW outer angle and lacks the submarginal black chevrons. Males are brown to brilliant iridescent purple, depending upon population, one's viewing angle, and the degree of wear of the individual. Male Purplish Coppers have much more extensive black spotting. Male Lilac-bordered Coppers have white, unchecked fringes and a more extensive orange marginal band. Females are similar to Purplish and Lilac-bordered Coppers but have checked fringes. *Habitat:* Moist openings in coniferous forests. *Abundance:* C-A, but R-U California Sierra Nevadas. Late June–Aug., mainly July–mid Aug. *Food:* Blueberries.

1 Purplish Copper

2 Purplish Copper ♀

3 Lilac-bordered Copper

4 Lilac-bordered Copper ♀

5 Mariposa Copper

6 Mariposa Copper ♀

7 Purplish Copper ♂

8 Purplish Copper ♂ ("Dorcas" type appearance)

9 Mariposa Copper ♂

10 Lilac-bordered Copper ♂

Hairstreaks (subfamily Theclinae)

The name of these small but intricately patterned butterflies is thought to be derived either from the many lines or streaks that tend to appear on the HW below or from the usual presence of fine, hairlike tails. Almost 40 species occur in the West, while about 1000 species of hairstreaks inhabit Central and South America. Many species have an eye-spot near the outer angle of the HW below that tends to attract the attention of predators to the wrong end of the butterfly. The subterfuge is usually enhanced by tails that resemble antennas. When the hairstreak lands with its head facing downward and its tails move in the air as it "saws" its HWs back and forth, the effect is complete. Many tropical species have this eye-spot pattern greatly developed, and it is not unusual to find individuals who have sacrificed the missing portions of their HWs to birds or other predators.

Most hairstreaks do not open their wings while landed and thus do not allow a view of their topsides, except in flight (often difficult to see), when "sawing" their HWs (see above) or by other unusual circumstances. Exceptions include the scrub-hairstreaks, which perch with their wings open fairly frequently, Arizona Hairstreak (and congeners), and Colorado and Golden Hairstreaks. Colorado and Golden Hairstreaks are also unlike other hairstreaks in that they rarely visit flowers for nectar. These last two species are unrelated to the 1000 or so New World species (which, together with a few of the Old World species, form a cohesive group), and instead are closely related to Old World hairstreaks.

Great Purple Hairstreak *Atlides halesus*

A very large, dramatically marked hairstreak. When it flies, one can see the flash from the shining iridescent blue (not purple) scales covering the entire wings above. Females have more restricted, non-iridescent, blue above. Below, both the **FW and HW have large red spots near their bases**. Also note the striking orange abdomen. Males have an iridescent turquoise patch on the FW below that females lack. *Habitat:* Canyons and streamsides with mistletoe-covered trees. *Abundance:* R-U. Southern Texas and the Arizona and California lowlands, March–Oct.; Rocky Mtns. and southern Oregon, April–May, July–Aug. *Food:* Mistletoes, especially on cottonwoods and oaks. *Comments:* A moderate hilltopper. The origin of the name "Great Purple Hairstreak" is hazy. But when this tropically oriented beauty kisses the sky with its brilliant blue topside, you will soar as high as Jimi Hendrix's music.

Colorado Hairstreak *Hypaurotis crysalus*

Note the **basal white stripe on the HW below**, unique among hairstreaks in the West. The **bright purple topside** is stunning. In males, the FW black diagonal band is restricted to near the costal margin. Male coppers that are purple above lack the black patch at the FW costal margin and are smaller. *Habitat:* Canyons with oak-covered hillsides. *Abundance:* U-LC. Late May–early Nov., but mainly July–early Sept. *Food:* Gambel's oak.

Golden Hairstreak *Habrodais grunus*

Note the unusual **HW submarginal pale ice-blue lunules** and the **tan legs**, unique among western hairstreaks. *Habitat:* Dry slopes in chaparral and foothill and lower mountain canyons. *Abundance:* LC-LA, but R in Arizona. One brood. June–mid Sept., mainly late June–mid Aug. *Food:* Canyon oak and chinquapin (in Oregon). *Comments:* Often crepuscular and best found perching on its foodplant.

1 Great Purple Hairstreak

2 Great Purple Hairstreak (caught by a crab spider)

3 Colorado Hairstreak

4 Colorado Hairstreak

5 Golden Hairstreak

6 Golden Hairstreak

Soapberry Hairstreak *Phaeostrymon alcestis*

Note the **strong white cell-end bars** on both wings and the **double "W"** over the HW blue spot. *Satyrium* hairstreaks lack the double "W" while Oak Hairstreaks and Gray Hairstreaks lack the cell-end bars (and have only single "W's"). *Habitat:* Sparsely wooded areas with the foodplant, including canyon watercourses and hedgerows. *Abundance:* LU. Mid May–June. *Food:* Western soapberry. *Comments:* Very closely associated with its caterpillar foodplant.

Striped Hairstreak *Satyrium liparops*

Striking white lines are aligned to form stripes. Also note the orange cap on the HW blue spot. *Habitat:* Thickets, woodland openings and brushy edges. *Abundance:* R-LU. Mid June–early Aug., mainly July. *Food:* Wild plums and wild cherries. *Comments:* There is a beautiful violaceous sheen on newly emerged individuals.

Coral Hairstreak *Satyrium titus*

A brown, **tailless** hairstreak with a **prominent row of red-orange spots** but no blue marginal spot. Acadian-group Hairstreaks have a tail, gray ground color and a blue spot. *Habitat:* Brushy fields and thicket edges, usually near water. *Abundance:* U-C, east of Continental Divide; LR west of Continental Divide. June–Aug., mainly July–early Aug. *Food:* Wild cherries and wild plums. *Comments:* A prize plum throughout much of the West.

Banded Hairstreak *Satyrium calanus*

Quite variable. Ground color varies from very pale ("white form" mainly in northwestern Colorado—inset to photo 4), to brown (photo 4), to gray (photo 5). **Spots of postmedian bands are elongated and almost contiguous** and are white edged distally. *Habitat:* Prefers open fields or glades, with nectar sources, within or adjacent to oak woodlands. *Abundance:* LR-LU. Texas, mainly late April–early June; Colorado, late June–early Aug.; South Dakota to Saskatchewan, July–mid Aug. *Food:* Oaks. *Comments:* Essentially an eastern butterfly, this denizen of oak woodlands enters a limited area of the western mountains through Colorado.

Behr's Hairstreak *Satyrium behrii*

A **gray, tailless** hairstreak with black postmedian and submarginal spots. California individuals somewhat lighter gray than individual shown. Fringe is uniformly dark. Desert Elfin is gray and tailless but lacks black spots. Mariposa Copper has black and white checked fringe and orange FW disk. *Habitat:* Rocky arid areas along foothill ridges and low mountaintops, brushy openings in coniferous forest, and sagebrush steppes. *Abundance:* C-A. May–Aug., mainly mid June–July. *Food:* Bitterbrush and other *Purshia*. *Comments:* Often swarms along the east slope of the California Sierra Nevada and the Oregon Cascades. Buckwheats are a top nectar source.

1 Soapberry Hairstreak

2 Coral Hairstreak

3 Striped Hairstreak

4 Banded Hairstreak (inset: NW Colorado)

5 Banded Hairstreak

6 Behr's Hairstreak

Sooty Hairstreak *Satyrium fulginosum*

Ground color is gray to brown. Spots, especially on HW are usually ill-defined and, on HW, circled with white. Most similar to Boisduval's Blue and Arctic Blues, but **lacks the strong FW cell-end black bar** of those species (some individuals do have a faint cell-end bar). *Habitat:* High sagebrush covered slopes and plateaus; high mountain meadows. *Abundance:* U-C. May–mid Sept., mainly July–Aug. *Food:* Lupines. *Comments:* Hilltops. Sooty is right! All the Sooty Hairstreaks I've seen looked as though they had soot thrown at them, even when fresh.

Acadian Hairstreak *Satyrium acadica*

Ground color is gray. Postmedian line is composed of black spots. Orange marginal spots extend up most of the HW. HW blue spot is capped with orange. California Hairstreak is extremely similar but usually with a darker, browner ground color. Note the position of the FW postmedian spot indicated in photo 2. On California Hairstreaks it is closer to the submarginal spotband than on Acadians. *Habitat:* Willow thickets. *Abundance:* LU-LC. Mid June–Aug., mainly July. *Food:* Willows. *Comments:* There is some evidence that this species is retreating northward, possibly due to global warming.

California Hairstreak *Satyrium californica*

Ground color gray-brown. Postmedian line is composed of black spots. Orange marginal spots extend a variable amount along the HW. HW blue spot is capped with orange. Sylvan Hairstreak has a paler ground color, has less extensive HW orange marginal spots, and lacks an orange cap on the HW blue spot. See Acadian Hairstreak description for separation from that species. *Habitat:* Chaparral, forest openings, foothill and lower mountain canyons, and sagebrush steppes. *Abundance:* U-C. Late May–mid Aug., mainly mid June–mid July *Food:* Oaks and mountain mahogany. *Comments:* Reports of this species feeding on willows are probably referable to Sylvan Hairstreaks.

Sylvan Hairstreak *Satyrium sylvinus*

Ground color gray-white to brown-gray. Postmedian line is composed of black spots. Orange marginal spots confined to near HW outer angle. HW blue spot without orange cap. See California Hairstreak description for separation from that species. *Habitat:* Willow-lined watercourses. *Abundance:* LU-LC. In lowlands and foothills, late May–mid July; at higher elevations, in Nevada and farther north, July–mid Sept. *Food:* Willows. *Comments:* Some populations in California and Nevada lack tails. The tailless California populations (Dryope) have sometimes been considered a separate species. In addition, some California willow-feeding populations, e.g., in Lake County, exhibit some California Hairstreak–like features—such as some orange over the HW blue spot—but they are pale with smaller, less intense, black HW spots than on California Hairstreaks.

1 Sooty Hairstreak

2 Acadian Hairstreak

3 California Hairstreak

4 California Hairstreak

5 Sylvan Hairstreak

6 'Dryope' Sylvan Hairstreak

Hedgerow Hairstreak *Satyrium saepium*

Dark brown ground color. Strong postmedian line but underside without orange or white markings (except in Utah–northern Arizona). **Often, but not always with characteristic pale cell-end bars.** Bright orange-brown topside usually visible in flight. *Habitat:* Chaparral, open pine forest, oak woodlands, and other situations with *Ceanothus. Abundance:* LC-A, but U in Washington and British Columbia. As early as April in southern California, as late as mid Sept., northern California through Washington. Mainly July–Aug. in the Rocky Mountains. *Food: Ceanothus.*

Gold-hunter's Hairstreak *Satyrium auretorum*

Yellowish-brown ground color. Postmedian line absent or weak. Fringe is brown. Note the **very short tail** of male; tail of female is somewhat longer. Cell-end bars are inconspicuous. *Habitat:* Oak-covered hills, chaparral with oaks. *Abundance:* R-LU. June–July. *Food:* Oaks.

Mountain Mahogany Hairstreak *Satyrium tetra*

Gray-brown ground color. Note the **white scaling** beyond the postmedian line. Cell-end bars absent or inconspicuous. Fringe is pale. Tail of male is similar to that of Gold-hunter's Hairstreak male. Unlike Hedgerow Hairstreak, upperside is dull. *Habitat:* Chaparral. *Abundance:* U-LC. June–July. *Food:* Mountain mahogany.

Ilavia Hairstreak *Satyrium ilavia*

Ground color light yellowish-brown. HW postmedian line with only a shallow "W." No cell-end bars. **Submarginal bands absent.** Orange-brown patches above are sometimes visible in flight. *Habitat:* Arid hills and slopes covered with desert scrub oaks. *Abundance:* LC. May–early July. *Food:* Desert scrub oak. *Comments:* Considered by some to be conspecific with Oak Hairstreak.

Poling's Hairstreak *Satyrium polingi*

Strong white HW postmedian line with a **"W" over the blue spot.** No orange cap on blue spot. Submarginal bands weakly developed, absent or nearly so on FW. The HW submarginal white spots do not reach the HW leading margin. *Habitat:* Sparse oak woodlands. *Abundance:* R-LC. two broods? May–June, Aug.–Sept. *Food:* Gray oak and Emory oak.

Oak Hairstreak *Satyrium favonius*

Strong white HW postmedian line with a **"W" over the blue spot.** **Orange cap on blue spot.** No cell-end bars. Submarginal bands well-developed with white spots reaching the HW leading margin. *Habitat:* Openings in and around oak woodlands. *Abundance:* R. April–May at the southern end of range, May–June farther north. *Food:* Oaks. *Comments:* Previously called Southern Hairstreak.

1 Hedgerow Hairstreak

2 Gold-hunter's Hairstreak

3 Mountain Mahogany Hairstreak

4 Ilavia Hairstreak

5 Poling's Hairstreak

6 Oak Hairstreak

The correct understanding of the populations of butterflies I treat here as Bramble and Sheridan's Hairstreaks is uncertain. See pg. 304 for more about this group.

Bramble Hairstreak *Callophrys dumetorum*

Most populations have a **variable amount of brown on the lower portion of the HW below**. Populations along the central California coast are more intense bluish-green with white fringes (*viridis*). Populations in the Great Basin are more yellowish-green. Populations in Arizona and New Mexico have a reddish-brown band inward of the usual white postmedian HW spots (*apama*). *Habitat:* Chaparral, sagebrush steppes, openings in foothill woodlands. *Abundance:* Southern California. C-A. Feb.–April; Pacific Northwest. LU. Mid April–May west of Cascades, mid May–June east of Cascades through the Great Basin; Rocky Mountains. U. April–June/July (as *affinis*); depending upon elevation and latitude; Arizona. LU. June–mid July (as *apama*). *Food:* Buckwheats, *Ceanothus* and deerweed.

Sheridan's Hairstreak *Callophrys sheridanii*

In the Rocky Mountains, this species is relatively easy to identify because its green coloration coupled with the strong and straight HW postmedian line is unique. With some populations farther west identification becomes more difficult. Sheridan's Hairstreaks have the area near the inner margin of the FW green, while most populations of Bramble Hairstreaks are brown there. At high altitudes in the California Sierra Nevadas and adjacent Nevada, 'Alpine' Sheridan's Hairstreaks (*C. s. lemberti*) perch on windy hilltops. *Habitat:* Sagebrush steppes and openings in coniferous forest and mixed forests. *Abundance:* Pacific states. LR-U. April–May at low-moderate elevations, June–July for *lemberti*; Rocky Mountains. LC. March–mid June. *Food:* Buckwheats.

'Desert' Sheridan's Hairstreak *C.s. comstocki*

In the Great Basin and Mojave Desert, 'Desert' Sheridan's Hairstreak is fairly distinctive, with a well-marked HW postmedian band that bulges outward, but intermediates occur at the eastern and northern edges of its range. *Habitat:* Arid canyons on lower slopes of desert mountains. *Abundance:* LU. Isolated colonies within the range shown. Mid March–early May (peak late March–early April) and late Aug.–mid Sept. *Food:* Buckwheats. *Comments:* Second brood individuals are noticeably more yellow-green than first brood individuals.

Arizona Hairstreak *Erora quaderna*

Its **green ground color coupled with its red-orange spots** makes this species unmistakable. *Habitat:* Mid-elevation oak-wooded canyons. *Abundance:* U. March–Aug. with occasional individuals in Nov. and Dec. *Food:* Oaks and *Ceanothus*. *Comments:* One of the few hairstreaks to routinely open its wings while landed. Both sexes visit mudpuddles, while males often perch on trees on hilltops.

1 Bramble Hairstreak (Los Angeles) (inset: Colorado)   2 Bramble Hairstreak (Arizona)

3 Bramble Hairstreak (San Francisco)   4 'Alpine' Sheridan's Hairstreak

5 'Desert' Sheridan's Hairstreak   6 Sheridan's Hairstreak

7 Arizona Hairstreak   8 Arizona Hairstreak

'Olive' Juniper

'Siva' Juniper

Juniper Hairstreak *Callophrys gryneus*

The intriguing Juniper Hairstreak complex consists of green-colored and brown to purplish-colored populations. The non-green populations are shown on pg. 97. See pg. 304 for more information about this group. 'Olive' Juniper Hairstreaks (*c. g. gryneus*) are immediately recognizable by the two white HW basal spots. From about Austin west through the Sacramento Mountains of New Mexico, these intergrade into 'Siva' Juniper Hairstreaks (*C. g. siva*), which lack the white basal spots. Rarely, individuals of Siva are largely purple (farther west 'Siva' becomes brown). Note the **strong HW marginal blue and black spots**. All green hairstreaks but Xami lack these spots. Xami is much yellower with pronounced outwardly directed "ears" on its HW postmedian line. *Habitat:* Anyplace with junipers. *Abundance:* U-C. two brood areas, March–May, June/July–Aug./Sept. (as early as Feb. and as late as Nov. in southeast Arizona). One brood areas, mainly late May–early July. *Food:* Junipers. *Comments:* Throughout much of the West the commonest green hairstreak is 'Siva' Juniper Hairstreak.

Sandia Hairstreak *Callophrys mcfarlandi*

The beautiful golden-green color of this New Mexican specialty is arresting. **HW postmedian band is white, thick, straight, and not broken into spots.** Note absence of prominent marginal spots or contrasting color and the unusual thin **black line forming a shallow pointed arch** past the postmedian line. *Habitat:* Arid hillsides with the foodplant. *Abundance:* LC-LA. Feb./March–June; rare partial 2nd brood, July–Aug. *Food:* Texas beargrass. *Comments:* Perches within the beargrass, back 1 to 2 feet from the blade tips. Nectars eagerly at beargrass flowers. Amazingly, only first discovered in 1960!

Silver-banded Hairstreak *Chlorostrymon simaethis*

Small but spectacular. **Note the large, maroonish HW marginal patch** and the **gray eye.** The HW postmedian band narrows to a sharp point near the outer angle. *Habitat:* Thorn scrub and dry tropical woodland. *Abundance:* R. Mid March–June, mid Sept.–mid Oct. RS to southern California, southern Nevada (one record) and southern New Mexico (one record). *Food:* Balloon-vine. *Comments:* Will sometimes perch with wings open—above, males are iridescent purple, females gray. In some years this essentially tropical animal wafts northward in numbers.

Xami Hairstreak *Callophrys xami*

Note the unusual yellowish brown-green ground color and the distinctive outwardly pointing "ears" on the HW postmedian line. *Habitat:* Steep canyon cliffs with the foodplant. *Abundance:* LR. Mid Feb.–mid Nov., seemingly most common in March. *Food: Graptopetalum*, stonecrops, and other succulents. *Comments:* Males are reported to perch at the bottoms of cliffs which hold foodplants at their tops. If you find an active colony of this ravishing beauty, please give me a call!

1 'Siva' Juniper Hairstreak

2 'Olive' Juniper Hairstreak

3 Sandia Hairstreak (New Mexico)

4 Sandia Hairstreak (Texas)

5 Silver-banded Hairstreak

6 Xami Hairstreak

Juniper Hairstreak *Callophrys (Mitoura) gryneus*

Please see page 304 for more information about this complex.

'Nelson's' Juniper

'Nelson's' Juniper Hairstreak *C.g. nelsoni*

When fresh, most populations of 'Nelson's' Juniper Hairstreak have a bright purple iridescence that quickly fades to brown. The HW postmedian line can be well-developed or almost absent. *Habitat:* Coniferous forests with the foodplants. *Abundance:* A. Mid April–early Aug., depending upon location and year, mainly mid May–mid July. *Food:* Incense cedar with some reports of junipers.

'Muir's' Juniper

'Siva' Juniper Hairstreak *C.g. siva*

Brown to purple populations are extremely similar to 'Nelson's' and 'Muir's' (postmedian line is pronounced and extremely angled—similar to appearance of individual in inset to photo 2). *Habitat:* Hillsides with junipers. *Abundance:* LU–C. April–May. *Food:* Junipers. *Comments:* Typical 'Muir's' is found in the California Coast Ranges where it feeds on Sargent cypress. See previous page for map of 'Siva.'

'Loki' + 'Thorne's'

'Loki' Juniper Hairstreak *C.g. loki*
'Thorne's Juniper Hairstreak *C.g. thornei*

These two subspecies are extremely similar, with a complicated and variable HW pattern of blue-gray, green-gray and brownish scales. *Habitat:* Hillsides and canyons with juniper (for 'Loki') or Tecate cypress (for 'Thorne's'). *Abundance:* LR ('Thorne's') or LC–A ('Loki'). March–April, Sept. *Comments:* 'Thorne's' is known only from the vicinity of Otay Mountain on the California/Mexico border in San Diego Co.

Thicket Hairstreak *Callophrys (Mitoura) spinetorum*

The **strong white postmedian line on the rich, dark reddish-brown ground color** is a unique combination except for Johnson's Hairstreak (this page). Note the **white FW cell-end bar** (sometimes faint or absent, especially in Cuyamaca Mtns.) that Johnson's Hairstreak lacks. Blue-gray upperside (rarely bright blue) can be glimpsed in flight. *Habitat:* Openings in coniferous forest. *Abundance:* U–C in most of Rockies, R west of Rockies and in Alberta. two broods areas, March–Aug./Sept. (mainly March–April, Aug.). One brood areas, May–July. *Food:* Dwarf mistletoes on conifers. *Comments:* Can be found hilltopping, mudpuddling, and nectaring.

Johnson's Hairstreak *Callophrys (Mitoura) johnsoni*

Similar to the commoner Thicket Hairstreak. Averages larger than Thicket Hairstreak. Ground color is somewhat duller and postmedian white line is less prominent with less of a "W" near the outer angle. Note the **absence of a FW cell-end bar**. **Orangish-brown upperside** color sometimes visible in flight. *Habitat:* Openings in coniferous forest. *Abundance:* LR. Mainly June–early Aug. Two broods in some lowland areas (too small to show). March–Aug./Sept. *Food:* Dwarf mistletoes on conifers. *Comments:* Very rarely has a "big" year.

1 'Nelson's' Juniper Hairstreak

2 'Siva' Juniper Hairstreak

3 'Loki' Juniper Hairstreak

4 'Thorne's' Juniper Hairstreak

5 Thicket Hairstreak

6 Johnson's Hairstreak

Elfins (subgenus *Incisalia* of the genus *Callophrys*)

Elfins are small, essentially tailless hairstreaks. They are often the first nonhibernating butterflies to appear, flying at the first sign of spring in the lowlands or just after snowmelt in the mountains.

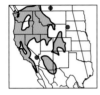

Brown Elfin *Callophrys augustinus*

Rich brown with a **brighter reddish-brown wide marginal border that tapers to a point at the HW apex.** Usually lacks white on the FW and HW postmedian lines. HW marginal line dark, or paler than ground color, but not normally white. *Habitat:* Varied. Chaparral, brushy forest edges *Abundance:* Mainly U-C. As early as Feb. in southern California and southeastern Arizona, mainly May–June in the mountains and north into Canada. *Food:* Many, in different families.

Moss' Elfin *Callophrys mossii*

Similar to Brown Eflin. HW reddish-brown marginal border is narrower and more defined than on almost all Brown Elfins. **FW and HW postmedian lines usually with white, often extensive.** Many populations have a grayish patch just beyond the bottom half of the HW postmedian line. The HW marginal line is normally at least partly white. *Habitat:* Rocky situations in mountains with the foodplant. *Abundance:* Mainly LR, but can be LC. Mainly March–April but as early as late Feb. in Pacific lowlands and as late as June in high mountains and Alberta. *Food:* Stonecrops. *Comments:* Some populations are best identified by association with the foodplant.

Henry's Elfin *Callophrys henrici*

Note the **"frosted" HW margin** and the **bold white marks at either end of the HW postmedian line.** Tail-like protuberances are usually visible. *Habitat:* Brushy woodlands. *Abundance:* U-LC. Feb.–April. *Food:* Redbud and Texas persimmon. *Comments:* West Texas population not as dark basally.

Hoary Elfin *Callophrys polios*

A small, dark, and dull elfin. Note the **"frosting" on the FW** and HW margins. *Habitat:* Barrens, ridges, and other areas with the foodplant. *Abundance:* Mainly LU-LC; LR, Oregon, and Washington. April–mid June (but short flight at any locality). *Food:* Bearberry. *Comments:* Closely tied to the foodplant.

Desert Elfin *Callophrys fotis*

Muted shades of gray. Eastern populations have the basal half of the HW more golden–brown but lack the reddish-brown or frosted borders of the other elfins. *Habitat:* Canyons and rocky areas, especially in pinyon/sageland. *Abundance:* LC-A. Late March–mid June. *Food:* Cliff rose.

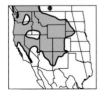

Western Pine Elfin *Callophrys eryphon*

Stunningly banded with rich reddish-brown and black. *Habitat:* Pine forest. *Abundance:* Mainly C, but R-U at southern edges of range. May–early July. *Food:* Pines. *Comments:* Males are aggressively territorial. Recently colonized San Francisco area using ornamental pines.

1 Brown Elfin

2 Brown Elfin

3 Moss' Elfin

4 Moss' Elfin

5 Henry's Elfin

6 Hoary Elfin

7 Desert Elfin

8 Western Pine Elfin

Eyes. Almost all western hairstreaks have jet-black eyes, but four of the five species on this page have gray eyes.

Leda Ministreak *Ministrymon leda*

A tiny gray hairstreak with a **"pebbly" appearance** and **gray eyes** and rust-colored crown. Most frequent form has HW postmedian line inwardly edged with red and, usually, a red spot in the middle of the HW leading margin. "Winter" form has reduced or absent red. Gray Hairstreak is much larger, lacks "pebbly" appearance, and has black eyes. *Habitat:* Arid region washes and canyons with mesquite. *Abundance:* C-A in two brood regions, where it is resident. Mid April–mid Dec., mainly late spring and late summer. R immigrant to regions shown with one brood. Mainly May–June but also July–Nov. Has strayed north to northern Nevada, Colorado, and Nebraska. *Food:* Mesquites.

Gray Ministreak *Ministrymon azia*

Gray with "pebbly" appearance, gray eyes, and prominent HW red postmedian line. Note the **red marginal lines** on both FW and HW. Even smaller than Leda Ministreak. *Habitat:* Thorn scrub. *Abundance:* RS north to San Antonio, Texas area, and West Texas. *Food:* Legumes, Mimosa subfamily.

Creamy Stripe-streak *Arawacus jada*

Its name tells you how to identify this rare visitor. *Habitat:* Thorn scrub. *Abundance:* RS to southeastern Arizona, possibly a temporary resident. Found all year in adjacent Sonora. *Food:* Horsenettles. *Comments:* Occasionally perches with wings open revealing a powdery blue topside.

Dusky-blue Groundstreak *Calycopis isobeon*

Postmedian line strongly edged with red and with a strong "W". Note that the **space over the HW blue spot is completely filled with red-orange**. Above (visible when "sawing" HWs), HW is shining, iridescent blue. *Habitat:* Tropical and subtropical woodlands. *Abundance:* U. All year in south-central Texas. RS northwest to southeastern New Mexico. *Food:* Detritus. *Comments:* This species is probably conspecific with the very similar Red-banded Hairstreak (*Calycopis cecrops*), which probably occurs regularly at the eastern border of the West in Texas (see *BTB: East* for photo). Records from Colorado and Saskatchewan are undoubtedly the results of mislabeling or of human-assisted movement.

Sonoran Hairstreak *Hypostrymon critola*

Note the **curiously striated FW** and gray eyes. Winter form is brown-gray; summer form is grayer with red on the HW postmedian line. Above, males are brilliant iridescent blue-purple while females are gray. *Habitat:* Thorn scrub. *Abundance:* RS to southeastern Arizona, appearing perhaps every 25–50 years. Records to date have been from May. *Food:* Unknown. *Comments:* Common in Sonora, Mexico, within about 60 miles of the U.S. border.

1 Leda Ministreak

2 Gray Ministreak

3 Creamy Stripe-streak

4 Dusky-blue Groundstreak

5 Sonoran Hairstreak (Winter)

6 Sonoran Hairstreak (Summer)

Scrub-Hairstreaks (genus *Strymon*)

Of this largely tropical group of roughly 60 species, only Gray Hairstreak ranges widely north of Mexico. Another 13 species have been recorded in the United States, seven of them in the West (see pg. 298 for Bromeliad Scrub-Hairstreak). Unlike most hairstreaks, scrub-hairstreaks will sometimes perch with their wings held open, usually at an angle, but occasionally almost flat. Many, but not all, have a red crown, and quite a few have males with orange abdomens. In the tropics, scrub-hairstreaks are characteristic inhabitants of arid thorn scrub and disturbed habitats.

Gray Hairstreak *Strymon melinus*

Ground color is usually true gray, sometimes brownish, especially when worn. Prominent HW postmedian line usually has at least some red, often with strong red, sometimes without any red (photo 3). Note that the large **orange HW marginal spot is flat inwardly and almost reaches postmedian line.** Has a "clean" appearance due to **lack of cell-end bars.** Males have orange abdomens, females gray. *Habitat:* A wide variety of open habitats. *Abundance:* C-A, south central Texas west through southern California, flying almost all year. R-U elsewhere, mainly March/April–Sept./Oct., but May–Aug. at high elevations and latitudes. *Food:* A wide variety. *Comments:* Hilltops. This widespread, common and variable species is found throughout much of the tropics.

Avalon Scrub-Hairstreak *Strymon avalona*

Looks like a washed-out, pale Gray Hairstreak. **HW marginal orange spot is very small. HW Postmedian line missing spot above "W".** *Habitat:* Can be found most anywhere on Santa Catalina Island. *Abundance:* U. Multiple broods, Feb.–Oct., but most common in March. *Food:* Silver-leaved lotus, deerweed and possibly buckwheats. *Comments:* Found only on Santa Catalina Island, off the southern California coast, Avalon Scrub-Hairstreak has long been isolated from Gray Hairstreak, its very close relative. Gray Hairstreaks have recently found their way to Santa Catalina, and it will be interesting to see whether these species will hybridize extensively, one swamping the other, or will develop mechanisms to maintain their genetic integrity.

Red-lined Scrub-Hairstreak *Strymon bebrycia*

Note the **HW grayish-white marginal lunules** and, on the the FW, relatively broad and diffuse submarginal spots. Gray Hairstreaks lack the HW pale lunules and FW submarginal markings, if present, are narrow and straight (like a sewing stitch). *Habitat:* Tropical woodlands and thorn scrub. *Abundance:* R immigrant to Big Bend, Texas. RS to southeastern Arizona. *Food:* Balloon-vine. *Comments:* Best chance to see this species in the United States may be in Big Bend National Park along the Rio Grande River.

1 Gray Hairstreak

2 Gray Hairstreak ♂

3 Gray Hairstreak

4 Gray Hairstreak ♀

5 Avalon Scrub-Hairstreak

6 Red-lined Scrub-Hairstreak

Mallow Scrub-Hairstreak *Strymon istapa*

HW with prominent postmedian band and **two basal black spots** (sometimes the more distal spot is faint). Other hairstreaks lack the black basal spots. Ceraunus Blues are smaller, lack tails, have extra dark spots on the basal half of the HW, and fly more slowly and less erratically. *Habitat:* Thorn scrub and tropical deciduous forest. *Abundance:* R-U, Central to west Texas; R immigrant, southeastern Arizona through southern California. March–Nov., but mainly mid Aug.–mid Oct. RS to North Texas and Nevada (one record). *Food:* Various mallow family plants. *Comments:* Our populations have been placed as a subspecies of *Strymon columella*, but recent work shows that *istapa* and *columella* are distinct species and that *columella* is restricted to the Antilles.

Lacey's Scrub-Hairstreak *Strymon alea*

Looks like a Gray Hairstreak with **very mottled ground color** and very irregular postmedian line. Note the **pale cell-end bars** and the **bold, black, HW marginal spot**. Mallow Scrub-Hairstreaks are less mottled and have black basal spots on the HW. *Habitat:* Thorn scrub and rocky canyons with the foodplant. *Abundance:* LR. All year. *Food:* Southwestern bernardia. *Comments:* Of the species of butterflies resident in the West, this is one of the most difficult to find.

Tailless Scrub-Hairstreak *Strymon cestri*

Tailless. Note the **falcate FW** and the highly patterned HW with a brown postmedian band and the black eyes. Lantana Scrub-Hairstreak lacks the falcate FW and the black spots near the HW outer angle and has gray eyes. *Habitat:* Tropical deciduous forest. *Abundance:* RS to southeastern Arizona (one record). Fairly common in central Sonora, Mexico. *Food:* Unknown.

Lantana Scrub-Hairstreak *Strymon bazochii*

Tailless. Note the **HW postmedian band of wide, brown spots** and the **brown spot in the middle of the HW leading margin. A white ray on the HW** is often present and the **HW apex forms a sharp angle.** So far as I know, this is the only scrub-hairstreak with a **gray eye**. *Habitat:* Anyplace with lantana, including suburban situations. *Abundance:* U, in Hawaii. All year. Possible, but unrecorded, stray along the United States–Mexican border. *Food:* In Hawaii, lantana. *Comments:* Introduced into Hawaii in a futile and misguided attempt to control lantana. The only individual I've seen in the United States (outside of Hawaii) was at the site of the future NABA Butterfly Park, in Mission, Texas—during the groundbreaking ceremonies!

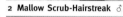

1 Mallow Scrub-Hairstreak   2 Mallow Scrub-Hairstreak ♂

3 Lacey's Scrub-Hairstreak   4 Tailless Scrub-Hairstreak

5 Lantana Scrub-Hairstreak   6 Lantana Scrub-Hairstreak

Blues (subfamily *Polyommatinae*)

Most blues can be recognized as blues on the wing. They are generally blue above (surprise!) and their flight is usually less rapid and erratic than hairstreaks.

Western Pygmy-Blue *Brephidium exile*

Tiny. Copper-colored above. Below, note the **four bold HW marginal eyespots** with iridescent highlights. FW is strongly two-toned—pale gray basally, copper-colored distally. *Habitat:* Arid country with saltbush or lambsquarters. *Abundance:* Mostly C-A in areas shown as three broods; R in areas shown as two broods. Flies all year in southeastern Arizona and southern California; mainly March–Oct. farther north; mainly June/July–Sept./Oct. in two-brood areas. *Food:* Saltbushes, lambsquarters, and others. *Comments:* The smallest butterfly in North America.

Cassius Blue *Leptotes cassius*

Its zebra-striping distinguishes Cassius Blue from all other Western blues except the darker Marine Blue. On the FW below, note that the **4th dark band in from the outer wing margin stops after four veins** leaving a white patch. Marine Blue has this band extending one stop farther down the wing and so lacks the white patch. *Habitat:* Subtropical open woodland. *Abundance:* R. All year. RS to West Texas and Kansas. *Food:* A wide variety, especially legumes.

Marine Blue *Leptotes marina*

A zebra-striped blue that periodically sweeps northward out of Mexico. Above, the males are purplish toward the wing bases. *Habitat:* Generally distributed in open areas. *Abundance:* C-A near the Mexican border, all year, but mainly March–Oct. Decreasing immigrant northward, usually reaching northern New Mexico about May and Kansas in June/July. *Food:* A wide variety, especially legumes. *Comments:* Emigrates northward and eastward each year, to a very variable extent, very rarely reaching Oregon and Saskatchewan.

Reakirt's Blue *Hemiargus isola*

Below, note that the **FW has a postmedian band of bold black spots**. Silvery and Boisduval's Blues are larger and lack the HW outer angle black spot. *Habitat:* A wide variety of open areas and open woodlands. *Abundance:* C-A, central Texas west through southeastern Arizona, mainly March–Oct.; U-C elsewhere. Variable immigrant northward. *Food:* Legumes.

Ceraunus Blue *Hemiargus ceraunus*

Small, with pale gray ground color. Note the **prominent two black spots along HW leading edge**. Other blues also have spots here, but they are not so prominent compared to the other HW spots. *Habitat:* Low deserts to mid-elevations. *Abundance:* U. All year along Mexican border; May–Nov. in Nevada. RS north to Kansas. Everywhere most common late summer/fall. *Food:* Many legumes. *Comments:* HW outer angle eyespots vary from two strong eyespots in Texas, to one strong and one weak eyespot in southeastern Arizona, to one eyespot in California.

1 Cassius Blue

2 Western Pygmy-Blue

3 Western Pygmy-Blue

4 Marine Blue

5 Marine Blue ♂

6 Marine Blue ♀

7 Reakirt's Blue

8 Reakirt's Blue ♂

9 Reakirt's Blue ♀

10 Ceraunus Blue

11 Ceraunus Blue ♂

12 Ceraunus Blue ♀

Western Tailed-Blue *Everes amyntula*

Along with Eastern Tailed-Blue, the only western blues with **tails**. Below, note the small orange spot at the base of the tail. Fringes are unchecked. HW black spots are faint on some northern populations. See Eastern Tailed-Blue for separation from that species. *Habitat:* Various, including moist mountain meadows, chaparral, sagebrush, poplar woods, and redwood forest. *Abundance:* Mainly U-C. March/April–Aug., depending upon elevation, latitude, and year; partial second fall brood in the southern lowlands. *Food:* Legumes, especially vetches.

Eastern Tailed-Blue *Everes comyntas*

Probably not separable without dissection from the more widespread Western Tailed-Blue. Eastern **males, above usually have some orange at the base of the tail** (but not always) while Westerns usually (but not always), lack the orange. Most female Easterns have little, if any, blue above, while most Western females have some blue. Below, Easterns usually have a fairly prominent orange spot at the base of the tail, along with some adjacent orange spots. Westerns usually have these orange spots reduced in size and intensity. Lastly, Easterns usually have the **outer margin of the FW slightly rounder** than do Westerns. *Habitat:* A wide variety of open habitats, but especially disturbed **lowland** riparian areas. *Abundance:* LR-LU. Continuously brooded during warm weather. *Food:* Legumes.

Small Blue *Philotiella speciosa*

FW with bold black spots. HW with or without postmedian black spots. FW fringe is checked. Tiny. Always **lacks an orange submarginal line on HW** (*most* Euphilotes populations have at least some orange here, see pg. 117). Small Blues have **zero to two HW basal black spots** (zero on individuals shown), while Euphilotes have 3. *Habitat:* Mainly desert gulches and hillsides, but also known from mixed chaparral-oak woodland in coastal Santa Barbara Co., California and pine forest in central Oregon, just east of the Cascades. *Abundance:* LR. Mainly March–April near the U.S.-Mexican border; April–mid June elsewhere. *Food:* Knotweed family, including punctured bract. *Comments:* Can occasionally be common following a wet winter, absent following dry winters.

Cyna Blue *Zizula cyna*

Small. Pale gray ground color. Fringes unchecked. Note the **whitish arrows pointing outward from cell-end bars**, the **black spots at the base of the HW**, and the absence of a black spot at the HW outer angle that Ceraunus Blue has. Spring Azure is larger, without such prominent black spots. *Habitat:* In Mexico, varied; often disturbed, including thorn scrub and oak-covered hillsides. *Abundance:* R immigrant and temporary colonist, May–Sept. *Food:* Reportedly acanthus family.

1 Western Tailed-Blue ♂

2 Eastern Tailed-Blue ♂

3 Western Tailed-Blue ♀

4 Eastern Tailed-Blue ♀

5 Western Tailed-Blue

6 Eastern Tailed-Blue

7 Small Blue

8 Cyna Blue

Spring Azure *Celastrina ladon*

Below, ground color is pale with various dark markings. The off-white to pale gray color, together with the lack of any orange color, of any strong black spots, and the lack of tails, should serve to differentiate this from other blues. In most of the West, the predominant form is the "pale" form shown in photo 1. In the Northwest and the Rocky Mountains some populations also contain many individuals with darker markings, either on the HW margin or the HW disk. Individuals with brown marginal markings are called form "marginata," while those that also have dark HW disk markings are called form "lucia" (photo 3). In actuality, there is a continuum among all of these forms. Above, males are completely bright blue, while females are a duller blue with wide black borders (but azures rarely perch with wings open). *Habitat:* A wide variety of woodlands. *Abundance:* C-A. One of the first nonhibernating butterflies to fly in the spring. Beginning Feb. in southern California to west Texas; March in low to moderate elevations in the rest of California north to Washington. April/May in most of the Rocky Mountain states; into early Aug. at high elevations. Flies essentially all year in southeastern Arizona. *Food:* A wide variety of shrubs and trees.

Summer Azure *Celastrina ladon neglecta* Not Illustrated

Essentially indistinguishable from Spring Azure or Hops Azure. There are only pale form individuals. Females above resemble female Hops Azures, with varying amounts of white suffusion. *Habitat:* Open woodland, edges, suburbia. *Abundance:* R-U. April–Oct. in Texas, tapering to mainly July in North Dakota and Saskatchewan. *Food:* A wide variety of shrubs and trees. *Comments:* Although previously considered to be a 2nd brood of the Spring Azure, these summer-flying azures are most likely a distinct species.

Hops Azure *Celastrina ladon humulus*

Not distinguishable from Spring Azure by wing pattern, although above, **females are often suffused with varying amounts of white**. Best guess for identification is flight date (Spring Azures rarely fly past mid June where Hops Azures are found) and association with hops. *Habitat:* Edges of canyon bottoms and steep rock slopes. *Abundance:* LC. One brood. June–July. *Food:* Hops (although one population is reported to use lupine). *Comments:* Recently described as a species, the correct placement of these populations is not certain.

Sonoran Blue *Philotes sonorensis*

Unmistakable. The combination of **bright blue with a bright orange FW patch** is unique. *Habitat:* Canyons and cliffs with the foodplants. *Abundance:* LU-LC. Mainly Feb.–April; into May at higher elevations. *Food:* Canyon dudleya and other dudleyas. *Comments:* Anza-Borrego State Park in San Diego Co., California, is a good place to see this stunning butterfly.

1 Spring Azure ♂

2 Spring Azure ♀

3 Spring Azure, form lucia

4 Hops Azure ♀

5 Hops Azure

6 Sonoran Blue ♂

7 Sonoran Blue

8 Sonoran Blue ♀

Euphilotes Blues (genus *Euphilotes*)

This complex group of interesting and handsome butterflies is frustratingly difficult to understand but will reward one's efforts at careful study by imparting a closer knowledge of plant–animal interactions.

Euphilotes blues usually are markedly black-spotted, especially on the FW with **checked fringes.** Note the **HW submarginal orange band** that almost all populations have. Other blues with HW submarginal orange bands are larger and have unchecked fringes. In addition Northern and Melissa Blues have black points on the HW marginal black line that *Euphilotes* blues lack while Acmon and Lupine Blues have iridescence on the HW marginal spots. Although there are sometimes useful identification clues on their uppersides, they mostly keep their wings closed while landed.

There are three species complexes within *Euphilotes*—Square-spotted Blue complex, Dotted Blue complex, and Rita Blue complex (with two species). Each complex is treated on its own two-page spread. I say "complex" because within each of these complexes the relationships among the many populations are very complicated and unclear. Please see pg. 305 for more information about this group.

Square-spotted Blue *Euphilotes battoides*

Below, intensity of black spotting varies. Note the **FW checked fringes.** Rita Blue has largely unchecked FW fringes. Above, orange or pink-orange HW submarginal band varies in intensity and width on both males and females, even within a population. Some females have moderate to extensive blue above. The extent of the blue is variable even within some populations, although most populations have females fairly consistently brown or showing some blue. Closely resembles Dotted Blue. Below, although varying in width and intensity, the **HW orange submarginal band usually is composed of bold and fused spots**, while in Dotted Blues they are *usually* separate and thinner. The black marginal line is thicker and more intense, especially at the FW apex, than is usual on Dotted Blues. Above, males usually have wider FW black borders than do male Dotted Blues. *Habitat:* Dry hillsides, slopes, and canyons with buckwheats. *Abundance: oregoniensis* and *glaucon*: Pacific Northwest south and east to northeastern California, northwestern Nevada and Idaho, U-LC, late May–early Aug.; *intermedia*: Oregon Siskiyous and Northern California, U, June–mid Aug.; *battoides*: High elevations in the California Sierra Nevadas, R-U, July–Aug.; *baueri*: The California–Nevada border, LU, mid April–late June; *centralis*: LU, Colorado, New Mexico and Arizona White Mountains, mid July–mid Aug.; *ellisi*: Utah, northern Arizona and southern Nevada, Aug.–Sept.; *martini*: Desert mountains of southeastern California through central Arizona (1 population in southwestern Arizona), U-C, April–early June; *bernardino*: southwestern California, C-A, late May–early July. *Food: glaucon, intermedia*: marifolium buckwheat; *battoides*: sulphur buckwheat and others; *baueri*: oval-leaved buckwheat and others; *centralis*: James' buckwheat and sulphur buckwheat; *martini* and *bernardino*: mainly California buckwheat (see photos on page 116).

1 Square-spotted Blue *(battoides)*

2 Square-spotted Blue *(bernardino)* ♀

3 Square-spotted Blue *(bernardino)*

4 Square-spotted Blue *(bernardino)* ♂

5 Square-spotted Blue *(martini)*

6 Square-spotted Blue *(centralis)* ♂

7 Square-spotted Blue *(centralis)*

8 Square-spotted Blue *(centralis)* ♀

Dotted Blue *Euphilotes enoptes*

Unfortunately, it is not yet known how to distinguish Dotted Blues from Square-spotted Blues in the field with anything approaching certainty, without recourse to location, date, and hostplant information (and even when all this is known, there are still times when identification will be uncertain). There are certain clues, but because these species are so similar and because there is so much variation over the range of these species, such clues are not conclusive.

The FW marginal black line on Dotted Blues is usually thin and not so intense as on Square-spotted Blues. The **HW submarginal orange band usually is composed of spots that are not connected.** Most, but certainly not all, populations of Square-spotted Blues and Rita Blues have a FW marginal black line that is thick and intense and their submarginal orange bands are usually composed of fused spots. Rita Blues lack black checks on the FW fringe.

For now, probably the best way to infer the identity of a population of *Euphilotes* blues is to note the location and date and to identify the hostplant. *Habitat:* Rocky hilltops, ridges and slopes; desert hills, canyons, and washes. *Abundance: ancilla*: Southern Alberta (Cypress Hills, LR) south through central Nevada, northern Utah and Colorado, C-A. Late May–July; *columbiae*: Washington and Oregon, LU. Late May–July; *enoptes*: extreme southern Oregon south through the Sierra Nevadas, U-C. Mainly June–July; *bayensis*: California coast from San Francisco north, C. June. *tildeni*: Inner coast range from San Francisco south to Los Angeles, U. July–Aug.; *mojavensis*: U. April–May; *dammersi*: U-C. Late Aug.–mid Oct. *Food:* From Alberta south to Colorado and west into Utah, mainly sulphur buckwheat; elsewhere mainly naked buckwheat, but also quite a few other buckwheats. 'Dammers' Dotted Blue on Wright's and elongated buckwheats. *Comments: E. enoptes dammersi* flies with *E. battoides ellisii* in some areas of Mojave desert, e.g., at Wildhorse Canyon in the Providence Mtns. See page 305 for more information.

Naked buckwheat

Sulphur buckwheat

1 **Dotted Blue** *(ancilla)*

2 **Dotted Blue** *(ancilla)* ♀

3 **Dotted Blue** *(enoptes)*

4 **Dotted Blue** *(bayensis)* ♀

5 **Dotted Blue** *(mojave)*

6 **Dotted Blue** *(bayensis)* ♂

7 **Dotted Blue** *(dammersi)*

8 **Dotted Blue** *(bayensis)*

Rita Blue *Euphilotes rita*

Below, usually **lacks black checks on the FW fringe** and usually has a strong black FW marginal line. The HW orange submarginal band is usually strong and composed of fused spots. The newly described subspecies (*calneva*), from Plumas County, California, and Washoe County, Nevada, entirely lacks the orange submarginal band and closely resembles Small Blue. *Habitat:* Prairies (in eastern Colorado), desert flats, foothills, and plateaus elsewhere. *Abundance:* LU. Mainly Aug.–mid Sept., at some locations as early as July. *Food:* Loose buckwheat in eastern Colorado; Wright's buckwheat in Arizona; various species of desert buckwheats in the rest of its range. Populations from Utah westward, 'pallid' Rita Blues (*E. r. pallescens*) are treated as a separate species by some. See page 305 for more information.

Spalding's Blue *Euphilotes spaldingi*

Below, this is the only *Euphilotes* blue with **orange on the FW**. Usually larger than other *Euphilotes* blues. Unlike Rita Blue, Spalding's Blue has the FW fringe strongly checked. Above, females have a strong orange FW band. *Habitat:* Ponderosa pine-juniper-pinyon slopes and flats. *Abundance:* LR-U. July–Aug. *Food:* Racemose buckwheat. *Comments:* At many locations Spalding's Blues will ignore noncaterpillar foodplant buckwheats for nectar, in favor of racemose buckwheat.

James' buckwheat

Racemose buckwheat

Buckwheats at right are foodplants for Square-spotted Blue, pg. 112

California buckwheat

1 Rita Blue (Colorado)

2 Rita Blue ♂ (inset: ♀)

3 Rita Blue (Arizona)

4 Rita Blue (Nevada)

5 Rita Blue *(calneva)*

6 Spalding's Blue ♂

7 Spalding's Blue

8 Spalding's Blue ♀

Arrowhead Blue *Glaucopsyche piasus*

Below, the **bold HW postmedian band of inwardly directed white arrow-heads** makes this blue a standout. Some California populations have less contrast between these white markings and their much paler ground color. Note also the large white spike on the HW disk. Extensiveness of the white varies, as shown. Above, both males and females lack cell-end bars and have strongly checked fringes. Silvery Blues above lack the checked fringes. *Habitat:* A variety of open habitats, including sagebrush and ponderosa pine woodland in the Pacific Northwest, chaparral-transition and forest openings in California, and gulches in high prairies and foothill canyons in Colorado and Alberta. *Abundance:* LR-U. Late March–May in southern and lowland California, May–June/July farther north and at high elevations. *Food:* Lupines. *Comments:* In the San Gabriel Mountains of Los Angeles County, California, Arrowhead Blues fly in April and May, while at higher elevations, a different subspecies flies in early June–early July. The caterpillars are often attended by ants.

Silvery Blue *Glaucopsyche lygdamus*

Below, ground color varies from gray to gray-brown. The **FW has a prominent row of postmedian black spots**. On the HW, postmedian black spots can be as bold as on the FW, can be much smaller and surrounded by white, or be almost absent. On both wings, note that **there are no marginal or submarginal spots**. Below, some Boisduval's Blues are quite similar, but have at least some marginal and/or submarginal spots. Above, both males and females lack cell-end bars and have unchecked fringes. Males are shining blue, while females vary from having extensive blue-gray as shown, to blue restricted to the wing bases, to all brown. *Habitat:* A variety of open situations, but mainly moist grassy areas and meadows. *Abundance:* LU-C. Feb.–April in southern California, May–June through much of range, late June–Aug. at high elevations and in Alberta and Saskatchewan. *Food:* A wide variety of legumes, especially lupines, deerweed, and rattleweeds. *Comments:* Caterpillars are attended by ants. Has a tendency to form small, isolated, somewhat differentiated populations. The extinct 'Xerces' Silvery Blue, considered to have been a full species by some, had all the bold black spots replaced with bold white spots, producing a striking effect that sadly can no longer be seen. Named by the Frenchman Boisduval for the Persian king (spelled Xerxes in English but Xerces in French), whose defeat by the Greek navy and death by murder eerily presaged the fate of the butterfly. The last colony on the coastal sand dunes of San Francisco was destroyed by the expansion of a military facility in 1943. A similar-appearing population on Santa Rosa Island, off the California coast, is the closest to the Xerces Blue you can see today.

1 Arrowhead Blue (Colorado)

2 Arrowhead Blue ♂

3 Arrowhead Blue (California)

4 Arrowhead Blue ♀

5 Silvery Blue

6 Silvery Blue ♂

7 Silvery Blue

8 Silvery Blue ♀

Boisduval's Blue *Plebejus icarioides*

A large and variable blue. Below, the usually **prominent black spots are encircled by white**, usually quite strongly. The **strong FW postmedian spotband is almost always noticeably more intense than the submarginal spotband**. Above, females vary from blue to brown. In parts of central and southern California and the western edge of the Willamette Valley in Oregon, populations contain individuals that are darker than most other Boisduval's Blues and that have more prominent submarginal and marginal markings (see photo 3). In the area of Point Reyes, California, individuals are almost completely unmarked below, except for a few black spots on the FW. Blue Coppers are similar but are whiter below without the white rings around the black spots and without a pronounced submarginal band. Silvery Blues are usually darker gray below and lack any submarginal or marginal markings. Arctic Blues are much smaller, have a darker ground color, and have a broad white postmedian band that abuts the large submarginal spots. Over most of their ranges, Boisduval's Blues have much more prominent HW white spotting than do Greenish Blues and have weaker submarginal markings. *Habitat:* A wide variety, including dunes, mountain meadows, forest openings, and prairies. *Abundance:* C-A. Mainly May–July. Flies as early as mid March in lowland California coast and through Aug./Sept. at high elevations and latitudes. *Food:* Many lupines (but each population usually uses just one). *Comments:* Adults are avid mudpuddlers. Caterpillars are tended by ants. Like many blues, this species has a tendency to form isolated colonies that are often one step from extinction. A number of these populations are formally listed as endangered by the United States government. These include the 'Mission' subspecies in San Francisco and 'Fender's' subspecies along the western edge of the Willamette Valley in Oregon.

Greenish Blue *Plebejus saepiolus*

Below, males are usually off-white while females are pale brown. **FW submarginal and marginal spotbands are usually as intense, or slightly less intense, than the FW postmedian spotband**. Usually with some faint orange at the HW outer angle between the submarginal and marginal spots, more intense and extensive in females. Above, both males and females have **FW cell-end bars**. Females vary from bluish-gray to brown with orange highlights to dark brown. Boisduval's Blue is very similar but usually larger. In most Boisduval's Blue populations males lack FW cell-end bars. *Habitat:* Moist meadows, mainly in the mountains up to and above treeline, but also down to sea level along the coast; boggy areas in sagebrush. *Abundance:* LC-A. Mainly June–July. As early as May in lowlands and as late as Aug./early Sept. at high elevations. *Food:* Clovers.

1 Boisduval's Blue

2 Boisduval's Blue ♂

3 Boisduval's Blue

4 Boisduval's Blue ♀

5 Greenish Blue ♀

6 Greenish Blue ♀

7 Greenish Blue ♂

8 Greenish Blue ♂

Lycaeides

The two species on this page are very closely related and often quite difficult to distinguish from each other but are fairly easy to separate from other Western blues. Look for an **orange HW submarginal band**, usually with iridescent blue-green distally, and **black points** where the HW veins intersect the outer margin. Fringes are unchecked. *Euphilotes* have orange submarginal bands but never have iridescence, lack the black points, and have checked fringes. Other blues have orange submarginal bands and iridescence but lack the black points.

Northern Blue *Lycaeides idas*

See top of page for distinguishing *Lycaeides* from other blues. Below, varies from very pale markings to essentially as well-marked as Melissa Blue. Populations from Cascadia (especially) south through the California Sierra Nevadas have black and orange markings pale and reduced. East of the Cascades, into Wyoming and Colorado, populations are more similar to Melissa Blue. Even here, however, individual Northern Blues are usually somewhat **paler and less well-marked than Melissa Blues**. Look especially for the **bluish-white ground color**, whiter than the smoky-gray ground color of Melissa Blues. Over most of the range, female Northern Blues have less pronounced orange bands above than do female Melissa Blues. Exceptions are Northern Blue populations in the California Sierras (*anna*) that have females with strong orange above and conversely, a population of Melissa Blues along the Sierra Nevada crest in which females have greatly reduced markings above. *Habitat:* Mainly moist meadows and bogs in coniferous forest, but also xeric areas above treeline. *Abundance:* LU-C. Mainly late June–Aug. *Food:* Mainly lupines, but also other legumes, including rattleweeds, vetches, and *lotus*. *Comments:* Like many blues, the males of Northern Blues are often found congregating at damp sand.

Melissa Blue *Lycaeides melissa*

See Northern Blue for distinguishing Melissa Blue from that species. Below, note the **orange HW submarginal band**, usually with iridescent blue-green distally, and **black points** where the HW veins intersect the outer margin. Fringes are unchecked. *Habitat:* A wide variety; from agricultural land and disturbed areas, to prairies, sagebrush steppes, mountain meadows in pine forest to windy rocky summits of mountain peaks. *Abundance:* C. Mainly two broods, May–Sept. but only one brood at high elevations. *Food:* A wide variety of legumes, including lupines, alfalfa, and rattleweeds. *Comments:* One of the most widespread blues of the West. Caterpillars are attended by ants.

1 Northern Blue (Washington)

2 Northern Blue ♂

3 Northern Blue (Montana)

4 Northern Blue ♀ *(anna)* (inset: Washington)

5 Melissa Blue (Sierra Nevada crest)

6 Melissa Blue ♀ (Colorado) (inset: Sierra Nevada crest)

7 Melissa Blue

8 Melissa Blue ♂

Acmon Blue *Plebejus acmon*

Below, the **orange HW submarginal band has iridescent blue spots. HW black marginal line is not swollen at the veins. Fringes are unchecked.** Females are usually brown above, but spring form cottlei in southern California has much blue. Melissa and Northern Blues have a HW black marginal line that is swollen at the veins while *Euphilotes* blues have checked fringes and lack iridescent spots. Also see other species on this page. *Habitat:* A wide variety of open habitats. *Abundance:* Mainly C, but R-U east of the Continental Divide. Mainly March/April–Aug./Sept. Almost all year in southeastern Arizona and southern California, June–July at high elevations and into Alberta and Saskatchewan. *Food:* Legumes (especially lotuses and rattle-weeds) and buckwheats in California and southern Oregon, mainly buckwheats elsewhere. *Comments:* Both Acmon and Lupine Blues use buckwheats in California, but they use different species. See page 308 for more information about Acmon and Lupine Blues.

Lupine Blue *Plebejus lupinus*

Very similar to Acmon Blue. In southern California, where these species fly together at some localities, most males can be distinguished by the color of the HW submarginal band above. Acmon Blues have this band distinctly pinkish, while on male Lupine Blues this band is orange, often with an inner bordering black line. The FW black border of Lupine Blue males is usually wider than on Acmon Blue males. Females cannot be reliably separated. *Habitat:* Chaparral, sage-brush/pinyon, and rocky slopes above treeline. *Abundance:* U-LC. Mainly May–July. *Food:* Sulphur and oval-leaved buckwheats; California buckwheat in southern California. *Comments:* The name of this nonlupine feeding species throws novitiates for a lupine. To maintain equilibrium, it is best to think of this "lupine" as in "lupine blue"—the color. See page 308 for more information.

San Emigdio Blue *Plebejus emigdionis*

Below, the HW orange submarginal band is pale and thin. The **FW cell is spotless.** Acmon and Lupine Blues have a FW cell-spot (although often small). Above, males lack a submarginal orange band, instead having an ill-defined dull brown marginal patch. *Habitat:* Arid wash-es. *Abundance:* LR. late April–May, late June–early July, Aug.–early Sept. 2nd and 3rd broods are partial and depend upon rainfall. *Food:* Saltbush.

Veined Blue *Plebejus neurona*

Below, very similar to Acmon Blue, but **HW submarginal band has iri-descent gold spots** (not blue). Above with striking **orange veining.** *Habitat:* Openings in coniferous forest, usually over 5000 ft. *Abun-dance:* LR. May–mid Aug. *Food:* Low, mat-forming varieties of Wright's buckwheat. *Comments:* The West's only blue whose males have no blue—the untrue blue.

1 Acmon Blue

2 Acmon Blue ♂ *(acmon)* **(California)**

3 Acmon Blue ♀ **(California)**

4 Acmon Blue ♂ *(texana)* **(Arizona)**

5 Acmon Blue ♀ (cottlei)

6 Lupine Blue ♂

7 San Emigdio Blue ♀

8 San Emigdio Blue ♂

9 Veined Blue

10 Veined Blue

Arctic Blue *Agriades glandon*

On the HW below **a broad white postmedian band abuts the inner edge of the large submarginal spots.** Boisduval's Blue is larger and has white postmedian spots that are round and separated from the submarginal spots. Reakirt's Blues have black eyespots at the HW outer angle. Populations in the California Sierra Nevadas north to the Siskiyous in southern Oregon (*podarce*) have bold black postmedian spots. **Above, males are an unevenly colored bluish-gray** that is unlike other blues (except for some female Greenish Blues in southern Utah and northern Arizona) and usually with cell-end bars on both FW and HW. *Habitat:* Mainly mountain meadows, but also rocky areas above treeline, and prairie hillsides and gulches in Alberta. Wet subalpine meadows for *podarce*. *Abundance:* Mainly U-C, but C-A in California Sierra Nevadas and LR in Siskiyous. June–Aug./early Sept. *Food:* A variety in a number of families, but especially in the primrose family, including rock-primroses. Shooting stars for *podarce*. *Comments:* The California and Oregon populations are isolated from other populations and are quite distinctive. Future work will determine whether they are best viewed as a full species.

Heather Blue *Agriades cassiope*

Extremely similar to Arctic Blue. The **wings are slightly less rounded** than on Arctic Blue. Below the HW cell is either spotless or has a small white spot. **Black spot in the HW cell is tiny or absent.** Arctic Blues have a prominent black spot in the HW cell. Habitat differs from co-occurring Arctic Blues. *Habitat:* Rocky slopes, near or above treeline, with seeps. *Abundance:* LR. Early July–early Sept. (mainly early July–early Aug.) (usually about 1–2 weeks later than Arctic Blues in the same area). *Food:* Mountain heather. *Comments:* This recently described species is currently known only from the western Lake Tahoe region south to Yosemite National Park and from the vicinity of Caribou Lake in the Trinity Alps.

Shasta Blue *Plebejus shasta*

Below, the HW has a pale orange submarginal band with iridescent spots. The **HW postmedian spots are dark brown to paler brown-gray**, but not black. Acmon and Lupine Blues have black postmedian HW spots. Above, males have strong cell-end bars on FW and HW. There is no orange submarginal band but they usually have a dull orange-brown marginal band. Females resemble female Acmon and Lupine Blues but usually have **strong HW cell-end bars** and the orange submarginal band is reduced to almost absent. *Habitat:* Northward in high meadows and forest openings or sagebrush steppes. Southward more restricted to high elevation rocky hilltops and ridges *Abundance:* LC. June–Aug./Sept. *Food:* Legumes, especially rattleweeds and clovers.

1 Arctic Blue (Washington)

2 Arctic Blue ♀

3 Arctic Blue (California)

4 Arctic Blue ♂

5 Heather Blue

6 Shasta Blue ♂

7 Shasta Blue

8 Shasta Blue ♀

Metalmarks (family Riodinidae)

Metalmarks derive their name, naturally enough, from the metallic marks that are often present on their wings. In the tropics, the variety of size, shape, and pattern of this large group is truly amazing. Like gossamer-wings, caterpillars are often attended by ants.

Arizona Metalmark *Calephelis arizonensis*
Ground color is fairly uniform, with only a slight darkening of the median bands on males. The FW fringe is strongly checked and the HW black submarginal spots are strongly expressed. *Habitat:* Moist situations in arid regions. *Abundance:* U-C. All year. *Food: Bidens.* *Comments:* Often more active in the afternoon.

Wright's Metalmark *Calephelis wrighti*
Ground color is uniform reddish-brown. **Outer margin of FW of male is uneven,** female less so. *Habitat:* Desert canyons and washes. *Abundance:* C. Feb.–Oct. (timing and abundance of summer and fall broods are determined by rainfall). *Food:* Sweetbush.

Rawson's Metalmark *Calephelis rawsoni*
Similar to the much more common Fatal Metalmark. The median bands are darkened, but less so than on Fatal Metalmarks. Individuals, especially females, usually have a brighter orange-brown color than do Fatal Metalmarks. The white check closest to the HW outer angle is usually weak to absent. *Habitat:* Moist situations in arid regions. *Abundance:* LR. *Food:* Mistflowers. *Comments:* Considered to be conspecific with Arizona Metalmark by some.

Rounded Metalmark *Calephelis perditalis*
The **FW postmedian metallic band bulges outward** (is rounded) at its center. The **FW fringe is only weakly checked** with the center white check usually missing. Fresh individuals, especially females, have a purplish-blue reflectance. On the HW, in the space between the postmedian and submarginal metallic bands, black spots are strongly expressed. *Habitat:* Tropical woodland and thorn scrub. *Abundance:* U-C. All year. *Food:* Mistflowers.

Fatal Metalmark *Calephelis nemesis*
Ground color above is **dull flat brown.** The **inside edge of the median band is greatly darkened**, especially in males, and especially at the ends of the FW and HW cells. On the FW the postmedian band is almost straight. On the HW, in the space between the postmedian and submarginal metallic bands, black spots are usually weakly expressed or absent. *Habitat:* Thorn scrub, chaparral, arid region riparian areas. *Abundance:* C west to southeastern Arizona, R-U westward. Almost all year. *Food:* Seepwillow (westward) and clematis (eastward). *Comments:* No known antidote if misidentified.

1 Arizona Metalmark

2 Arizona Metalmark

3 Wright's Metalmark

4 Rawson's Metalmark ♀

5 Rawson's Metalmark ♂

6 Rounded Metalmark ♀

7 Rounded Metalmark ♂

8 Fatal Metalmark

Zela Metalmark *Emesis zela*
Above, the gray-brown FW contrasts with the brighter orange-brown HW. Note the **dark patch just distal to the FW cell**. *Habitat:* Sycamore-lined canyons through mid-elevation oak woodland. *Abundance:* C. Two broods, mainly March–April, July–Sept. RS to Big Bend, National Park, Texas (one recent record). *Food:* Unknown (but oaks suspected). *Comments:* While nectaring, often seems oblivious to observers. Moves over flowerheads with a rigid rotation.

Ares Metalmark *Emesis ares*
Above, gray-brown FW contrasts with brighter orange-brown HW. Both above and below, note the presence of **black FW marginal spots** (absent or faint on Zela). Above the **HW orange patch is sharply cut-off along the trailing margin** (broader and more diffuse on Zela). *Habitat:* Mid-elevation oak woodland. *Abundance:* U. One brood, June–Sept., mainly July–Aug. *Food:* Oaks. *Comments:* Some individuals appear to be intermediates between Zela and Ares. Whether these are due to normal variation or to hybridization is not known.

Crescent Metalmark *Apodemia phyciodoides*
This little-known species resembles a crescent, but has **two white FW subapical spots**. *Habitat:* The vicinity of steep cliffs in riparian areas. *Abundance:* Not currently known from U.S. *Food:* Clematis. *Comments:* Two specimens from the early 1900s are labeled as having been collected in the Chiricahua Mtns. of Arizona. This species is known to occur in nearby Sonora and Chihuahua, Mexico.

Nais Metalmark *Apodemia nais*
This snappy species is bright orange above, with black markings, but its **green eyes** tell you this is a metalmark, not a brushfoot or a copper. Unlike Chisos Metalmark, the bases of the wings have much gray. *Habitat:* Open areas with ceanothus in mountain pine forest, 6000–9000 ft. *Abundance:* C-A, but LU in southeastern Arizona. One brood, mainly mid June–mid July (northward), into August (southward). *Food:* *Ceanothus fendleri.*

'Chisos' Nais Metalmark *Apodemia nais chisosensis*
Very similar to Nais Metalmark. Above, with less gray at wing bases than on Nais Metalmark and with black markings less extensive. **Below**, there is **no orange in the center of the HW** and the **HW postmedian black spots are strong and form a straight line** (zig-zag on Nais Metalmark). The two species do not occur together. *Habitat:* Middle elevations in the Chisos, mainly 3500–5000 ft. *Abundance:* U-C. One brood, April–June. *Food:* Havard's plum. *Comments:* This species is obviously very closely related to Nais Metalmark. But, given that the Chisos Metalmark population is separated by a very large distance from Nais Metalmarks, that each individual is easily identifiable, and that a very different hostplant is used, it seems entirely possible that these will eventually be treated as separate species. Look for it in the Basin area of Big Bend National Park, and especially along the trail into Pine Canyon.

1 Zela Metalmark ♂

2 Zela Metalmark ♀

3 Zela Metalmark

4 Ares Metalmark

5 Ares Metalmark

6 Crescent Metalmark

7 Nais Metalmark

8 Nais Metalmark

9 'Chisos' Nais Metalmark

10 'Chisos' Nais Metalmark

Mormon Metalmark *Apodemia mormo*

Above, pattern and size are variable but the **combination of black and orange with many white spots is distinctive**. Populations vary from being almost entirely orange (*mejicanus* and *duryi*), to mixtures of orange (ranging from red-orange to yellow-orange) and black on both FWs and HWs (*virgulti* and some *mormo*), to black HWs with a mix of orange and black on the FWs (some *mormo* and some *mejicanus*), to almost entirely black (some populations in the San Bernardino Mountains of southern California and the Chiricahua Mountains of southeastern Arizona—not shown), all with white spots. **Below, the HW is silvery gray with large white spots.** *Habitat:* Arid regions, including sand dunes, rocky canyons and hillsides, sagebrush steppes and sparse grassland with buckwheats. *Abundance:* LR-LC, mainly LU, most common along the Mexican border. One–two broods. Some populations have a spring (March–April) and a fall flight (Aug.–Oct.); others have a single brood either in the spring (April–June), or fall (Aug.–Nov.), with a flight period of about 1 1/2 months. Some populations in southern California and southeastern Arizona may have three broods. *Food:* Mainly buckwheats, but also ratanys (especially *duryi*). *Comments:* A candidate for ritalin if I've ever seen one—these guys just won't sit still. Difficult to follow while flying, when they finally decide to nectar they often keep walking around the flowers, waving their antennas and flapping their wings constantly. Mormon Metalmark is a complex assemblage of populations. As is the case with the buckwheat-feeding blues, local populations are adapted to particular hosts and have flight-times that synchronize with optimal growth and flowering of the buckwheat species. This leads to diminished gene flow between populations. Whether this has led to enough genetic differentiation to consider some of these populations as bona fide species is not yet known. What *is* certain is that, given our present lack of knowledge, any provisional attempt to group these populations into separate species will almost certainly prove to be wrong in detail. One subspecies, 'Lange's' Mormon Metalmark, an inhabitant of sand dunes in Antioch, California, is federally listed as an endangered species.

Palmer's Metalmark *Apodemia palmeri*

Recognize this as a metalmark by its green eyes. Smaller than Mormon Metalmark. Above, ground color varies from a dark blackish-brown (Texas) to a paler orange-brown (California). Bases of wings with much gray. Marginal area of wings with at least some orange (black on Mormon Metalmark). FW with submarginal white spots. *Habitat:* Arid regions, especially low deserts. *Abundance:* C-A, southeastern Arizona; LU, southern California and west Texas. Three broods, April–Oct. *Food:* Mesquites, including honey and screwbean mesquites.

Hepburn's Metalmark *Apodemia hepburni*

Similar to Palmer's Metalmark but **lacks submarginal white FW spots** and HW with white spots reduced. *Habitat:* Subtropical thorn scrub. *Abundance:* RS to southeastern Arizona (one record) and Big Bend. *Food:* Unknown.

1 Mormon Metalmark *(virgulti)*

2 Mormon Metalmark *(virgulti)* **(Los Angeles)**

3 Mormon Metalmark *(mormo)*

4 Mormon Metalmark *(mejicanus)* **(SE Arizona)**

5 Mormon Metalmark *(mejicanus)*

6 Mormon Metalmark *(duryi)* **(Big Bend, Texas)**

7 Palmer's Metalmark

8 Palmer's Metalmark **(Texas)**

9 Palmer's Metalmark **(California)**

10 Hepburn's Metalmark

Brushfoots *(family Nymphalidae)*

Called brushfoots because of the greatly reduced male forelegs, this family includes many of our best known and most conspicuous butterflies. Some treat a number of the groups included here (such as satyrs and the monarchs) as separate families.

American Snout *Libytheana carinenta*
The **extremely long snout** (palps) is obvious on this otherwise quite variable butterfly. **FW apex is blunt**. HW below varies from highly mottled as shown to evenly dark gray to evenly pale. *Habitat:* Thorn scrub, thickets and open woodland with hackberries. *Abundance:* Three-brood areas. C-A. All year; Two-brood areas. U-C. Mainly May–Sept.; One-brood areas. R-U. Mainly a late summer/fall immigrant. RS north to North Dakota, Utah, and central Nevada. *Food:* Hackberries. *Comments:* Sometimes swarming in the millions (in the Rio Grande Valley), this is the chameleon of the butterfly world. When you are searching for a special butterfly, American Snouts will magically assume the appearance of that butterfly, or perhaps it's vice versa. Butterflies as varied as Chisos Banded-Skippers, Red Satyrs, and a large hairstreak with a silvery reflection, have all turned into American Snouts—right before my eyes! A Rorschach test for butterfliers.

Gulf Fritillary *Agraulis vanillae*
A long-winged, low-flying nymphalid that, with its brilliant silvered spots below, resembles the greater fritillaries. Note the **black-ringed white spots in the FW cell** above. *Habitat:* Thorn scrub, open woodland and gardens. *Abundance:* U-C. Three-brood areas. All year; Two-brood areas. Mainly May–Oct. RS north to northern California, Colorado, and South Dakota. *Food:* Passionvines. *Comments:* Range has been expanding in coastal California.

Variegated Fritillary *Euptoieta claudia*
Dull orange-brown above, often with a pinkish sheen when fresh. Below, HW has pale median and marginal patches. *Habitat:* Open areas, including open fields, prairie, and thorn scrub. *Abundance:* C-A in three-brood areas, mainly March–Nov.; U-C in two-brood areas, mainly May–Sept.; R-U in one-brood areas, mainly July–Sept. Immigrant northward. Has strayed to British Columbia, central Nevada, and southern California. *Food:* Many, including violets, passionvines and flax. *Comments:* Size and wing shape (from squarish to elongated) both are much more variable than for most species. Abundance also varies greatly from year to year and it is occasionally abundant far northward.

Mexican Fritillary *Euptoieta hegesia*
Brighter orange than Variegated Fritillary, but with **no HW median black line**. *Habitat:* Thorn scrub. *Abundance:* R. May–Oct. *Food:* Passionvines. *Comments:* An occasional temporary colonist along the Arizona–Mexican border.

1 American Snout

2 American Snout

3 Gulf Fritillary

4 Gulf Fritillary

5 Variegated Fritillary

6 Variegated Fritillary

7 Mexican Fritillary

8 Mexican Fritillary

Greater Fritillaries (genus *Speyeria*)

These are some of the largest and most beautiful butterflies in the West; unfortunately they are the most difficult group to identify to species. Most of the species are exceptionally variable. Travel a hundred miles and you'll think you're looking at a completely different animal. A species may be confused with two other species at one location and with a different set of species at a different location! Making matters even worse is that, in general, most of the identification cues, such as they are, are on the underside of the HW and, more often than not, greater fritillaries will only show you their topsides. I have tried to show some of the variation for most species, but the reality is that in many cases you're going to have to accept that your best identification is that it's a greater fritillary. In many cases, people who believe they can identify individual butterflies are wrong. We'll start with some easy ones! See page 309 for more information.

Nokomis Fritillary *Speyeria nokomis*

Below note the **very wide, yellow or cream-colored HW submarginal band**. Populations in California–Nevada have HW almost completely yellow (males) or with a somewhat darker greenish-gray disk (females, see photo 5). Eastward populations have darker HW disks (see photo 1). The boldly silvered HW disk spots are strongly ringed with black. **Eyes are yellow-green.** Above, **lacks a black spot along the base of the FW inner margin**. Females have very strong, connected HW black submarginal marks. Comparable marks on female Great Spangled Fritillaries are not as strong nor connected. Compared to Great Spangled Fritillaries, males have an extra black mark in the HW cell and the last black bar in the FW cell angles in to touch the penultimate black bar (not so on Great Spangled Fritillaries). *Habitat:* Seeps and wet meadows in arid regions and high mountains. *Abundance:* LR-LU. Mid July–mid Oct., mainly Aug.–Sept. *Food:* Violets. *Comments:* A population with bluish females (*coerulescens*) previously flew high in the Santa Catalina Mountains on the north side of Tucson, Arizona. None has been seen since 1938 and the colony is presumably extirpated. Similar populations still can be found in northern Mexico.

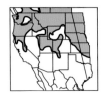

Great Spangled Fritillary *Speyeria cybele*

Below note the **wide, yellow or cream-colored HW submarginal band**. Most populations have **reduced HW silver spots. Eyes are yellow-green.** Above, note the **lack of a black spot along the base of the FW inner margin**. Especially above, males and females in Western populations (*leto*) are quite different, with females being black and buffy and males orange; in Eastern populations (*cybele*) sexes are similar (orange). *Habitat:* Prairies, meadows, open woodlands. *Abundance:* LC-C south to Oregon, Idaho, and Montana; R-U southward. Late June–Sept., mainly July–Aug. *Food:* Violets. *Comments:* Eastern and western populations have sometimes been considered separate species, but they reportedly intergrade where they meet in Alberta and Montana.

1 Nokomis Fritillary ♂

2 Nokomis Fritillary ♂

3 Great Spangled Fritillary ♂

4 Great Spangled Fritillary ♂

5 Nokomis Fritillary ♀ (inset: eye)

6 Nokomis Fritillary ♀

7 Great Spangled Fritillary ♀

8 Great Spangled Fritillary ♀

Regal Fritillary *Speyeria idalia*

A large and distinctive fritillary. Below, the **HW is completely dark brown with white spots**. Above, the HW is extremely dark brown to black with white spots. Note the **brownish-black body** (other greater fritillaries have orange-brown bodies). *Habitat:* Tall-grass prairie, wet fields and meadows and, to a lesser extent, short-grass prairie. *Abundance:* R-U. Mainly mid June–mid Sept. *Food:* Violets. Primarily uses prairie violet in Kansas, elsewhere, little information is available. *Comments:* As with many greater fritillaries, the females fly much later in the season than do males. Until recently (thirty years ago) this species ranged throughout the northeastern United States. It is now completely gone from this vast area, except for one very fragile colony in Pennsylvania. Reasons for the precipitous decline are not known, but changes in land use are strongly suspected. This species is probably one of the few butterflies to require large expanses of near pristine habitat. The continuing fragmentation of essential habitats bodes ill for the long-term fate of this truly magnificent animal—one of our largest and most splendid butterflies. The stronghold of this vanishing species is the tall-grass prairie province, and although strong colonies still exist in this region, even here the species appears to be in trouble.

Coronis Fritillary *Speyeria coronis*

A **large to mid-sized** fritillary. Similar to Callippe and, especially, Zerene Fritillaries, but usually larger. **Bright orange above**. Below, the FW usually has a reddish-orange flush, especially on females. The HW **marginal silvered spots are inwardly rounded**, almost egg-shaped (Great Basin and eastward) **or are shaped like tents** (north and west of Great Basin). HW disk color varies from dark brown in the Rocky Mountains, becoming paler and slightly green-tinged in western Colorado and eastern Utah, changing to greenish-gray in the Great Basin to paler brown westward. Through much of their ranges, Coronis and Zerene are very similar. In California, especially along the central coast, Coronis and Callippe may be indistinguishable, except that Coronis, on average, is larger and somewhat brighter orange above and paler below, and the underside HW pale postmedian spots show through the topside to a lesser extent. *Habitat:* Moist openings in mountain forest, chaparral, and sagebrush and other brushy habitats. *Abundance:* California coast ranges from Sonoma Co. south through San Lui Obispo Co. (*coronis*) U. May–Aug.; California San Gabriels south (*semiramis*), C-A. July–Aug.; California Mt. Pinos region and Tehachapis (*hennei*), R. late June–early Aug.; Great Basin (*snyderi*), C. June–Sept.; Northwest (*simaetha*), C. June–mid Sept.; East of the Continental Divide in Colorado and southeastern Wyoming (*halcyone*), U. Late May–early Sept. *Food:* Violets.

1 Regal Fritillary

2 Regal Fritillary ♂

3 Coronis Fritillary (Colorado)

4 Regal Fritillary ♀

5 Coronis Fritillary (Nevada)

6 Coronis Fritillary ♀

7 Coronis Fritillary (S. California)

8 Coronis Fritillary ♂

Aphrodite Fritillary *Speyeria aphrodite*

A large to mid-sized fritillary. Below, **HW disk is brown to reddish-brown**, the **disk color extending beyond the postmedian white spots**, often completely obliterating the submarginal band (see photo 1 inset). In the Rocky Mountains, Great Spangled Fritillary, Coronis Fritillary, this species and the Atlantis Fritillary complex have dark brown or red-brown HW disks. Note the **dull yellow-green eyes** (see photo 1 inset) that separate this species from all other similar species except for Great Spangled (and some southern Atlantis Fritillaries—see Atlantis Fritillary comments). Above, **males do not have swollen black areas along FW veins**. The **FW has a black basal spot along the trailing margin** that Great Spangled Fritillary lacks. *Habitat:* Woodland openings and native prairie. *Abundance:* C. Late June–Aug. *Food:* Violets. *Comments:* Some believe that populations in western Montana and eastern British Columbia that are traditionally mapped as Aphrodite Fritillary, are misidentified Atlantis Fritillaries. Hopefully a look at eye color in the field will clarify the situation.

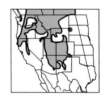

Atlantis Fritillary *Speyeria atlantis*

A mid-sized to small fritillary. In the Rocky Mountains, Great Spangled Fritillary, Coronis Fritillary, this complex and Aphrodite Fritillary have dark brown or red-brown HW disks, usually with contrasting submarginal pale band. Note the **blue-gray eyes** (see photo 3 inset and comments). Below, HW disk is reddish-brown to dull brown and, in different populations, spots can be silvered or unsilvered (although almost all individuals in any particular population will, with a few populations as exceptions, normally be similar to each other). **Disk is usually fairly evenly colored**, not mottled with included pale areas as is usual for the disk of Great Basin Fritillaries. Aphrodite Fritillaries can be very similar but have yellow-green eyes. Populations in the Oregon Cascades and California Sierra Nevadas are unsilvered below. **Above, FW borders are usually black** and **males have swollen black areas along FW veins**. Populations in Alberta, Saskatchewan, and Montana lack the FW basal spot that Great Spangled Fritillaries also lack (see photo 6) but can be separated by eye color. *Habitat:* Openings in mountain coniferous and mixed forests. *Abundance:* Mainly C-A. Mid June–mid Sept., mainly July in most areas. *Food:* Violets. *Comments:* Strangely, the eye color of Atlantis Fritillaries in the Arizona White Mountains and adjacent New Mexico (the very large and brightly colored subspecies *nausicaa*) is dull yellow-green. As this goes to press, the eye color of Atlantis in Utah and north-central New Mexico is not yet known. In parts of Alberta, Colorado, and the Black Hills of South Dakota, there appears to be both reddish-brown disked and gray-brown disked populations of "Atlantis" Fritillaries flying together. Many believe that these are separate species. Please see page 312 for more information.

1 Aphrodite Fritillary

2 Aphrodite Fritillary ♂

3 Atlantis Fritillary (red-disked)

4 Atlantis Fritillary ♂

5 Atlantis Fritillary (gray-disked)

6 Atlantis Fritillary ♀

7 Atlantis Fritillary (Arizona)

8 Atlantis Fritillary (Arizona, White Mtns.)

Hydaspe Fritillary *Speyeria hydaspe*

A small fritillary, usually with a **wine-toned HW disk** and mainly with **unsilvered spots** (silvered on Vancouver Island). Some populations are darker than shown and some lack the paler submarginal band. Some purplish Zerene populations closely resemble Hydaspe, but because Hydaspe has larger, less elongated spots than does Zerene and because Hydaspe has the bottom two spots in the postmedian band fairly aligned while Zerenes have the upper of these two spots displaced inwardly, the **outer edge of the postmedian spotband appears to be fairly smooth and coherent**; more jagged and less coherent on Zerene Fritillaries. Some Atlantis populations in the Pacific Northwest and California Sierra Nevada also resemble Hydaspe. They also have the 2nd from bottom postmedian spot displaced inwardly and also have larger HW marginal spots. *Habitat:* Coniferous/aspen forest openings. *Abundance:* U-C. Mid June–mid Sept., mainly July–Aug. *Food:* Violets. *Comments:* Will hilltop.

Zerene Fritillary *Speyeria zerene*

A mid-sized fritillary that is **extremely variable**. HW disk color ranges from strongly purple (California Sierra Nevada to the Oregon Klamath Mountains) to dark brown to pale brown to buff (mainly east of the Cascades-Sierra Nevada crests)—generally paler in drier areas. Marginal white/silver spots can be relatively flat or quite broad and rounded or angled inwardly, with or without "caps," silvered or unsilvered (California Sierra Nevada and Trinity Alps). Above, color varies from deep orange to pale yellow. Most often confused with Coronis Fritillary but also, for some populations, with Hydaspe Fritillary, with Great Basin Fritillary and with others! Compared to Coronis (and most others), Zerene Fritillaries usually have **very strong wide FW median spots**, especially the 2nd spot up from the inner margin. See Hydaspe Fritillary for separation from it. *Habitat:* Woodland openings, grasslands, coastal meadows and dunes. *Abundance:* Mainly C-A. Mid May–Sept. Most populations peak mid July–early Aug. Others include: California Trinity Alps, R-U; Central California coast, C. Mid May–early July; northern California and Oregon coasts, R. Aug.–Sept. *Food:* Violets. *Comments:* Three subspecies of Zerene Fritillary in northern California and Oregon, 'Oregon,' 'Behren's,' and 'Myrtle's' Zerene Fritillaries are listed as federally endangered. 'Carol's' Zerene Fritillary (*S. zerene carolae*) is an isolated population in the Spring Mountains of Nevada (where it is the only greater fritillary) that some believe should be treated as a full species.

1 Hydaspe Fritillary (California) (inset: WA)

2 Hydaspe Fritillary ♂

3 Zerene Fritillary (Trinities, CA)

4 Zerene Fritillary ♂

5 Zerene Fritillary (Mono County, CA)

6 Zerene Fritillary (Washington)

7 Zerene Fritillary (Colorado)

8 Zerene Fritillary (Nevada)

Edwards' Fritillary *Speyeria edwardsii*

Large and brightly colored, both above and below. Has **strong green reflections below** on brownish ground, narrowing or obscuring the pale HW postmedian band. Pale spots are large, rounded and silvered. **HW marginal pale spots are rounded inwardly**; these are more pointed on Callippe Fritillaries in the range of Edwards' Fritillary. Bright orange above with strong black borders. Note that, counting from the body, the **3rd FW black bar doesn't touch the 2nd black bar**. Callippe Fritillaries usually have the 3rd bar just touching the 2nd bar. *Habitat:* Prairies and foothills. *Abundance:* U-C. Late May–early Sept. *Food:* Violets. *Comments:* One of the least variable greater fritillaries.

Callippe Fritillary *Speyeria callippe*

Medium-sized. East of the California Sierra Nevada–Cascades crests, HW disk below has variable amounts of green reflections (bright or dull) and the pale spots are silvered. There may be a tan postmedian band, or it may be obscured by the green color. Only Edwards' Fritillary also is usually green below. Coronis Fritillaries in the Great Basin and a few populations of Mormon and Great Basin Fritillaries also have green below. In California and southwestern Oregon, the HW disk is brown-disked, almost always without green, and the pale spots are often unsilvered (see photo 5). Some of these populations are easy to confuse with populations of Coronis Fritillary. In almost all populations, the **marginal pale spots on the HW below are usually triangular-shaped and usually bordered inwardly by only a thin dark border**. Other species *usually* have differently shaped marginal spots with darker and wider borders. The **median and submarginal pale spots show through the wings above**, especially on females. Especially along the Pacific Coast, these buffy pale spots give Callippe a two-toned appearance above. Other species usually have these pale spots less pronounced. *Habitat:* Prairies, sagebrush flats, chaparral, and open woodlands. *Abundance:* C-A. Mainly May/June–July/Aug. As early as late April in southern California. *Food:* Violets. *Comments:* In many areas this is one of the first greater fritillaries flying in each new season, and is sometimes the only greater fritillary in a locality in May and early June. Along the central California coast, even many experienced observers are unable to determine whether some individuals are Callippe or Coronis Fritillaries.

1 Edwards' Fritillary

2 Edwards' Fritillary

3 Callippe Fritillary (Colorado)

4 Callippe Fritillary ♂ (Colorado)

5 Callippe Fritillary (Trinities)

6 Callippe Fritillary ♀ (California Trinities)

7 Callippe Fritillary (California coast)

8 Callippe Fritillary ♀ (California coast)

Great Basin Fritillary *Speyeria egleis*

Confusingly variable. Can resemble Atlantis, Coronis, Zerene Callippe and Mormon Fritillaries!—but not all at the same time. Small to mid-sized, it **most often, has a brown disk below (pale to dark brown) that is usually mottled in appearance.** Populations vary from almost all silvered to some individuals silvered and some unsilvered (for example, in the Wasatch and Uinta Mountains of Utah) to almost all unsilvered. Above, **males have prominent wide black areas along the FW veins. Above, especially on females, the bases of the wings are usually quite darkened and contrast with the outer portion of the wings.** In central Nevada, some populations are very pale below with a HW disk that is yellow with strongly silvered spots. On the prairies of Montana and Alberta many individuals have a dull greenish tint to the disk, somewhat similar to Callippe Fritillary but the disk is usually mottled. *Habitat:* Varied, but usually at fairly high elevations in openings of mixed or coniferous forest. *Abundance:* U-C. Sometimes A in California Sierra Nevadas and Trinities. LR in southern California. June–Sept. Mainly late June–Aug. *Food:* Violets.

Unsilvered Fritillary *Speyeria adiaste*

A beautiful ghost of a fritillary. Below, the **absence of silver markings** and the delicate **lavender-pink reflections** give these butterflies a fragile, otherworldly appearance. Above, bright orange with **thickened black FW veins** on males and, only slightly less pronounced, on females. *Habitat:* Openings in redwood forest in San Mateo and Santa Cruz Counties, California. High mountain meadows in Monterey and San Luis Obispo Counties, California. *Abundance:* LR-LU. June–July/early Aug. *Food:* Violets. *Comments:* Its fragile and otherworldly appearance may reflect the precarious existence of this species—it may be headed for another world. A large, pale population, formerly found in the Tehachapi and Tejon Mountains and in the Mt. Pinos area in Los Angeles, Kern, and Ventura Counties, California, was last seen in 1959. The reasons for its extirpation are unknown. Given the very limited areas they inhabit, the future of the existing populations is not that bright.

SHOWN LIFE SIZE

1 Great Basin Fritillary (Colorado)

2 Great Basin Fritillary ♀ (Montana)

3 Great Basin Fritillary (Utah)

4 Great Basin Fritillary ♀ (Wyoming)

5 Great Basin (California Sierra Nevadas)

6 Great Basin Fritillary ♂ (Lake County, California)

7 Unsilvered Fritillary

8 Unsilvered Fritillary

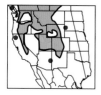

Mormon Fritillary *Speyeria mormonia*

This mountain meadow gem is **small**—about the size of a lesser fritillary (lesser fritillaries on pages 151 to 155 appear larger because they are shown at 1 1/4 life size). The **FWs are short and rounded** with **veins that are thin, without black scaling**. There is usually little basal darkening of the wings above. The marginal spots are often quite pale, creating the effect of a dark and light patterned border, especially on females. **Below, the ground color is usually pale**, with the HW disk varying from pale yellow to pale brown, sometimes tinged with green, or, as in populations in the Cascades of Washington, with strong green tones. Some individuals in the Black Hills of South Dakota have a dark brown HW disk. Although there can be variation even within a population, by and large pale spots are silvered but sometimes only partially (California Sierra Nevadas) or they are unsilvered as is the distinctive population in the Arizona White Mountains. Another distinctive set of populations occurs in northern Nevada and southeastern Oregon in the Ruby, Jarbidge, and Steens Mountains. Individuals are unsilvered below with a yellow ground color and very little pattern. They resemble yellow Unsilvered Fritillaries. This species is most likely to be confused with Great Basin Fritillary. Usually it is somewhat smaller, but some populations that occur together—for example, in the California Sierra Nevadas, are the same size. Above, male Great Basin Fritillaries can be distinguished because they have relatively wide areas of black scales running along the FW veins. Females are more difficult, but because Sierra Nevada Great Basin Fritillaries prefer dry meadows while the local Mormon Fritillaries prefer wet meadows, the habitat where you see the butterfly is a clue to its identity. *Habitat:* High elevation mountain meadows. *Abundance:* Mainly C-A. Mainly July–Aug. As early as late June in the California Sierra Nevadas, as late as Sept. at some locations. RS to Nebraska (one record). *Food:* Violets. *Comments:* Flight is close to the ground. The population in the White Mountains of Arizona is very isolated from other populations and is quite distinctive. Further study may provide grounds for treating it as a separate species.

1 Colorado: San Juan Mountains

2 Colorado: San Juan Mountains ♂

3 Wyoming: Wind River Mountains

4 Wyoming: Wind River Mountains ♀

5 California: Sierra Nevadas

6 California: Sierra Nevadas ♀

7 Arizona: White Mountains

8 Nevada: Ruby Mountains

Lesser Fritillaries (genus *Boloria*)

These delightful, diminutive, but intricately marked fritillaries of the North can sometimes cause frustration because of their tendency to be constantly in motion— viewing their much more distinctive undersides can be a problem. Of the almost 30 species found worldwide, twelve are found in the West. Above, they are orange with black markings, as are crescents and checkerspots. But the lesser (and greater) fritillaries have a complete FW submarginal band of black spots that these other groups lack. Many species have a set of marks that resemble a duck's head—an "eye" in the HW cell with a narrow "bill" extending outward from the cell. Many of the lesser fritillaries have distributions that include Eurasia in addition to North America.

Bog Fritillary *Boloria eunomia*

Below, the HW has bright white median and marginal spots and black-outlined, **white postmedian spots**. Above, the HW black border, with inward pointing black chevrons, encloses pale spots. **"Duck bill" paler than ground color.** *Habitat:* Bogs and also moist areas above treeline. *Abundance:* LR-LU. June–early Aug. *Food:* A wide variety of plants in a number of families have been reported.

Silver-bordered Fritillary *Boloria selene*

Below, the **HW has bright silvered-white median and marginal spots** and solid black (or red-brown) postmedian spots. Above, the HW black border with inward pointing black chevrons, encloses pale spots. **"Duck bill" the same color as ground color.** *Habitat:* Wet meadows, moist aspen groves, and willow bogs. *Abundance:* LC-LA, Alberta and Montana. LR-LU elsewhere. Late May–early Sept., but only one brood in mountains in mid June–July. *Food:* Violets.

Meadow Fritillary *Boloria bellona*

Above and below, **outer margin of FW comes to a shallow point**—it is not evenly rounded. Submarginal chevrons do not point outward. **Above, HW without black border.** Below, HW without strong postmedian band. Some populations are darker, duller and more uniform on the HW than indiividual shown. *Habitat:* Moist meadows and willow thickets. Found in a greater variety of open habitats eastward. *Abundance:* LR-LU, but LC in Saskatchewan. May–early Sept. in most locations (with only one brood at high elevations), June–July in Pacific Northwest. *Food:* Violets.

Pacific Fritillary *Boloria epithore*

Above and below, outer margin of FW is evenly rounded. Above, HW without black border. **Both above and below, the submarginal black (above) or brown (below) chevrons point *outward*,** except that populations from Montana north and west to central British Columbia have this trait very weakly developed above. *Habitat:* Moist forest openings and mountain meadows. *Abundance:* C-A. Late May–Aug., mainly June–July. *Food:* Violets.

1 Bog Fritillary

2 Bog Fritillary

3 Silver-bordered Fritillary

4 Silver-bordered Fritillary

5 Meadow Fritillary

6 Meadow Fritillary

7 Pacific Fritillary

8 Pacific Fritillary

Frigga Fritillary *Boloria frigga*

Below, usually with **pinkish frosting on the HW outer one-third**. The HW is more well-marked than Meadow Fritillary with the white spot at the base of the HW leading margin especially prominent. The FW outer margin is evenly rounded, not coming to a shallow point as on Meadow Fritillary. Above, usually darker basally than Meadow Fritillary with the HW margin darker and with the FW cell-end bar solidly black. Meadow Fritillary has the cell-end bar enclosing some orange ground color. *Habitat:* Black spruce bogs and willow thickets. *Abundance:* LR-LU. Late May–mid July, but only about one week at any given locality. *Food:* Shrubby willows.

Freija Fritillary *Boloria freija*

Below, note the **prominent white postmedian band, broken by the long white "duck bill"** and the **horizontal white marginal bars**. *Habitat:* Subalpine willow thickets. *Abundance:* LC. May–Aug., mainly May–June, but only a few weeks at any given locality, usually while the snowpack is melting. *Food:* Bearberry, blueberry, and other heath family plants. *Comments:* Where they occur, Freija Fritillaries are some of the first butterflies to fly in a new season. The Norse goddess Freija, for whom this species is named, is known to favor love songs and so it may become a tradition among butterflier lovers to seek this northern fritillary to invoke her blessing.

Dingy Fritillary *Boloria improba*

Wings are very rounded. Below, HW has strong median spotband, with a long "duck bill," but no postmedian spotband. Above, dingy with **strong FW postmedian spots that blur into one another**. *Habitat:* Moist areas above treeline with the foodplant. *Abundance:* LR. Mainly mid July–early Aug. in San Juan Mountains of Colorado (*acronema*) and mainly early Aug.–mid Aug. in Wind River Mountains of Wyoming (*harryi*). *Food:* Prostrate willows, including snow willow and arctic willow. *Comments:* The population in the San Juan Mountains of Colorado, 'Uncompahgre' Dingy Fritillary, is listed as federally endangered. Some believe that the Colorado and Wyoming populations merit full species status.

Relict Fritillary *Boloria kriemhild*

Only Relict and Pacific Fritillaries have **submarginal black chevrons that point *outward***. Above, Relict has these **spots more continuous and band-like** while Pacific has orange areas separating the chevrons. Below, Pacific Fritillary is very different. *Habitat:* Moist openings in high mountain coniferous forest. *Abundance:* LR-LU. July–early Aug. *Food:* Violets. *Comments:* One of the few butterflies whose range is restricted to the Rocky Mountains in the United States.

1 Frigga Fritillary

2 Frigga Fritillary

3 Freija Fritillary

4 Freija Fritillary

5 Dingy Fritillary

6 Dingy Fritillary

7 Relict Fritillary

8 Relict Fritillary

Purplish Fritillary *Boloria montinus*

Variable. Below, many populations are tinged with reddish-purple. Note the **FW submarginal horizontal white lines.** Usually with **HW marginal row of white spots.** (see photo 3). Above, usually with black inwardly pointing triangles **with flat bottoms** along the HW submargin. *Habitat:* Openings in coniferous forest. *Abundance:* C-A. July–Aug./Sept. (flying until frost). *Food:* Willows and violets. *Comments:* Recently shown to be distinct from the Old World's Titania Fritillary, *Boloria titania.* The oldest available scientific name is *montinus.* Some treat this as a subspecies of the tundra-dwelling Arctic Fritillary, *Boloria chariclea,* and this was the treatment mistakenly given in *Butterflies through Binoculars: The East.*

Mountain Fritillary *Boloria napaea*

Both above and below, the **HW comes to a shallow point**—it is not evenly rounded. Above, wing bases are very dark. *Habitat:* Moist sloping meadows above treeline. *Abundance:* LR. Early Aug.–mid Aug. *Food:* Knotweeds. *Comments:* Although common in parts of Alaska and also found in the northern Canadian Rocky Mountains, the only place in the lower U.S. where this species occurs is over 11,500 ft. in the Wind River Mountains of Wyoming. The inaccessible nature of its spectacularly beautiful habitat (a horse is helpful), coupled with its short flight period and the unpredictable vagaries of the weather pattern each year (changing the flight period by weeks) and each week (it was about 40°F and cloudy/rainy the first year I tried) makes the romance of this butterfly irresistible.

Alberta Fritillary *Boloria alberta*

Large. Both above and below, **very dull colored.** Below, **FW with postmedian black spots either very faint or absent** but with small black marginal black points at veins. HW with gray smudges. *Habitat:* Windswept scree slopes and ridges above treeline in the high Rocky Mountains. *Abundance:* LR. July–mid Aug. Mostly flying in even-numbered years. *Food:* Mountain avens. *Comments:* One of the least seen butterflies of North America.

Astarte Fritillary *Boloria astarte*

Large. Below, HW has a pale postmedian white spotband with a row of black spots just beyond it. Silver-bordered Fritillary is smaller, brighter orange above and on the FW below and with darker ground color on the HW below. *Habitat:* High, rocky, windswept ridges above treeline. *Abundance:* R-LU. Late July–early Aug. Usually flies every year in Alberta, but only in even-numbered years in Washington. *Food:* Spotted saxifrage.

1 Purplish Fritillary (Wyoming)

2 Purplish Fritillary

3 Purplish Fritillary (Alberta)

4 Mountain Fritillary

5 Alberta Fritillary (museum specimen)

6 Alberta Fritillary (museum specimen)

7 Astarte Fritillary (museum specimen)

8 Astarte Fritillary (museum specimen)

Patches, Checkerspots and Crescents
(subfamily Melitaeinae)

Most of the species in this group are orange-colored, with black reticulations. Unlike the greater and lesser fritillaries, they do not have a complete FW submarginal band of black spots. The patches and the *Thessalia* checkerspots have a white spot in the middle of their crowns.

California Patch *Chlosyne californica*

Bright orange with a black postmedian band containing small white spots. Above, note the **orange marginal spots**. Both above and below, note that the **outer edge of the second and third spots of the FW median orange band are almost aligned**. The **FW cell is orange below**. The orange median bands can be narrower than on the individuals shown. *Habitat:* Desert canyons and washes. *Abundance:* C. March–April. Partial, less common 2nd and 3rd broods in June and Sept.–Nov., their abundance depending upon rainfall. Occasionally strays outside range shown. *Food:* Desert sunflower.

Bordered Patch *Chlosyne lacinia*

This is one of the most variable butterfly species in the world. Individuals similar to those shown from Texas predominate in the eastern part of the range, ones similar to those shown from Arizona and New Mexico predominate in the western portion. Below, there is usually a cream-colored median band, of varying width, and marginal cream-colored HW spots. The black postmedian area almost always has a row of small white spots. Unlike California Patch, the **second and third spots of the FW median spotband are not aligned, and the second spot is displaced inwardly.** Above, the HW margin is black, **lacking HW orange marginal spots** that California Patch exhibits. Almost every individual varies in some fashion from others. Some individuals (more often in South America) have more extensive orange than on the individual shown in photo 4, while other rare individuals are almost entirely black, showing less orange and white than the individuals in photos 7 and 8. *Habitat:* A wide variety of open situations, including brushy fields, thorn scrub, and woodland edges. *Abundance:* C, three-brood areas west to southeastern Arizona, becoming U-R westward. Mainly March–Oct. Decreasing immigrant northward. R late summer immigrant north to Kansas and Utah. RS north to Nebraska. Everywhere, most common in late summer/fall. *Food:* Aster family, especially sunflowers. *Comments:* Although Bordered Patches frequent hilltops and mud puddles, they are often easiest to find in flatlands on flowers. While I've never seen orange HW marginal spots on a Bordered Patch in the United States, some South American Bordered Patches do have some orange HW marginal spots, so this is within the genetic repertoire of the species.

1 California Patch

2 California Patch

3 Bordered Patch (Texas)

4 Bordered Patch (Texas)

5 Bordered Patch (Arizona)

6 Bordered Patch (Arizona)

7 Bordered Patch (New Mexico)

8 Bordered Patch (New Mexico)

Crimson Patch *Chlosyne janais*

Below, the **HW basal yellow patch is dotted with black** and there is a **yellow marginal spotband**. Above, the **bold red-orange HW patch** against a black ground color is distinctive (but see Rosita Patch). *Habitat:* Tropical woodland and thorn scrub. *Abundance:* LR. Mainly June–Nov. RS north to northern Texas and west to southeastern New Mexico. *Food:* Acanthus family. *Comments:* In southern Texas, this gorgeous species' abundance is very variable, but at times it can be quite common.

Rosita Patch *Chlosyne rosita*

Very similar to Crimson Patch, but smaller. Below, the **HW basal yellow patch lacks black spots on its outer half** and there is **no yellow marginal spotband**. Above, the **HW patch is two-toned, paler inwardly, darker outwardly** and is more orange than red. *Habitat:* Thorn scrub. *Abundance:* RS to southeastern Arizona, mainly late Aug.–mid Oct. *Food:* Acanthus family.

Definite Patch *Chlosyne definita*

Above this rarely seen species closely resembles a Theona Checkerspot. Both above and below, note the **reduced size of the middle spot of the HW submarginal spotband**. Below, the middle spot, in addition to being small, is white, not orange. Also note the inverted orange "Y" dangling from the HW leading margin. *Habitat:* Thorn scrub, especially in limestone areas but also along rocky or clay embankments. *Abundance:* R-LU. March–Nov. *Food:* Shaggy tuft. *Comments:* Your best chance for seeing one of these probably is in the Guadalupe Mountains in west Texas and southeastern New Mexico, or in the Franklin Mountains in El Paso County, Texas.

Banded Patch *Chlosyne endeis*

Above, similar to Bordered Patch. Note the red-orange HW submarginal spots and the white neck. Below, similar to Definite Patch, with small white spot at the center of the orange submarginal spotband and inverted orange "Y" dangling from the HW leading margin, but Banded Patch is larger. Note the **black outer FW**. The **HW white median area is bounded by a black continuous line**. Definite Patches have this line discontinuous, with one end attached to an arm of the orange inverted "Y." Some Leanira Checkerspots are very similar above but ranges do not overlap and the Leanira Checkerspots have orange spots behind the eyes that Banded Patches lack. *Habitat:* Thorn scrub. *Abundance:* LR. March–Nov. Has been reported from the Del Rio, Texas, area. *Food:* Unknown. *Comments:* This species is one of the least seen butterflies of those that are resident in the United States.

1 Crimson Patch

2 Crimson Patch

3 Rosita Patch

4 Rosita Patch

5 Definite Patch

6 Definite Patch

7 Banded Patch

8 Banded Patch

Elada Checkerspot *Texola elada*

Tiny. Below, alternating bands of orange and white are dramatic. **HW marginal band is orange.** Above, heavily reticulated with black. Vesta Crescents are similar above but are not quite so heavily reticulated with black and have pale HW marginal crescents and submarginal black spots. *Habitat:* Thorn scrub. *Abundance:* C-A. March–Nov. but mainly April–Oct. *Food:* Acanthus family. *Comments:* Flight is often slow and floating. In some desert canyons there can be a lot of Eladas. In many areas this species flies with Tiny Checkerspots and one must look closely to distinguish them.

Tiny Checkerspot *Dymasia dymas*

Tiny. Below, alternating bands of orange and white are dramatic. **HW marginal band is white.** Above, note the **red-brown crown spot.** Often with a **pale area near the middle of the FW costal margin.** Black reticulations form an "open" network. *Habitat:* Low elevation arid regions, including desert canyons and foothills. *Abundance:* Mainly U-C, occasionally A in southeastern Arizona and southern California. Feb.–Nov. Usually most common March/April–May and Sept. *Food:* Acanthus family, including chuperosa.

Arachne Checkerspot *Poladryas arachne*

Below, the **white median band has rows of black dots.** Above, note the **orange body bands** on the abdomen and the blue-gray eyes. See Dotted Checkerspot (below). Similar checkerspots (Northern Checkerspot and others), have white body bands, except for Variable and Edith's Checkerspots, which have brown eyes. *Habitat:* Mountain meadows and arid grasslands. *Abundance:* R-LC. April–Oct. Mainly April/May–June, Sept. High elevation populations, including the California population (*monache*), are single brooded, June–Aug. *Food:* Beardtongues. *Comments:* Look for this species in the morning, especially on grassland knolls.

Dotted Checkerspot *Poladryas minuta*

Below, the **white median band has rows of black dots.** Above, note the **orange body bands** on the abdomen and the blue-gray eyes. Arachne Checkerspot has more extensive black markings above and narrower orange bands below. Above, Dotted Checkerspot has HW marginal black bands that are strongly crescent-shaped while Arachne Checkerspot has these lines more gently rounded. *Habitat:* Limestone ridges with sparse woods. *Abundance:* R-LU. April/May–Sept. *Food:* Beardtongues. *Comments:* Presumably occurring over most of Texas in the recent past, the reasons for this species' apparent decline are unknown. Considered by some to be conspecific with Arachne Checkerspot.

1 Elada Checkerspot

2 Elada Checkerspot

3 Tiny Checkerspot

4 Tiny Checkerspot

5 Arachne Checkerspot

6 Arachne Checkerspot

7 Dotted Checkerspot

8 Dotted Checkerspot

Theona Checkerspot *Thessalia theona*

Below, only Chinati Checkerspot resembles this species. The **bold HW pattern of orange postmedian and basal bands on a white ground color** makes identification easy. Note the orange along the bottom vein of the HW. Above, Theona Checkerspots are extremely variable, even within the same population. Although patterns range, as shown, from very dark (photo 1) to very light-colored (photo 4), the majority of individuals probably come closest to the individual shown in photo 3. *Habitat:* Thorn scrub and brushy canyons. *Abundance:* U-C. March–Oct. Peaks in April and Aug. *Food:* Mainly Indian paintbrushes in Arizona and silverleafs in Texas.

Chinati Checkerspot *Thessalia chinatiensis*

Very similar to Theona Checkerspot. **Below, note the absence of orange along the bottom vein of the HW.** Above, there is a **complete absence of any black postmedian bands on both the FW and HW**. Also note the **solid black HW border**, without any included pale spots. Theona Checkerspot usually have strong black postmedian bands, but sometimes these are faint (photo 4). They also almost always have at least some submarginal pale spots in the HW border (outside the area of this guide, in southeastern Texas and northeastern Mexico, many Theona individuals lack submarginal pale spots in the HW border). *Habitat:* Open brushy situations at mid-elevations. *Abundance:* R-U. April–Oct. *Food:* Silverleafs. *Comments:* The status of Chinati Checkerspot is uncertain. Found in a limited geographical area and very closely related to Theona Checkerspot, Chinati Checkerspot may be only a subspecies or form of that species. One finds individuals in West Texas that may be hybrids between Chinati and Theona, such as the individual shown in photo 8, but it is not certain that these actually are hybrids. Even if they are, one needs more information about how frequently such hybrids occur before concluding that there is only one species. If there is but one species and Chinati and Theona freely interbreed, it would seem that Chinati genes would be quickly swamped by the ocean of Theona genes surrounding it, especially considering that I found individuals that seemed to be "pure" Theona at the exact location I found Chinati seven months earlier. Hopefully, further studies will help us resolve this issue.

1 Theona Checkerspot

2 Theona Checkerspot

3 Theona Checkerspot

4 Theona Checkerspot

5 Theona Checkerspot

6 Chinati Checkerspot

7 Chinati Checkerspot

8 Chinati Checkerspot

Thessalia checkerspots (in part)

The three species of *Thessalia* checkerspots on this page are characterized by their bold underside pattern. The HW has a dramatic **black postmedian band enclosing white spots.** Above, all three have **median and postmedian white or cream-colored HW spotbands.** The **spots in the postmedian band are usually small and closely aligned.**

Leanira Checkerspot *Thessalia leanira*

Below, **HW with black postmedian band enclosing white spots.** West of the California Sierras most individuals also have a basal black band on the HW. Both above and below, note the **orange palps.** Above, mainly black west of the Sierra Nevadas and the coastal and transverse ranges of southern California, mainly orange eastward, with intermediates occurring, mainly in Los Angeles, Kern, and Tulare Counties, California. **Abdomen is black** (Fulvia has at least some orange). *Habitat:* Varied, including open pine and aspen woodlands, sagebrush steppes, chaparral, desert hills, and sand dunes *Abundance:* LR-LU. March–July, mainly April–May, except mainly May–June in northern California/Oregon. Occasional late season emergences have been reported. At Oso Flaco Lake in San Louis Obispo County, California, the population is reportedly two-brooded, flying mid April–mid May, late June–July. *Food:* Indian paintbrushes. *Comments:* Rare individuals lack the black bands below. An entire population, formerly in the vicinity of San Rafael, Marin County, California, now probably extirpated, lacked these black bands.

Fulvia Checkerspot *Thessalia fulvia*

Below, **HW with black postmedian band enclosing white spots.** Both above and below, note that the **palps are black above and white below.** Above, similar to Leanira Checkerspot, but note **at least some orange on the abdomen.** *Habitat:* Open hillsides covered by pinyon-juniper, prairie, or grassland, often in limestone areas. *Abundance:* LR-U. Peaks in April, June, and Aug.–Sept. in three-brood area; mainly May–July and Aug.–Sept. in two-brood area. *Food:* Indian paintbrushes.

Black Checkerspot *Thessalia cyneas*

Below, **HW with black postmedian band enclosing white spots.** Extremely similar to Fulvia Checkerspot. Above, mainly black with **orange HW marginal spotband.** *Habitat:* Mid-elevation mountain canyons with permanent water. *Abundance:* R-C. Abundance seems to be cyclical. It will become common for a period of years and then become rare again. Continually brooded—April–Nov. with rainfall the primary controlling factor in emergences. Most common in the fall. Known only from Cochise Co., Arizona, in the United States but also occurs in the states of Sonora and Durango in Mexico and is possible in the southwestern mountains of New Mexico. *Food:* Indian paintbrushes.

1 Leanira Checkerspot (black)

2 Leanira Checkerspot (black)

3 Leanira Checkerspot (orange)

4 Leanira Checkerspot (orange)

5 Fulvia Checkerspot

6 Fulvia Checkerspot

7 Black Checkerspot

8 Black Checkerspot

Gorgone Checkerspot *Chlosyne gorgone*

Below, the **zigzag brownish gray and white HW pattern is unique**. Above, note the **wide, black FW borders** that other checkerspots lack (except for Silvery). Gorgone usually has pronounced **pale chevrons in the HW black border** that Silvery usually lacks (when pale spots are present in Silvery borders they tend to be relatively flat). *Habitat:* Although the heart of its range is the prairie province, this species can occur in a great variety of open situations, including waste areas, streamsides and roadsides. *Abundance:* C. April–Oct. in three-brood area; May–Aug. in two-brood area; May–early July in one-brood areas (sometimes with a partial second brood in late July). *Food:* Sunflowers and other aster family plants. *Comments:* A widely wandering, colonizing species. There have been temporary colonies in (for example) western Montana, the Salt Lake City area, and southwestern Idaho. All now seem to be gone.

Silvery Checkerspot *Chlosyne nycteis*

Note the **very broad pale median band on the HW below, with individual spots bulging outward**. Above, note the **wide black FW borders** that other checkerspots lack (except for Gorgone). Silvery Checkerspots usually lack the pronounced pale chevrons in the HW black border that Gorgone Checkerspot usually have. Also, Silvery Checkerspots average larger and the less extensive orange on the basal half of the wings gives Silvery Checkerspots an overall darker appearance. *Habitat:* Moist openings in deciduous and mixed woodland; stream edges in open country. *Abundance:* LR-U. May–Oct. in the southern portion of green area, mid June–Aug. in the northern portion of green area; June–July in yellow areas. *Food:* Sunflowers and other aster family plants.

Harris' Checkerspot *Chlosyne harrisii*

Below, similar to Silvery Checkerspot, with HW median band that bulges outward. Note the **HW margin with a complete row of large white spots**. *Habitat:* Wet shrubby meadows and marsh borders. *Abundance:* LR. Late June–mid July. *Food:* Flat-topped white aster. *Comments:* Barely enters the West. Like its relatives, eggs are laid in clusters and caterpillars are colonial.

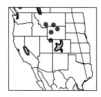

Rockslide Checkerspot *Chlosyne whitneyi*

Very similar to Northern Checkerspot, and especially to Sagebrush Checkerspot. Below, median band is white. Median band below on Northern Checkerspot is slightly off-white—buffy. Although Rockslide Checkerspots average darker and duller above than Sagebrush and Northern Checkerspots, identification is really only possible by habitat—a *Chlosyne* checkerspot flying over a rockslide above treeline can reasonably be assumed to be this species. *Habitat:* High elevation rockslides and scree slopes above treeline. *Abundance:* R-U. July–Aug. *Food:* Fleabanes.

1 Gorgone Checkerspot

2 Gorgone Checkerspot

3 Silvery Checkerspot

4 Silvery Checkerspot

5 Harris' Checkerspot

6 Harris' Checkerspot

7 Rockslide Checkerspot

8 Rockslide Checkerspot

Charidryas **Checkerspots**
(subgenus *Charidryas* of genus *Chlosyne*)

These five species (with Rockslide Checkerspot on previous page) are very similar. All have a HW below with a pale median band flanked by red-orange bands. The **postmedian red-orange band stops well short of the leading margin.** Also see *Euphydryas* checkerspots, next pages.

Gabb's Checkerspot *Chlosyne gabbii*
Below, **HW median spotband is white**. Above, as shown. Rockslide Checkerspot doesn't occur within range. Sagebrush Checkerspot is extremely similar and variable, but populations that occur near Gabb's Checkerspots are bright orange with much reduced black markings (see photo 4). *Habitat:* Chaparral, low canyons, dunes, and washes. *Abundance:* U. Late March–June. *Food:* Beach aster and others in aster family.

Sagebrush Checkerspot *Chlosyne acastus*
Below, **HW median spotband is white**. Above, ground color varies from bright orange with weak black markings (*neumoegeni* in southeastern California and western Arizona) to almost all black. *Habitat:* Open arid areas, including desert flats and hills, sagebrush steppes, and pinyon-juniper hillsides. *Abundance:* Mainly C, but LR to the northeast. March–May in the southern deserts, with a partial second brood in Aug.–Oct.; elsewhere, mid May–mid July, depending upon location. *Food:* Rabbitbrush (most populations) and desert aster (*neumoegeni*). *Comments:* This species and Gabb's and Rockslide Checkerspots are very closely related.

Northern Checkerspot *Chlosyne palla*
Below, **HW median spotband is usually off-white**. Along the inner edge of the HW median spotband, the **2nd and 3rd small pale spots (counting from leading margin) are equal**. Above, extremely variable. Ground color varies from almost all orange to orange and black, to almost entirely black (in some areas females are blacker than photo 6 inset). *Habitat:* A wide variety, from woodland openings to sagebrush. *Abundance:* C. April–Aug. *Food:* Asters and rabbitbrush.

Hoffmann's Checkerspot *Chlosyne hoffmanni*
Below, **HW median spotband is off-white**. Along the inner edge of the HW median spotband, the **2nd and 3rd small pale spots (counting from leading margin) are unequal** (in most populations), with the second spot narrower and not extending as far inward. Above, **wings are darkened at their bases**, with a **strong contrast between basal and median areas**. Also, the three HW median band spots nearest the trailing margin tend to be more aligned than on Northern Checkerspot. *Habitat:* Openings in mountain coniferous forest. *Abundance:* C-A in California; R-LU northward. June–Aug. *Food:* Asters.

1 Gabb's Checkerspot

2 Gabb's Checkerspot

3 Sagebrush Checkerspot

4 Sagebrush Checkerspot

5 Northern Checkerspot

6 Northern Checkerspot

7 Hoffmann's Checkerspot

8 Hoffmann's Checkerspot

Euphydryas Checkerspots (genus *Euphydryas*)

The three to five species in the West (depending upon who's counting) are easy enough to recognize as a group, but often impossible to identify to species. The patterns both above and below, while amazingly variable, even within a single population, are similar enough that an individual can usually be recognized as belonging to this group. If in doubt, check the eyes. *Euphydryas* eyes are brown while other checkerspots have blue-gray eyes.

chalcedona + colon

anicia

Variable Checkerspot *Euphydryas chalcedona*

Also see next page. Extremely variable. Varies from primarily red-orange above, to primarily black, to very white and everything in between. This species and Edith's Checkerspot are often extraordinarily difficult to distinguish in the field (however, unlike the greater fritillaries, they can be distinguished by an examination of inner anatomy). Many, but not all, populations of Variable Checkerspots have **at least some white spots on the abdomen**, set off-center. Edith's Checkerspots always lack white abdominal spots. Many, but not all, populations of Variable Checkerspots have **luminous yellow antennal clubs**, with little if any black at their base. I believe, but am not yet certain, that in California, Edith's Checkerspots always have much black on the bottom halves of their antennal clubs. So, if your checkerspot has white spots on the abdomen or, in California, luminous yellow antennal clubs, you can safely conclude that it's a Variable Checkerspot. If you are in California and your checkerspot lacks white spots and has much black on the antennal clubs, you can probably conclude that it's an Edith's. Elsewhere, it's going to be a guess. In general, the outer margin of the HW on Variable Checkerspot often comes to a very slight point, while that of Edith's is more gently rounded. Also, see comments section, below. *Habitat:* Many open situations, including mountain meadows, desert canyons and high elevation barrens. *Abundance:* C-A. March–May in southern California, southeastern Arizona-southwestern New Mexico (*hermosa*); mainly May–July elsewhere. *Food:* Beardtongues, Indian paintbrushes, snowberries (*colon*), and others. *Comments:* Included here are both *colon* and *anicia*, which at least some consider to be separate species. In some areas two of these three subspecies fly at the same location or nearby, but in other areas they seem to intergrade. Further careful, large-scale studies are needed to clarify the situation. Of some help in identification, Variable Checkerspot is the sole alpine species of *Euphydryas* in the high mountains of Arizona (*magdalena*, see photo 5) and throughout the Rocky Mountains south of Wyoming (including the Wasatch Plateau).

1 Orange County, California

2 Orange County, California

3 Olympic National Park, Washington

4 San Mateo County, California

5 Apache County, Arizona (July)

6 Sublette County, Wyoming

7 Apache County, Arizona (May)

8 Tuolumne County, California

anicia

Variable Checkerspot *Euphydryas chalcedona*

Also see previous page. Sometimes with **white, off-center spots on the abdomen** and with **luminous yellow antennal clubs**. Edith's Checkerspots always lack the white abdomen spots and usually (but not always) have much black on the lower half of the antennal clubs. *Habitat:* Foothills to alpine open areas, but rarely in true alpine habitats north of Wyoming. *Abundance:* C-A. March–Aug. Mainly June–July. *Food:* Beardtongues, paintbrushes, and others.

Edith's Checkerspot *Euphydryas editha*

Extremely similar to, and often impossible to distinguish in the field from, the more common Variable Checkerspot. Edith's Checkerspots always **lack white, off-center abdomenal spots** that Variable Checkerspots sometimes have (the faint white spots visible in the center of the abdomens in photos 4 and 6 is an artifact of photo flash) and often have much **black on the lower half of the antennal clubs**. Below, the **pale HW median band is sometimes narrowed, so that the black line outward of this median band separates two reddish areas**, but many populations do not exhibit this feature. Variable Checkerspots have the black line separating the white median inwardly and a red band outwardly. Unfortunately, the butterflies rarely show off their spiffy undersides. Edith's Checkerspots average smaller than Variable Checkerspots and the wing shape tends to be more rounded than Variable Checkerspot, but these are subtle and inconsistent points, and probably not much use in the field. *Habitat:* Mainly in stressed habitats, including ocean bluffs, desert hills, ridgetops in sagebrush scrub and rocky outcrops above treeline. *Abundance:* Mainly LR-U, but C at high elevations in the California Sierra Nevadas (*nubigena*). March–April in southern lowlands and coast; April–June in southern mountains and northern lowlands; mainly June–early Aug. elsewhere. *Food:* Indian paintbrushes, Chinese houses, louseworts, and others.

Gillette's Checkerspot *Euphydryas gillettii*

Easy to recognize, both above and below by **wide red-orange submarginal band** on both FW and HW. *Habitat:* Wet mountain meadows. *Abundance:* LR. Late June–July, with a short flight season. *Food:* Twinberry honeysuckle. *Comments:* Most frequently encountered in Alberta.

1 Variable Checkerspot (Wyoming)

2 Variable Checkerspot (Colorado)

3 Variable Checkerspot (Colorado)

4 Edith's Checkerspot (Jacumba, California)

5 Edith's Checkerspot (Nevada)

6 Edith's Checkerspot (Nevada)

7 Gillette's Checkerspot

8 Gillette's Checkerspot

Crescents (genus *Phyciodes*)

As with many butterfly groups, it is easy to recognize a butterfly as a crescent, but often extemely difficult to determine to which species the individual belongs. Also as with other groups, because of geographical variation it is often easier to distinguish two species at a particular locality than to describe how to separate them everywhere in their range. Named for the crescent-shaped spot near the HW margin, most of the crescents are common butterflies. Although all North American species are not dissimilar, the group is very diverse in the American tropics, with species mimicking heliconians and other butterfly groups.

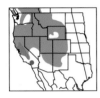

Field Crescent *Phyciodes campestris*

Variable. Both above and below, **antennal tips are dark brown or black**. Generally, other crescents in the range of Field Crescents have orange antennal tips. The presence of a **pale bar in the FW cell below** (except in the California Sierra Nevadas) is often useful. Individuals in eastern populations are browner with more a more patterned HW (see inset to photo 1). Individuals in most populations resemble the individual in photo 2, **appearing to be primarily black above**, with extensive dark areas strongly contrasting with the pale median band and with the HW postmedian orange band enclosing black dots. Most other crescents register primarily as orange. At mid to high elevations in the California Sierra Nevadas individuals are generally more orange above and are almost unmarked below. Intermediates occur. *Habitat:* Extremely varied, including open weedy fields, prairies, roadsides, taiga, and moist mountain meadows, ranging from sea level to above treeline. *Abundance:* Mainly C-A. May–Sept.; March–Nov. in the California lowlands. Only one brood at high elevations, mainly July–early Aug. *Food:* Asters.

California Crescent *Phyciodes orseis*

Populations in Trinity Alps and Siskiyous areas differ from those in the Sierra Nevada. In Trinities and Sikiyous the upper side resembles a Field Crescent but the antennal tips are orange, while the underside resembles a Mylitta Crescent, with fairly strong mottling. At high elevations in the California/Nevada Sierra Nevadas, upperside resembles a Mylitta Crescent while the underside resembles the high-elevation populations of Field Crescents! *Habitat:* Mountain creeksides. *Abundance:* LR. April–June in most of the range, July–Aug. at high elevations in the Sierra Nevadas. *Food:* Thistles. *Comments:* Populations formerly occurred north of San Francisco, but these populations have not been found for many years. The reasons for their extirpation are unknown.

1 Field Crescent

2 Field Crescent

3 Field Crescent (Sierra Nevadas)

4 Field Crescent (California Sierra Nevadas)

5 California Crescent (Sierras)

6 California Crescent (Sierras)

7 California Crescent (Trinities)
(museum specimen)

8 California Crescent (Trinities)
(museum specimen)

Pearl Crescent *Phyciodes tharos*

Exact pattern is quite variable. Usually with orange antennal clubs. Above, orange with black reticulations. Usually with FW median band not much paler than the postmedian band. HW reticulation of males is similar to that of females. *Habitat:* Widespread in moist open situations southward, including fields, meadows, woodland edges, and suburbia; more frequent in drier habitats northward. *Abundance:* C-A. April/May–Sept./Oct. *Food:* Asters.

Northern Crescent *Phyciodes selenis*

Variable. Usually with orange antennal tips. Above, males have reduced HW black reticulations, leaving the **orange postmedian area of males more "open."** Females usually have the FW median band somewhat paler than the postmedian band but are often not separable from female Pearl or Tawny Crescents. *Habitat:* Mainly woodland openings and edges, but occurs wherever there are asters, including suburban and urban areas. *Abundance:* C-A. Mainly June–July, but as early as mid May and as late as early Sept. Partial second broods have been reported. *Food:* Asters. *Comments:* Northern and Pearl Crescents seem to behave as separate species in some areas and as subspecies in others. This complex does not comfortably fit within the neat boxes we like to construct. If you consider all individuals as Pearl Crescents you'll not only make your identifications easier, you'll probably be closer to the biological reality.

Tawny Crescent *Phyciodes batesii*

Variable. Below, the bottom of the black spot in the middle of the FW inner margin is usually wide. Unfortunately, this can almost never be seen in the field. The individual in photo 7 is from North Carolina; many individuals in western populations much more closely resemble Pearl and Northern Crescents, but the HW ground color on most individuals is yellower (others are browner). The **antennal tips are black** (except for the Colorado populations). The black median bar that is perpendicular to the FW costal margin may be helpful. In Tawny Crescents it is characteristically (but not always) longer, with straighter sides (more rectangular) than on Northern and Pearl Crescents. Above, tends to be darker than Northern and Pearl Crescents (especially comparing males). Males resemble Pearl Crescents above, usually lacking the "open" HW orange area of Northern Crescent males. Females usually have a FW median band that is paler than the postmedian band. *Habitat:* Mainly woodland openings and edges. *Abundance:* LR-U. June–early Aug. *Food:* Asters. *Comments:* Some Colorado crescents have recently been described as a subspecies of this species. They look quite different from the eastern populations, and it is not certain that they are actually Tawny Crescents. A thorough study of this group using molecular systematics is needed.

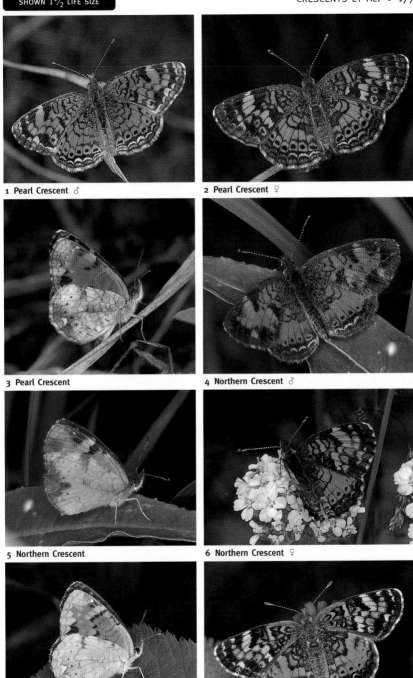

1 Pearl Crescent ♂

2 Pearl Crescent ♀

3 Pearl Crescent

4 Northern Crescent ♂

5 Northern Crescent

6 Northern Crescent ♀

7 Tawny Crescent

8 Tawny Crescent

Mylitta Crescent *Phyciodes mylitta*

Above, most populations have black areas greatly reduced, so that Mylitta Crescents are **the most orange crescents**. From southern Colorado through New Mexico and eastern Arizona, the FW above closely resembles that of Pale Crescent, but that species does not occur there. *Habitat:* A wide variety, including urban areas, dry fields and wet meadows, woodland openings and mountain canyons, from sea level to treeline. *Abundance:* U–C. March–Sept./Oct. at low to moderate elevations. Probably two broods, April/May–Aug./Sept. at higher elevations. *Food:* Thistles. *Comments:* As with almost all the crescents, males will generally differ from females, wet season individuals from dry season individuals, and there is great variability from individual to individual. Males often patrol along small streams, gully bottoms, or trails.

Pale Crescent *Phyciodes pallida*

Pale Crescents average larger than Mylitta Crescents, but the diagnostic mark that best separates this species from Mylitta is the large black spot in the middle of the FW trailing margin below. Unfortunately, in the field this spot is almost always obscured by the HW. However, a similar **large black spot is in the middle of the FW trailing margin above**, and where the two occur together, Mylitta Crescents usually have only a small black spot at this position, or lack the spot entirely. *Habitat:* Woodland openings, streambeds in arid regions, prairie, and foothill gulches. *Abundance:* R–LU in Pacific Northwest, mid April–mid June. LU–C in Colorado, June–Aug. *Food:* Thistles. *Comments:* Tends to be more colonial and local than other crescents.

Vesta Crescent *Phyciodes vesta*

The postmedian chain of black encircled orange spots on the FW below is diagnostic, but often difficult to see in the field. Some individuals have black lines crossing the FW cell below and these can be separated from Pearl Crescents which have much paler brown lines. Above, Vesta Crescents are highly reticulated with black. Elada Checkerspot have even thicker black reticulations and have wide black wing borders. *Habitat:* Thorn scrub and other dry open situations. *Abundance:* C. March–Oct. RS and temporary colonist to southeastern Arizona. RS north to Kansas and Colorado. *Food:* Hairy tubetongue.

1 Mylitta Crescent (California)

2 Mylitta Crescent (California)

3 Mylitta Crescent (Arizona)

4 Mylitta Crescent (Arizona)

5 Pale Crescent

6 Pale Crescent

7 Vesta Crescent

8 Vesta Crescent

Phaon Crescent *Phyciodes phaon*

Below, HW is tan with darker markings. **FW ground color is bright orange**. Above, note the **cream-colored FW median band, contrasting with the orange postmedian band**. *Habitat:* Moist situations with low vegetation that includes its low, mat-forming hostplant. Often along roadsides, trails, lake beds, or in suburban plantings. *Abundance:* C-A eastward; becoming U in West Texas and California. Mainly April/May–Oct./Nov. RS to Nebraska, Colorado, southeastern Arizona, and southern Nevada. *Food:* Fogfruits.

Painted Crescent *Phyciodes picta*

Below, **HW is cream to pale yellow with dark markings greatly reduced or absent**. FW apex is pale and unmarked. Above, note the **pale FW median band and pale subapical spots**. *Habitat:* Moist areas in arid grasslands, prairies, and deserts. *Abundance:* LU-LC. March–Oct. in southeastern Arizona. Mainly mid May–Aug. northward. Strays to Nebraska. *Food:* Asters and (non-native) bindweed.

Texan Crescent *Phyciodes texana*

Both above and below, FW outer margin has a concavity. Below, **FW with orange base and large black patch**. Above, black with a white median spotband and variable amounts of red-brown basally. Much blacker than other Western crescents. *Habitat:* Open woodland, thorn scrub, roadsides, and parks. *Abundance:* C. Can occur all year, but mainly March–Oct. Probably not resident in northern Texas and Oklahoma, mainly June–Oct. Strays widely, north to Nebraska, Colorado, Utah, and southern Nevada. *Food:* Small acanthus family plants. *Comments:* Males often patrol small sections of a trail or gulch, flying less than one foot off the ground.

Pale-banded Crescent *Phyciodes tulcis*

RS only. Very similar to Texan Crescent. Above, FW pale spots are yellower and larger than on Texan Crescents and HW pale median band is yellow and wider. **HW has partial pale postmedian band** in addition to pale submarginal band. Texan Crescent has only a submarginal band. Below, lacks the orange FW base of Texan Crescent and has a pale HW. *Habitat:* Tropical woodland and edges. *Abundance:* RS to San Antonio area, West Texas, and southeastern Arizona. *Food:* Unknown. Small acanthus family plants are suspected. *Comments:* Treated as a subspecies of Cuban Crescent, *Phyciodes frisia*, on the first edition of the NABA *Checklist*.

Elf *Microtia elva*

Nothing else resembles this diminutive stray. *Habitat:* Thorn scrub. *Abundance:* RS to southeastern Arizona. Mainly late Aug.–Oct. *Food:* Unknown. *Comments:* Small size and weak flight close to the ground make it easy to overlook.

1 Phaon Crescent

2 Phaon Crescent

3 Painted Crescent

4 Painted Crescent

5 Texan Crescent

6 Texan Crescent

7 Elf

8 Pale-banded Crescent

True Brushfoots (subfamily Nymphalinae)
Anglewings and Tortoiseshells
(genuses *Polygonia* and *Nymphalis* respectively)

These two groups are best considered together, since they share many traits and are very closely related. Unlike most of our butterflies, adult anglewings and tortoiseshells rarely nectar at flowers. Instead, they often can be seen taking sap from trees, congregating at rotting fruit, or even deriving sustenance from animal scat or carrion. These butterflies are closely associated with woodlands where one is likely to see them along dirt roads and trails or at creeksides. Also unlike any other western butterflies, species in these groups overwinter in cold areas as adults. The adult butterflies crawl into narrow cavities in trees, or into cracks in human dwellings. On warm days in the dead of winter, they can sometimes be found flying in the sunshine! The overwintering adults usually mate in the early springtime.

Question Mark *Polygonia interrogationis*
Larger than other anglewings. Note the **silvered "question-mark" below**. Varies from almost unpatterned to highly patterned. This is the only anglewing with a **small black horizontal bar on the subapical FW above**. HW margin is often violaceous. Black or "summer" form has much black on the HWs which the orange or "fall" form lacks. *Habitat:* Woodlands and adjacent open areas. *Abundance:* U-C from West Texas eastward and north to Colorado and Oklahoma. Elsewhere, R-U. Early spring and again from mid summer to fall. *Food:* Hackberries, nettles, elm family, and others. *Comments:* Very rarely a Question Mark will have the dot of its "question mark" missing, leaving you to question the correct punctuation of the species!

Eastern Comma *Polygonia comma*
Below, brown-toned. **HW black postmedian line below "comma" is very jagged. FW apex is usually two-toned**, outwardly pale, inwardly darker. Distinguished from Question Mark by smaller size, the "comma" on the HW below and the lack of a small black horizontal bar on the subapical FW above that Question Mark has. Like Question Mark, has a fall "orange form" with greatly reduced HW black. Range barely overlaps other Western commas, except for Gray Comma. Below, Gray Commas are heavily striated. Satyr Commas have a less jagged postmedian line below the comma. *Habitat:* Woodlands. *Abundance:* R-U. Late May/late June–mid Oct. 2nd brood overwintering as adults and flying again next spring, mainly April–May. *Food:* Elms and nettles.

Satyr Comma *Polygonia satyrus*
Below, brown-toned. Most other western commas are darker and grayer below. Above, the **two black spots on the inner margin of the FW** (top spot sometimes pale), **black spot in the middle of the HW and the pale HW margin**, and **pale submarginal band** separate this species from other commas. *Habitat:* Woodlands. *Abundance:* Mainly R-U. Single brood flies June/July (early Aug. in Canada)–Oct/Nov., overwinters, then flies again the following spring. *Food:* Nettles.

1 Question Mark

2 Question Mark (orange form)

3 Question Mark

4 Question Mark (black form)

5 Eastern Comma

6 Eastern Comma

7 Satyr Comma

8 Satyr Comma

Hoary Comma *Polygonia gracilis*

Below, varies from paler than shown to even darker gray than shown, **usually with a two-toned appearance** with outer portions of the wings whitish-gray and inner portions darker gray. Above, the **HW submarginal yellow spots run together** forming a band. HW lacks a black spot in the middle of the wing. *Habitat:* Openings and edges of varied woodlands and brushy areas, especially along streams, from prairie and foothills to treeline. *Abundance:* C. Early spring–late fall. *Food:* Currants *Comments:* Some consider the western populations, Zephyr Comma (*P. gracilis zephyrus*) to be a separate species from the more eastern Hoary Comma.

Green Comma *Polygonia faunus*

Usually, the **wings are more jagged** than other anglewings. Note the **bluish-green submarginal band below** (faint in Colorado). Above, note the two black spots on the inner margin of the FW (top spot sometimes faint) and the black spot in the middle of the HW. Eastern, Gray, and Hoary Commas usually have only the FW bottom spot or if the top spot is present it is faint; Gray and Hoary Commas lack the middle HW black spot. **The black HW border has yellowish spots and is bordered inwardly by a dark brown band.** *Habitat:* Streamsides and openings in coniferous or mixed mountain woodlands. *Abundance:* R-U. Single brood flies July–Sept./Oct., overwinters, then flies again the following spring. *Food:* Willows and birches and others.

Gray Comma *Polygonia progne*

Below, very heavily striated. "Comma" is thin and tapered at both ends. The outer portion of the FW is whitish, but the outer portion of the HW below the "comma" is the same dark color as the inner wing area. Above, HW black border (very wide and diffuse in black form—as shown) with small yellow spots. FW lacks top spot on the inner margin and HW lacks black spot in the middle of the wing. *Habitat:* Deciduous woodlands. *Abundance:* R-U. Mainly June–July, Aug.–early Oct. with overwintering adults in April–May. *Food:* Gooseberries.

Oreas Comma *Polygonia oreas*

Below, usually two-toned. **Above, the HW dark border is the same color on both sides of the enclosed HW pale submarginal band.** *Habitat:* Moist woodlands, especially in the vicinity of streams. *Abundance:* R-U. Late June/July–Sept. with overwintering adults in early spring. *Food:* Gooseberries. *Comments:* Some consider Oreas Comma to be a subspecies of Gray Comma.

1 Hoary Comma

2 Hoary Comma

3 Green Comma

4 Green Comma

5 Gray Comma

6 Gray Comma

7 Oreas Comma

8 Oreas Comma

Mourning Cloak *Nymphalis antiopa*

Unmistakable. A large, dark nymphalid. Below, dark striated brown with pale yellow borders. Dark brown above with yellow borders and blue submarginal spots. ***Habitat:*** Though characteristic of hardwood forests, Mourning Cloaks can be found in almost any habitat, including woodlands, fields, suburbs, and cities. ***Abundance:*** Generally C, but R-U in much of Texas and in southern California. Adults emerge in mid summer, fly into the fall, overwinter, then fly again early the following spring. There may be multiple broods in some areas, but more likely is that after emerging and briefly flying, many adults enter a resting stage, becoming active again in the fall. ***Food:*** Willows and many other trees and shrubs. ***Comments:*** Often glides in flight. Seems to move south and downslope in the fall, north and to higher elevations in the spring.

Compton Tortoiseshell *Nymphalis vau-album*

Note the **white spot on the HW above**. Below, dark gray and heavily striated. Gray Comma, similar below, is much smaller. ***Habitat:*** A wide variety of wooded situations. ***Abundance:*** LU-LC. Adults fly late July–early Sept., overwinter, and then fly again the following spring. Subject to cyclical population explosions and range expansions. R immigrant south to Oregon, Utah, Colorado, and Nebraska (and probably farther). ***Food:*** Birches and willows. ***Comments:*** The aristocratic and boldly patterned Compton Tortoiseshell often glides through the woodlands, seemingly surveying its realm. Named after Compton County, Quebec, so, like California Tortoiseshell (not California's Tortoiseshell), this species is Compton Tortoiseshell, not Compton's Tortoiseshell.

California Tortoiseshell *Nymphalis californica*

Below, very similar to commas and Compton Tortoiseshell, but lacks "comma" and wing margins are less jagged than commas. Above, bright brown-orange with bold black borders. ***Habitat:*** Coniferous and mixed woodland. ***Abundance:*** Usually R-U but A during irruptions (see Comments). Adults fly mid summer to fall, overwinter, then fly again the following spring. ***Food:*** Ceanothus. ***Comments:*** This species, often quite rare, has periodic irruptions and migratory movements. In irruption years the butterfly may be everywhere, with the caterpillars completely covering Ceanothus-covered hillsides.

Milbert's Tortoiseshell *Nymphalis milberti*

This colorful nymphalid has bright orange and yellow FW borders above. Below, dark, striated brown with a **pale submarginal band**. Mourning Cloak is much larger and has a pale marginal band. ***Habitat:*** Moist woodland openings. ***Abundance:*** Mainly R-U but C in the Pacific Northwest. Adults emerge mid summer, fly into the fall, overwinter, and fly again the following spring. ***Food:*** Nettles.

1 Mourning Cloak

2 Mourning Cloak

3 Compton Tortoiseshell

4 Compton Tortoiseshell

5 California Tortoiseshell

6 California Tortoiseshell

7 Milbert's Tortoiseshell

8 Milbert's Tortoiseshell

Red Admiral *Vanessa atalanta*

Naturally enough, Red Admirals are patriotic—sporting red, white and blue along the FW costa below. Above, the reddish-orange bands on both FWs and HWs make confusion of this species with any other very difficult. *Habitat:* Open situations with flowers, including fields, beaches, suburbia, and especially moist meadows near woodlands. *Abundance:* Mainly U-C but often R in Nevada, the California Sierras, and the Pacific Northwest. March–November in southern California east to central/northern Texas. Mainly May–Oct. northward. *Food:* Nettles. *Comments:* A cross-dresser of sorts, this species is a lady, not an admiral.

American Lady *Vanessa virginiensis*

Both above and below, note the **protruded FW apex.** Below, note the distinctive cobweb pattern and the pink patch on the FW. To distinguish from similar Painted and West Coast Ladies remember, "American Ladies have big eyes and an open mind." The big eyes refer to the **two large eyespots on the HW below.** The open mind refers to the lack of a horizontal "closing" line connecting the black lines in the lower middle FW above. Most individuals have a **white spot on the FW** above that other ladies lack. *Habitat:* Widespread in open situations. *Abundance:* Mainly U, but R in the Pacific Northwest. Mainly March–Nov. in southern California east to central/northern Texas. May–Oct. northward. RS north to British Columbia and Montana. *Food:* Pearly everlastings and others in aster family.

West Coast Lady *Vanessa annabella*

Both above and below, note the **protruded FW apex** and the **black bar that completely crosses the FW cell.** Other ladies have two incomplete black bars in the FW cell. The region just **outside the black FW cell bar is pink below.** *Habitat:* Open situations, often disturbed. *Abundance:* R-U. Almost all year, but mainly March–Nov. in southern and coastal lowlands. May–Sept./Oct. elsewhere. *Food:* Mallows and others in the mallow family.

Painted Lady *Vanessa cardui*

Averages larger than other ladies, without protruded apex. Note the **four small HW eyespots below.** Often with a pink suffusion above. The FW median black band is wider and bolder. *Habitat:* Can be encountered in any type of open habitat. *Abundance:* Mainly C-A, but R-C in Pacific Northwest. March/April–Oct./Nov. *Food:* Thistles and many others. *Comments:* Each year Painted Ladies stream out of northern Mexico during March and April in often impressive swarms to repopulate the West. Numbers of butterflies, and the extent of the territory they reach, vary widely from year to year. This is the most cosmopolitan butterfly in the world.

1 Red Admiral

2 Red Admiral

3 American Lady

4 American Lady

5 West Coast Lady

6 West Coast Lady

7 Painted Lady

8 Painted Lady

Common Buckeye *Junonia coenia*

Note the **prominent eyespots** along the margins of both wings and the **two orange bars in the FW cell**. *Habitat:* Open fields, beaches, and many disturbed situations. *Abundance:* Mainly R-U, but C-A through much of eastern New Mexico, Texas, and Oklahoma. March–November from southern California, southern Nevada, southeastern Arizona east to the Dallas–Fort Worth area. Moves northward as the season progresses, in variable numbers each year, usually reaching northern California, northern New Mexico, and Kansas by June. RS to northern Nevada and North Dakota. *Food:* Monkeyflowers, snapdragons, and others.

'Dark' Tropical Buckeye *Junonia genoveva nigrosuffusa*

Below, HW has a narrow white median stripe. Above, **dark overall, without pale FW band** of Common Buckeye. *Habitat:* Arid open situations. *Abundance:* R-U. Mainly May–Nov. R fall immigrant to western portion of range. *Food:* Fogfruits, ruellias, and others. *Comments:* The degree of "darkening" varies.

White Peacock *Anartia jatrophae*

Below, when fresh, with beautiful red markings on the silvery white ground color. Above, silvery white all over with a pale orange HW border. *Habitat:* Open and/or disturbed areas. *Abundance:* R San Antonio area. Decreasing stray northward. RS north to southern Nebraska and southeastern New Mexico. *Food:* Fogfruits, ruellias, and others.

Admirals (genus *Limenitis*) and Relatives (subfamily Limenitidinae)

This is an eclectic group of butterflies, including admirals, sisters, sailors, crackers, and beauties! among others. Although mainly a tropical group, with quite a few species barely entering the West as strays, the West does have some pretty spiffy admirals. Most of these butterflies do not spend much time at flowers, preferring sap and carrion.

Blue-eyed Sailor *Dynamine dyonis*

Below, unlike any other Western butterflies. White HW postmedian region enclosed two bull's-eyes with blue at their centers. Above, males are iridescent greenish-gold, while females are brown and white. *Habitat:* Tropical and subtropical woodlands. *Abundance:* RS to the San Antonio area with reports as far north as the Dallas–Fort Worth area. *Food:* Noseburn.

Common Mestra *Mestra amymone*

A very small white nymphalid with an apricot-colored HW border and a **very slow fluttering flight**. *Habitat:* Openings and edges of tropical woodland and thorn scrub. *Abundance:* R. Mainly Aug.–Oct. Wanders widely. RS north to Kansas, Colorado, and northern Arizona. Probably does not survive the winter most years anywhere in the West. *Food:* Noseburn.

1 Common Buckeye

2 Common Buckeye

3 'Dark' Tropical Buckeye

4 'Dark' Tropical Buckeye

5 White Peacock

6 White Peacock

7 Blue-eyed Sailor

8 Common Mestra

White Admiral

Red-spotted Admiral *Limenitis arthemis*

There are two basic color forms—White Admiral (shown opposite, map at left) and Red-spotted Purple (shown page 195). See Comments section. Below, note the **red spots on the bases of the wings** that give this species its name. Above, with a bold white band. Note the **HW marginal blue crescents** and the submarginal band of red spots. *Habitat:* Openings in moist coniferous and mixed forests and adjacent areas. *Abundance:* U-C. Late May–early Sept., mainly mid June–mid Aug. *Food:* Birches, poplars, and others. *Comments:* Populations of this species come in two basic color patterns, the white-banded pattern (White Admiral) is characteristic of the northern, single-brooded populations, while the blue-purple pattern (Red-spotted Purple) is found in southern, multiple-brooded populations. These populations meet in a wide band across the northeastern United States where they form a hybrid swarm.

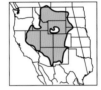

Weidemeyer's Admiral *Limenitis weidemeyerii*

Large. Below, **inner half of HW off-white with restricted black markings**. Above, with a bold white band. Usually (but not always) with a small white spot in the FW cell. Note the **HW marginal bluish-white dashes**, not crescents. Submarginal red spots usually, but not always, reduced. **FW apex is black**, not orange-brown. *Habitat:* Moist mountain forest; washes and riparian areas in arid country. *Abundance:* U-C. Mainly mid June–mid Aug. *Food:* Willows, aspens, and others. *Comments:* Will soar high among the trees, but comes down to perch on trees, usually about 7 to 15 feet above the ground. Occasionally hybridizes with Lorquin's Admiral where their ranges meet and some consider them to be conspecific.

Lorquin's Admiral *Limenitis lorquini*

Below, **inner half of HW with brown markings**, usually more extensive than on individual shown. Above, with bold white band. **FW apex has a linear orange patch that reaches the outer margin**. FW cell with white spot. *Habitat:* Openings and edges of moist forest and riparian areas. *Abundance:* C-A. April–Sept. where two-brooded; June–Aug. where single-brooded. *Food:* Willows, poplars, and others. *Comments:* Males patrol short stretches of trails, sallying forth from their perches, usually about 7 to 15 feet above the ground.

California Sister *Adelpha bredowii*

Both above and below, **FW apex has a large round orange patch that doesn't reach the outer margin**. Below, with lilac-toned wing bases. *Habitat:* Oak woodland, often in canyons or washes. *Abundance:* C. April/May–Sept./Oct. *Food:* Oaks. *Comments:* Fresh individuals have shimmering blue, green, and purple sheens that can be seen as they puddle at damp sand. Otherwise, adults mainly fly swiftly, high through the oak trees.

1 Red-spotted Admiral

2 Red-spotted Admiral

3 Weidemeyer's Admiral

4 Weidemeyer's Admiral

5 Lorquin's Admiral

6 Lorquin's Admiral

7 California Sister

8 California Sister

Red-spotted Purple

Red-spotted Admiral *Limenitis arthemis*

There are two basic color forms—Red-spotted Purple (shown opposite, map at left) and White Admiral (shown on previous page). See Comments section. Below, the brilliant iridescent blue will excite all but the most jaded. Note the **red spots at the bases of the wings** that give this species its name. Above, HW with brilliant iridescent blue. Pipevine Swallowtails are tailed. *Habitat:* Moist woodlands, including riparian canyon woodlands in arid country. *Abundance:* U-C. April–Oct. north to southeastern Arizona and Dallas–Fort Worth; May–Sept. northward; mid June–mid Aug. in South Dakota. *Food:* Cherries, poplars, aspens, and others. *Comments:* Populations of this species come in two basic color patterns. The blue-purple pattern (Red-spotted Purple) shown here is characteristic of southern, multiple-brooded populations, while the white-banded pattern (White Admiral), is found in northern, single-brooded populations. These populations meet in a wide band across the northeastern United States, where they form a hybrid swarm.

Viceroy *Limenitis archippus*

Bright orange all over, with a **black HW postmedian band.** This band is faint or absent on individuals in southwestern populations, often with white replacing the black. Monarchs and Queens lack the HW black band. Viceroys are smaller than Monarchs and they often glide on flat wings while Monarchs and Queens sail with their wings in a V. *Habitat:* Open areas adjacent to watercourses or wet areas with willows, westward mainly in riparian canyons and along rivers. *Abundance:* U-C west to the Rocky Mountains; LR westward. April–Oct southward; mainly June–Aug./Sept. northward *Food:* Willows. *Comments:* Well known as a mimic of the Monarch, the appearance of Viceroys is radically different from that of other admirals. For a long time it was thought that birds avoided eating palatable Viceroys because they confused them with distasteful Monarchs. Recent evidence suggests that, at least in Florida, Viceroys are also distasteful to birds. Presumably, a greater number of similar-looking unpalatable individuals in an area results in a faster learning curve for birds, sparing butterflies.

Malachite *Siproeta stelenes*

How many other big, bright green butterflies have you seen flying around? *Habitat:* Tropical woodland. *Abundance:* Strays to San Antonio area. Also RS north to Kansas (one record), West Texas, and southeastern Arizona (one record). *Food:* Ruellias and others in acanthus family. *Comments:* Not many people can remain stoic after sighting one of these flying emeralds. This species is a true brushfoot (subfamily nymphalinae) and is placed here only for convenience. The admiral and relatives subfamily continues on the next page.

1 Red-spotted Admiral

2 Red-spotted Admiral

3 Viceroy

4 Viceroy

5 Viceroy

6 Viceroy

7 Malachite

8 Malachite

Red Rim *Biblis hyperia*

Brilliant red (above) or icy pink (below) bands are set against a black velvet ground color. **Habitat:** Tropical woodlands and thorn scrub. **Abundance:** RS to San Antonio area and West Texas. **Food:** Noseburn. **Comments:** Usually quite wary, landing 6–10 feet up on leaves—just out of camera range.

Blackened Bluewing *Myscelia cyananthe*

Below, closely resembles the tree bark on which it habitually perches, head downward. Above, gorgeous deep blue bands are set against black, but usually perches with wings closed. **Habitat:** Thorn scrub. **Abundance:** RS to southern Arizona. **Food:** Noseburn and other euphorbia family. **Comments:** In the population that reaches Arizona, males and females are similar except that females have a few white spots around the FW margins. Farther south in Mexico, the females of this species very closely resemble Mexican Bluewings.

Mexican Bluewing *Myscelia ethusa*

Below, closely resembles the tree bark on which it habitually perches, head downward. Mottling varies from lighter than shown to darker than shown. Perhaps not separable from Blackened Bluewing below. Above, spectacular bright blue and black bars are punctuated by bold white spots, but usually perches with wings closed. **Habitat:** Tropical woodland. **Abundance:** RS to West Texas. **Food:** Adelias (according to the late Joe Ideker of the Lower Rio Grande Valley). **Comments:** Bluewings can appear to be either blue or purple, depending upon the angle the light glints off the wings.

Dingy Purplewing *Eunica monima*

Below, note the HW postmedian circular areas, the upper circular area containing two spots—the top one gray-white. Above, a dull, iridescent purple. Unfortunately, it doesn't usually open its wings while landed. **Habitat:** Tropical woodland. **Abundance:** RS to southeastern Arizona and central Texas. **Food:** Gumbo-limbo.

Gray Cracker *Hamadryas februa*

Large. Pale gray both below and above. Characteristic undulating flight takes it between tree trunks, where it lands head downward with its wings spread. Only rarely can one get a good look at the underside of a cracker. **Habitat:** Tropical woodland. **Abundance:** RS to southwestern New Mexico (one record). **Food:** Noseburns. **Comments:** Male crackers are capable of making a clicking, or cracking sound. Two other species of crackers, Black-patched (*atlantis*) and Glaucous (*glauconome*), have strayed to southeastern Arizona. Above, Black-patched is darker blue-gray than Gray Cracker and the HW submarginal eyespots are filled in with black. Glaucous lacks red in the FW cell above.

1 Red Rim

2 Red Rim

3 Blackened Bluewing

4 Blackened Bluewing

5 Mexican Bluewing

6 Mexican Bluewing

7 Dingy Purplewing

8 Gray Cracker

Ruddy Daggerwing *Marpesia petreus*

Above and below with characteristic dagger-tails. Unlikely to be confused with other species. *Habitat:* Openings and edges of tropical woodlands. *Abundance:* RS, mainly in late summer/fall, to southern Arizona, West Texas, north to eastern Colorado and Kansas. *Food:* Figs.

Many-banded Daggerwing *Marpesia chiron*

Above and below with characteristic dagger-tails. Below, two-toned. Unlikely to be confused with other species. *Habitat:* Openings and edges of tropical woodlands. *Abundance:* RS to southeastern Arizona (one record), West Texas, the San Antonio area, and Kansas (one record). *Food:* Figs.

Leafwings (subfamily Charaxinae)

The leafwings are medium-sized to large, swift-flying butterflies, found mainly in the American and African tropics. Rarely visiting flowers, they are often seen at sap and rotting fruit. Above, many of the tropical species have patterns of iridescent blue, while others are bright red. The undersides of the wings of most of the species resemble dead leaves. The mimicry of some of the tropical species is amazing. On one occasion, a butterflier spying a leafwing at some rotting fruit exclaimed "Here's a leafwing! Wait a minute, my mistake, it's actually a leaf." It was actually a leafwing!

Goatweed Leafwing *Anaea andria*

Larger than anglewings. Red-orange to orange-brown above (males are brighter), with a short HW tail. Behavior, flight, and wing-shape are different from other orange butterflies in its range except for Tropical Leafwing. See the latter for distinction. *Habitat:* Open woodlands with its foodplants and adjacent areas. *Abundance:* U-LC. June/July–Aug.; Aug.–Oct. overwintering as adults and flying March/April–May. *Food:* Crotons. *Comments:* Often flies as if swooping up and down on ocean waves. Overwintering individuals have more pointed FWs than summer individuals.

Tropical Leafwing *Anaea aidea*

A slightly smaller (on average), redder above (on average) version of the Goatweed Leafwing. Look for **slightly uneven wing margins**, pointing out at the veins, especially on the HW above the "tail." Below, also note the **well-developed HW submarginal band** that Goatweed Leafwings lack. *Habitat:* Tropical woodlands and thorn scrub. *Abundance:* C. All year. RS north to southeastern New Mexico and Kansas. *Food:* Crotons. *Comments:* Adults are long-lived. Some consider *aidea* a subspecies of *troglodyta*.

1 Ruddy Daggerwing   2 Ruddy Daggerwing

3 Many-banded Daggerwing   4 Many-banded Daggerwing

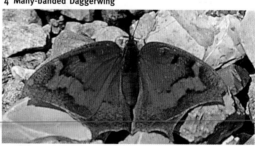

5 Goatweed Leafwing   6 Goatweed Leafwing

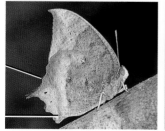

7 Tropical Leafwing   8 Tropical Leafwing

Emperors (subfamily Apaturinae)

Emperors are found worldwide, but mainly in the tropics. They rarely visit flowers, but these are the butterflies most likely to visit butterfliers, frequently landing on people in search of the salts in our perspiration. All four of the Western species have landed on me!

Hackberry Emperor *Asterocampa celtis*

A nervous, rapidly flying nymphalid that often appears quite pale in flight as the sun flashes off the creamy gray-brown undersurface. Note the **black FW eyespot(s)**. Northern populations have one eyespot, southern populations (*antonia*) have two. Note the **two black spots in the center of the FW cell** (these spots occasionally come close to coalescing). *Habitat:* Anyplace with hackberries, but mainly woodlands and thorn scrub. Often in riparian canyons. *Abundance:* Mainly C-A. But R-U, Arizona westward and in the Dakotas. March/April–Oct./Nov. north to southeastern Arizona and northeastern Texas; mainly late May–Sept. through Nebraska; June–July in the Dakotas. *Food:* Hackberries. *Comments:* Closely tied to hackberry trees. Geographically variable, some populations have previously been considered separate species.

Empress Leilia *Asterocampa leilia*

Note the combination of **two FW eyespots** and a **solid brown inner bar in the FW cell**. Tawny Emperor lacks FW eyespots and Hackberry Emperor has two black spots in the FW cell. *Habitat:* Tropical and subtropical scrub, desert washes and canyons. *Abundance:* C. March–Nov. *Food:* Hackberries, especially desert hackberry. *Comments:* Found much more frequently landed on the ground than other emperors, which usually land on tree trunks and tree leaves.

Tawny Emperor *Asterocampa clyton*

Above, warm orange-brown with HW borders that can be either mainly orange or mainly black. **There are no FW black eyespots.** *Habitat:* Anyplace with hackberries, but mainly woodlands and thorn scrub. *Abundance:* Generally U-C, but R-U West Texas westward. Mainly May/June–Sept./Oct. *Food:* Hackberries. *Comments:* Very variable in size, females are often very much larger than are males. Males (not shown) are more angular with black near the FW apexes.

'Cream-banded' Dusky Emperor *Asterocampa idyja argus*

A Mexican species with emperor wing shape, behavior, and HW pattern. Note the **FW with a diagonal cream-colored band**, quite unlike other emperors. *Habitat:* Thorn scrub. *Abundance:* RS to southeastern Arizona (two occasions—Sonoita Creek, Oct. 1990; Coronado Peak, Oct. 1999). *Food:* Hackberries. *Comments:* The Mexican subspecies, *argus*, is quite different from the West Indian *idyja*, and is probably best considered a separate species Unlike other western emperors, this species hilltops. Hang out on those hilltops overlooking the Mexican border in October, and you just might see one.

1 Hackberry Emperor

2 Hackberry Emperor

3 Empress Leilia

4 Empress Leilia

5 Tawny Emperor

6 Tawny Emperor

7 'Cream-banded' Dusky Emperor

8 'Cream-banded' Dusky Emperor

Satyrs (subfamily Satyrinae)

These brown, medium-sized butterflies have a **characteristic bobbing flight,** often weaving through the grasses that are their foodplants. Most species rarely visit flowers. The **wood-nymphs** (this page) **all have two FW eyespots tightly ringed with yellow.**

Common Wood-Nymph *Cercyonis pegala*

Large. Comes in two basic color forms, each with many variations. From Texas through eastern New Mexico and Colorado, individuals have a bright yellow patch on the FW, similar to photo 1. Elsewhere, they resemble the individual shown in photo 2 and more closely resemble the other wood-nymphs. Note that the **FW bottom eyespot is as large as or larger than the top eyespot** and that the **FW postmedian band is prominent and extends to the top of the top eyespot.** HW eyespots vary from prominent to almost absent. *Habitat:* Moist grassy areas. *Abundance:* C-A. Late May–mid Sept. Mainly July–Aug. As early as late May in Pacific lowlands and as late as Sept. at many locations. *Food:* Grasses.

Great Basin Wood-Nymph *Cercyonis sthenele*

Note that the **FW bottom eyespot is smaller than the top eyespot** (sometimes the same size). The **FW postmedian band is present, but extends only about halfway up the top eyespot**, and is often less prominent than on Common Wood-Nymph. HW eyespots vary from prominent to almost absent. *Habitat:* Open grassy woodlands especially pinyon pine-juniper; moist canyons in arid country. *Abundance:* U-C. Mainly July–Aug. As early as mid May in the San Francisco area, as late as mid Sept. at many locations. *Food:* Grasses.

Mead's Wood-Nymph *Cercyonis meadii*

Very similar to Great Basin Wood-Nymph but with a pronounced **reddish flush on the FW**. The HW postmedian line is variable, but very rarely shaped like two adjacent mountain peaks. *Habitat:* Open grassy woodlands and canyons. *Abundance:* Southern populations U-LC. July–Sept. Northern populations R. Late July–Aug. *Food:* Grasses. *Comments:* Possibly conspecific with Great Basin Wood-Nymph.

Small Wood-Nymph *Cercyonis oetus*

Note that the **FW bottom eyespot is much smaller than the top eyespot** and that the **outer edge of the bottom eyespot is much closer to the FW outer margin than is the outer edge of the top eyespot.** The FW postmedian line is usually absent, if present it stops at the bottom of the top eyespot. The **HW postmedian line is shaped like two adjacent mountain peaks** (peaks pointing outward) in most individuals. *Habitat:* Grasslands, sagebrush flats, scrub, and open woodland. *Abundance:* C-A. Mainly June–Aug., as late as late Sept. at some locations. *Food:* Grasses. *Comments:* Nectars more avidly than other wood-nymphs.

1 Common Wood-Nymph

2 Common Wood-Nymph

3 Great Basin Wood-Nymph (Nevada)

4 Great Basin Wood-Nymph (California)

5 Mead's Wood-Nymph

6 Small Wood-Nymph (Wyoming)

7 Small Wood-Nymph (Colorado)

8 Small Wood-Nymph (Arizona)

Ridings' Satyr *Neominois ridingsii*
FW subapex with a patch shaped like a bear-claw. *Habitat:* Short-grass prairie, sagebrush, and open grassy woodland. *Abundance:* LR-LC. June–Sept. *Food:* Blue grama grass and wheatgrasses. *Comments:* Spotted in low flight, this only North American representative of an Old World group is difficult to relocate after landing, blending with the soil, rocks, and grass.

Red-bordered Satyr *Gyrocheilus patrobas*
Large and dark. **HW with a broad pink-red border**. *Habitat:* Coniferous and mixed woodland in mountain canyons. *Abundance:* C-A. Mainly Sept.–Oct., but as early as mid Aug. *Food:* Bull grass.

Eyed Brown *Satyrodes eurydice*
Pale with **strong submarginal eyespots that are individually surrounded by white rings**. Northern and Southern Pearly-eyes, which barely enter the West, are larger and darker and have submarginal eyespots that are surrounded as a group by a white line. *Habitat:* Very wet meadows, marshes with sedges. *Abundance:* R. Late June–July. *Food:* Sedges.

Pine Satyr *Paramacera allyni*
FW apex with eyespot. HW with submarginal eyespots and a pale postmedian band. *Habitat:* High-elevation pine forest in the Chiricahua and Huachuca Mountains. *Abundance:* LR-LC. One brood. June–mid Aug., mainly mid June–mid July. *Food:* Bentgrasses are suspected.

Hayden's Ringlet *Coenonympha haydenii*
Pale gray-brown HW with marginal eyespots ringed with orange. Common Alpines are much darker with fewer, less orderly, HW eyespots. Other satyrs have HW eyespots that are either not submarginal or are not ringed with orange. *Habitat:* High-elevation subalpine and alpine meadows. *Abundance:* C. Late June–mid Aug. *Food:* Grasses. *Comments:* Flight is slow with much wing movement. A soft gray/black in flight.

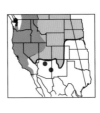

Common Ringlet *Coenonympha tullia*
Small. Variable, but distinctive. Usually with a single FW subapical eyespot (sometimes faint or absent) and a straight FW postmedian line. HW ground color varies (mainly geographically) from green-gray to brown to pale gray or off-white. HW postmedian line characteristically jagged. HW eyespots prominent or almost absent. *Habitat:* Grasslands, meadows, coastal dunes and open grassy woodlands. *Abundance:* C-A. Mainly April–Sept. in two-brood areas; late May–Aug., peaking June–July, in single-brood areas. *Food:* Grasses. *Comments:* As the Supreme Court has said about pornography, it is difficult to define, but you'll recognize it when you see it.

1 Ridings' Satyr

2 Ridings' Satyr

3 Red-bordered Satyr

4 Eyed Brown

5 Pine Satyr

6 Hayden's Ringlet

7 Common Ringlet (WY)

8 Common Ringlet (AZ)

9 Common Ringlet (CA)

Red Satyr *Megisto rubricata*

Both above and below, the **FW disk is flushed with red-orange**. Usually **opens its wings immediately after landing**, then closes them again. This is an excellent identification clue, since other satyrs do not behave this way. *Habitat:* Dry woodlands. *Abundance:* C-A, but becoming LR at northeastern edge of range. Mainly mid May–Sept. *Food:* Grasses. *Comments:* There are unverified rumours claiming that McCarthyites held secret congressional hearings, in the 1950s, about the alarming range expansion of this species.

Little Wood-Satyr *Megisto cymela*

A medium-brown butterfly that "bounces" along the tops of grasses, shrubs, and just inside the canopy of small trees. Its characteristic flight, color, and size make it immediately recognizable on the wing. This is good, because it rarely rests. When it does, note the two large eyespots on each wing. *Habitat:* Mainly at the grassland/woodland interface, but also in more open situations. *Abundance:* U-C, Oklahoma south; R-U northward. May/June–Aug. *Food:* Grasses.

Carolina Satyr *Hermeuptychia sosybius*

Small. Much more at home *within* the woods than is Little Wood-Satyr. Below, similar to Little Wood-Satyr but has a **HW cell-end bar**. Also note the **gray eyes**. Eyes of Little Wood-Satyr are black. **Without eyespot above** and uniformly brown. *Habitat:* Woodlands, especially moist forest. *Abundance:* U-C. April–Nov. *Food:* Grasses.

Nabokov's Satyr *Cyllopsis pyracmon*

The distinctive **HW marginal patch, gray and "gemmed"** tells you this is one of the gemmed-satyrs. Unlike other gemmed-satyrs, **the postmedian line runs to the HW leading margin**. The spring brood lacks the outwardly directed spikes on the postmedian band. *Habitat:* Oak woodland in mountains. *Abundance:* C-A. Mid April–July, Aug.–mid Nov. *Food:* Grasses.

Canyonland Satyr *Cyllopsis pertepida*

HW marginal patch, gray and "gemmed." The **HW postmedian line dies (falls into a canyon) without reaching the leading margin**. FW is flushed with red. *Habitat:* Mountain canyons and gulches. *Abundance:* Mid May–July, late Sept.–Nov. in two brood areas. June–mid Sept. in one brood areas. *Food:* Grasses.

Gemmed Satyr *Cyllopsis gemma*

Similar to Canyonland Satyr but **without red flush** and (in U.S.) range is farther east. *Habitat:* Moist grassy areas within woodlands. *Abundance:* R-LU. March–Oct. *Food:* Grasses.

1 Red Satyr

2 Red Satyr

3 Little Wood-Satyr

4 Little Wood-Satyr

5 Carolina Satyr

6 Carolina Satyr

7 Nabokov's Satyr

8 Canyonland Satyr

9 Gemmed Satyr

Alpines (genus *Erebia*)
and Arctics (genus *Oeneis*)

Found circumpolarly, these butterflies are mainly specialties of the far north and of high altitudes. Because the growing season is so short in these regions, many of these species require two years to complete their life cycle. So, in some regions a particular species only (or mainly) appears once every two years. Alpines are dark satyrs of alpine meadows and tundra. Their flight is less "bouncy" than the flight of wood-nymphs or ringlets and less skittering than that of most arctics. Chasing arctics over rocks at 12,000 ft. in order to get a good look at them is not for the faint of heart.

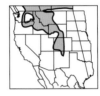

Common Alpine *Erebia epipsodea*
Fringes are unchecked. Both above and below with an irregular **burnt orange FW patch enclosing black eyespots** (occasionally lacking). Below, blackish-brown with a few HW orange-circled eyespots. Small Wood-Nymphs are not as dark and lack the burnt orange FW patch. *Habitat:* Moist meadows and prairies, from Rocky Mountain foothills to high elevations, occasionally above treeline. *Abundance:* U-C. May (low elevations)–Aug. (high elevations). *Food:* Grasses. *Comments:* The most wide-ranging alpine in the West.

Vidler's Alpine *Erebia vidleri*
Fringes are checked. Below, note the **pale postmedian band**, especially white at the HW leading margin. Below, most individuals lack the postmedian HW eyespots of Common Alpine. *Habitat:* Moist alpine/subalpine mountain meadows. *Abundance:* C. Late June–Aug. *Food:* Grasses. *Comments:* Luckily for butterfliers, Vidler's Alpines are found in beautifully lush mountains meadows filled with kaleidoscopic flower displays.

Colorado Alpine *Erebia callias*
Gray in flight with a visible reddish flush. The soft gray HW and red-orange FW disk is distinctive. Above, the FW has a wedge-shaped red-orange patch and often has green sheens when fresh. *Habitat:* Alpine meadows. *Abundance:* LU. July–Aug. *Food:* Unknown, probably grasses or sedges.

Red-disked Alpine *Erebia discoidalis*
Both above and below note the **reddish-brown FW disk**. Below, the HW has the outer one-third heavily frosted. *Habitat:* A wide variety of open grassy situations, including pine glades, ridge tops, meadows, and sedge marshes. *Abundance:* R-LU. April–Aug., mainly May–early June. One record from the Turtle Mountains of North Dakota. *Food:* Bluegrass.

Taiga Alpine *Erebia mancinus*
Fringes are checked. Note the **single small white spot in the middle of the postmedian HW**. *Habitat:* Black spruce and tamarack bogs. *Abundance:* R. Mainly June–July. *Food:* Unknown, probably grasses or sedges. See pg. 313 for more information.

1 Common Alpine

2 Common Alpine

3 Vidler's Alpine

4 Vidler's Alpine

5 Colorado Alpine

6 Colorado Alpine

7 Red-disked Alpine

8 Taiga Alpine

Theano Alpine *Erebia theano*

Both above and below, the **FW has a smooth postmedian band of rectangular spots without black eyespots**. Below, also note the cream-colored HW postmedian band. *Habitat:* Dry or moist alpine (mainly) and subalpine meadows. *Abundance:* LU. Mainly July–mid Aug., occasionally as early as early June. At some localities, only flies every other year. *Food:* Unknown.

Magdalena Alpine *Erebia magdalena*

Black, with green/purple sheens when fresh. Males patrol back and forth across rockslides. *Habitat:* Rockslides and scree slopes above treeline. *Abundance:* R-U. July–early Aug. *Food:* Grasses. *Comments:* The butterfly version of a black hole—when you see one, you can't take your eyes off of it.

Melissa Arctic *Oeneis melissa*

Variable. **FW without eyespots and somewhat translucent**. HW tightly mottled, with overall appearance varying from almost black to brownish. **HW basal and postmedian lines absent or poorly developed**. *Habitat:* Rocky alpine areas with grasses, including hilltops and ridges. *Abundance:* U-C. Late June–early Aug. *Food:* Sedges. *Comments:* In the clouds and wind these glacial relics look much like the lichen-covered rocks on which they rest. Sunshine induces brief, skittering, low flight.

White-veined Arctic *Oeneis taygete*

FW without eyespots. HW with median band set off by **strongly developed basal and postmedian lines, edged with white**. Note the **whitened veins**. Other arctics, e.g., Alberta and Chryxus, can have whitened veins but they have a FW eyespot. *Habitat:* Moist alpine meadows. *Abundance:* LR-LU. Late June–mid Aug. *Food:* Sedges. *Comments:* Some believe that the North American populations are best treated as conspecific with the Old World species *Oeneis bore*.

Polixenes Arctic *Oeneis polixenes*

FW without eyespots and somewhat translucent. **HW with basal and postmedian lines strongly developed, setting off darker median band**. *Habitat:* Alpine grassy knolls and hillsides. *Abundance:* LR. Mid June–early Aug. *Food:* Sedges and grasses. *Comments:* Flies fast, low, and straight.

1 Theano Alpine (Wyoming)

2 Theano Alpine

3 Theano Alpine (Colorado)

4 Magdalena Alpine

5 Melissa Arctic (Colorado)

6 Melissa Arctic (Alberta)

7 White-veined Arctic

8 Polixenes Arctic

Great Arctic *Oeneis nevadensis*

Large. The **leading edge of the HW is whitened**, with a dark triangle at the postmedian line. The **HW outer margin appears to be scalloped**. There is no FW postmedian line. *Habitat:* Openings in moist mountain coniferous forest. *Abundance:* LU-LC. Mid May–July in lowlands, mid July–Aug. at high elevations. Much more common in even-numbered years. *Food:* Grasses. *Comments:* Fond of landing on dirt trails and fallen trees. Macoun's Arctic (not shown—see *BTB: East*), found in British Columbia just east of the Okanogan Valley and in the Alberta mountains south to Kananaskis Provincial Park, closely resembles Great Arctic but the HW leading margin is not as whitened and it flies mainly in odd-numbered years.

Chryxus Arctic *Oeneis chryxus*

Variable. Usually bright tawny above, visible in flight. Below, usually with **at least some orange visible on the FW**. Postmedian FW line with "bird beak" pointing outward. *Habitat:* Mountain meadows and grasslands; openings in coniferous forest. *Abundance:* C-A. June–early Sept., mainly July. *Food:* Sedges and grasses. *Comments:* Along the crest of the California Sierra Nevadas are found both very pale Chryxus Arctic (both below and above) and the more usual form. Its flight is usually fairly slow, high, and nondirectional.

Uhler's Arctic *Oeneis uhleri*

FW without postmedian line or "bird beak." Usually with **four or five small, dark eyespots spread along the HW submarginal line**. HW usually with "strata" pattern, like sedimentary rock. *Habitat:* Dry prairies, ridgetops, and other dry, open, grassy situations. *Abundance:* Mid May–mid July. *Food:* Grasses. *Comments:* Flight is generally high off the ground, but slow, making them easy to follow.

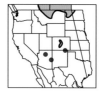

Alberta Arctic *Oeneis alberta*

Smaller and duller above than Chryxus Arctic. Below, overall aspect is paler than Chryxus Arctic. The **FW is brown-gray, without orange**. FW postmedian line with "bird beak" pointing outward. HW usually with one small, dark eyespot (0–2) in submarginal area. HW veins whitened. *Habitat:* Dry grasslands, often over volcanic rock fields. *Abundance:* LR-LC. Mid April–early July. *Food:* Grasses. *Comments:* Flight is low, fast, and erratic.

Jutta Arctic *Oeneis jutta*

Look for the **combination of a HW that is uniformly dark and a FW with an eyespot surrounded by orange**. FW with faint postmedian line (or none). *Habitat:* Openings in lodgepole pine forest. *Abundance:* LU. Late June–mid Aug. *Food:* Sedges. *Comments:* Sometimes nectars—note the pollen clinging to the butterfly's body in photo 7.

1 Great Arctic

2 Chryxus Arctic (Colorado—low)

3 Chryxus Arctic (Colorado—high)

4 Chryxus Arctic (California)

5 Uhler's Arctic

6 Alberta Arctic

7 Jutta Arctic

8 Jutta Arctic

Monarchs (subfamily Danainae)

Many of these butterflies are distasteful to predators because of the accumulation of toxic chemicals derived from the caterpillar foodplants.

Monarch *Danaus plexippus*

A large orange butterfly with a powerful flight. Often sails with its wings held in a V. The male has a black scent patch on the HW above. See Viceroy, below. *Habitat:* Open fields, roadsides, canyons, suburban areas. While migrating it can be anywhere. *Abundance:* Mainly C, but R-U in Pacific Northwest. Mainly March/April–Oct./Nov. Reaches Oregon, Alberta and North Dakota in June. Overwinters along the central/southern California coast. *Food:* Milkweeds. *Comments:* The best-known butterfly of North America. Huge numbers of Monarchs move south through the Midwest in Sept. and Oct. The spectacle at congregation points is awe-inspiring. Millions of Monarchs from North America eventually find their way to communal sites high in the fir-clad Mexican mountains, where they spend the winter. West of the Continental Divide, most Monarchs migrate to the central/southern California coast, where they spend the winter. In early spring, the overwintering adults mate and begin to move north and east and lay eggs. Their offspring then continue migrating east and/or northward.

Viceroy *Limenitis archippus*

The species is not related to Monarchs and is shown here for comparison. Small. Note the **HW black postmedian band**. Viceroy's flight is weaker than Monarch's, with shallower wingbeats, often gliding on flat wings. See page 194 for more information about this species.

Queen *Danaus gilippus*

Rich mahogany brown, darker than Monarchs. This closely related species lacks Monarch's black subapical band and has **white spots in the FW postmedian area** that are visible both above and below. *Habitat:* General in open areas, such as brushy fields and roadsides. *Abundance:* C in 3+ brood areas, mainly March/April–Nov.; R-U in two brood areas, mainly May–Sept. *Food:* Milkweeds and milkweed vines. *Comments:* Many falls, tremendous numbers of Queens migrate southward through southern Texas. Whether these butterflies congregate at specific sites, à la Monarchs, is unknown.

Soldier *Danaus eresimus*

Deep reddish-brown. Similar to Queen but **lacks the white spots in the FW postmedian area**. Note the **blackened FW veins**; Queen veins are not blackened. Below, the HW median area is dark, contrasting with the paler postmedian area, which often appears as if it has a watermark. *Habitat:* General in open areas and woodland edges. *Abundance:* RS to San Antonio area and southeastern Arizona, mainly in late fall. *Food:* Milkweeds and milkweed vines.

1 Monarch

2 Monarch ♂

3 Viceroy

4 Monarch ♀

5 Queen

6 Queen

7 Soldier

8 Soldier

Skippers (family Hesperiidae)

Skippers derive their name from their characteristic rapid darting flight. They are generally distinguishable from true butterflies by their relatively large bodies (compared to their very angular wings) and by the thin extension (apiculus) of the antennal club. There are four subfamilies of skippers in the West.

Firetips (subfamily Pyrrhopyginae)

This tropical group of often brilliantly colored skippers is represented in the West by one species. The great majority of the species are characterized by the brilliant red of their abdomen tips—thus the name firetip.

Dull Firetip *Pyrrhopyge araxes*
Large. **Below, bright yellow-orange** is distinctive. Above, **FW has curved median band of three white spots**, narrowing at the bottom. *Habitat:* Oak woodland in mountains. *Abundance:* C-A. Mid July–early Oct., mainly Aug.–early Sept. *Food:* Oaks. *Comments:* Usually nectars with its wings partly open. "Dull" refers to the abdomen tip, which lacks the brilliant red color characteristic of this group.

Spread-wing Skippers (subfamily Pyrginae)

Generally larger than grass-skippers, most species land with their wings spread flat. Unlike the grass-skippers, they always open their FW and HW in unison.

Silver-spotted Skipper *Epargyreus clarus*
A large powerful skipper that flashes its **silvered spot in the middle of the HW below** even as it flies. *Habitat:* Wide-ranging in open habitats. Woodland borders and openings, fields, gardens, riparian canyons, etc. *Abundance:* Mainly C, but LU in northern California and the Pacific Northwest. Mainly May–Sept., as early as April and as late as Oct./Nov. in southern Texas, southeastern Arizona, and Pacific lowlands. June–July in the north—North Dakota, Canada. *Food:* Locusts and many other legumes.

Short-tailed Skipper *Zestusa dorus*
Both above and below, note the **short tail-like projection of the HW**. Below, **HW with unusual postmedian band of four cream-yellow spots**. *Habitat:* Oak woodlands in mountains. *Abundance:* C. Mid March–mid May, with a partial summer brood in southeastern Arizona. *Food:* Oaks. *Comments:* An avid mudpuddler. When hilltopping, lands on trees and shrubs.

Hammock Skipper *Polygonus leo* .
Often **perches upside down under a leaf** (photo 7 has been flipped right side up). Below, with a black spot near the base of the HW. Above, with **blue iridescent sheen** and three large white FW spots. *Habitat:* Tropical woodland. *Abundance:* R immigrant, July–Oct., mainly Aug.–early Sept. Strongly migratory. RS north to central California, northern Nevada, and central New Mexico. *Food:* Legumes.

1 **Dull Firetip**

2 **Dull Firetip**

3 **Silver-spotted Skipper**

4 **Silver-spotted Skipper**

5 **Short-tailed Skipper**

6 **Short-tailed Skipper**

7 **Hammock Skipper**

8 **Hammock Skipper**

Acacia Skipper *Cogia hippalus*

HW is soft gray-brown with mauve overcast and a **white fringe**. Submarginal areas are pale. Note the **small black spots on the HW marginal line**. Other similar skippers with white HW fringes are browner and lack the black spots on the HW marginal line. *Habitat:* Rocky canyons and hillsides in arid situations. *Abundance:* U-LC. April–Sept. *Food:* Acacias.

Outis Skipper *Cogia outis*

FWs are long and narrow. Note the semicircle of white spots on the FW and the white patch just below the antennal club. Cloudywings lack these features. *Habitat:* Acacia prairie, parks. *Abundance:* U. April–May, July–Aug. *Food:* Acacias. *Comments:* One of our least-known butterflies.

Gold-costa Skipper *Cogia caicus*

As with many desert skippers, the HW fringe is white. The **gold costa** is distinctive. *Habitat:* Rocky canyons. *Abundance:* U. Mid March–May, mid July–early Sept. *Food:* One report of fern acacia. *Comments:* Males perch at the bottoms of gullies.

Arizona Skipper *Codatractus arizonensis*

Large. HW with strong black and white markings and slightly elongated at outer angle. *Habitat:* Foothill canyons and arroyos. *Abundance:* C, Southeastern Arizona. R-U, West Texas. Late March–mid Oct. *Food:* Kidneywoods. *Comments:* Males are very territorial, landing with wings closed on an exposed piece of vegetation, dead branch, etc. (often jutting out from a canyon wall), a few feet off the ground.

Potrillo Skipper *Cabares potrillo*

Note the saddle-shaped pale spot on the FW. *Habitat:* Tropical woodland. *Abundance:* RS to southeastern Arizona and San Antonio, Texas area. *Food:* Privas. *Comments:* Potrillo means colt in Spanish, so the saddle should be easy to remember.

Valeriana Skipper *Codatractus mysie*

Closely resembles a Northern Cloudywing, but almost never opens wings while perched. FW apex is more mottled and HW fringe is more strongly checked black and tan below. *Habitat:* Red-rock canyons. *Abundance:* R. Late July–Aug. *Food:* *Tephrosia leiocarpa*. *Comments:* Foodplant is colonial. Few people have seen this species in the United States. Even fewer knew that they were seeing it! See page 313 for more information.

Fritzgaertner's Flat *Celaenorrhinus fritzgaertneri*

Large. **HW with soft checkerboard pattern**. FW with darkened spot near base of wing. *Habitat:* Tropical woods and thorn scrub. *Abundance:* RS to southeastern Arizona, July–Aug. *Food:* Unknown. *Comments:* This species is crepuscular; during the day it is most often found in highway culverts.

1 Acacia Skipper

2 Outis Skipper

3 Gold-costa Skipper

4 Gold-costa Skipper

5 Arizona Skipper

6 Potrillo Skipper

7 Valeriana Skipper

8 Fritzgaertner's Flat

Long-tailed Skipper *Urbanus proteus*

Note the long, broad "tails." Below, the **FW dark submarginal band is unbroken**. Note the **striking blue-green iridescence** above. Usually lands with its wings partly open. *Habitat:* Open fields and woodland edges, especially brushy and disturbed situations. *Abundance:* R. Immigrant, mainly Aug.–Oct. RS to West Texas. *Food:* Legumes. *Comments:* Temporarily established in southern California in the 1950s.

Dorantes Longtail *Urbanus dorantes*

Note the long, broad "tails." Below, the **FW dark submarginal band is almost completely interrupted** by a finger of the paler interior ground color pushing through from the inside. **Above, without blue-green iridescence**; brown with yellowish spots. Usually lands with its wings closed or only partly open. *Habitat:* Open woodland, woodland edges, and gardens. *Abundance:* U. Mainly Aug.–Oct. *Food:* Beggarticks and other legumes.

White-striped Longtail *Chioides catillus*

Look for that **white stripe** going straight across the middle of the HW below. Note the very long tails (so long that—unlike other longtails' tails—they dangle as the butterfly flies) and the black upside-down triangle at the FW subapex. This species rarely opens its wings. *Habitat:* Tropical and subtropical scrub and open woodland. *Abundance:* R. Almost all year. RS to Austin, Texas area and West Texas, Sept.–Oct. *Food:* Legume family vines.

Zilpa Longtail *Chioides zilpa*

Long tails. Below, dramatically mottled. Note the **black upside-down triangle at the FW subapex** and the large **black spot and trailing white patch along the HW trailing margin**. Rarely opens its wings. *Habitat:* Thorn scrub. *Abundance:* RS to San Antonio, Texas, area and southeastern Arizona. Sept.–Oct. *Food:* Legume family vines.

Brown Longtail *Urbanus procne*

Long tails. Note the **uniform brown ground color** above. Other longtails have prominent pale spots above. Usually lands with its wings open. *Habitat:* Tropical woodland. *Abundance:* RS to southern California, southeastern Arizona, and Austin, Texas, area, Sept.–Oct. *Food:* Grasses. *Comments:* The tropical Teleus, *U. teleus*, and Plain, *simplicius*, Longtails are very similar to Brown. Both have been reported from southeastern Arizona, neither definitely. Teleus has a very pronounced pale median stripe on the FW above. Brown Longtails also can have a pale median stripe but, when present, it is not as strong as that of Teleus. Plain Longtails are even more similar to Brown Longtail. They have a faint pale FW median stripe with characteristic vague darker markings within the stripe.

1 Long-tailed Skipper

2 Long-tailed Skipper

3 Dorantes Longtail

4 Dorantes Longtail

5 White-striped Longtail

7 Zilpa Longtail

6 Brown Longtail

Golden Banded-Skipper *Autochton cellus*

Those luminous golden-yellow bands make identifying this species easy. *Habitat:* Riparian canyons and gulches. *Abundance:* U-C. March–Sept. in two brood areas; Mid June–Aug. in one-brood areas. *Food:* Legumes. *Comments:* Although you can certainly see Golden Banded-Skippers during the middle of the day, they are most active nectaring early in the morning and late in the afternoon. Most of the day is spent perching in the shade in gullies and narrow canyons.

Chisos Banded-Skipper *Autochton cincta*

Similar to the tremendously more common Golden Banded-Skipper, but the **HW fringe is pure white**, not checked. Also note that the FW median band is narrower and paler. *Habitat:* Oak woodlands. *Abundance:* R. March–Aug. *Food:* Beggar-ticks. *Comments:* This Mexican species is a difficult-to-find specialty of Big Bend National Park, mainly in Green Gulch.

Gold-spotted Aguna *Aguna asander*

The **pale stripe down the middle of the HW** varies from wide and bright white to wide and pale, to narrow and bright white. Usually, the stripe is fuzzy outwardly. The gold spots on the FW above are rarely seen. *Habitat:* Thorn scrub. *Abundance:* RS to southeastern Arizona (one record). *Food:* Unknown.

Sonoran Banded-Skipper *Autochton pseudocellus*

Although on average smaller, this species is essentially identical to Golden Banded-Skipper except that there is a prominent **white patch just below the antennal club** that Golden Banded-Skipper lacks. *Habitat:* Canyons in pine-oak woodland. *Abundance:* Formerly occurred June–mid July in the Huachuca and Chiricahua Mountains, especially in Ramsey Canyon, but, despite much searching, none has been seen in the United States since 1936. *Food:* Beggar-ticks. *Comments:* Still common in much of Mexico.

Brown-banded Skipper *Timochares ruptifasciatus*

Male is shown; female is similar but darker. Note the three brown bands on the HW. *Habitat:* Tropical woodland. *Abundance:* RS to southeastern Arizona and southwestern New Mexico, mainly Sept.–Oct. *Food:* Barbados cherry.

Hermit Skipper *Grais stigmaticus*

Large. Brown bands on both HW and FW. Note the **HW postmedian band composed of separate spots, pointed on their outsides**, and the characteristic **FW postmedian dark blotch**. Males sometimes lack the white FW spots. *Habitat:* Tropical woodland and thorn scrub. *Abundance:* RS throughout Texas and north to Kansas (one record), mainly Sept.–Oct. *Food:* Unknown. *Comments:* Rarely closes its wings.

1 Golden Banded-Skipper

2 Golden Banded-Skipper

3 Chisos Banded-Skipper

4 Chisos Banded-Skipper

5 Gold-spotted Aguna

6 Sonoran Banded-Skipper

7 Brown-banded Skipper (Shown Life Size)

8 Hermit Skipper (Shown Life Size)

Cloudywings (genuses *Achalarus* and *Thorybes*)

Cloudywings are largish skippers with an even, dark brown ground color above with pale or golden spots. They often land with their wings held half open. Dusky-wings have an upperside ground color that is very mottled. Species treated on this two-page spread have **white fringes**; brown-fringed species are on the next two-page spread.

Hoary-edge *Achalarus lyciades*
Large and dark. Note the **conspicuous wide white patch on the HW margin below**. Silver-spotted Skipper has its silver spot in the middle of the HW. Desert Cloudywing doesn't occur in range, has a narrower white patch on the HW margin below, and lacks the wide golden band on the FW. *Habitat:* Open situations near woodlands. *Abundance:* R. April–Sept. *Food:* Beggar-ticks.

Coyote Cloudywing *Achalarus toxeus*
The **FW postmedian band is a pale golden tracing**, unlike that of any other species. *Habitat:* Tropical woodland and thorn scrub. *Abundance:* RS to San Antonio, Austin, and Del Rio, Texas, areas. In addition, this and/or a closely related species, Skinner's Cloudywing (*A. albociliatus*), have strayed to southeastern Arizona. *Food:* Texas ebony. *Comments:* Very wily.

Desert Cloudywing *Achalarus casica*
Very large and very dark. Note the conspicuous white patch on the HW margin below. Gold-costa Skipper is smaller with a gold costa. Also, see Hoary-edge, this page. *Habitat:* Canyons and washes in desert foothills and mountains. *Abundance:* R-U. April–Sept., mainly May and Aug. *Food:* Beggar-ticks and other legumes.

Drusius Cloudywing *Thorybes drusius*
Basically like a Northern Cloudywing with white HW fringes (but see white-fringed form of Northern Cloudywing, this page). FW white markings are reduced. Below, note that the HW marginal area is only slightly frosted and paler than the rest of the wing. *Habitat:* Mid-elevation grassy areas in oak and pine-oak woods. *Abundance:* R-U. July–Aug. *Food:* Cologania and probably other legumes.

Northern Cloudywing *Thorybes pylades albosuffusa*
A white-fringed form of Northern Cloudywing is sometimes found in West Texas, more commonly in northeastern Mexico. Below, note that the **HW marginal area is widely frosted and paler than the rest of the wing**. Otherwise, extremely similar to Drusius Cloudywing. *Habitat:* Pine-oak woodland. *Abundance:* R. *Food:* Unknown.

1 Hoary-edge

2 Coyote Cloudywing

3 Desert Cloudywing

4 Desert Cloudywing

5 Drusius Cloudywing

6 Drusius Cloudywing

7 Northern Cloudywing

8 Northern Cloudywing

Northern Cloudywing *Thorybes pylades*

Usually larger than Western or Mexican Cloudywings. Below, dark with darker HW median and spikey postmedian bands. Over most of the range, the face (palps) is dark gray or brown, but in southwestern New Mexico and southeastern Arizona it is almost white. Above, pale markings are usually restricted. *Habitat:* A wide variety of open habitats. *Abundance:* Mainly C, but U in California and the Pacific Northwest. Two brood areas, March/April–Aug./Sept. One brood areas, mainly May–June, June–July in Canada. *Food:* Beggar-ticks, clovers, and other legumes. *Comments:* By far the most common and widespread cloudywing.

Western Cloudywing *Thorybes diversus*

Below, the **HW has the median and postmedian bands very poorly developed**. The outer portion of the HW is only barely paler than rest of wing. *Habitat:* Openings in moist coniferous forests. *Abundance:* R-LU. June–July. *Food:* Clovers and possibly other legumes. *Comments:* This species is restricted to the western slope of the California Sierra Nevadas and a relatively small area of northwestern California and southwestern Oregon. Even within these areas, you are not likely to stumble upon it.

Mexican Cloudywing *Thorybes mexicana*

Usually small. **Below, the outer portion of the HW is very pale**. Above, **spots often have dark outlines**, but vary from extensive, as shown, to almost absent. *Habitat:* Openings in mountain coniferous forests. *Abundance:* C. May–June southward; June–Aug.northward. *Food:* Clovers and other legumes.

Confused Cloudywing *Thorybes confusis*

Many individuals cannot be distinguished from Northern Cloudywings in the field. Below, outer portion of wings is often pale, face is white. Above, spot pattern varies usually very restricted (like Northern) to extensive (like Southern). In range shown, individuals with **white face and very restricted markings above** are probably this species. *Habitat:* Dry open situations, such as dry prairie, hillside fields, and sand barrens. *Abundance:* R-U. April–May, July–Aug. *Food:* Probably legumes.

Southern Cloudywing *Thorybes bathyllus*

Both above and below, note the **white patch just where the antennal club bends**. Other cloudywings lack such a patch. Above, white markings are usually strongly expressed. *Habitat:* Many open situations, especially dry, fields with low brushy areas. *Abundance:* U. May–June, Aug.–Oct. *Food:* Legumes.

1 Northern Cloudywing 2 Northern Cloudywing

3 Western Cloudywing 4 Western Cloudywing

5 Mexican Cloudywing 6 Mexican Cloudywing

7 Confused Cloudywing 8 Southern Cloudywing

Texas Powdered-Skipper *Systasea pulverulenta*

The unusual **soft brown appearance** and **scalloped HW** makes powdered-skippers quite distinctive. The two western species are very similar. Distinguish them by the FW pale median band. Texas Powdered-Skippers have a **smooth inner edge to the FW pale median band**. Arizona Powdered-Skippers have a jagged inner edge. The pale underside becomes prominent in flight. *Habitat:* Tropical and subtropical woodland, thorn scrub, and arid canyons. *Abundance:* R-U. Immigrant, mainly July–Nov. *Food:* Mallow family.

Arizona Powdered-Skipper *Systasea zampa*

The unusual **soft brown appearance** and **scalloped HW** makes powdered-skippers quite distinctive. Arizona Powdered-Skippers have a **jagged inner edge to the FW pale median band**. Texas Powdered-Skippers have a smooth inner edge. The pale underside becomes prominent in flight. *Habitat:* Desert canyons. *Abundance:* U. All year, but mainly early spring and fall. *Food:* Mallow family. *Comments:* Flight is quite "fluttery" and back and forth—doesn't fly as powerfully or linearly as most other skippers.

Sickle-winged Skipper *Achlyodes thraso*

The **FW apex is curved outward—like a sickle**. Above, with various mottled bluish-purplish sheens. Females are paler brown with less iridescence. *Habitat:* Tropical woodlands, thorn scrub and adjacent gardens. *Abundance:* R. Mainly Aug.–Oct. RS to West Texas. *Food:* Lime prickly-ash. *Comments:* Unpublished work by Andy Warren indicates that the correct name for this species may well be *Eantis tamenund*, with the genus *Achlyodes* split and *thraso* referring to a South American species. In any event, the English name will still be Sickle-winged Skipper!

White-patched Skipper *Chiomara asychis georgina*

Above, mottled dark gray, black and white. White is more extensive on males. Female FW looks like a pale version of a duskywing (which are close relatives). *Habitat:* Open tropical woodlands, thorn scrub, and gardens. *Abundance:* R. Immigrant and probably temporary colonist. Mainly Aug.–Oct. *Food:* Barbados cherry. *Comments:* Northern *georgina* is probably separate from the South American *asychis*.

White Spurwing *Antigonus emorsus*

A largely white skipper (summer form; winter form with white bands, but much less extensive white). Note the **scalloped outer margin of the HW**. White-patched Skipper is smaller, with extensive black, and a less pronounced scalloped HW. Northern White-Skipper lacks the scalloped HW and has a less defined HW dark border. *Habitat:* Tropical woodland and thorn scrub. *Abundance:* RS to southeastern Arizona and adjacent New Mexico. July–Sept. *Food:* Unknown.

1 Texas Powdered-Skipper

2 Arizona Powdered-Skipper

3 Arizona Powdered-Skipper

4 Sickle-winged Skipper

5 White-patched Skipper ♀

6 White-patched Skipper ♂

7 White-patched Skipper

8 White Spurwing

Duskywings (genus *Erynnis*)

Duskywings constitute one of the butterfly world's more difficult challenges. Many duskywings are so similar that it is common to find misidentified museum specimens. Thus the astute observer will often say "That's a duskywing," or "That's a Juvenal's Duskywing group duskywing." The butterfly's size and the amount of white spots on the FW are useful in grouping species. The "wake me when you see a colorful butterfly group," comprised of Dreamy and Sleepy Duskywings, normally lacks any white spots above, while all others have at least some white spots on the FW. Members of the Juvenal's Duskywing group (Juvenal's, Scudder's, Horace's, Rocky Mountain, Meridian, and Propertius Duskywings) are generally large. Persius group species (Persius, Afranius, and Wild Indigo Duskywings), along with Pacuvius and Mottled Duskywings, are mid-sized. And lastly, Mournful and Funereal Duskywings are large with white fringes. In identifying duskywings, it is often useful to know if one is viewing a male or a female. One can usually distinguish duskywing sexes, even in the field, by viewing the FW costal margin. Males have a fold along the costal margin and the presence of this fold often creates a slight angle at the FW "wrist." Females lack the fold and have a smoothly curved FW costal margin.

Male Afranius Duskywing

Female Propertius Duskywing

Rocky Mountain Duskywing *Erynnis telemachus*

Large. HW fringe is brown. Below, HW usually with **two pale subapical spots** and with pale marginal spots. Above, with **much gray on the FWs**. Postmedian pale spots usually large. Shoulders are black and the **thorax is prickled with bright gray hairs** (except, of course, when well worn). Juvenal's Duskywing lacks bright gray thorax hairs. *Habitat:* Oak, and mixed oak, woodlands. *Abundance:* Mainly C, late April–early July, mainly May–June but as early as March near southern edge of range. *Food:* Oaks. *Comments:* Occasionally, very small males are encountered.

Propertius Duskywing *Erynnis propertius*

Large. HW fringe is gray. Above, with much gray on the FWs, males looking especially "furry." In California and Pacific Northwest, only Pacuvius Duskywing is similar (others have white fringe, lack FW pale spots, or are much smaller). Pacuvius is smaller, lacks the gray of this species, usually has a brown patch just beyond the FW cell. *Habitat:* Oak, and mixed oak, woodlands. *Abundance:* C-A. March/April–June/July. *Food:* Oaks.

Meridian Duskywing *Erynnis meridianus*

Large. Similar to Rocky Mountain Duskywing but lacks bright gray thorax hairs, brown **HW fringe is tipped with off-white** and, below, pale marginal spots are lacking. *Habitat:* Oak woodlands. *Abundance:* U-C. March/April–May, late June–mid Sept. *Food:* Oaks. *Comments:* A strong hilltopper.

1 Rocky Mountain Duskywing ♂

2 Rocky Mountain Duskywing ♀

3 Rocky Mountain Duskywing

4 Propertius Duskywing

5 Propertius Duskywing ♂

6 Propertius Duskywing ♀

7 Meridian Duskywing ♂ (museum specimen)

8 Meridian Duskywing ♀ (museum specimen)

'Arizona' Juvenal's Duskywing *Erynnis juvenalis clitus*

Medium-sized to large with white fringe. **HW fairly evenly colored, both above and below**. In southeastern Arizona there are four other white-fringed duskywings—Scudder's, Mournful, Funereal, and Pacuvius. In Arizona, Mournful has a white HW marginal patch below that this species lacks. Both Funereal and Pacuvius have brown patches on the FW. Scudder's Duskywing is extremely similar but more rarely encountered—see below. **Habitat:** Oak woodland in mountains. **Abundance:** R-U. Mid March–Aug., mainly April–May and July–Aug. **Food:** Oaks. **Comments:** I suspect that these Mexican-Arizona populations will eventually be considered a separate species from the eastern populations.

Juvenal's Duskywing *Erynnis juvenalis*

A large, strong-flying duskywing with well-expressed FW postmedian pale spots. For the eastern brown-fringed populations, the only other species that one is likely to confuse this with is Horace's Duskywing (see discussion there). Rocky Mountain Duskywing has bright gray hairs on its thorax. **Habitat:** Oak woodlands. **Abundance:** C, east Texas. LU, the Dakotas, and Saskatchewan; LR, Palo Duro Canyon and Big Bend. April/May–June. **Food:** Oaks.

Scudder's Duskywing *Erynnis scudderi*

See inset to photo 2. Although usually considered to be inseparable in the field from 'Arizona' Juvenal's Duskywing, I believe that individuals strongly exhibiting the three **dark half-checks encroaching on the HW white fringe** are Scudder's. Averages perhaps 25% smaller than 'Arizona' Juvenal's Duskywing. Also see Mournful Duskywing. **Habitat:** Oak and pine-oak woodlands above 6000 ft. **Abundance:** R. Mid April–mid Sept., mainly May with a partial second brood in Aug. **Food:** Presumed to be oaks. **Comments:** Hilltops.

Horace's Duskywing *Erynnis horatius*

A large brown-fringed duskywing, similar to Juvenal's and Rocky Mountain. Below, **Horace's lacks two pale subapical spots near the HW apex** that Juvenal's and Rocky Mountain Duskywings *almost* always have. Above, **usually with chestnut shoulders (Rocky Mountain—black) and thorax without bright pale gray hairs**. Horace's is more sexually dimorphic than Juvenal's or Rocky Mountain and males are less mottled, more uniform dark brown, lacking gray overscaling. Horace's females are more boldly mottled than Rocky Mountain or (especially) Juvenal's females. Spring individuals are smaller and can resemble Afranius Duskywing. **Habitat:** Oak woodlands, especially those on poor soils and adjacent open areas. **Abundance:** C, east Texas and Oklahoma, March–Sept.; R-LC, Colorado and New Mexico, April–May, July–Aug. **Food:** Oaks.

1 'Arizona' Juvenal's Duskywing

2 'Arizona' Juvenal's Duskywing ♂ (inset: Scudder's)

3 Juvenal's Duskywing

4 Juvenal's Duskywing ♂

5 Horace's Duskywing

6 Juvenal's Duskywing ♀

7 Horace's Duskywing ♂

8 Horace's Duskywing ♀

Mournful Duskywing *Erynnis tristis*

HW fringes are white. Large. Below, populations from **Arizona eastward have vertically elongated white marginal spots on the HW**. In California these spots are weak to absent. The FW is usually quite mottled and without a pale brown patch beyond the cell. *Habitat:* Oak woodlands. *Abundance:* R-U. California. March/April–Sept.; U-C. Southeastern Arizona to west Texas. Feb./March–Sept./Oct.; R-U northward. May–Aug.; RS to northwestern Arizona, north central New Mexico and Austin, Texas, area. *Food:* Oaks. *Comments:* A strong hilltopper. In California, Mournful and Funereal Duskywings are the only duskywings with white HW fringes.

Funereal Duskywing *Erynnis funeralis*

HW fringes are white. Large. Below, without HW marginal white spots or with narrow, horizontally elongated white spots. Above, the **FW is largely black** with a **pale brown patch beyond the cell**. The FW white spots are weakly expressed. *Habitat:* A wide variety, including desert, woodland edges, and spruce forest, but preference is for hot, dry situations. *Abundance:* U-C. California southeast to southeastern Arizona to West Texas and eastward. Almost all year, mainly March–Oct.; R-U elsewhere. Mainly May–Sept.; RS to Nebraska, northern Colorado, and northern California. *Food:* Legumes.

Pacuvius Duskywing *Erynnis pacuvius*

Small. HW fringes are usually white in eastern part of range, including most of Colorado (individuals in northwestern Colorado have dark fringes), dark in California and Pacific Northwest. Below, there are no white marginal spots. **Above, black and brown**. Eastern range individuals with more contrast between these areas, western range individuals with less (almost entirely black along the northern California coast). Note the **multiple gray rings on the abdomen**. HW usually with less distinct pale spots and cell-end bar than on Persius Duskywings. *Habitat:* Extremely varied—from pine forest to mixed woodlands to chaparral. *Abundance:* R-U. In two-brooded areas, late March/April–Sept./Oct. In single-brooded areas, May–mid July. *Food:* Ceanothus. *Comments:* Hilltops.

Mottled Duskywing *Erynnis martialis*

Small. HW fringes brown. A brighter, more mottled skipper than other duskywings, especially on the HW above. Note the **narrow and relatively sharply delineated HW postmedian dark band** and the **multiple gray rings on the abdomen**. Fresh individuals have a purplish sheen. *Habitat:* Open wooded areas with sites for hilltopping. *Abundance:* C. Colorado. May–June; R-U. Black Hills of South Dakota. Late May–mid July; R-U elsewhere. March/April–July–Aug. *Food:* Ceanothus. *Comments:* A strong hilltopper.

1 Mournful Duskywing (Arizona)

2 Mournful Duskywing

3 Mournful Duskywing (California)

4 Funereal Duskywing

5 Funereal Duskywing

6 Pacuvius Duskywing (Colorado)

7 Pacuvius Duskywing (Oregon)

8 Mottled Duskywing

Dreamy Duskywing *Erynnis icelus*

Small. **FW without white spots and with broad, chain-like postmedian bands**. Dreamy is smaller than Sleepy, has the last segment of the **palps longer,** has the **inner one-third of the FW above blacker than the rest of the ground color,** and flies later in the year. *Habitat:* Openings in moist forest. *Abundance:* C. Canada and Montana; Mainly R-U elsewhere; Everywhere, May–mid July. *Food:* Willows and poplars. *Comments:* Doesn't hilltop.

Sleepy Duskywing *Erynnis brizo*

A small to medium-sized duskywing, **without white spots on the FW above** and with a **broad, chain-like FW postmedian band**. See Dreamy Duskywing for comparison. *Habitat:* Openings in oak woodlands with scrubby oaks. *Abundance:* LR-U. California; C. Rockies; R-U. Texas; Mainly March/April–May/June. As early as mid Feb. in southeastern Arizona, as late as early July at some high elevations. *Food:* Scrubby oaks and oak seedlings. *Comments:* Hilltops.

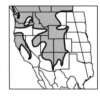

Persius Duskywing *Erynnis persius*

Small to medium-sized. **Males have gray hairs over much of the FW, creating a soft appearance.** Basal third of the female FW is blackened and HW has small pale spots and a cell-end bar that are less prominent on Pacuvius Duskywings. *Habitat:* Mainly mountain meadows and forest openings but also in prairie. *Abundance:* Mainly U-C. Mainly May–July *Food:* Golden banners and other legumes. *Comments:* Hilltops.

Afranius Duskywing *Erynnis afranius*

Small to medium-sized. Males **often have a small brown patch just past the FW cell** and lack the gray hairs of Persius Duskywings, creating a sharper pattern. HW pale spots are usually paler than on Persius. Males **patrol in gulches,** while Persius males are usually found on hilltops. *Habitat:* High prairie, badlands, canyons, and chaparral. *Abundance:* U-C. March/April–May, Late June/July–Aug./Sept. *Food:* Legumes. *Comments:* Females are perhaps not separable from Persius.

Wild Indigo Duskywing *Erynnis baptisiae*

Medium-sized. Basal 1/3 of FW often appears dark and "oily." Note the **brown patch just past the FW cell.** Females can be mistaken for Horace's Duskywings but have small pale spots on the HW margin below. *Habitat:* Roadsides and embankments. *Abundance:* U-LC. April–Sept. *Food:* Crown vetch and wild indigo. *Comments:* Adapting to use of the alien crown vetch about 25 years ago, this is now one of the commonest duskywings in the East. It may well spread westward.

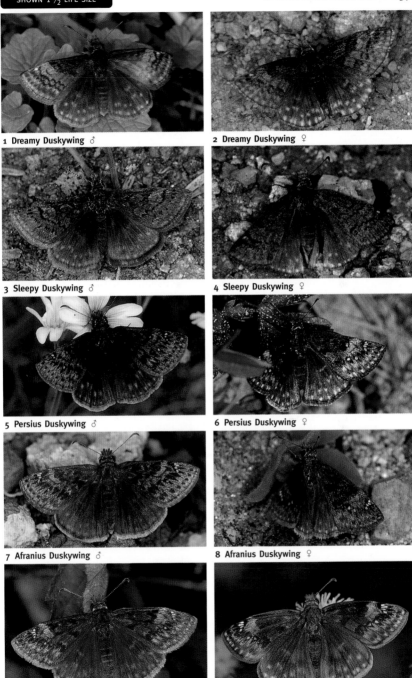

1 Dreamy Duskywing ♂

2 Dreamy Duskywing ♀

3 Sleepy Duskywing ♂

4 Sleepy Duskywing ♀

5 Persius Duskywing ♂

6 Persius Duskywing ♀

7 Afranius Duskywing ♂

8 Afranius Duskywing ♀

9 Wild Indigo Duskywing ♂

10 Wild Indigo Duskywing ♀

Checkered-Skippers (genus *Pyrgus* and relatives)

The checkered-Skippers are small, but delightful, black and white energy machines. You'll need your close-focusing binoculars and some patience to get good looks at these animals; but your efforts will be rewarded. Although there are useful field marks below, checkered-skippers usually land with their wings open (but often allowing a fleeting view of their undersides).

'Common'

'White'

Common Checkered-Skipper *Pyrgus communis*

The extensive white spots on the black background coupled with the blue-tinged hair creates the effect of a blue-gray blur as this little skipper whirs by you. It is larger, more common, and more widespread than other checkered-skippers. Below Commons have a "telephone" at the base of the HW that Tropicals lack. Remember, telephones are common. *Habitat:* A wide variety of open situations, often disturbed. Mainly in lowlands, but also occurs at high elevations. *Abundance:* C. Three-brood areas, almost all year; two-brood areas, mainly May–Sept. *Food:* Mallow family. *Comments:* Along the Mexican border flies the 'White' Common Checkered-Skipper, *P. communis albescens*. Treated as a subspecies on the NABA *Checklist*, recent, as yet unpublished, evidence indicates that it is best considered a separate species. Although, on average, 'White' Checkered-Skippers *are* slightly whiter than Common Checkered-Skippers, both species are extremely variable and it is not known how to separate them in the field.

Tropical Checkered-Skipper *Pyrgus oileus*

Very similar to Common Checkered-Skipper, but above, note the **white spot at the FW apex** that is a continuation of the marginal spot-band. This spot is almost always missing from Commons. The **FW fringe just below the apex is blackened** or with the black checks very closely spaced. Commons have this portion of the FW similar to the rest of the FW. The FW cell has a prominent white spot (see photo) where Commons have a faint spot or none. Lastly, the HW marginal white spots are usually not too much smaller than the submarginal white spot. Commons usually have the marginal spots much smaller than the submarginal spots. Below, Tropicals are tanner and more smudged and have a brown spot in the middle of the HW leading margin that Commons lack. *Habitat:* A variety of open situations. *Abundance:* C. Southern Texas. All year; R immigrant, southeastern Arizona. March–Oct. *Food:* Mallow family. *Comments:* Perhaps becoming more common northward.

Desert Checkered-Skipper *Pyrgus philetas*

Above, very similar to Tropical, but **FW fringe just below the apex is not blackened**. Below note the **even, tan** coloration and the row of small dark spots. *Habitat:* Thorn scrub. *Abundance:* R-U. All year. *Food:* Mallows. *Comments:* A more avid flower visitor than Common or Tropical Checkered-Skippers, it is also fond of damp sand.

1 Common Checkered-Skipper

2 Common Checkered-Skipper ♂

3 'White' Checkered-Skipper

4 Common Checkered-Skipper ♀

5 Tropical Checkered-Skipper

6 Tropical Checkered-Skipper ♂

7 Desert Checkered-Skipper

8 Desert Checkered-Skipper

Grizzled Skipper *Pyrgus centaureae*

Large. Larger than the West's other mountain Checkered-Skippers (except Common Checkered-Skipper). Note the **missing white spot in the FW basal spotband**. In the Rocky Mountains, most individuals seem to have a faint yellowish cast. *Habitat:* Alpine meadows and talus slopes. *Abundance:* R-U. June–late July/early Aug. More common in odd-numbered years. *Food:* Cinquefoils.

Two-banded Checkered-Skipper *Pyrgus ruralis*

The FW has two white bands forming an "X." Note the **white spot at the base of the HW** (sometimes quite small). Small Checkered-Skippers lack this spot. **Below, HW bands are reddish-brown**. Mountain Checkered-Skippers are grayer and duller. Males have a costal fold that male Mountain Checkered-Skippers lack, but it can be very difficult to determine the sex of individuals of these species in the field. An added problem is that the presence or absence of a costal fold in these species is often not obvious. *Habitat:* Mountain meadows and openings in cool coniferous forests, down to sea level on the Pacific Coast. *Abundance:* R. Southern California (endangered). April–May; C. Northern California and the Pacific Northwest. March/April–Aug.; R-U. Rockies. June–mid July. *Food:* Cinquefoils and horkelias.

Mountain Checkered-Skipper *Pyrgus xanthus*

On *some* individuals, the FW white bands do not form as strong an "X" as on Two-banded Checkered-Skippers. This is because the position of the spot indicated in photo 6 is sometimes closer to the FW outer margin than is the equivalent spot on Two-bandeds. Note the white spot at the HW base (sometimes small). Small Checkered-Skippers lack this spot (except in spring). Best identification is from below. Mountain Checkered-Skippers have **dull gray-brown HW bands**, while Two-banded Checkered-Skippers have a redder tint to the HW bands. *Habitat:* High, dry mountain meadows and gullies. *Abundance:* LR-U. May–June. *Food:* Cinquefoils.

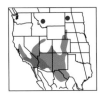

Small Checkered-Skipper *Pyrgus scriptura*

Small. Above, white spotting is usually (but not always) reduced, especially on the HW. Note the **absence of a white HW basal spot** (except some spring individuals) that both Two-banded and Mountain Checkered-Skippers have and that, at the HW apex, the **black fringe checks only go halfway across the fringe**. The FW costal margin usually has a pale gray area that other checkered-skippers lack. Below, the ground color is pale and soft. *Habitat:* Roadsides, gulches, alkali fields, and disturbed open situations. *Abundance:* LR-U. Three-brood areas: March–Sept./Oct.; single-brood areas: July–Aug. *Food:* Alkali-mallows and other mallow family.

1 Grizzled Skipper

2 Grizzled Skipper

3 Two-banded Checkered-Skipper

4 Two-banded Checkered-Skipper

5 Mountain Checkered-Skipper

6 Mountain Checkered-Skipper

7 Small Checkered-Skipper

8 Small Checkered-Skipper

Northern White-Skipper *Heliopetes ericetorum*

A medium-sized white-colored skipper, unlikely to be confused with anything else. Common Checkered-Skippers are black and white, but they have much less white than white-skippers. Like most white-skippers, females have more extensive black markings than males. Note the inward-pointing HW submarginal white chevrons. See Erichson's White-Skipper for separation from that species. *Habitat:* Chaparral and arid canyons. *Abundance:* C. Southern California north and east to southern Nevada; R-U elsewhere. Mainly April–June, Aug–Oct. *Food:* Shrubby mallows and other mallow family. *Comments:* In almost all of its range, this is the only species of white-skipper normally encountered.

Erichson's White-Skipper *Heliopetes domicella*

The well-defined basal portions of the wings make this a **banded** white-skipper. Males and females are similar. Above, only likely to be confused with female Northern White Skippers. Erichson's White-Skippers have the white bands above very defined, while female Northern White-Skippers have them more diffuse. Also, the HW submarginal white spots on Erichson's White-Skippers are not inward-pointing chevrons as they are in female Northern White-Skippers. Below, note the dark FW patch that other white-skippers, occurring in the United States, lack. *Habitat:* Thorn scrub. *Abundance:* U. Almost all year, but especially spring and fall. R immigrant to Colorado River area of southeastern California, Sept.–Oct. *Food:* Mallow family.

Laviana White-Skipper *Heliopetes laviana*

Below, note that the **brown HW median band slants in toward the body.** Northern and Erichson's White-Skippers have this band perpendicular to the HW leading margin. The **inner edge of the dark HW marginal patch is approximately straight** and does not follow the contour of the outer margin. Females have somewhat more extensive black above. *Habitat:* Open tropical woodland and thorn scrub. *Abundance:* R immigrant. Mainly April–early May, Sept.–mid Nov. RS to Austin area and north Texas. *Food:* Mallow family.

Turk's-cap White-Skipper *Heliopetes macaira*

Both above and below, note the **white ray that shoots through the FW black border to the margin.** Below, note that the brown HW median band slants in toward the body. Northern and Erichson's White-Skippers have this band perpendicular to the HW leading margin. The **inner edge of the dark HW marginal patch is convex** and follows the contour of the outer margin. Females have somewhat more extensive black above. *Habitat:* Tropical woodland and thorn scrub. *Abundance:* RS to San Antonio area. *Food:* Mallow family.

1 Northern White-Skipper

2 Northern White-Skipper ♀ (inset: ♂)

3 Erichson's White-Skipper

4 Erichson's White-Skipper

5 Laviana White-Skipper

6 Laviana White-Skipper ♂

7 Turk's-cap White-Skipper

8 Turk's-cap White-Skipper ♂

Mottled Bolla *Bolla clytius*

Extremely similar to scallopwings but averages slightly larger and **HW is rounder, less scalloped**. Both males and females have 0–3 inconspicuous white spots at the FW subapex. Note the **diffuse, broad, dark band in the middle of the FW** above. *Habitat:* Tropical woodlands and thorn scrub. *Abundance:* RS to southeastern Arizona and possibly north to San Antonio, Texas area. Mainly Aug.–Oct. *Food:* Unknown.

Mazans Scallopwing *Staphylus mazans*

Often not distinguishable in the field from Hayhurst's. HW fringe is unchecked (sometimes alternating black and gray), while many Hayhurst's have definite white checks to the fringes. *Habitat:* Open areas within and adjacent to woodlands. *Abundance:* U. March–Nov. *Food:* Lambsquarters and pigweeds. *Comments:* May be moving north of range shown.

Hayhurst's Scallopwing *Staphylus hayhurstii*

Small. **HW margin scalloped**. Dark brown (females) or black (males) with even **darker bands forming concentric semicircles on the HW**. Variably **strewn with tiny pale silver or gold flecks**. Usually with HW fringe with some white checkering. No white on head. *Habitat:* Moist open woodland, gardens, and disturbed areas. *Abundance:* U-C. Texas–Oklahoma. March–Oct.; R-U. Kansas–Nebraska. May–Aug. *Food:* Lambsquarters.

Golden-headed Scallopwing *Staphylus ceos*

I don't think you'll usually need help with this one, but females and worn individuals sometimes lack a gold head. But even then, they usually have a trace of gold, often have white at the FW apex and have a less scalloped HW margin than other scallopwings. *Habitat:* Washes, canyons and riparian areas in arid regions. *Abundance:* U-C. Almost all year, but mainly March/April–Sept./Oct. *Food:* Lambsquarters.

Common Sootywing *Pholisora catullus*

Small. Black with a variable number of **white spots, including some on the head**. *Habitat:* Varied, including weedy areas, desert washes, agricultural lands, and suburban gardens. *Abundance:* Three-brood areas: C, March–Oct.; two-brood areas. Mainly U-C, but R in mountains. April–Aug./Sept. *Food:* Lambsquarters and pigweeds.

Mexican Sootywing *Pholisora mejicana*

Identical to Common Sootywing except that below, the **veins are jet black** and wings have a bluish tinge (occasional on Common Sootywing also). *Habitat:* Gulches and canyons. *Abundance:* LR. May–June, July–Aug. *Food:* Pigweeds. *Comments:* Even when they stop, undersides are rarely shown.

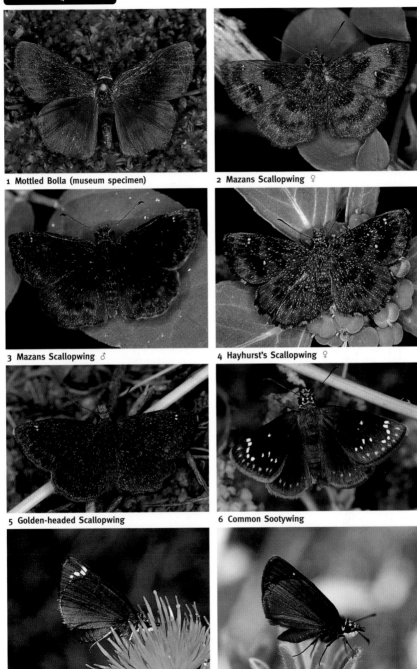

1 Mottled Bolla (museum specimen)

2 Mazans Scallopwing ♀

3 Mazans Scallopwing ♂

4 Hayhurst's Scallopwing ♀

5 Golden-headed Scallopwing

6 Common Sootywing

7 Common Sootywing

8 Mexican Sootywing

Mojave Sootywing *Hesperopsis libya*

A small black skipper **flying around saltbush** is likely to be this or the next species. Two-brooded populations (see photos 1 and 2) look quite different from single-brooded populations. Below, they are soft gray-brown with **large white spots**. Quite distinctive. Above, they are dark brown with FW white spots organized into median and post-median bands. Individuals in single-brooded populations have greatly reduced white spots, both above and below, and much more closely resemble Saltbush Sootywings. Note the **smooth dark brown/black ground color above**. Saltbush Sootywings have a more mottled appearance. Common Sootywings are blacker with white spots on the head. *Habitat:* Saltbush concentrations along desert washes and alkaline salt flats. *Abundance:* R-U. Two-brood areas March–Oct.; single-brood areas June–early Aug. *Food:* Saltbushes.

Saltbush Sootywing *Hesperopsis alpheus*

A small black skipper **flying around saltbush** is likely to be this or the previous species. Below, usually with a white bar in the middle of the HW. Common Sootywings are blacker with white spots on the head. *Habitat:* Saltbush concentrations, along desert washes and rivers, and in alkaline sage flats. *Abundance:* Mainly R-U. Two-brood areas: May–June, July–mid Sept.; California–southern Nevada. March/April–mid June; Other single-brood areas: May/June–July. *Food:* Saltbushes. *Comments:* Reportedly abundant at Butterbredt Peak in Kern County, California. Some consider 'MacNeill's' Saltbush Sootywing, *Hesperopsis alpheus gracielae*, to be a distinct species. It is found along the Colorado River and its tributaries, mainly along the California–Arizona border. It is little different from the other subspecies.

'MacNeill's'

Common Streaky-Skipper *Celotes nessus*

A tiny scrap of crinkled brown aluminum foil that flies away is sure to be this species. I believe that the technical term for the group is pleatedoptera. *Habitat:* Thorn scrub. *Abundance:* U-C. Mainly March/April–Aug./Sept. *Food:* Mallow family. *Comments:* How much more fun can butterflies be?

Scarce Streaky-Skipper *Celotes limpia* Not Illustrated

It is not currently known how to separate this species from Common Streaky-Skipper without dissection. *Habitat:* Mountain gullies and washes and along riparian areas. *Abundance:* R? March–Sept. *Food:* Mallow family. *Comments:* Because of the difficulty of determining whether one is viewing this species, its habits, range, and abundance remain little known.

1 Mojave Sootywing

2 Mojave Sootywing

3 Saltbush Sootywing

4 Saltbush Sootywing

5 'MacNeill's' Saltbush Sootywing

6 'MacNeill's' Saltbush Sootywing

7 Common Streaky-Skipper

8 Common Streaky-Skipper

Skipperlings (subfamily Heteropterinae)

These small skippers share some traits with grass-skippers and others with spread-wing skippers. They open their FWs and HWs in unison, like the spread-wing skippers, but they feed on grasses and have other obvious affinities with the grass-skippers. They also lack the tapering terminal extension of the antenna (apiculus) that other skippers have.

Arctic Skipper *Carterocephalus palaemon*
A small, but choice, gift from the north. Marked rather like a miniature fritillary. *Habitat:* Moist grassy openings in coniferous and mixed forest. *Abundance:* LR-U. Mid April–early Aug, mainly May–July. *Food:* Grasses. *Comments:* Has a strong fondness for wild geraniums.

Russet Skipperling *Piruna pirus*
Below, HW is unmarked, FW disk is black with white spots. Above, there are a variable number of white spots on the FW, but none on the HW. Note the blue-gray body hairs. *Habitat:* Moist grassy streamsides and other riparian situations in woodlands from prairie canyons to high elevations. *Abundance:* Mainly LU-LC. Mainly June–July, as early as May in some areas. Recently discovered colony in Jeff Davis Mtns. flies in Aug. *Food:* Grasses. *Comments:* Flight is quite slow.

Four-spotted Skipperling *Piruna polingi*
Below, with four large white spots, or an approximation thereof. Above, with variable FW white spots. Note the **two HW white spots**, the **spot in the middle of the HW large and doubled**. Russet Skipperling lacks HW white spots. *Habitat:* Very moist, grassy situations in high-elevation woodland. *Abundance:* LC. July–Aug. *Food:* Grasses.

Many-spotted Skipperling *Piruna cingo*
Below, with many large white spots. Above, similar to Four-spotted Skipperling (in different habitat), but **HW fringe is white** (usually buffy on Four-spotted Skipperling). *Habitat:* Mid-elevation grassy arroyos in arid oak-covered hillsides. *Abundance:* LR-LU. Aug. *Food:* Grasses. *Comments:* Comparing the underside patterns of this species and Arctic Skipper, it is easy to see the relationship between the many tropical skipperlings and the handful of northern representatives of this group.

Chisos Skipperling *Piruna haferniki*
Below, HW dark brown with base and outer angle gray, giving the appearance of a **dark inverted triangle** sitting on the HW leading margin. Above, dark brown with a few FW white spots and a **black marginal line** on both wings. *Habitat:* Mountainous pine-oak woodland. *Abundance:* R. March–Sept. *Food:* Unknown. *Comments:* In the United States, known only from the Chisos Mountains in Big Bend National Park.

1 Arctic Skipper

2 Arctic Skipper

3 Russet Skipperling

4 Russet Skipperling

5 Four-spotted Skipperling

6 Four-spotted Skipperling

7 Many-spotted Skipperling

8 Many-spotted Skipperling

9 Chisos Skipperling

10 Chisos Skipperling

Grass-Skippers (subfamily Hesperiinae)

Generally smaller than spread-wing skippers, most grass skippers have a rapid, darting flight. When landed, their wings are kept completely closed (often), or with the HWs more or less completely open but with the FWs only partially opened, forming a V or U. Males usually have a black "stigma" on the FW that contains specialized sex scales. The characteristics of the stigma are sometimes useful for identification.

Tropical Least Skipper *Anycloxypha arene*
Small. **Below, note the tiny dark spots on the HW margin.** Above, bright orange with a **dull black FW border**. Orange Skipperling lacks tiny marginal spots below or a black FW border above. *Habitat:* Edges of permanent streams and ponds, cienegas. *Abundance:* LR-LU. Mid Feb.–mid May, mid July–mid Nov. RS north to the Austin, Texas, area. *Food:* Grasses that have their roots in water.

Least Skipper *Anycloxypha numitor*
Small. Bright orange with **much black above** that can be seen in flight. Note the **rounded wings**. Flight is weak. *Habitat:* Wet meadows, marshes, grassy roadside ditches, etc. *Abundance:* Three-brood areas: LC. April–Oct.; two-brood areas: LR-LU, June–Sept. Strays west of range shown. The one report from Alberta is unlikely to have been of an individual who arrived there under its own power. *Food:* Grasses.

Orange Skipperling *Copaeodes aurantiaca*
Very small. Bright orange with **angular wings**. No distinctive markings. Flight is rapid. *Habitat:* Widespread in arid regions, especially in canyons and gulches. *Abundance:* Mainly C-A. Becoming U-R at northern edges of range. Almost all year in southern lowlands, but mainly March–Oct. Mainly May–Aug. at high elevations. *Food:* Bermuda grass and other grasses. *Comments:* "Jet plane" position shown in photo 6 is typical.

Southern Skipperling *Copaeodes minima*
Tiny. Bright orange with very angular wings. Note the **very narrow and sharp white ray on the HW below.** Above, essentially indistinguishable from Orange Skipperling. *Habitat:* A variety of open grassy habitats, but usually not in very wet nor very dry situations. *Abundance:* Three-brood areas: C-A, almost all year; two-brood areas: U-C, March–Oct.; one-brood areas: R-U, Sept.–Oct. *Food:* Bermuda grass and other grasses.

Sunrise Skipper *Adopaeoides prittwitzi*
Small. Bright orange with a **very pale yellow (not bright white) HW ray below**. Also note the **evenly orange fringes**. Southern Skipperling has a narrower, white HW ray. *Habitat:* Cienegas. *Abundance:* LR-LU. Mid May–mid Oct. *Food:* The grass, *Paspalum disticum* (Poaceae). *Comments:* In order to get a good look at this elusive beauty, you'll probably need to get your feet wet.

1 Tropical Least Skipper

2 Tropical Least Skipper

3 Least Skipper

4 Least Skipper

5 Orange Skipperling

6 Orange Skipperling

7 Southern Skipperling

8 Southern Skipperling

9 Sunrise Skipper

10 Sunrise Skipper (museum specimen)

Julia's Skipper *Nastra julia*

Below, **almost unmarked dull brown**. Above, usually with two small pale spots in the middle of the FW. Eufala Skipper is larger with somewhat more elongated wings and is usually grayer below. *Habitat:* Many open grassy habitats. *Abundance:* C. Texas. March–Nov.; LR. California–Arizona, immigrant to Colorado River Valley late Aug.–early Oct. *Food:* Bermuda grass and other grasses. *Comments:* Although not recorded from adjacent Sonora, Mexico, I have included this area on the range map with the thought that the late-summer immigrants to California must come from somewhere. Or perhaps the butterflies just say, "Beam me up, Scottie." Swarthy Skipper, *Nastra lherminier* (see *BTB:East* for illustration), looks similar, but ground color below is yellow-brown and veins are slightly paler. Above, there are usually no pale spots at all.

Swarthy Skipper

Garita Skipperling *Oarisma garita*

The **HW below has white veins and fringe** on this small orange skipper. **Variably blackened orange above** and with a white FW costal margin. *Habitat:* Mountain meadows and short-grass and mixed-grass prairies. *Abundance:* C. June–mid Aug. *Food:* Grasses. *Comments:* Flight is weak and weaving.

Edwards' Skipperling *Oarisma edwardsii*

Larger than an Orange Skipperling with a slower flight. Note the **black-tipped fringe, below**. Above, orange, without blackened wings of Garita Skipperling. *Habitat:* Open mountain woodland, usually pine-oak between 5000 and 8000 ft. *Abundance:* U-C. Late May–mid Aug. Mainly July–Aug. in southeastern Arizona and southwestern New Mexico, mainly June–July northward. *Food:* Unknown.

European Skipper *Thymelicus lineola*

A small, weak-flying skipper with an unmarked orange HW (sometimes with white overscaling) and usually with **orange fringe below** (occasionally pale). Note the **short and squat** appearance. *Habitat:* Dry fields and roadsides with tall grasses. *Abundance:* LC. June–early Aug. *Food:* Timothy. *Comments:* A native of Europe, this skipper was introduced into Ontario in 1910 and is now abundant in much of the East. First recorded from Colorado and Montana in the mid-1980s and from Utah in 1999, it is still expanding its range.

Alkali Skipper *Pseudocopaeodes eunus*

Below, **HW is pale orange with even paler, off-white ray** and dark marginal spots. Other rayed skippers are brighter orange without dark marginal spots (Tropical Least Skipper, with different range and habitat, often has a faint ray). *Habitat:* Grassy desert seeps. *Abundance:* LR. June–Sept. *Food:* Saltgrasses.

1 Julia's Skipper

2 Julia's Skipper

3 Garita Skipperling

4 Garita Skipperling

5 Edwards' Skipperling

6 Edwards' Skipperling

7 European Skipper

8 European Skipper

9 Alkali Skipper

10 Alkali Skipper

Morrison's Skipper *Stinga morrisoni*

Below, the **big silver spike at the base of the HW** is almost unique. Also note the **white marginal line.** Some Sonoran Skippers have a very similar pattern, but have a paler ground color, no white marginal line, and evenly colored pale fringes. *Habitat:* Open pine or pine-juniper woodlands. *Abundance:* R-U. Southeastern Arizona to West Texas. March–May, mainly April. Northward, mainly May–June. *Food:* Grasses. *Comments:* A strong hilltopper.

Hesperia Skippers (genus Hesperia)

Many of these interesting skippers are very similar to one another. The HW pattern often includes a prominent postmedian chevron of white spots and some basal white spots, while the FW below has two pale subapical spots near the outer margin. Color of "felt" in center of male stigma can sometimes be used for identification. They feed on perennial bunchgrasses and most are single-brooded. **Also see female Sachem.**

Green Skipper *Hesperia viridis*

Below, ground color is yellower and lighter than most similarly patterned *Hesperia*. Note that **taken together, the outer margins of the bottom three spots of the postmedian spotband form a concavity** (some female Pahaska Skippers share this trait and are not separable). Above, **male has black felt** in stigma. *Habitat:* Low- to mid-elevation canyons and gulches. *Abundance:* Mainly U-C, but R southeastern Arizona, Austin area, and Kansas–Nebraska. Two-broods areas: April/May–June/July, Aug.–Sept./Oct.; one-brood areas: mainly June–July. *Food:* Grasses. *Comments:* Fresh individuals are reported to have a green tint—perhaps they do. This species congregates in canyons and gulches, not on hilltops.

Pahaska Skipper *Hesperia pahaska*

Below, ground color is yellower and lighter than most similarly patterned *Hesperia*. Above, **male has yellow felt** in stigma and females usually have more contrast on their FW than do Green Skipper females. Most Common Branded Skippers below have the HW lower basal white spot shaped somewhat like a C. See Green Skipper for distinction from that species. Also see Juba Skipper. *Habitat:* A wide variety, from sparsely wooded grassland in desert ranges to open pine forest. *Abundance:* Mainly U-C. Two-brood areas: March–Oct.; one-brood areas, May–July. *Food:* Grasses. *Comments:* Hilltops. Females are seen much less frequently than are males.

Apache Skipper *Hesperia woodgatei*

Below, **ground color is dark brown**, sometimes green-brown. Both above and below, note the **white patches just below the clubs** of the jet black antennas. *Habitat:* Openings in high mountain pine and pine-oak forest. *Abundance:* LU-LC. Mid Sept.–Oct. *Food:* Grasses.

1 Morrison's Skipper

2 Morrison's Skipper ♂

3 Morrison's Skipper ♀

4 Green Skipper

5 Green Skipper ♂

6 Green Skipper ♀

7 Pahaska Skipper

8 Pahaska Skipper ♂

9 Pahaska Skipper ♀

10 Apache Skipper

11 Apache Skipper ♂

12 Apache Skipper ♀

Common Branded Skipper *Hesperia comma*

This species, the most widespread and generally common *Hesperia,* is difficult to characterize due to the extreme individual and geographical variation. The underside ground color varies from brassy green to dull brown-gray to chocolate to yellow-brown, as shown, in part, on the opposite page. Some populations in northwestern California and southwestern Oregon are chocolate brown beneath with only traces of the HW chevron or none at all. Note that most populations have the **HW basal white spots forming a C,** with the spots connected, or almost connected. Even when not connected, the lower of the two white basal spots almost always curves back toward the body. Differentiation from other *Hesperia* Skippers is generally given under those species. Juba Skippers have the inner edge of the FW black border above very jagged and have the bottom spot of the HW chevron displaced inwardly (some northern Common Branded Skippers also share this latter trait but lack the jagged border above). *Habitat:* A wide variety, including rocky outcrops above treeline, open coniferous forest, sagebrush steppes, and prairies. *Abundance:* Mainly C-A. June–Sept., depending upon elevation, location, and year—much less at any given locality in a given year, as early as May in southern California and southern Nevada, occasionally as late as Nov. July–Aug. is the peak flight period over most of the range. *Food:* Grasses. *Comments:* Will hilltop. About the various named subspecies, a few of which are now treated as full species by some (*H. c. assiniboia* on the plains of Montana and Alberta, east to Saskatchewan and North Dakota), Ferris and Brown (in *Butterflies of the Rocky Mountain States*) said, "Often one must be satisfied to [identify individuals] to the species, a job made simpler by considering Holarctic [Common Branded Skipper] as a single species."

Sierra Skipper *Hesperia miriamae*

Below, note the **partially checked fringes.** Ground color below is **dark brown with scattered bluish-white overscaling.** *Habitat:* Found only above treeline (over 10,500 ft.) on the highest peaks of the California Sierras and the White Mountains of California and Nevada. *Abundance:* LR. July–Aug. *Food:* Grasses. *Comments:* Hilltops.

Columbian Skipper *Hesperia columbia*

Bright, pale to medium brownish-yellow. **HW without the upper of the two white basal spots** and with the upper section of the HW white chevron missing or partial. **FW with very faint subapical spots along costal margin.** *Habitat:* Chaparral and oak woodlands, but will hilltop into other habitats. *Abundance:* LR-LU. Southern Californa: March/April–May (occasionally through June), Sept.–Oct.; Northern California: Late May–June, Sept. *Food:* Grasses *Comments:* Hilltops and mudpuddles.

1 Common Branded (WA) 2 Common Branded ♂ (WA) 3 Common Branded ♀ (MT)

4 Common Branded (MT) 5 Common Branded (CA) 6 Common Branded ♀ (CA)

7 Common Branded (CA) 8 Common Branded (WY) 9 Common Branded ♂ (CO)

10 Sierra Skipper 11 Columbian Skipper 12 Columbian Skipper ♂

Cobweb Skipper

Uncas Skipper *Hesperia uncas*

Below, **extensive HW white chevron with connected spots, white veins** (usually), and **blotchy dark brown/black markings** make this skipper unlike any other except Rhesus and some Sandhill. Above, females usually have more prominent FW white spots than do other *Hesperia* skippers. Rhesus Skipper is smaller and has pure white fringes without the HW marginal dark spots that Uncas Skippers possess. Populations in Mono County, California (*macswaini* and *giulanii*), have the HW white veining greatly reduced or absent but often have the blotchy dark brown/black markings. *Habitat:* Short-grass grasslands and grassy alkaline flats. *Abundance:* Mainly R-U. Two-brood areas: May–June, late July–Sept.; one-brood areas, mainly June–July. *Food:* Blue grama grass and other grasses. *Comments:* Cobweb Skipper (*Hesperia metea*) (See *BTB: East* for illustration) looks like a very small, dark Uncas Skipper. It is LR-LU and flies April–early June in dry fields with bluestem grasses.

Juba Skipper *Hesperia juba*

Large. Below, ground color is dark yellow-brown to dark green-brown and the **bottom spot of the HW chevron is displaced inwardly.** Above, **FW black border is very jagged** and is especially prominent on females. **Females also have a double black spot in the middle of their FW** above. *Habitat:* Mountain meadows and sagebrush grasslands. *Abundance:* Mainly C, but R in eastern Colorado, in much of the California Sierra Nevadas and in the Spring Mountains of Nevada. April–June, late Aug.–Sept./Oct. *Food:* Grasses. *Comments:* Not a hilltopper.

Lindsey's Skipper *Hesperia lindseyi*

Below, the **HW chevron on males is cream-colored**, not white. The **outer edge of the chevron spots is very spikey** (usually), extending along the veins. Above, the FW border is indistinct, blending into the ground color. *Habitat:* Open grassy areas within chaparral or open oak woodland in foothills. *Abundance:* LR-U. Southern California; U-C. Northern California. Mainly mid May–early July. *Food:* Grasses.

Nevada Skipper *Hesperia nevada*

Below, the HW ground color is green-toned and the **bottom spot of the HW chevron is displaced inwardly, barely touching the spot above it**. HW **chevron spots are often edged with black**. Above, FW borders are not sharply defined. *Habitat:* High-elevation grasslands, mountain meadows, and northern prairies. *Abundance:* Mainly U-C, but LR in Saskatchewan. May–early Sept. Much shorter at any given locality. *Food:* Grasses. *Comments:* Hilltops.

1 Uncas Skipper

2 Uncas Skipper ♂

3 Uncas Skipper ♀

4 Juba Skipper

5 Juba Skipper ♂

6 Juba Skipper ♀

7 Lindsey's Skipper

8 Lindsey's Skipper ♂

9 Lindsey's Skipper ♀

10 Nevada Skipper

11 Nevada Skipper ♂

12 Nevada Skipper ♀

Ottoe Skipper *Hesperia ottoe*

Large. Below, dull yellow-orange without a HW chevron of white spots. Sometimes with a faint, paler HW postmedian area. Above, males' stigmas have gray "felt." Western populations of Leonard's Skipper are very similar but fly later in the year and males have yellow "felt" (occasionally one can see this in the field, but it is quite tricky). Dakota Skipper males are extremely similar except that they are much smaller. *Habitat:* Tall grass and short grass prairies, especially along ridgetops. *Abundance:* R-U. June–early Aug. *Food:* Grasses.

Dakota Skipper *Hesperia dacotae*

Below, males are dull yellow-brown with a faint HW postmedian band. Females vary from mouse brown with strong spots (most common form) to gray-yellow (similar to male) but usually have a basal white spot at the HW leading margin. Dotted Skippers lack this basal spot and are larger. Above, female Sachems look surprisingly similar but have a black patch at the center of the FW that Dakota Skippers lack. *Habitat:* Moist or dry, ungrazed, calcareous (alkaline) prairies. Often associated with pale purple coneflower. *Abundance:* LR. Mid/late June–mid July. *Food:* Grasses. *Comments:* The few remaining colonies of this prairie species need all the help they can get. Small, isolated colonies are certain to die out, the only question is when. Since native prairie is one of our most endangered habitats, prairie restoration is the only hope for this and similarly situated species.

Leonard's Skipper *Hesperia leonardus*

Below, pale yellow-orange with the HW chevron variable, usually reduced to a few small white spots or completely absent. **Above, females have extensive black with strongly contrasting pale spots.** Often difficult to distinguish from Ottoe Skipper except by flight time. *Habitat:* Prairie. *Abundance:* LC. Mid Aug.–Sept. *Food:* Bluestem grasses. *Comments:* The local and federally protected *montana* subspecies in the South Platte River Canyon of Colorado is more like eastern populations, often with more extensive chevron spots and a redder HW.

Dotted Skipper *Hesperia attalus*

Below, ground color varies from pale yellow-orange to yellow-brown to olive-brown. HW "dotted" spotband can be as extensive as on the individual shown in photo 10 (this individual is from the slightly different eastern population) or completely absent. Ottoe and Leonard's Skippers are very similar but are usually brighter and more orange, both above and below. *Habitat:* Short-grass prairie. *Abundance:* LR. May–mid June, mid Aug.–Sept. *Food:* Grasses. *Comments:* The Texas–Oklahoma populations of this skipper are rarely seen and little known.

1 Ottoe Skipper

2 Ottoe Skipper ♂

3 Ottoe Skipper ♀

4 Dakota Skipper

5 Dakota Skipper ♂

6 Dakota Skipper ♀

7 Leonard's Skipper

8 Leonard's Skipper ♂

9 Leonard's Skipper ♀

10 Dotted Skipper

11 Dotted Skipper ♂

12 Dotted Skipper ♀

Fiery Skipper *Hylephila phyleus*

This southern species has the "measles"—many small black spots on the HW below—giving it a fever and making it "fiery." Below, males are bright orange with spots varying from faint dull brown to sharp black. Above, note the **very wavy black borders on the FW and HW.** Females are similar but the ground color is dull yellow-brown with a greenish tinge. Usually with an **"arrow" on the HW above.** *Habitat:* Lawns and other low open grassy areas such as dry fields and roadsides. *Abundance:* Three + brood areas: Mainly C-A. Mainly March–Sept. Almost all year in southeastern Arizona, where it is U. Immigrant to two-brood areas: Mainly R-U occasionally more common. Mainly late summer. RS to northern California and northern Nevada. *Food:* Bermuda grass and other grasses. *Comments:* A very variable immigrant northward.

Whirlabout *Polites vibex*

Below, male is orange-yellow with large smudged brown or black spots. These spots are larger and not as numerous as on Fiery Skipper. Above, note the smooth black border on the HW. Females are olive-gray below and sometimes (as on the individual in photo 5) have the marginal dark spots coalesced into a border. *Habitat:* Woodland edges, roadsides, disturbed grassy fields. *Abundance:* Immigrant to two-brood areas. Mainly R-U. April–Sept. RS to West Texas. *Food:* Grasses. *Comments:* The flight pattern of the Whirlabout lives up to its name.

Sachem *Atalopedes campestris*

Below, the ground color of males is yellow. There is a **squarish brown patch at the center of the HW bottom margin** and broad borders. Very rarely these darker markings are extremely faint so that superficially the HW appears to be all yellow. Above, the **large, black rectangular stigma** of males is unmistakable. **Females are large, with a characteristic dull brown ground color below**, and with a **HW postmedian chevron that closely resembles *Hesperia* skippers.** Unlike *Hesperia* skippers, the outer edge of the three subapical spots along the costal margin often curves outward and at least some of the spots are often hyaline. Note the two **very large, white hyaline spots on the FW** and the **black patch at the center of the FW** above. *Habitat:* Open disturbed fields, roadsides, suburban and urban lots, barrens. *Abundance:* A. South Texas north through Kansas. Feb./March–Nov.; U-C. Nebraska northward. Mainly June–Oct.; Mainly R-U, West Texas westward. March/April–Oct.; RS to North Dakota and Nevada. *Food:* Bermuda grass, crabgrass, and other grasses. *Comments:* This species is the source of many reports of rare *Hesperia* skippers. It could turn up almost anywhere.

1 **Fiery Skipper** ♂

2 **Whirlabout** ♂

3 **Sachem** ♂

4 **Fiery Skipper** ♀

5 **Whirlabout** ♀

6 **Sachem** ♀

7 **Fiery Skipper** ♂

8 **Whirlabout** ♂

9 **Sachem** ♂

10 **Fiery Skipper** ♀

11 **Whirlabout** ♀

12 **Sachem** ♀

Draco Skipper *Polites draco*

"Draco" is Latin for dragon, and so it seems fitting that this skipper has a **"lightning bolt" (with jagged inner edge) in the middle of the HW chevron**, both above and below. Some populations of Sandhill Skipper are similar, but usually have white HW veining. Hesperia Skippers lack the "lightning bolt." *Habitat:* Dry mountain meadows and forest openings. *Abundance:* Mainly U-C, but A in the White Mountains of Arizona and LR in the Cypress Hills of Saskatchewan. Late May/June–July. *Food:* Grasses. *Comments:* In most of its range, Draco Skippers are found only at high elevations, ranging up to treeline, but in Alberta they are reported to occur in foothills grasslands and forest openings.

Sonoran Skipper *Polites sonora*

Below, HW with a pale postmedian band and an **elongated pale basal spot**. Long Dash has a postmedian band that is wider and a pale basal spot that is not as elongated. Ground color below ranges from green-gray-brown in the Rocky Mountains (inset to photo 4), to yellow-brown most of the rest of the range (photo 4), to dark reddish-brown along the Pacific coast. Above, the ground color of males can be as shown or almost entirely orange. *Habitat:* Cool, wet meadows. *Abundance:* Mainly U-C, but R in the San Bernardino Mountains of southern California. Late May–Aug. Much shorter at any given locality. *Food:* Grasses.

Long Dash *Polites mystic*

Below, **HW with a broad pale yellow postmedian band** and a pale basal spot. Sonoran Skipper has a HW postmedian band that is narrower and a HW pale basal spot that is usually more elongated. Peck's Skippers have an even broader HW postmedian band and a more prominent outwardly-pointing central spot. Above, **males have a black patch outward from the stigma**—the stigma and the patch together creating the long dash. Females have a pattern similar to the males, with a dark area where the males have a stigma. *Habitat:* Moist to wet grassy habitats, including meadows and roadside ditches. *Abundance:* Mainly U-C but LR at the western edge of its range. Mainly June–July but as late as mid Aug. *Food:* Grasses.

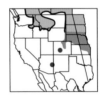

Peck's Skipper *Polites peckius*

Below, note the **very broad HW postmedian yellow patch** with the **central spot jutting outward** and the second smaller yellow patch at the base of the HW. *Habitat:* Wet mountain meadows, prairie marshes, and also disturbed moist areas. *Abundance:* Mainly LU-LC. Two-brood areas: May–Sept.; one-brood areas (including Arizona White Mountains): mainly mid June/late June–early Aug. *Food:* Grasses. *Comments:* The population in the White Mountains is separated by about 400 miles from other populations but looks remarkably similar.

1 Draco Skipper

2 Draco Skipper ♂

3 Draco Skipper ♀

4 Sonoran Skipper

5 Sonoran Skipper ♂

6 Sonoran Skipper ♀

7 Long Dash

8 Long Dash ♂

9 Long Dash ♀

10 Peck's Skipper

11 Peck's Skipper ♂

12 Peck's Skipper ♀

Rhesus Skipper *Polites rhesus*

This inhabitant of high grasslands is like a small Uncas Skipper, with a **bold white HW chevron** and **dark chocolate markings**. Note the **pure white fringes**. Above, dark with some white FW spots. Note the **white shoulders**. Uncas Skippers, and other similar species, have at least some dark markings on the fringes and some orange above. *Habitat:* High-elevation short grass prairie, often on high-quality blue grama grassland. *Abundance:* Mainly R. Some locations and occasional years, C. Mainly May–mid June, as late as mid July at some localities. *Food:* Blue grama grass. *Comments:* In the Arizona White Mountains, look for this species in iris-filled gullies on high, dry, open grassland. The yummy dark chocolate markings on the HW are Rhesus pieces.

Carus Skipper *Polites carus*

Below, **ground color is brown-gray**. Wing **fringes are gray**. HW has **distinct postmedian and basal white bands**. Above, with white shoulders. *Habitat:* Arid, open oak grassland. *Abundance:* R-U. Mid March–mid May, July–Sept. Perhaps only an immigrant to northern part of range, moving northward in late summer. July–Sept. Frequently strays outside the range shown—to extreme eastern California, northern Texas, and undoubtedly elsewhere. *Food:* Unknown. *Comments:* Unlike most species, Carus Skippers hilltop just *below* the tops of hills. With their precise markings and small black spots, Carus Skippers look like pen and ink drawings.

Sandhill Skipper *Polites sabuleti*

A widespread, variable species. Below, the HW has a prominent postmedian chevron that ranges from pale yellow to almost white. Mostly as shown in photo 7. The postmedian chevron extends outwardly along the veins and is connected inwardly to basal spots. Most populations have a **pattern inside the chevron that resembles a portion of a hand with an outward-pointing finger**. Many desert populations have the HW pattern washed out (see photo 8), while populations at high elevations in the California Sierra Nevadas and in south-central Colorado are the most distinct (see photos 10–12). Other similar species lack the finger-pointing pattern. Uncas Skippers have a sort of "finger," but it is wider (two veins wide), giving a quite different appearance. *Habitat:* A wide variety of dry grasslands. Most frequently on sandy areas, but also on lawns and high-elevation dry meadows. *Abundance:* LU. Three-brood areas (*chusca*); April–Sept.; R-U. Two-brood areas: May–June, Aug.–Sept.; U. One-brood areas (*tecumseh*); June–Sept. *Food:* Saltgrasses, Bermuda grass and other grasses. *Comments:* Single-brooded populations also occur at higher elevations in the Rocky Mountains, flying mainly late June–mid July.

1 Rhesus Skipper

2 Rhesus Skipper ♂

3 Rhesus Skipper ♀

4 Carus Skipper

5 Carus Skipper ♂

6 Sandhill Skipper ♀

7 **Sandhill Skipper** *(sabuleti)*

8 **Sandhill Skipper** *(chusca)*

9 **Sandhill Skipper** ♂ *(sabuleti)*

10 **Sandhill Skipper** *(ministigma)*

11 **Sandhill Skipper** *(tecumseh)*

12 **Sandhill Skipper** ♂ *(tecumseh)*

Tawny-edged Skipper *Polites themistocles*

Small. Below, usually unicolorous drab olive with a **strongly contrasting tawny orange FW margin**. However, some individuals and populations have a faint HW postmedian band and rarely individuals or a population will have a well-marked postmedian band (inset to photo 1). Above, **males have an intense thick black stigma** bordered by a bright orange FW costal margin. *Habitat:* Many open grassy situations, including low meadows, roadsides, mountain meadows and lawns. *Abundance:* C. Two-brood areas: May–June, Aug.–Sept.; U. one-brood areas. Mainly June–July. *Food:* Grasses.

Crossline Skipper *Polites origenes*

Medium-sized. Usually larger than Tawny-edged Skipper, the disjunct populations in Colorado and New Mexico being especially large. Below, the yellowish-brown ground color is usually lighter than on Tawny-edged Skipper, often with a "brassy" look, and there is less contrast between the HW and the costal margin of the FW. There is **usually at least a faint HW postmedian band**, occasionally strong. Above, **males have a less intense stigma than Tawny-edged and it narrows toward the base of the FW**. Note the **additional yellow spot just past the FW stigma**. Females above usually have a brighter FW costal margin and the HW yellow overscaling stops well short of the outer margin (usually reaching the outer margin on female Tawny-edged Skipper). *Habitat:* Low-elevation grassy meadows and fields. *Abundance:* LU-C. Mid June–July. *Food:* Purple top and other grasses in most of range, big bluestem and other grasses in Colorado–New Mexico.

Mardon Skipper *Polites mardon*

Wings are short and stubby with a rounded FW apex. Very similar to Long Dash, but Long Dash is found in a different range and habitat. Also similar to some Woodland Skippers, but FW subapical spots near outer margin are weaker on Mardon. *Habitat:* In Washington State, lowland pastures and grassy slopes. In northwestern California, mainly grassy areas in rhododendron/conifer forest in the fog belt. *Abundance:* LR. California–Oregon. Early June–early July; Oregon–Washington. Mid May–July. *Food:* Red fescue and probably other grasses.

Southern Broken-Dash *Wallengrenia otho*

Below, **HW postmedian band is often shaped like a 3** and ground color is bright reddish-brown. *Habitat:* Woodland openings and edges. *Abundance:* U. April–Oct. *Food:* Grasses. *Comments:* Northern Broken-Dash, *W. egeremet* (See *BTB: East* for illustration), is similar but is a much duller yellow-brown. It strays westward along the West's eastern border between Nebraska and Texas.

1 Tawny-edged Skipper

2 Tawny-edged Skipper ♂

3 Tawny-edged Skipper ♀

4 Crossline Skipper

5 Crossline Skipper ♂

6 Crossline Skipper ♀

7 Mardon Skipper ♀

8 Mardon Skipper ♂

9 Mardon Skipper ♀

10 Mardon Skipper ♂

11 Southern Broken-Dash

12 Southern Broken-Dash ♀

Arogos Skipper *Atrytone arogos*

Below, orange-yellow with **white HW fringes** and **whitish HW veins**. Note the **broad blackish border on the FW above**. Males have the orange portion of the FW unmarked, females with a black streak in the center of the orange portion. *Habitat:* Tall and mixed grass prairies. *Abundance:* LR-U. Two-brood areas: May/June–early July, Aug.–Sept.; one-brood areas: June–July. *Food:* Bluestem grasses. *Comments:* Very wary.

Delaware Skipper *Anatrytone logan*

Below, **clear bright unmarked yellow-orange below**. Usually the **fringes are orange**, sometimes tan. Above, orange with black borders and at least some **black veining**. Females have a black arrowhead at the base of the FW and another smaller black patch in the middle of the FW. Other orange skippers are larger and not so bright (Ottoe, Leonard's) or are much smaller (Least Skipper, Orange Skipperling). *Habitat:* Wet brushy areas in prairies or open foothills, such as stream or marsh edges or shrubby ravines. *Abundance:* Mainly R-U, becoming LC along eastern edge of the region. Two-brood areas: May/June–Sept./Oct.; one brood areas: Mid June–July. *Food:* Grasses

Two-spotted Skipper *Euphyes bimacula*

Large. Below, orange to brownish-orange with **paler veining** and a **striking white ray along the HW trailing margin**. Above, males have a restricted dull orange patch on both sides of the stigma. *Habitat:* Bogs and acidic sedge marshes. *Abundance:* LR. Mid June–mid July. *Food:* Sedges. *Comments:* This is perhaps the rarest and most local of any butterfly with an extensive range. The widely scattered colonies generally have a very low population density—usually only a few individuals are seen. Extensive wetland draining has made this species even rarer than it was historically. Dion Skipper, *Euphyes dion* (See *BTB:East* for illustration), barely enters the West in northeastern Texas. It is large and orange, with a pale ray through the middle of the HW.

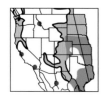

Dun Skipper *Euphyes vestris*

Dark brown all over. Below, occasionally with a faint postmedian patch and with a purplish sheen when fresh. Above, males are dark brown with a black stigma. In many populations, the **head is bright golden-orange, in most it is at least gold-green**. Female above is dark brown with two small pale spots near the center of the FW, the inner spot often shaped like a half moon. *Habitat:* Varied. Woods and edges, prairies and roadsides, seeps and springs in southern California. *Abundance:* Mainly U-LC, but LR in southern California and Saskatchewan. Two-brood areas: May–Sept.; one-brood areas: Mid May–early Sept., mainly June–July. *Food:* Sedges. *Comments:* Probably because it tolerates drier conditions than its relatives, this is the most common and widespread *Euphyes*.

1 Arogos Skipper

2 Arogos Skipper ♂

3 Arogos Skipper ♀

4 Delaware Skipper

5 Delaware Skipper ♂

6 Delaware Skipper ♀

7 Two-spotted Skipper

8 Two-spotted Skipper ♂

9 Two-spotted Skipper ♀

10 Dun Skipper

11 Dun Skipper ♂

12 Dun Skipper ♀

Woodland Skipper *Ochlodes sylvanoides*

Below, ground color is usually red- or yellow-brown (brown along the northern California coast north through Oregon), but pattern is variable. Individuals (often in the same population) vary from having a prominent broad HW pale chevron of large "blocky" spots (most frequent) to having only a faint trace of the chevron, to everything in between. Above, **FW has a jagged black border** and a dark patch past the FW cell that is not as black as on Long Dash. *Habitat:* Almost everywhere but in the deserts. *Abundance:* C-A. Mid June–early Oct. Mainly Aug.–Sept. *Food:* Grasses. *Comments:* One of the most widespread grass-skippers of the West. In many areas in late summer and fall, Woodland Skippers are the most common butterflies to be found.

Rural Skipper *Ochlodes agricola*

Small. Below, males are mainly unmarked, but usually have a somewhat darkened area in the middle of the HW. There are usually **prominent dark spots in the center of females' HW and often a pink blush.** Woodland Skipper is somewhat larger, usually more well-marked below and with jagged FW borders above. *Habitat:* Woodland openings and edges, roadsides and riparian habitats, all at low to moderate elevations. *Abundance:* U-C. May–July. *Food:* Grasses.

Yuma Skipper *Ochlodes yuma*

Large. Below, almost unmarked, usually with a washed-out look and a ground color of yellow to off-white. A very dark population flies in the Rio Grande Gorge of Taos County, New Mexico. Above, females often have a pale tracing of white spots on the FW. *Habitat:* Arid-country **seeps and marshes with giant reed** colonies. *Abundance:* LR (Colonies are mainly very localized and separated from other colonies by large distances, although once located a colony will usually contain a fair number of individuals). Two-brood areas: June–July, Aug.–Sept.; one-brood areas: July–Aug. *Food:* Giant reed. *Comments:* There are almost certainly undiscovered colonies of Yuma Skippers waiting for you to find them.

Snow's Skipper *Paratrytone snowi*

Medium-sized. Below, ground color is red-brown. The HW postmedian spotband is variably expressed. The **HW fringe is usually snowy white**, varying to off-white. Note the three prominent FW pale subapical spots along the costal margin. Above, rich brown with the same spot pattern on males and females, including an hourglass-shaped spot near the end of the FW cell. *Habitat:* High-elevation moist openings in pine forest. *Abundance:* LR-U. July–Aug./Sept. *Food:* Grasses. *Comments:* Flight is often very fast.

1 Woodland Skipper

2 Woodland Skipper ♂

3 Woodland Skipper ♀

4 Rural Skipper ♂ (inset: ♀)

5 Rural Skipper ♂

6 Rural Skipper ♀

7 Yuma Skipper

8 Yuma Skipper ♂

9 Yuma Skipper ♀

10 Snow's Skipper

11 Snow's Skipper ♂

12 Snow's Skipper ♀

Hobomok Skipper *Poanes hobomok*

Below, males and most females have an **extensive brown patch at the HW base and broad brown borders** enclosing a yellow postmedian area. Some females below (form pocahontas, photo 10) are suffused with dark brown but usually retain some of the usual pattern. They are very similar to female Umber Skippers, but their range is very different. *Habitat:* Woodland trails, openings, and edges. *Abundance:* U. Mid May–early July. *Food:* Grasses. *Comments:* Form pocahontas is unknown from Colorado populations.

Taxiles Skipper *Poanes taxiles*

Below, **male HW is mainly pale yellow with scattered brown rectangles** and a narrow brown border. Above, males are lustrously golden. **Below, females have a silvery white HW leading margin** and are dark yellow-brown with vague darker blotches (photo 11). *Habitat:* Woodland openings and edges, parks and gardens, small patches of woods in prairie. *Abundance:* Mainly C-A. June–July/mid Aug., as late as Sept. in southeastern Arizona. *Food:* Grasses. *Comments:* Zabulon Skipper, *Poanes zabulon* (see *BTB:East* for illustration), is similar but males are brighter and the brown patch at the base of the HW below is more extensive and encloses a small yellow patch. Females have the white along the HW costal margin placed more at the apex. Two broods, May–Sept.

Zabulon Skipper

Umber Skipper *Poanes melane*

Below, blotchy rusty-brown and yellow-brown with frosted margins. **Above, note the black area in the center of the FW** and the adjacent roundish yellow (male) or whitish (female) spot. *Habitat:* Woodland trails and openings, lowland and foothills canyons; often near water. *Abundance:* Mainly U-C. California (becoming R north of San Francisco); R, elsewhere. March/April–June, July–Sept./Oct. *Food:* Grasses.

Clouded Skipper *Lerema accius*

Both below and above, note the **three white subapical FW spots that usually curve outwardly.** Below, the HW frosting at the margin and at the lower middle of the wing sets off a dark vertical band that extends from the center of the HW trailing margin. The FW lacks the two white subapical spots near the outer margin that *Poanes* skippers have. *Habitat:* Prefers moist grassy areas in or near woods but wanders widely. *Abundance:* Three-brood areas: A. Almost all year; two-brood areas: C eastward, R-U westward, April–Nov. *Food:* Grasses. *Comments:* Taxonomically, this skipper is usually placed close to Least and Julia's Skippers, but it is shown here because of its similar appearance to *Poanes* skippers. One of the earliest-rising skippers, Clouded Skippers will be seen perching and courting early in the morning before their relatives have woken.

1 Hobomok Skipper

2 Hobomok Skipper ♂

3 Hobomok Skipper ♀

4 Taxiles Skipper ♂

5 Taxiles Skipper ♂

6 Taxiles Skipper ♀

7 Umber Skipper

8 Umber Skipper ♂

9 Umber Skipper ♀

10 Hobomok Skipper ♀
form Pocahontas

11 Taxiles Skipper ♀

12 Clouded Skipper

Dusted-Skippers (genus *Atrytonopsis*)

These are brown to gray, largish skippers with strong white eyebrows. Most species have an affinity for rocky canyons or boulder-strewn washes. The species on these pages have dull HWs both below, mainly with two slightly darker bars, and above. The four species on pages 278–279 have more prominent HW white markings, both above and below.

Dusted Skipper *Atrytonopsis hianna*

Below, because the white eyeline does not go completely around the eye, the black eye with white above and below gives this species a **masked appearance**. Wings have few markings but margins are frosted. *Habitat:* Dry prairies, barrens, and openings in oak-pine woodlands with bluestem grasses. *Abundance:* LU. Mainly mid/late May–mid June. As early as late April in Texas, as late as early July in South Dakota. *Food:* Bluestem grasses. *Comments:* Flight is low and difficult to follow.

Viereck's Skipper *Atrytonopsis vierecki*

Below, gray-brown, usually with a **faint pale spot near the base of the HW**. The **HW fringe is gray, not white**. The white eyeline is continuous. Above, note the **hourglass-shaped pale spot in the FW cell**. Dusted Skipper is smaller, and darker with a masked appearance. Deva and Moon-marked Skippers have white HW fringes below and Deva lacks the FW cell hourglass spot. *Habitat:* Washes through sparse oak-juniper-pinyon woodland and dry gulches on high prairies. *Abundance:* U-C. West Texas. April–May; elsewhere, mainly May–June. *Food:* Unknown. *Comments:* Often chooses small rocks for perching.

Moon-marked Skipper *Atrytonopsis lunus*

Large. Below, against the dark brown ground color the bold **white HW fringe** looks like a crescent moon. There are usually no pale spots on the HW. Note the **hourglass-shaped spot in the FW cell** above. *Habitat:* Openings in mid-elevation mountain oak woodland, especially in canyons. *Abundance:* U-C. July–Aug. *Food:* Bull grass. *Comments:* In love with thistles.

Deva Skipper *Atrytonopsis deva*

Below, HW fringe is off-white. Above, with only a few pale markings, lacking an hourglass-shaped spot in the FW cell. Viereck's Skipper has a gray fringe below and has an hourglass-shaped spot in the FW cell above. *Habitat:* Openings in mid-elevation mountain oak woodland, especially in canyons. *Abundance:* C-A. Southeastern Arizona. Late April–early July, mainly May–June; Becoming R northward. Mainly June–early July. *Food:* Unknown. *Comments:* Some years, the flowering shrubs in southeastern Arizona canyons swarm with Deva Skippers. Even then, their beautiful song is heard only by the cognoscenti.

1 Dusted Skipper

2 Dusted Skipper

3 Viereck's Skipper

4 Viereck's Skipper

5 Moon-marked Skipper

6 Moon-marked Skipper

7 Deva Skipper

8 Deva Skipper

White-barred Skipper *Atrytonopsis pittacus*

Below, the **HW has a white postmedian bar of translucent pale spots** that can be obvious or difficult to see, depending upon the light. **HW fringe is unchecked white.** The FW above has an hourglass-shaped spot in the cell and the **HW above has a straight white bar.** Other species with white postmedian bands below have checked fringes. Above, Viereck's Skipper has no HW white spots, while Python Skipper has a curved HW white band. *Habitat:* Mid-elevation grassy oak woodlands. *Abundance:* U-C. Arizona; R. West Texas. March–May, sometimes a partial second brood Sept.–Oct. *Food:* Unknown. *Comments:* An avid mudpuddler and sometime hilltopper.

Python Skipper *Atrytonopsis python*

Both below and above, there is a white patch just below the antennal club. Below, the HW is strikingly marked with white, lavender-tinged gray and some black. Note the **prominent, narrow white postmedian band that cuves outward** and the checked fringes. **Above, FW has yellowish spots** and the **HW has a curved pale spotband.** Cestus Skipper has a wider postmedian band and lacks the white patch just below the antennal club. *Habitat:* Openings in mid- to high-elevation oak woodland. *Abundance:* C. Southeastern Arizona; Mainly R-U elsewhere. May–June/early July. *Food:* Unknown.

Cestus Skipper *Atrytonopsis cestus*

Both below and above, there is no white patch just below the antennal club. Below, the HW is strikingly marked with white, gray, and some black. Both below and above, note the **prominent, wide white postmedian band** and the checked fringes. **Above, the FW cell spot looks more like a Z** than an hourglass. *Habitat:* The saguaro/mesquite grassland interface. *Abundance:* LR-LU. Mid April–May. Mid Aug.–early Oct. *Food:* Bamboo muhly. *Comments:* Usually perches on steep rock faces where it can be difficult to see. A rock thrown parallel to the rock face often looks like a speeding Cestus Skipper to the intently gazing male, inducing a brief investigatory sortie that allows you to determine his position.

Sheep Skipper *Atrytonopsis edwardsii*

Large. Below, ground color of dull brown with extensive gray overscaling. HW variably expresses some pale yellowish spots. Fringe is checked. FW is more rounded than that of other co-occurring *Atrytonopsis.* Above, similar to Python Skipper but spots are not so yellow. *Habitat:* Openings in low- to mid-elevation oak grassland, especially in rocky canyons. *Abundance:* R-U. Mid April–June, Aug.–mid Oct. Mainly May and Aug. *Food:* Side oats grama. *Comments:* Quite partial to perching on rock ledges.

1 White-barred Skipper

2 White-barred Skipper

3 Python Skipper

4 Python Skipper

5 Cestus Skipper

6 Cestus Skipper

7 Sheep Skipper

8 Sheep Skipper

Roadside-Skippers (genus *Amblyscirtes*)

The great pleasure derived from learning the roadside-skippers is, fortunately, as close as most of us will get to understanding sadomasochism. They are small, dully colored, and many of the species closely resemble one another, while the others are not far off!

Texas Roadside-Skipper *Amblyscirtes texanae*

Below, dull blurry gray, often with an olive cast when fresh. Above, FW spots are pale yellow, including a small spot in the FW cell. *Habitat:* Canyons and washes in low-elevation arid regions. *Abundance:* R-U. Eastward. May–Sept.; Westward perhaps there is only a single brood as it is reported only mid July–early Sept. *Food:* Bulb panicgrass. *Comments:* Males often perch on rocks in washes or gullies.

Bronze Roadside-Skipper *Amblyscirtes aenus*

Below, variable. Most populations are relatively unmarked below, with **gray overscaling over the entire HW** and a few vague pale spots. Some individuals, especially in lowland southeastern Arizona, are more strongly marked (see inset to photo 3). Fringes are checked. **Both below and above, there are at least some orange/copper-colored scales on the FW.** Above, the FW spots are usually yellow-tinged. There is **usually no spot in the FW cell**, or, if present, it is small and vague. Also see Common Roadside-Skipper. *Habitat:* Woodland openings and prairie gulches. *Abundance:* Mainly U-C, but R along limits of range. Late April–Sept. Mainly May–June northward and June–Aug. elsewhere. *Food:* Grasses. *Comments:* Males often perch on rocks in washes or gullies.

Cassus Roadside-Skipper *Amblyscirtes cassus*

Below, **FW with bright orange and with a pale spot in the cell** (often obscured by the HW). The fringes are strongly checked. The HW is a pepper-and-salt gray-brown, with vague paler spots, especially a short median and longer postmedian band, giving the effect of two parallel pale bars. **Above, with extensive bright orange** on both FW and HW, including large orange spots on the FW. Bronze Roadside-Skippers are usually darker below and not as orange above. *Habitat:* Moist open situations in mid- to high-elevation woodland. *Abundance:* C. Mid June–mid Aug. *Food:* Grasses.

Slaty Roadside-Skipper *Amblyscirtes nereus*

Both below and above, **fringes are almost completely unchecked**. Below, ground color is a buffy yellow-brown wearing to a dull gray-brown. The **HW postmedian band is irregular**, often shaped vaguely like a loose 3. Above, the ground color is black. The FW has a white postmedian spotband and the **HW has a spotband** (occasionally absent) that replicates the spotband below. *Habitat:* Grassy openings in mid-elevation oak-juniper and pine woodlands. *Abundance:* R-U. July–Aug. *Food:* Common beardgrass.

1 Texas Roadside-Skipper

2 Texas Roadside-Skipper

3 Bronze Roadside-Skipper

4 Bronze Roadside-Skipper

5 Cassus Roadside-Skipper

6 Cassus Roadside-Skipper

7 Slaty Roadside-Skipper

8 Slaty Roadside-Skipper

Large Roadside-Skipper *Amblyscirtes exoteria*

Large (for a roadside-skipper). Below, with scattered gray overscaling when fresh that very rapidly wears to a **flat brown ground color**. HW with scattered white spots. The **spots in the postmedian spotband are pointed outwardly** and are aligned in a straight line, but the **4th spot up is smaller and slightly displaced inwardly, making the 5th spot seem to stick outward**. Above, often with dull orange overscaling. *Habitat:* Openings in mid- to high-elevation oak and coniferous woodland. *Abundance:* C-A in southeastern Arizona; becoming R-U northward. Mid June–Aug. *Food:* Bullgrass.

Dotted Roadside-Skipper *Amblyscirtes eos*

Striking when fresh. **Below, bold white rounded HW spots are outlined by black** that becomes difficult to see on worn individuals. Postmedian spotband is irregular. Above, there is no white spot in the FW cell. *Habitat:* Grassy areas in sparse oak woodland. *Abundance:* R-U. Two-brood areas: Mid March–mid Oct.; mainly mid March–April/May, July–Aug.; one-brood areas: mainly mid June–July. *Food:* Obtuse panic-grass.

Toltec Roadside-Skipper *Amblyscirtes tolteca*

Below, similar to Dotted Roadside-Skipper but usually with a **white spot in the middle of the HW trailing margin** (sometimes faint) that Dotted and Elissa Roadside-Skippers lack. Note the **prominent hourglass-shaped white spot in the FW cell**, both below and above, and the **pale bar in the middle of the HW** above. *Habitat:* Canyons and washes at low to mid elevations in desert ranges. *Abundance:* LR. Mid May–mid Sept. *Food:* Grasses.

Elissa Roadside-Skipper *Amblyscirtes elissa*

Similar to Dotted Roadside-Skipper but, both below and above, with a **small oval white spot in the FW cell**. Toltec Roadside-Skipper usually has a white spot in the middle of the HW trailing margin that this species lacks, has a pale bar in the middle of the HW above, and has a larger hourglass-shaped spot in the FW cell. *Habitat:* Edges of desert canyons and washes. *Abundance:* LR. Mid July–mid Aug. *Food:* Side-oats grama. *Comments:* Adults typically nectar early in the morning. Males perch and display from about 8 A.M. to 9:30 A.M., after which locating an individual becomes problematical.

1 Large Roadside-Skipper

2 Large Roadside-Skipper

3 Dotted Roadside-Skipper

4 Dotted Roadside-Skipper

5 Toltec Roadside-Skipper

6 Toltec Roadside-Skipper

7 Elissa Roadside-Skipper

8 Elissa Roadside-Skipper

Common Roadside-Skipper *Amblyscirtes vialis*

Both below and above, note the **strongly checkered fringes**. Below, the **HW is almost black with gray "frosting"** over the outer portion, but not along the HW leading margin. The **FW subapical spots are usually wider at the costal margin**, forming a white wedge. Other small dark skippers such as female Taxiles or Dusted Skippers lack the checkered fringes. Bronze Roadside-Skippers have frosting over the entire HW and usually do not have wedge-shaped FW subapical spots. *Habitat:* Woodland edges and grassy openings. *Abundance:* Two-brood areas: U. April–June, partial second brood July–Aug.; one-brood areas: R-LU. mainly May–July, as late as Aug./Sept. in parts of Oregon and the California Sierra Nevadas. *Food:* Grasses. *Comments:* Rarely common anywhere, this is the most widespread roadside-skipper in North America.

Nysa Roadside-Skipper *Amblyscirtes nysa*

The **mottled pattern below** nysally distinguishes this species from our other roadside-skippers (to paraphrase Klots). *Habitat:* Thorn scrub and canyons and washes in sparsely wooded arid regions; also lawns and gardens and roadsides in disturbed areas eastward. *Abundance:* Mainly R-U. March/April–Sept./Oct., most common March–April, July–Sept. *Food:* Grasses. *Comments:* Males love to perch early in the morning in the middle of trails, roads, or gullies.

Orange-headed Roadside-Skipper *Amblyscirtes phylace*

An orange-headed stunner trimmed with white fringe. How could you go wrong? Well, some populations of Dun Skippers, especially in northern Mexico, have heads that are almost as bright orange as this species. They are much larger than this species and their fringes are pale, but not white. Golden-headed Scallopwings are spreadwing skippers and open their wings in unison. *Habitat:* High prairie gulches and canyons in sparsely wooded regions. *Abundance:* R. Southeastern Ariz. July–early Aug.; U-C northward. Mainly May–June/early July. *Food:* Big bluestem grass. *Comments:* Did I forget to mention the lovely ultramarine blue color below? Or the fact that those pesky Dun Skippers can be rather blue-purply below also?

Orange-edged Roadside-Skipper *Amblyscirtes fimbriata*

An orange fringed version of Orange-headed Roadside-Skipper. The fringe wears to a pale orange that, if desperate enough, you can turn into white. *Habitat:* Moist grassy openings in high-elevation pine forest. *Abundance:* LC. Late May–Aug. Mainly mid June–July. *Food:* Grasses. *Comments:* North of Mexico, this winsome species is found only high in the Huachuca and Chiricahua Mountains of extreme southeastern Arizona. Individuals will sometimes move downslope into oak woodlands late in the season.

1 Common Roadside-Skipper

2 Common Roadside-Skipper

3 Nysa Roadside-Skipper

4 Nysa Roadside-Skipper

5 Orange-headed Roadside-Skipper

6 Orange-headed Roadside-Skipper

7 Orange-edged Roadside-Skipper

8 Orange-edged Roadside-Skipper

Celia's Roadside-Skipper *Amblyscirtes celia*

Below, dark grizzled gray-brown-black with vague, small white HW spots. Above, HW has white spots. This species resembles members of the Dotted Roadside-Skipper group on page 283 but only Dotted Roadside-Skipper itself overlaps it in range. Dotted Roadside-Skipper is not as dark below and has larger, brighter, and more well-defined white spots. Above, Dotted Roadside-Skipper lacks the HW white spots that this species has. **Habitat:** Woodland trails, creek bottoms, moist open woodland, suburban lawns and gardens. **Abundance:** C eastward, becoming R in West Texas. April/May–early June, late

June–early Sept. **Food:** Grasses. **Comments:** Bell's Roadside-Skipper, *Amblyscirtes belli* (See *BTB: East* for illustration), barely enters the West. It is extremely similar to Celia's Roadside-Skipper. It is usually even blacker than Celia's Roadside-Skipper, often with a purplish sheen but, unlike Celia's Roadside-Skipper, the HW apex is not frosted. The HW pale spots are often even more indistinct than on Celia's Roadside-Skipper. It is found along trails through moist, rich wood-

Bell's Roadside-Skipper

lands and along woodland creeksides, where it is LR-LU, flying April/May–early June, July–early Sept.

Oslar's Roadside-Skipper *Amblyscirtes oslari*

Below, the **soft gray HW has a pale postmedian band** and the **FW disk has some orange**. The **HW fringe is unchecked, pale gray-brown**, often white-tipped. Above, largely unmarked with extensive, scattered dull-orange scales. Cassus Skipper is more aggressively gray-brown below with a checked fringe. Simius Roadside-Skipper has a well-developed HW median band below and its fringe is whiter. **Habitat:** A species of the high prairies and Rocky Mountain foothills. Most often found in prairie ravines, badlands, stream beds, and canyons and gulches in arid regions. **Abundance:** R-U (sometimes LC in Colorado). Mainly mid May–July, but mid July–early Sept. in southeastern Arizona. **Food:** Side-oats grama. **Comments:** Mating occurs in gully and canyon bottoms.

Simius Roadside-Skipper *"Amblyscirtes" simius*

Below, the **soft gray HW has both median and postmedian pale bands** and the **FW disk is orange**. Above, very variable. From almost all orange, to mixed orange and black, to almost all black. Note the pale gray FW costal margin. **Habitat:** High, short grass prairie. **Abundance:** Mainly R-U, but LC in parts of Wyoming and Colorado. Mid May–Aug. Mainly mid July–Aug. in southeastern Arizona; possibly two broods in West Texas and southeastern New Mexico, April–May, June–July; mainly June–July elsewhere. RS? to southern Saskatchewan (three records). **Food:** Blue grama grass. **Comments:** "Hilltopping" takes place on small knolls on gently rolling grassland. Known not to be an *Amblyscirtes*, the species is, for now, without a genus that it can call home.

1 Celia's Roadside-Skipper

2 Celia's Roadside-Skipper

3 Oslar's Roadside-Skipper

4 Oslar's Roadside-Skipper

5 Simius Roadside-Skipper

6 Simius Roadside-Skipper

7 Simius Roadside-Skipper

8 Simius Roadside-Skipper

Eufala Skipper *Lerodea eufala*

Grayish-brown with a **pale body**. Often identifiable at a distance because it frequently gives two quick "wing-claps" after landing. Below, often with faint traces of a pale HW postmedian band vaguely shaped like a 3. Above, the FW cell often has one or two small pale spots. *Habitat:* A wide variety of open situations. *Abundance:* Three + brood areas: U-C, mainly C eastward and U westward, almost all year; two-brood areas: C immigrant eastward, mainly June–Oct., R-U immigrant in California, mainly Aug.–Oct. *Food:* Grasses.

Wandering Skipper *Panoquina errans*

Below, yellow-brown with some **HW cream-colored spots** and usually with **pale yellow veins**. The **abdomen is striped lengthwise**. *Habitat:* Coastal marshes along river mouths and other brackish waters. *Abundance:* LR-LU. July–Sept. *Food:* Saltgrasses. *Comments:* Disappearing from many areas.

Ocola Skipper *Panoquina ocola*

The **wings are long and narrow**. Plain, dull yellowish-brown below with the **distal one-quarter of the wings darker brown**. Sometimes with a purple sheen when fresh. Note the **lengthwise-striped abdomen**. *Habitat:* A wide variety. *Abundance:* Three + brood areas: C, almost all year; two-brood areas: R, mainly July–Oct.; RS to southeastern Arizona. *Food:* Grasses. *Comments:* Another species whose influx northward varies greatly from year to year.

Violet-clouded Skipper *Lerodea arabus*

Below, **HW has a dark central blotch** (often like an inverted triangle), and pale areas at the wing base and outer margin. Fresh individuals are tinged with violet. Eufala Skipper is smaller and a weaker flyer. *Habitat:* Arid gullies and canyons, spilling out into nearby flower gardens. *Abundance:* LU. All year, mainly early spring and late fall. *Food:* Grasses.

Violet-banded Skipper *Nyctelius nyctelius*

Below, the **HW has alternating pale and dark bands**, the pale bands with a violaceous sheen when fresh. A **black spot is near the middle of the HW leading margin**. Abdomen with black and white rings. *Habitat:* Thorn scrub. *Abundance:* RS to southeastern Arizona and the Austin area. *Food:* Grasses.

Brazilian Skipper *Calpodes ethlius*

Very large. Red-tinged brown below with **three or four large white or translucent spots in an angled line** on the HW. *Habitat:* Suburban and urban gardens with cannas. *Abundance:* R. Very variably abundant immigrant, mainly July–Oct. *Food:* Cannas. *Comments:* This species possesses a strong emigrational drive. Strays have been recorded in southern California, Utah, west Texas, and eastern Nebraska. Keep your canna ready!

1 Eufala Skipper

2 Eufala Skipper

3 Wandering Skipper

4 Ocola Skipper

5 Violet-clouded Skipper

6 Violet-banded Skipper

7 Brazilian Skipper (Shown at 1½ x Life Size)

Giant-Skippers (subfamily Megathyminae)

The aptly named giant-skippers are big, fat, and powerful. The *Megathymus* feed on yuccas, while *Agathymus* caterpillars feed on agaves. The yucca-feeders occasionally open their wings while landed, the agave-feeders more rarely do, making field identification even more difficult. Some species, for example, Orange Giant-Skipper, have been treated as consisting of seven different species, each with tiny ranges. The adults of some species, such as Ursine Giant-Skipper, are rarely seen. Typically, people locate caterpillars and raise them to adults.

Yucca Giant-Skipper *Megathymus yuccae*
Very large and black with some marginal frosting. Other giant-skippers are not so black. Above, the HW marginal yellow band has a smooth inner border. On Strecker's Giant-Skipper it is usually scalloped inwardly. *Habitat:* Yucca grassland and semidesert. *Abundance:* LR-U. Feb.–early June, mainly March–April. *Food:* Yuccas. *Comments:* Adults are rarely seen.

Strecker's Giant-Skipper *Megathymus streckeri*
Very large. Grayer, not as black as Yucca Giant-Skipper and with **a few scattered HW white spots** that Yucca Giant-Skipper lacks. Note the **pale HW margin** that agave giant-skippers lack. *Habitat:* Rolling yucca grassland. *Abundance:* R-LC. Mid May–early July. *Food:* Yuccas. *Comments:* In flight, rapidly beating HWs look like a black tail with a white border.

Ursine Giant-Skipper *Megathymus ursus*
Huge and unmistakable with **white antennas**. There is **blue-white overscaling over more than two-thirds of the wing** below. *Habitat:* Yucca grassland/oak woodland interface. *Abundance:* R. Mainly July–Aug. but reported April–June in the Big Bend, Texas, area. Strangely, the reported flight period in nearby southeastern New Mexico is July–Aug. *Food:* Yuccas. *Comments:* Extremely rarely seen as an adult.

Mojave Giant-Skipper *Agathymus alliae*
Individuals are probably not separable from Arizona Giant-Skipper. For now, field identification must rely on location and foodplant. *Habitat:* Mid-elevation dry rocky limestone hillsides with pinyon-juniper. *Abundance:* LR-LU. Sept.–Nov., mainly late Sept.–Oct. *Food:* Utah agave. *Comments:* Perhaps most common in the Spring Mountains of Nevada.

Poling's Giant-Skipper *Agathymus polingi*
The **smallest giant-skipper** often has the most **contrastingly patterned HW** below. Very similar to Huachuca and Arizona Giant-Skippers. Use size and association with shindaggers for identification. *Habitat:* Dry, shindagger-covered slopes. *Abundance:* LC-LA. Oct. *Food:* Shindagger. *Comments:* Adults of this little giant-skipper are sometimes so common on shindagger-covered hillsides that the pain from your bloody ankles will melt away. Hey, maybe I should have worn boots!

1 Yucca Giant-Skipper

2 Yucca Giant-Skipper

3 Strecker's Giant-Skipper

4 Strecker's Giant-Skipper

5 Ursine Giant-Skipper

6 Mojave Giant-Skipper (museum specimen)

7 Poling's Giant-Skipper

8 Poling's Giant-Skipper

Arizona Giant-Skipper *Agathymus aryxna*

Very similar to Huachuca Giant-Skipper but normally found at lower elevations. Also similar to Orange Giant-Skipper but **fringes are almost always checked white and black** and there is almost no overlap in range. *Habitat:* Low- to mid-elevation arid grassland/open woodland. *Abundance:* U–C. Sept.–Nov., mainly Oct. *Food:* Palmer's agave, desert agave, and others. *Comments:* Most likely to be found mudpuddling.

California Giant-Skipper *Agathymus stephensi*

Often more mottled than other giant-skippers, **usually with some rusty-brown spots**, especially where indicated on photo 2. *Habitat:* Desert hillsides and canyons along the western edge of the Colorado desert. *Abundance:* U. Sept.–early Oct. *Food:* Desert agave. *Comments:* Usually lands with its head up.

Huachuca Giant-Skipper *Agathymus evansi*

Averages larger and more well-marked than Arizona Giant-Skipper, but this is not much to go on. Probably not separable except by higher-elevation habitat and association with foodplant. *Habitat:* North of Mexico, found only above about 5500 ft. in open pine-oak forest in the Huachuca Mountains and vicinity. *Abundance:* C. Mid Aug.–mid Nov., mainly Sept. *Food:* Parry's agave, var. huachucensis. *Comments:* Most likely to be found mudpuddling.

Orange Giant-Skipper *Agathymus neumoegeni*

Usually with **orange hairs on the thorax and abdomen** and with **fringes checked buffy and black**. Arizona Giant-Skippers have fringes checked white and black. *Habitat:* Arid grassland/open woodland usually at mid-elevations. *Abundance:* R–U. Aug.–Oct. *Food:* A variety of agaves.

Mary's Giant-Skipper *Agathymus mariae*

Usually with a **silvery reflection below**. HW may be unmarked or strongly marked. See Coahuila Giant-Skipper for separation from that species. *Habitat:* Lecheguilla-covered, rocky Chihuahuan desert. *Abundance:* R–U. Sept.–Nov., mainly Oct. *Food:* Lecheguilla. *Comments:* If you love 100° heat and laugh at a baking sun, are inspired by desolate landscapes virtually devoid of butterflies, and shrug off the pain of jabbing plant spines, then searching for this butterfly is right up your alley!

Coahuila Giant-Skipper *Agathymus remingtoni*

Below, brownish HW is strongly marked. **Spots in the HW postmedian spotband are strongly pointed outwardly** both below and above, and, especially above, **individual spots are very thin**. There is no orange on the wings, including bases of FW and HW where Mary's Giant-Skipper has orange. *Habitat:* Lecheguilla-covered, rocky Chihuahuan desert. *Abundance:* LR. Aug.–Nov., mainly mid Sept.–mid Oct. *Food:* Lecheguilla.

1 Arizona Giant-Skipper

2 California Giant-Skipper

3 Huachuca Giant-Skipper

4 Orange Giant-Skipper

5 Mary's Giant-Skipper

6 Mary's Giant-Skipper

7 Mary's Giant-Skipper

8 Coahuila Giant-Skipper (museum specimen)

Hawaiian Butterflies

Butterflies in Hawaii fly essentially all year and, for the most part, species are found throughout all the major islands, in gardens and parks. There are only two species of butterflies native to the Hawaiian Islands—Hawaiian Blue and Kamehameha Lady, neither of which is found elsewhere in the world. Both of these are great butterflies.

Kamehameha Lady *Vanessa tameamea*

This is a big butterfly, only a little smaller than a Mourning Cloak. Although Painted Lady and American Lady are now found in Hawaii, the bright red coloration of Kamehameha Lady, along with its bold black markings and large size, make it unmistakable. Its flight is very high, comfortably flying 15–20 feet off the ground—unlike other ladies. Although very attracted to flowing sap, it will nectar at flowers, including the yellow blossoms of a tree legume. This species is uncommon and generally restricted to the ever-fewer areas with native vegetation. Its major caterpillar foodplant is mamaki.

Hawaiian Blue *Vaga blackburni*

This butterfly is a minty shade of green, somewhat like an Arizona Hairstreak. It is most closely related to some Asian species that are relatives of the azures. Who would think that there would be a violet-topped, green-bottomed blue? It also is uncommon and restricted to native highlands habitat where its main caterpillar foodplant is the native acacia, koa.

Another 13 species have found their way to the islands in historical times, almost all of them introduced intentionally or accidentally by humans. Species that occur elsewhere in the West are treated on the previous pages, another three are shown here, and one, Banana Skipper, is unillustrated. With so few species, identification is easy. The 13 introduced species are:

Chinese Swallowtail *Papilio xuthus* Opposite page
The only swallowtail in Hawaii. A widespread Asian species.

Cabbage White *Pieris rapae* Pg. 55
Lantana Scrub-Hairstreak *Strymon bazochii* Pg. 105
Introduced in an absurd attempt to control introduced lantana.

Red-spotted Hairstreak *Tmolus echion* Opposite page
Ditto.

Pea Blue *Lampides boeticus* Opposite page ˙
Ranges through much of Eurasia and Africa.

Western Pygmy-Blue *Brephidium exile* Pg. 107
Gulf Fritillary *Agraulis vanillae* Pg. 135
Painted Lady *Vanessa cardui* Pg. 189
American Lady *Vanessa virginiensis* Pg. 189
Red Admiral *Vanessa atalanta* Pg. 189
Monarch *Danaus plexippus* Pg. 215
Very pale to almost white individuals are fairly common.

Fiery Skipper *Hylephila phyleus* Pg. 263
Banana Skipper *Erionota torus*
A large, crepuscular, banana-loving Asian species.

1 Chinese Swallowtail ($^2/_3$ x Life Size)

2 Chinese Swallowtail ($^2/_3$ x Life Size)

3 Kamehameha Lady ($^3/_4$ x Life Size)

4 Kamehameha Lady ($^3/_4$ x Life Size)

5 Red-spotted Hairstreak

6 Hawaiian Blue

7 Hawaiian Blue

8 Pea Blue

9 Pea Blue

Photos 5–9 shown at $1^1/_4$ x Life Size

RARE STRAYS AND EASTERN SPECIES
MARGINALLY ENTERING THE WEST

White-dotted Cattleheart *Parides alopius*
A small, black Mexican swallowtail with a HW postmedian row of white spots. One record from southeastern Arizona.

Zebra Swallowtail *Eurytides marcellus* See *BTB: East* for illustration
The black-striped white triangular wings on this small swallowtail are distinctive. Strays just west of the eastern border of the region in Texas, Kansas, and Nebraska.

Broad-banded Swallowtail *Papilio astyalus*
Very similar to Ornythion Swallowtail. Males have a yellow spot in the FW cell above that Ornythion males lack. Females can be tailed or untailed. RS to southeastern Arizona, late July–mid Sept.

Three-tailed Swallowtail *Papilio pilumnus*
Resembles Pale Swallowtail with black bands much wider so that cream-yellow bands are narrow. Also has red-orange postmedian spots along the HW inner margin and three tails. RS to southeastern Arizona.

Palamedes Swallowtail *Papilio palamedes* See *BTB: East* for illustration
Dark brown with yellow postmedian and submarginal bands. Has strayed to the San Antonio, Texas, area and been reported from northern New Mexico (once). A butterfly of the southeastern United States with disjunct populations in northeastern Mexico.

Ruby-spotted Swallowtail *Papilio anchisiades*
Black with pink-red median and postmedian spots on the HW. RS to San Antonio, Texas, area, west Texas, and southeastern Arizona.

Mexican Dartwhite *Catasticta nimbice*
A medium-sized white that is black! with wide median band of yellow or yellowish white. In the 1970s and '80s, a small colony was apparently established in the Green Gulch area of Big Bend NP. Although now gone, probably still a RS to Big Bend, Texas.

Giant White *Ganyra josephina*
A very large Mexican white, usually larger than *phoebis* sulphurs, with a strong black spot at the end of the FW cell. RS to New Mexico (1 record) and western Kansas (1 record).

Howarth's White *Ganyra howarthi*
Very similar to Giant White but about 3/4 the size. A stray and irregular colonist to southwestern Arizona, especially at Organ Pipe Cactus National Monument. Mainly found in thorn scrub woodland on sand dunes along the coast or along sandy washes. RS to southeastern Arizona. Multiple broods. All year.

Florida White *Appias drusilla* See *BTB: East* for illustration
A large white with pale antennal clubs. FW has solid black border, not extending inward along the veins. Some orange at the base of the HW leading margin. RS to Kansas, Colorado, and southeastern Arizona.

Great Southern White *Ascia monuste* See *BTB: East* for illustration
A large white with turquoise antennal clubs. FW has wavy black border with black extending inward along the veins. RS to Kansas, Colorado, southeastern Arizona.

Sonoran Marble *Euchloe guaymasensis*
Pale yellow above. Sparsely marbled below. Common in Sonora, Mexico, north to about Imuris, about 25 miles south of the Arizona border; there is one U.S. record from Bisbee, Arizona, late March 1997. This species hilltops.

Apricot Sulphur *Phoebis argante*
Similar to Large Orange Sulphur but the FW diagonal band is unbroken. RS to west Texas.

Statira Sulphur *Phoebis statira* See *BTB: East* for illustration.
Similar to Cloudless Sulphur but the outer 1/3 of the wings below appear to be "puckered." There is some yellow at the base of the FW costal margin and along the FW disk. RS to north and west to western Kansas and New Mexico.

Tailed Sulphur *Phoebis neocypris*
Similar to Large Orange Sulphur but HW with very definite tail. RS to southeastern Arizona.

Harvester *Feniseca tarquinius* See *BTB: East* for illustration
A medium-sized gossamer-wing that is bright orange above with bold black markings. Below, the FW disk is orange and the HW is dull reddish-brown with delicate white markings. Strays to eastern edge of region in Texas and, to a lesser extent, Kansas and Nebraska.

Marius Hairstreak *Rekoa marius*
A fairly large hairstreak. Below, similar to Red-lined Scrub-Hairstreak but browner and without any red in the postmedian line. Above, males are dull iridescent blue and females are pale gray. RS to southeastern Arizona.

White M Hairstreak *Parrhasius m-album* See *BTB: East* for illustration.
HW red-orange spot is displaced inwardly. Brilliant iridescent blue above. Resident west to about Fort Worth, Texas. Strays west to Austin, Texas, area.

Edwards' Hairstreak *Satyrium edwardsii* See *BTB: East* for illustration
Similar to Banded Hairstreak, but usually browner with HW postmedian band broken into spots surrounded by white. RS along eastern edge of the region.

Yojoa Scrub-Hairstreak *Strymon yojoa*
Similar to Lacey's Scrub-Hairstreak but with a white FW cell-end bar, a straighter HW postmedian line, and a more definite white band just outside the HW postmedian line. One recent report from southeastern Arizona.

Bromeliad Scrub-Hairstreak *Strymon serapio*
Similar to Red-lined Scrub-Hairstreak but red on HW postmedian band is much broader. RS? Has been found on limestone hills overlooking the Rio Grande River in Big Bend NP, Texas. Associated with a terrestrial bromeliad (*Hechtia scarisoa*).

Clytie Ministreak *Ministrymon clytie*
Looks like a small Red-spotted Hairstreak (pg. 295) but with an red-orange FW cell-end bar. U in the Lower Rio Grande Valley, it occurs north to Uvalde County, Texas, possibly as a temporary colonist.

Red-bordered Metalmark *Caria ino*
Tiny. Dark iridescent ultramarine blue above with orange borders, a metallic submarginal line, and a very wavy FW costal margin. RS from the Lower Rio Grande Valley to the San Antonio, Texas, area.

Mexican Silverspot *Dione moneta*
Similar to Gulf Fritillary but the ground color above is darker and there are no black-rimmed white spots in the FW cell above. RS to west Texas.

Julia (Heliconian) *Dryas iulia* See *BTB: East* for illustration
About the size of a Gulf Fritillary with even longer and narrower wings. Males are almost completely orange above, while females have a black diagonal line on the FW. RS north to Kansas and Colorado.

Zebra (Heliconian) *Heliconius charithonia* See *BTB: East* for illustration
The black and yellow horizontal stripes make this species unmistakable. RS north and west to Nebraska, Colorado, southeastern Arizona, and southern California.

However, because unethical commercial interests are shipping these butterflies for release at special events (to unwitting victims who don't realize the environmental damage this may cause), I would hesitate to place much credence in any out-of-range occurrence of this species.

Isabella's Heliconian *Eueides isabella*
Somewhat larger than Gulf Fritillary, with black and orange horizontal stripes. RS north and west to Austin, Texas, area, west Texas, and southeastern Arizona.

White Morpho *Morpho polyphemus*
A huge and powerful all-white Mexican butterfly. One record from extreme southeastern Arizona.

Southern Pearly-eye *Enodia portlandia* See *BTB: East* for illustration
Similar to Eyed Brown but larger and darker with HW submarginal eyespots that are surrounded as a group by a white line. Antennal clubs are orange-yellow. RS to western North Dakota, central Nebraska, and central Kansas.

Northern Pearly-eye *Enodia anthedon* See *BTB: East* for illustration
Very similar to Southern Pearly-eye but antennal clubs have a black base. RS to western North Dakota, central Nebraska, and central Kansas.

Mercurial Skipper *Proteides mercurius* See *BTB: East* for illustration
Very large, with a golden head and thorax. HW below mottled dark and pale. One recent report from southeastern Arizona.

Mexican Longtail *Polythrix mexicana*
Similar to Dorantes Longtail, but in addition to white spots in the middle of the FW, there is an unusual violet-tinged spot toward the base of the FW, about 1/3 out along the inner margin. One record from southeastern Arizona.

Two-barred Flasher *Astraptes fulgerator*
A very large skipper, about the size of a Dull Firetip. Brilliant turquoise blue above on the base of the wings and on the body. FW with a strong white median band and a shorter subapical white band. RS to southeastern Arizona (2 records) and San Antonio, Texas, area.

Glassy-winged Skipper *Xenophanes tryxus*
About the size of a White-patched Skipper and somewhat similar to that species, but white marks on the FW are translucent. One record from Hidalgo County, New Mexico.

Chiomara mithrax
Resembles a female White-patched Skipper without any of the white. Instead, ground color is slaty-gray with blue reflectances. One record from southeastern Arizona.

False Duskywing *Gesta gesta invisus* See *BTB: East* for illustration
About the size of a White-patched Skipper. Duskywing-like with a brown patch, distal to the FW cell, that curves outward in characteristic fashion, enclosing a darker black patch. Resident along the south Texas coast, RS to south central Texas.

Faceted Skipper *Synapte syraces*
About the size of a male Sachem with wide black FW borders both above and below. Below, with the HW very striated by fine lines and with an inverted black triangle along the HW leading margin. Two records from southeastern Arizona. Commonly found from central Sonora, Mexico, south.

Neamathla Skipper *Nastra neamathla* See *BTB: East* for illustration
Extremely similar to Julia's Skipper but tends to have ground color duller brown below and to have less prominent pale spots on the FW above. An eastern species occurring west to about Freestone and Brazoria Counties, Texas. One report from southeastern Arizona was probably of a Julia's Skipper.

Little Glassywing *Pompeius verna* See *BTB: East* for illustration
Similar to Dun Skipper and Northern Broken-Dash, but has a white patch just below the antennal club. Two reports from central Nebraska.

Broad-winged Skipper *Poanes viator* See *BTB: East* for illustration
A large, dull-colored, weak-flying marsh skipper. Below, dull orangish-brown with a somewhat pale ray. Usually lands with its head up. R-U. April–Aug. in shrubby marshes and bogs along the West's eastern border in Texas.

Purple-washed Skipper *Panoquina sylvicola*
See *BTB: East* for illustration
Like an Ocola Skipper with extensive violet iridescence below. Also with a spot in the FW cell above that Ocola Skipper lacks. One record from southeastern Arizona (one record—10/30/85) and two from the Austin, Texas, area.

SPECIES DUBIOUSLY REPORTED
TO HAVE OCCURRED NATURALLY

The following species have been reported as having occurred naturally in the West, but those reports are either clearly erroneous—for example, *Dynamine tithia*—or are unsubstantiated.

Thoas Swallowtail *Papilio thoas*
Conflicting reports of one individual on July 18, 1935, or two individuals on July 5, 1935, from Scott County, Kansas, and some vague reports from Colorado. Giant Swallowtails are commonly misidentified as this species. Since I have never seen a legitimate record of this tropical species from south Texas, I strongly suspect that specimens were misidentified, or that if this species was in Kansas it was brought in with tropical fruit.

Cyanophrys longula

Cyanophrys amyntor

Florida Purplewing *Eunica tatila*
One report from west Texas seems unlikely.

Rusty-tipped Page *Siproeta epaphus*
One museum specimen that probably is of Mexican origin.

Dynamine tithia
Reportedly collected on March 15, 1977 at the Woodward Ranch, 20 miles south of Alpine, Brewster County, Texas (see Kendall and McGuire, 1984). This species is found in southeastern Brazil. The same collector reportedly also collected a specimen of *Cyanophrys amyntor* (another tropical species not otherwise ever recorded from the United States) at the same location on the same date. The most charitable interpretation of this information is that some errors were made.

Diaethria anna
One unlikely report from Big Bend

Historis acheronta
One recort from Presidio Co. Texas, Aug. 13, 1969. Not reported from any northern Mexican states.

Blomfild's Beauty *Smyrna blomfildia*

Waiter Daggerwing *Marpesia coresia*

Angled Leafwing *Anaea glycerium*
One uncorroborated report from southeastern Arizona.

Tiger Mimic-Queen *Lycorea cleobaea*

Mercurial Skipper *Proteides mercurius*

Epargyreus windi
Unsubstantiated reports from southern Arizona and California.

Mimosa Skipper *Cogia calchas*
One report from southern California. This species is unknown from any adjacent Mexican areas.

Windia windi
One unpublished and unsubstantiated report from southeastern Arizona.

Fawn-spotted Skipper *Cymaenes odilia*
One unconfirmed report from southeastern Arizona.

Chestnut-marked Skipper *Thespieus macareus*

Supplementary Text

Sara Orangetip *Anthocharis sara*

The possibility that there is more than one species in the Sara Orangetip complex arises mainly from the work of Geiger and Shapiro (1986). Electrophorectic data led them to conclude that populations of *stella* in the high California Sierra Nevadas were genetically different from *sara* at lower elevations on the west slope. As a control, they used Colorado individuals believed to be of the subspecies *julia* and found that these individuals were different from both *sara* and *stella*.

To my knowledge, there is no published information about the genetics of populations in the Pacific Northwest, nor has there been a genetic examination of populations between Colorado *julia* and California *stella* to see whether there is a gradual change or a marked discontinuity. In addition, in the Pacific Northwest, where there are two taxa in the complex, *flora* and *stella*, basically west and east of the Cascades respectively, very experienced observers maintain very different views. Some are of the opinion that *flora* and *stella* are not really distinguishable and that they form a cline. Others are of the opinion that *flora* and *stella* are distinguishable and are separate species, with *flora* as a subspecies of *sara*. Still others are certain that *flora* and *stella* are one species, but that this species is distinct from *sara*.

In Colorado, the relationships between high-elevation *julia* to pinyon-juniper populations (*ingrahami*) and to *stella* to the northwest is very little understood. To the south, *ingrahami* in northern New Mexico superficially more closely resembles *julia* than it does *thoosa* of the California–Nevada desert ranges.

Western Sulphur *Colias occidentalis*

Populations in the Wasatch Mountains of Utah and from central Idaho to Walla Walla County, Oregon, are *pseudochristina*, considered as a full species by some. Males are orange-flushed above, females are pale yellow or off-white with greatly reduced or absent FW black borders. Below, the HW cell spot is usually single or weakly doubled and the red rimming is narrower than on Orange Sulphurs. Most individuals lack HW postmedian spots, but they are sometimes weakly present. Found in rocky openings in coniferous forest, reportedly in areas with mule-ears (*Wyethia*) (Compositae) in bloom, late May–late July, depending upon locality and elevation.

Queen Alexandra's Sulphur *Colias alexandra*

Christina's Sulphur (*C. alexandra christina*) may well be a distinct species. It is mainly orange above, flies mainly in June–July and is more an inhabitant of coniferous forest openings than is Queen Alexandra's Sulphur. Unlike Orange Sulphur, the HW cell-spot below is usually single. Populations in the Black Hills of South Dakota and Bear Lodge Mountains of northeastern Wyoming, are *krauthii* are allied with *christina*, but are considered a full species by some. They are found in coniferous forest openings, mainly July–early Aug.

Bramble and Sheridan's Hairstreaks
Callophrys dumetorum and *C. sheridanii*

There is great variability in the expression of the white postmedian line in both of these species, in some cases with individuals in the same population varying greatly. Also varying, again sometimes within the same population, is the ground color below, from blue-green, to green, to yellow-green. Some recent authors have treated populations I place as Bramble Hairstreak as four species and populations I place as Sheridan's Hairstreak as three species. Others consider that there are two species in Bramble and two in Sheridan's. As Ernst Dornfeld said in *Butterflies of Oregon*, "Separating the different species . . . is often perplexing even to experts." As an example of the level of confusion, some populations in Oregon traditionally considered to be 'Alpine' Sheridan's Hairstreaks (*C. s. lemberti*) are now considered by some to be 'Coastal' Bramble Hairstreaks (*C. d. viridis*). Unfortunately, some books give little inkling of the lack of consensus, instead giving the idea that the way it is presented in that particular book is the current considered opinion of the scientific community.

Juniper Hairstreak *Callophrys gryneus*

Lepidopterists try to divide the Juniper Hairstreak by wing color and pattern and/or by caterpillar foodplant. However, to date it is not certain which, if any, of these populations merit species status, and more work is required. In the Great Basin, populations traditionally treated as 'Siva' Juniper Hairstreaks, feeding on junipers, become progressively browner and then more purple as one travels from east to west, until one reaches the California Sierra Nevadas. Here, essentially identical-appearing populations use incense cedar as the hostplant and are called 'Nelson's' Juniper Hairstreaks (*C.g. nelsoni*). But note that there really aren't any junipers for this population to use and that caterpillars of *nelsoni* will feed on junipers in the laboratory. Farther west and south, certain populations also use nonjuniper hosts. 'Muir's' Juniper Hairstreak (*C.g. muiri*) is found in the California Coast Ranges where it feeds on Sargent cypress while 'Thorne's' Juniper Hairstreak (*C.g. thornei*) (known only from the vicinity of Otay Mountain on the California/Mexico border) uses Tecate cypress. Each of these is most similar to juniper-feeding populations found nearby; juniper-feeding populations in the Inner Coast range south of San Francisco for Muir's and juniper-feeding populations just miles away ('Loki' Juniper Hairstreak) for Thorne's. Northward, one finds brown siva-like populations (*C.g. barryi*) feeding on junipers and extremely similar populations (*C.g. rosneri*) using giant cedar (*Thuya plicata*) as a hostplant.

Euphilotes **Blues**

More than most butterflies, the life of a *Euphilotes* blue revolves around its host-plant—in each case a species or variety of buckwheat. Eggs are laid on the host-plant, caterpillars feed on the hostplant flowers, while adults nectar at the flowers. Rarely does the butterfly fly far from the stand of hostplants, which is often isolated from other potential hostplants by a large distance.

Given this intensive involvement with the hostplant, it is not surprising that many populations of *Euphilotes* blues are adapted for optimal use of the host, including timing of the flight of adults. Because different varieties of buckwheats flower at different times, the different populations of *Euphilotes* blues tend also to fly at different times. Flying at different times of the year erects some barriers to gene flow among the populations—it would be a pretty good trick for an April-flying female to mate with a September-flying male! But because there are so many different populations with different flight times, it is possible that an April-flying population sometimes overlaps with a May-flying population that sometimes overlaps with a June-flying population . . . And so on.

It seems to me that one of the hallmarks of a "species" is that it is consistently different from related species and thus each individual should be identifiable as belonging, or not belonging, to that species. Usually the difference will be obvious upon visual inspection, but it may be that the difference is in some internal structure(s), or in some particular DNA sequence(s). So if two species occur together, the fact that each retains its genetic integrity and remains identifiably different is reason to consider each a full species.

With this group of blues, identification as to Square-spotted Blue, Dotted Blue, Rita Blue, or Spalding's Blue is possible for all individuals, although sometimes only by dissection, and so we treat them as full species. But for most *Euphilotes* blues individuals it is impossible to identify, with certainty, the subspecies an individual belongs to without reference to exact locality, flight date and hostplant.

When two related populations do not occur together, either because their ranges are different and nonoverlapping (allopatric), or the time of year at which adults fly is different and non-overlapping (allochronic), it seems reasonable to impose another criterion for deciding whether or not to consider them as separate species: just how different are they? Admittedly, this will be arbitrary—there are many ways to measure differences, and some differences may be more important than others. But we can at least ask that the differences we measure, regardless of how we are measuring them, be as great as the differences between closely related, but clearly separate, species that fly together. Is the genetic distance between *Euphilotes battoides baueri* and *Euphilotes battoides intermedia* equivalent to the genetic distance between Greenish and Boisduval's Blues? So far as I can tell, there is no published information that would allow one to answer this question.

Another unanswered question relating to allochronic populations is what percentage of individuals emerge at the "wrong" time of the year and potentially interbreed with populations that normally fly at that time. We know that while most butterflies in a population with a synchronous brood are programmed to emerge at roughly the same time of year, sometimes an individual, either because of environmental factors or a mutation or other genetic factors, emerges at a time very different from normal. But we don't know if *Euphilotes* blues populations produce 0.0001%, 1%, or 10% of such individuals. Since their numbers would be low they would be very easily overlooked, especially because they would probably emigrate from the colony's home area (due to lack of flowers on the traditional hostplant) and because if encountered they would probably be assumed to be a member of the population normally flying at that time of year.

Until we can identify individuals with certainty to population and have obtained information about the degree of relatedness of these populations, my advice is to retain your sanity and identify these butterflies to "complex" (even this may not be possible in all cases in the field), while at the same time noting exact location, date, and hostplant used, if possible, for future reference. The following (simplified!) table, giving the subspecies flying in various locations along with their usual flight times and foodplants (bring your buckwheat field guide), may be a useful aid to identification.

	Square-spotted	Dotted	Rita
BC	glaucon LC, July *E. umbellatum*	—	—
AB	—	ancilla LR, mid May–early July *E. umbellatum*	—
WA	glaucon LC, late March–late July *E. umbellatum*	columbiae LU, mid April–mid Aug. *E. compositum, E. heracleides*	—
OR	glaucon (includes oregonensis) LC, late May–July *E. umbellatum* intermedia (Siskiyous) LR, June–July *E. marifolium*	columbiae (north & east) LC, mid May–early Aug. *E. compositum, E. heracleides* enoptes (southwest) U-C, late May–July *E. nudum*	—
MT	glaucon July *E. umbellatum*	ancilla May–early Aug. *E. umbellatum*	—
ID	glaucon U, June–July *E. umbellatum*	columbiae-ancilla U, mid May–July *E. compositum, E. umbellatum*	—
WY	—	ancilla *E. umbellatum*	coloradensis *E. effusum*

	Square-spotted	**Dotted**	**Rita**
CO	**centralis** LU, July–Sept. *E. jamesii* **ellisi** (extreme west) LR, Aug.-Sept. *E. corymbosum*	**ancilla** C-A, April–July *E. umbellatum*	**coloradensis** LU, July–early Aug *E. effusum*
UT	**ellisi** (extreme east & south) U, Aug.–Sept. *E. corymbosum*	**ancilla** U, June–July *E. umbellatum*	**rita** (southeast) LU, Aug. *E. wrightii* **pallescens** R, July various
NM	**centralis** LU, mid July–early Aug. *E. jamesii*	—	**coloradensis** (northeast) LU, July–early Aug. *E. effusum* **rita** (west) LU, Aug. *E. wrightii*
AZ	**centralis** LU, July–Sept. *E. jamesii* **ellisi** (north) U, Aug.–Sept. *E. corymbosum* **martini** (sw quadrant) LU, April–mid May *E. fasciculatum* **baueri** (NV border) *E. ovalifolium*	**dammersi** LU, mid Aug.–Sept. *E. wrighti* **mojave** (NV border) LU, April–June *E. pusillum* & *E. reniforme*	**rita** LC, Aug. *E. wrightii* **pallescens**
NV	**glaucon** (north) U, May–June *E. umbellatum* **baueri** (west) C, April–June *E. ovalifolium* **intermedia** (Carson Range) R, June–Aug. foodplant unknown	**ancilla?** (north 2/3) C, late May–July *E. umbellatum* **opacapulla** (south 1/3) LC, Sept.–Oct *E. wrightii* & *E. plumatella* **enoptes ssp.** (Carson Range) LC, June–Sept. *E. wrightii* & *E. elatum*	**pallescens** LA, June–Sept. *E. nummulare*

	Square-spotted	Dotted	Rita
NV (cont.)	martini (south)	purpura (Spring Mtns.)	
	C-A, March–May	C, June–Aug.	
	E. fasciculatum	E. umbellatum	
	ellisi (south)	giulianii (Grapevine Mtns.)	
	LC, Aug.–Sept.	LR, July	
	E. heermannii	E. umbellatum	
		mojave (Virgin Mtns.)	
		LC, April–June	
		an annual Eriogonum	
CA	intermedia (Trinities region)	enoptes (north & Sierras)	pallescens (southeast)
	C, June–mid Aug.	U-C, June–Aug.	LU, Aug.–mid Oct.
	E. umbellatum &	E. nudum	E. plumatella,
	E. marifolium		E. microthecum
	battoides (Sierra Nevadas)	bayensis (north coast)	
	LU, July–Aug.	C, June	
	E. umbellatum	E. nudum	
	bernardino (southwest)	smithi (Monterey coast)	
	C, late May–early July	LR, July–Aug.	
	E. fasciculatum	E. parvifolium	
	martini (southeast)	tildeni (SF-LA, inner coast range)	
	C, late April–early June	U, July–Aug.	
	E. fasciculatum	E. nudum	
	ellisi (southeast)	dammersi (southeast)	
	LR, Aug.–early Oct.	LU, Sept.–Oct.	
	E. heermanii	E. elongatum	
	baueri (east of Sierras)	mojave (southeast)	
	May–June	LU, April–May	
	E. ovalifolium	E. pusillum, E. reniforme	

Acmon and Lupine Blues Plebejus acmon and P. lupinus

The ranges given of Acmon and Lupine Blues reflect the traditional view of these species. Recently, a few individuals have argued that most populations throughout the West are actually Lupine Blues and that Acmon Blue is essentially restricted to California. Given the fact that these two species are extremely closely related—although they behave as separate species in southern California, it is possible that when enough information is available that they will be considered to be one species—it isn't impossible that this is correct. However, no new information was presented in support of this radical realignment. One argument given was that "Acmon" in much of the West outside of California uses only buckwheats as caterpillar foodplants, as does Lupine Blue, while "Acmon" in California uses legumes in addition to buckwheats. However, in both Alberta and Arizona knowledgeable butterfly enthusiasts are fairly certain that the Acmon Blues in their areas (lutzi and texana, respectively) are using legumes in addition to buckwheats. This is based on their finding Acmon populations to be common in certain areas where they are unable to locate any buckwheats, but that have a profusion of the suspected leguminous foodplants. Until there is a reliable scientific study of the situation, it is best to adhere to the traditional view.

Identification of Greater Fritillaries in Colorado

by Andrew D. Warren

Probably the most difficult of the greater fritillaries to identify with certainty in Colorado are the Atlantis group fritillaries. These are so difficult to identify that most specialists studying the group don't even agree on where to draw species and subspecies lines. Silvered and unsilvered Atlantis fritillaries can often be found together in Colorado's mountains between 7000 and 9000 feet, where they mostly behave as separate species. Always-silvered Atlantis fritillaries tend to prefer higher elevation habitats (above 8000 feet), while throughout the state 'Hesperis' Atlantis fritillaries are found at lower elevations, down to 6000 feet or lower. These Hesperis fritillaries are silvered west of the Continental Divide, and mostly unsilvered east of the divide. In the southeastern part of Colorado (Raton Mesa and Mesa de Maya) flies a silvered form of Hesperis, which also has a very pale disk on the HW below. Partly silvered individuals are common around La Veta Pass, while farther north, partly silvered individuals are very scarce (and then mostly females) along the Front Range west of Denver and Fort Collins. On the west slope, where Atlantis and Hesperis are both silvered, they are very difficult to tell apart. Here, Atlantis can usually be distinguished from Hesperis by the darker coloration on the HW below, with well-defined dark and black markings. Below, the FW of most Hesperis individuals has a prominent orange flush, strongest basally. Most Atlantis individuals have a less pronounced orange flush on the FW below. Female Hesperis are a deep, almost red-orange on the upperside, while the upperside of Atlantis females is generally paler. The dark basal coloration on the upperside of all wings of Atlantis females is usually less extensive than it is on Hesperis females. Female Atlantis fritillaries almost always have a dark cinnamon brown disk, while females of Hesperis have a reddish-brown disk.

Great Basin Fritillaries in Colorado are only found in the northwestern part of the state (roughly 7000–10,000 feet), and are essentially always silvered. They can usually be told apart from all other fritillaries there by their smaller size (only Mormon Fritillaries are smaller) and the dark reddish-brown color of the HW disk below. The extent of the submarginal pale band on the HW below is quite variable, and this band is often overscaled with the reddish-brown scaling of the disk. The topside coloration of Great Basin fritillaries is paler orange than is that of Hesperis. On Great Basin fritillaries, the male FWs below are very pale, and the HW disk lacks the greenish-gray patches usually found on Atlantis.

In Colorado, Coronis Fritillaries do not show a great amount of geographic variation, but may show variation at the same location. Below, the hindwing disk typically varies from a light cinnamon brown to a greenish-brown. Coronis individuals are most likely to be confused with Zerene Fritillaries, since both of them have large, rounded silver spots on the HW below, and may have similarly colored HW disks. Fortunately, Zerene is restricted to the northwestern part of the state (where Coronis is scarce), so Coronis can be easily determined along the Front Range. Where the two species may fly together, Coronis is larger than Zerene and always has a thick, well-defined brown lining on the basal edge of the marginal silver spotband of the HW below. This lining is poorly developed in Zerene and is usually green or greenish-brown.

Zerene Fritillaries are extremely variable in the state. Below, the color of the HW disk ranges from light cinnamon brown to light green to pale tan. Zerene can almost always be separated from Callippe and Mormon Fritillaries by Zerene's larger, more rounded, very lustrous silver spots on the HW below—these spots are narrower with more pointed edges in Callippe and Mormon Fritillaries.

Callippe and Edwards' Fritillaries are the only two species in Colorado that always have a totally green HW disk below. Edwards' is always much larger than Callippe, and the marginal silver spots on the HW below of Edwards' tend to be slightly larger and less pointed than are the same spots on Callippe. Male Callippe Fritillaries have a reduced orange flush on the FW below (which is prominent on Edwards'), and the upperside of all wings on Callippe have bolder black markings than on Edwards'.

Great Spangled Fritillaries occur in two distinct populations in Colorado. In the southwest, populations look like a small version of Great Spangled Fritillary from eastern North America. Males and females above are similarly colored, the HW below has large, rounded silver spots and a narrow submarginal band. In the northwestern part of the state, Great Spangled has reduced silver spotting on the HW below, and a wide, pale submarginal band. Males and females are strongly dimorphic (very pale females), and, below, both sexes have a darker HW disk than do the southwestern populations. These two populations are reported to intergrade on the south side of Grand Mesa in Delta and Mesa Counties, but the situation there requires further study.

Identification of Greater Fritillaries in the Great Basin

by George Austin

Unlike the situation in the eastern United States, where five species of greater fritillaries are relatively distinct in appearance and generally unvarying over broad areas, the several western species of greater fritillaries are confusingly similar and vary greatly and often in a parallel fashion where as many as eight species may be seen together. Geographic segregates within species are often easier to identify than are different species whose patterns may converge. Knowledge of flight times, location, and subtle differences in color and pattern, gleaned from a thorough examination of many individuals, is often necessary for determination. Useful characters include size; wing shape; intensity of color; thickness of veins and black markings; amount of basal dusting; color of the HW disk below; size, shape, and extent of silvering; and the width of the postmedian band below.

The first step in the identification of a greater fritillary in the Great Basin (California east of the Sierra Nevadas, Nevada, and western Utah) is to consider only species potentially found at the location where the fritillary is flying. Then the "easy" species can be eliminated. 'Carol's' Zerene Fritillary is found only in the Spring Mountains of southern Nevada and is the only greater fritillary found there. An easy call! Both Great Spangled and Nokomis Fritillaries are large and striking, with black and cream-colored females. They are the only greater fritillaries in the Great Basin with green-brown eyes, rather than blue-gray eyes. In the Great Basin, nearly all Callippe Fritillaries are easily identified by the intensely green HW disk below. Above, Callippe Fritillaries also differ from other Great Basin greater fritillaries. They are pale yellow-orange with the females tinted (almost) greenish. On the HW above, both males and females have conspicuously pale ghosts of the underside silvered spots.

The remaining species can then be categorized as small or large. In northeastern Nevada, the generally encountered small species that is unsilvered is Mormon Fritillary (but see Atlantis Fritillary, below). Their HWs below are nearly uniformly dull yellow to yellow-orange. A minority of individuals here have silvered spots and a somewhat browner HW disk often tinged with green. These latter individuals resemble the Mormon Fritillaries of central Utah on which the disk is yet darker and the silvering more prominent. Small individuals from western Nevada and eastern California include both Mormon and Great Basin Fritillaries (Great Basin Fritillaries from eastern Nevada are much larger). Male Great Basin Fritillaries are distinguished from Mormon Fritillaries by their thickened black veins, but females of these two species are very similar. Some Great Basin Fritillaries lack any silvering, while, in western Nevada, Mormon Fritillaries have at least a hint of silver in the HW spots below.

This leaves us with Zerene, Coronis, Atlantis, Great Basin (in the eastern Great Basin), and, in central Utah, Hydaspe. Coronis Fritillary is large (and females are sometimes huge), bright orange, and the females have a very dark, often nearly solidly colored, outer margin above. The FWs of Coronis are slightly more elongated at the apex than the other species. Below, the HW disk is evenly colored, not mottled, and brownish—often with a hint of green. The silvered spots are large, squarish, and bold.

Great Basin Fritillary, from central Nevada to central Utah, is smaller than is Coronis and the HW disk below is mottled, ranging from dark to pale brown or yellowish, often with distinct (but not strong) greenish tints. In the Stansbury Mountains of Utah, the disk is especially variable and of a strange yellow-brown to yellow-green color unlike that seen on any other greater fritillary. The silvered spots are smaller and somewhat more elongated. Males often have noticeably thickened FW veins. Above, the ground color is darker, more brownish orange than it is on Coronis Fritillaries. The greener-tinged disk individuals could be confused with Callippe Fritillary, but that species has an intensely bluish-green disk in this region with the green often obliterating the pale postmedian band.

Except in extreme western Nevada, Zerene Fritillary is pale orange above with a yellowish to pale brown HW disk below. The silvered spots are squarish, but not as large as on Coronis. The FW veins above are not noticeably thickened. In western Nevada Zerene Fritillary has a purplish to pale purple-brown HW disk below.

Atlantis Fritillary occurs in Elko County, Nevada, and rarely in the Carson range. Two different subspecies are unsilvered and have tan HW spots instead. One of these occurs in the Jarbidge and Independence mountains, the other is in the Carson Range. In the Ruby and East Humboldt mountain ranges, Atlantis Fritillary is silvered and looks like a small Zerene. Besides its smaller size, the disk of this Atlantis population is somewhat darker (red-brown on females) than on the Zerenes in the area. In the mountains of central Utah, Atlantis Fritillary is a medium-sized species that is relatively bright orange above. The HW spots below range from brightly silvered to whitish or pale cream. They may be best distinguished from their sympatric congeners by their bright red-brown disks.

Hydaspe Fritillary barely enters the Great Basin in Utah. This medium-sized species is broadly marked with black above. Below, the disk is dull purple-brown (with this color running across the postmedian pale band) and the spots are square, dull, and unsilvered.

Habitat preferences also differ somewhat among the greater fritillaries. In Nevada, Nokomis Fritillary is found in the wettest meadows and seeps, usually at lower elevations. Great Spangled Fritillaries are found in those same habitats but also range into somewhat drier areas. Mormon Fritillary prefers wet meadows at high elevations. Great Basin Fritillary is usually found in drier areas, often at the edges of meadows, but also in more arid situations in eastern and central Nevada where males frequently are encountered on hilltops (as are Callippes). Zerene, Coronis, and Callippe Fritillaries prefer even drier habitats and so are more widespread in Nevada than the other species. The different subspecies of Atlantis Fritillaries are found in a variety of habitats from relatively dry draws and canyons to woodlands.

Atlantis Fritillary *Speyeria atlantis*

As mentioned in the Comments section of the main text, in some areas there appears to be two populations of Atlantis Fritillaries flying at the same location and many believe that these are separate species. Although I personally believe that at least two species are likely, it is also possible that populations that behave as separate species in one area may merge and behave as a single species over much wider areas. Another problem with the two species concept for the Atlantis complex is that there is essentially no information as to which of the two species to assign many of the separate populations. Reddish-tinged HW disk vs. gray-tinged HW disk may, or may not have anything to say about species assignment. The thought that one of the two species is always silvered while the other may be silvered or not, may or may not be correct. In many populations of greater fritillaries, an occasional unsilvered individual can be found. Populations in Oregon, California and Idaho are unsilvered. In the Wasatch and Uinta ranges of Utah, and in much of Montana, individuals may be either silvered or unsilvered. In Colorado and the Black Hills of South Dakota, silvered and unsilvered populations fly together.

Of all the Atlantis complex populations I have seen, only *nausicaa*, in the White Mountains of Arizona and adjacent New Mexico, has the dull yellow-green eye color typical of the Aphrodite group of greater fritillaries. But, I have not seen live (butterfly eye-color changes upon death) individuals of populations in southern Utah (*chitone*), northern Arizona (*shellbachi*) and central New Mexico (*dorothea*) and I would not be surprised if these also had yellow-green eyes. The possibility that these populations are a separate species should be investigated.

Taiga Alpine *Erebia mancinus*
Until recently, these butterflies were treated as a subspecies of Disa Alpine, *Erebia disa*. However, new evidence, presented in *The Butterflies of Canada* (Layberry et.al. 1998), shows that the populations inhabiting taiga habitat are very distinct from those inhabiting tundra. The second edition of the NABA *Checklist* will reflect this change.

Valeriana Skipper *Codatractus mysie*
In the first edition of the NABA *Checklist*, this species was called Valeriana Cloudy-wing and its scientific name was *Thorybes valeriana*. Recent work has demonstrated that this species belongs in the genus *Codatractus*, not in *Thorybes*, and so it is not a cloudywing. In addition, and most confusingly, the correct scientific name for the species appears to be *mysie*, not *valeriana*. It is possible that the English name will be changed in the second edition of the NABA *Checklist*. This entire mess demonstrates a major downside to using a scientific name as the basis of an "English" name.

Photo Dates, Locations and Credits

All photographs were taken by Jeffrey Glassberg, except as indicated below. The author used a Minolta 7000i camera equipped with a Minolta 100 mm macro lens and a Minolta AF1200 ring flash. Page numbers followed by photo number; dates are given as month/day/year.

43.1: 6/19/99 Crawford Creek, Siskiyou Co., CA
43.2: 6/19/99 Crawford Creek, Siskiyou Co., CA
43.3: 7/17/98 Harts Pass, Okanogan Co., WA
43.4: 5/30/97 Apex Park, Jefferson Co., CO
43.5: 6/14/98 Mt. Lindo, Jefferson Co., CO
43.6: 8/9/99 Libby Flat, Snowy Range, Albany Co., WY
43.7: 7/24/95 Above Frog Lake, Carson Pass, Alpine Co., CA
43.8: 6/13/98 Tinytown, Jefferson Co., CO

45.1: 9/29/98 Juno, Val Verde Co., TX
45.2: 10/12/97 Sycamore Canyon, Santa Cruz Co., AZ
45.3: 3/20/97 Ft. Lauderdale, Broward Co., FL
45.4: Ft. Lauderdale, Broward Co., FL. Photo by Ron Boender
45.5: 9/4/97 Sierra Picachos, Nuevo Leon, Mexico
45.5: inset. 9/5/98 Chipinque Park, Monterrey, Nuevo Leon, Mexico
45.6: 9/3/97 Sierra Picachos, Nuevo Leon, Mexico
45.7: 6/1/99 Green Gulch, Big Bend NP, TX
45.8: 10/22/99 Chaparral WMA, LaSalle Co., TX

47.1: 9/29/98 Juno, Val Verde Co., TX
47.2: 9/29/98 Juno, Val Verde Co., TX
47.3: 6/5/97 Royal Gorge overlook, Fremont Co., CO
47.4: 6/12/98 Mt Lindo, Jefferson Co., CO
47.5: 6/17/86 Fort Collins, Larimer Co., Co., Photo by Paul A. Opler
47.6: 5/25/99 16 mi. w. of Springerville, Apache Co., AZ
47.7: 6/12/98 Mt. Lindo, Jefferson Co., CO
47.8: 5/25/97 Butterbredt Peak, Kern Co., CA. Photo by Jack N. Levy

49.1: 7/16/98 Winthrop, Okanogan Co., WA
49.2: 7/19/98 Black Canyon, Okanogan Co., WA
49.3: AMNH specimen. 6/21/75 St. Mary, MT
49.4: 6/5/97 6/5/97 Royal Gorge Overlook, Fremont Co., CO
49.5: 7/22/95 West of Sonora Pass, Tuolumne Co., CA
49.6: 7/6/97 Rabbit Ears Pass, Routt Co., CO
49.6: inset. 6/13/98 Mt. Lindo, Jefferson Co., CO
49.7: 2/27/98 Plum Canyon, Anza-Borrego SP, San Diego Co., CA
49.8: 2/27/98 Plum Canyon, Anza-Borrego SP, San Diego Co., CA

51.1: 7/5/97 Rabbit Ears Pass, Routt Co., CO
51.2: 6/19/99 Crawford Creek, Siskiyou Co., CA
51.3: 8/21/94 Spruce Run Rec. Area, Hunterdon Co., NJ
51.4: 8/16/96 McKinney, Collin Co., TX
51.5: 6/28/96 McNair, Lake Co., MN
51.6: 6/19/97 Chew's Ridge, Monterey Co., CA
51.7: 6/28/99 Rustler Park, Cochise Co., AZ
51.8: 6/29/99 Onion Saddle, Cochise Co., AZ

53.1: 6/6/97 south of Florence, Fremont Co., CO
53.1: inset. 9/19/93 Sentenac Canyon, Anza-Borrego SP, San Diego Co., CA
53.2: 6/17/98 Descanso, San Diego Co., CA
53.3: 7/18/92 Lake Louis, Wind River Mtns., Fremont Co., WY
53.4: 7/19/98 Harts Pass, Okanogan Co., WA
53.5: 5/31/97 Above Tinytown, Jefferson Co., CO
53.6: Same individual as 53.5
53.7: 8/5/97 Nye Co., NV
53.8: 7/29/98 Mesa Verde NP, Montezuma Co., CO

55.1: 7/7/97 Fort Collins, Larimer Co., CO
55.2: 6/12/97 Hobergs, Lake Co., CA
55.3: 4/10/98 San Gabriel Canyon, Los Angeles Co., CA
55.4: 7/31/99 Campbell Blue River, Greenlee Co., AZ
55.5: 7/22/92 Togwotee Pass, Teton Co., WY
55.6: 6/16/97 Purisima Creek Redwood Preserve, San Mateo Co., CA
55.7: 7/31/99 Campbell Blue River, Greenlee Co., AZ
55.8: 7/31/99 Campbell Blue River, Greenlee Co., AZ
55.9: 6/30/99 Marshall Gulch, Mt. Lemmon, Pima Co., AZ
55.10: 6/30/99 Marshall Gulch, Mt. Lemmon, Pima Co., AZ
55.11: 9/9/97 Sawmill Canyon, Cochise Co., AZ
55.12: Same individual as 7.9

57.1: 6/20/99 Mt. Ashland, Jackson Co., OR
57.1: inset. AMNH specimen. 6/1/68 Mayo Lake,Yukon
57.2: 5/30/97 Apex Park, Jefferson Co., CO
57.3: March 1993 Tucson, AZ. Photo by Jim Brock

57.4: 4/9/98 Lucerne Valley, San Bernardino Co., CA
57.5: 4/3/98 Jacumba, San Diego Co., CA
57.6: 4/4/98 Jacumba, San Diego Co., CA
57.7: 5/31/97 above Tinytown, Jefferson Co., CO
57.8: 4/23/94 Larenim Park, Mineral Co., WV
57.9: 6/21/99 northeast of Crescent City, Del Norte Co., CA
57.10: 6/23/99 Spike Buck Meadow, Humboldt Co., CA

59.1: 4/28/98 Vogel Flat, Big Tujunga Canyon, Los Angeles Co., CA
59.2: 3/1/98 Jacumba, San Diego Co., CA
59.3: 4/27/95 O'Neill Regional Park, Trabuco Canyon, Orange Co., CA
59.4: 7/24/95 Carson Pass, Alpine Co., CA
59.5: 8/4/98 Osborn Mtn., Sublette Co., WY
59.6: 7/21/95 east of Sonora Pass, Mono Co., CA
59.7: June 1998, Golden Gate Park, Jefferson Co., Co., Photo by Rick Cech
59.8: 5/10/98 Sandia Mtns., Bernallilo Co., NM
59.9: 4/8/95 Clark Mtn., San Bernardino Co., CA
59.10: 3/3/98 Scissors Crossing, Anza-Borrego SP, San Diego Co., CA
59.11: 3/4/98 Scissors Crossing, Anza-Borrego SP, San Diego Co., CA
59.12: 2/27/98 Plum Canyon, Anza-Borrego SP, San Diego Co., CA
59.13: 4/18/99 Assunpink WMA, Monmouth Co., NJ
59.14: same individual as 59.13
59.15: 4/2/93 Gray Ranch, Hidalgo Co., NM. Photo by Steven J. Cary

61.01: 6/17/98 Descanso, San Diego Co., CA
61.01: inset. 6/1/99 Big Bend NP, TX
61.02: 9/19/93 Anza-Borrego SP, CA
61.03: 9/25/99 Goshen, Cape May Co., NJ
61.04: 7/14/93 Glazier Arboretum, New Castle, Westchester Co., NY
61.05: 7/7/97 Westridge Estates, Fort Collins, CO
61.06: 8/8/99 Elkhart Park, Pinedale, Sublette Co., WY
61.07: 6/19/98 Ridge Route, Los Angeles Co., CA
61.08: 6/17/98 Descanso, San Diego Co., CA

63.01: 6/19/99 Cecileville, Siskiyou Co., CA
63.02: 7/22/98 Hurricane Ridge, Olympic NP, WA
63.03: 8/5/97 Kingston Canyon, Lander Co., NV
63.04: 8/3/98 Green River Lakes Trailhead, Sublette Co., WY
63.05: 8/1/00 Banff NP, Alberta, Canada. Photo by Ahmet Baytas
63.06: 7/22/97 Plateau Mountain, Alberta, Canada
63.07: 8/7/97 Dana Meadows, Yosemite NP, CA
63.08: 7/27/98 Mt. Uncompahgre, Hinsdale Co., CO

65.01: 7/19/97 Southeast of Polebridge, Flathead Co., MT
65.02: 7/19/97 Southeast of Polebridge, Flathead Co., MT

65.03: Darby MT. Photo by Steven Kohler
65.04: Darby MT. Photo by Steven Kohler
65.05: 8/3/98 Green River Lakes trailhead, Sublette Co., WY
65.06: 7/23/92 Yellowstone NP, WY
65.07: 7/25/98 American Basin, 11,000 ft., near Lake City, Hinsdale Co., CO
65.08: 8/9/99 Snowy Range, 9900 ft. Carbon Co., WY

67.01: 10/9/97 Garden Canyon, Cochise Co., AZ
67.02: 10/26/95 La Gloria, Starr Co., TX
67.03: 6/11/97 Pepperwood Preserve, Santa Rosa, Sonoma Co., CA
67.04: 6/17/97 Pozo, San Luis Obispo Co., CA
67.04: inset. 6/11/97 Pepperwood Preserve, Santa Rosa, Sonoma Co., CA. In flight
67.05: 6/11/97 Pepperwood Preserve, Santa Rosa, Sonoma Co., CA
67.06: 9/23/98 21 miles north of Del Rio, Val Verde Co., TX
67.06: inset. 10/23/99 Santa Ana NWR, Hidalgo Co., TX. Caught by an ambush bug
67.07: 2/6/95 6 miles south of Mismaloya, Jalisco, Mexico
67.08: 10/26/93 Mission, Hidalgo Co., TX

69.01: 9/23/98 21 miles north of Del Rio, Val Verde Co., TX
69.01: inset. 10/27/96 La Joya, Starr Co., TX. Road-killed
69.02: 10/9/97 Sawmill Canyon, Cochise Co., AZ
69.03: 3/22/94 Kendall, Dade Co., FL
69.03: inset. 3/26/90 South Miami, Dade Co., FL
69.04: 9/29/98 Juno, Val Verde Co., TX
69.05: 10/16/99 Santa Ana NWR, Hidalgo Co., TX
69.06: 10/16/99 Santa Ana NWR, Hidalgo Co., TX
69.06: inset. 10/14/94 Roma, Starr Co., TX

71.01: 10/9/97 Garden Canyon, Cochise Co., AZ
71.02: 8/29/99 Methodist Thicket, Weslaco, Hidalgo Co., TX
71.03: 9/23/98 21 miles north of Del Rio, Val Verde Co., TX
71.03: inset. 10/25/99 North of Hargill, Hidalgo Co., TX
71.04: 10/20/99 Amistad National Rec. Area, Val Verde Co., TX
71.04: inset. 6/18/96 Brazos Bend SP, Fort Bend Co., TX
71.05: 10/14/94 Peñitas, Hidalgo Co., TX
71.06: 10/27/95 Santa Ana NWR, Hidalgo Co., TX
71.07: 10/23/99 Santa Ana NWR, Hidalgo Co., TX
71.07: inset. 1/19/97 Catemaco, Veracruz, Mexico
71.08: 3/19/94 Gainesville, Alachua Co., FL

73.01: 9/23/98 20 miles north of Del Rio, Val Verde Co., TX
73.02: 9/27/98 Laguna Meadow Trail, Big Bend NP, TX
73.02: inset. 9/23/98 20 miles north of Del Rio, Val Verde Co., TX
73.03: 9/27/98 20 miles north of Del Rio, Val Verde Co., TX
73.04: 10/9/97 Saw Mill Canyon, Cochise Co., AZ

73.05: 10/9/97 Garden Canyon, Cochise Co., AZ
73.06: 5/23/94 Bauer Camp, Miami-Dade Co., FL
73.07: 5/20/94 Bauer Camp, Miami-Dade Co., FL
73.08: 4/30/98 Sonoita, Santa Cruz Co., AZ
73.08: inset. 12/13/99 South of Cd. Victoria, Tamps., Mexico

75.01: 7/7/97 Fossil Creek, Fort Collins, Larimer Co., CO
75.02: 7/7/97 Fossil Creek, Fort Collins, Larimer Co., CO
75.02: inset. 7/7/97 Fossil Creek, Fort Collins, Larimer Co., CO
75.03: 7/18/95 Crane Flat, Yosemite NP, CA
75.03: inset. 7/15/97 West Glacier, Flathead Co., MT
75.04: 7/22/95 West of Sonora Pass, Tuolumne Co., CA
75.05: 6/20/97 Mines Rd. Alameda Co., CA
75.05: inset. 4/22/95 Santa Clarita Valley, Los Angeles Co., CA
75.06: Same individual as 75.05 inset
75.07: 7/23/92 Yellowstone NP, WY
75.08: 6/12/97 Middletown, Lake Co., CA

77.01: 7/30/94 Roan Mtn., Carter Co., TN
77.02: Southeast of Chief Mtn. entrance to Glacier NP, MT
77.03: 7/23/95 Niagara Creek Rd., Tuolumne Co., CA
77.03: inset. 7/21/97 Carthew Ridge, Waterton NP, Alberta
77.04: 8/4/98 Osborne Mtn., Sublette Co., WY
77.05: 7/20/95 Lee Vining, Mono Co., CA
77.06: 7/22/92 Togwotee Pass, Teton Co., WY
77.07: 6/21/97 Mines Rd., Alameda Co., CA
77.08: 6/20/97 Mines Rd., Alameda Co., CA

79.01: 6/19/97 Chew's Ridge, Monterey Co., CA
79.02: 6/19/99 Cecileville, Siskiyou Co., CA
79.03: 7/3/96 Dakota Dunes, Union Co., SD
79.04: 6/19/99 Cecileville, Siskiyou Co., CA
79.05: 6/12/94 Descanso, San Diego Co., CA. Photo by Jack N. Levy
79.06: 7/2/96 Pipestone National Monument, Pipestone Co., MN
79.07: June 1993, near Descanso, San Diego Co., CA. Photo by Jack N. Levy
79.08: 6/5/90 Middle Creek WMA, Lancaster Co., PA

81.01: 7/30/99 Big Lake Rd., Alpine, Apache Co., AZ
81.02: 7/21/95 1 mile east of Devil's Gate Pass, Mono Co., CA
81.03: 8/8/99 Pinedale, Sublette Co., WY
81.04: 8/6/99 Pinedale, Sublette Co., WY
81.05: 8/2/97 10 miles north of Bridgeport, Mono Co., CA
81.06: 8/1/98 Pinedale, Sublette Co., WY
81.07: 7/2/97 Apex Park, Jefferson Co., CO
81.07: inset. 5/30/97. Apex Park, Jefferson Co., CO
81.08: 7/17/98 Winthrop, Okanogan Co., WA

83.01: 7/17/98 Below Hart's Pass, Okanogan Co., WA
83.02: 8/6/99 Bondurant, Sublette Co., WY
83.03: 7/17/98 Below Hart's Pass, Okanogan Co., WA
83.04: 7/21/95 West of Sonora Pass, Tuolomne Co., CA
83.05: 7/18/97 West Glacier, Flathead Co., MT
83.06: 7/18/97 West Glacier, Flathead Co., MT
83.07: 7/27/98 Mt. Uncompahgre, Hinsdale Co., CO
83.08: 7/20/92 Togwotee Pass, Teton Co., WY
83.09: 7/21/98 Hurricane Ridge, Olympic NP, WA
83.10: 7/22/95. Niagara Rd., Tuolomne Co., CA

85.01: 9/26/98 Chisos Basin, Big Bend NP, TX
85.02: 9/24/94 Gainesville, Alachua Co., FL
85.03: 7/28/98 Mesa Verde NP, Montezuma Co., CO
85.04: same individual as 85.03
85.05: 7/18/95 Crane Flat, Yosemite NP, CA
85.06: 6/12/97 R.L. Stevenson SP, Napa Co., CA

87.01: 6/9/95 Wagoner, Wagoner Co., OK
87.02: 7/7/97 Westridge Estates, Fort Collins, Larimer Co., CO
87.03: 7/2/97 Apex Park, Jefferson Co., CO
87.04: 7/29/98 Mesa Verde NP, Montezuma Co., CO
87.04: inset. 8/3/85 27 miles south of Hayden, Rio Blanco Co., Co., Photo by Paul A.
    Opler
87.05: 6/25/88 Rock Creek Park, El Paso Co., CO
87.06: 7/2/97 Apex Park, Jefferson Co., CO

89.01: 8/2/97 Sonora Pass, Tuolonmne Co., CA
89.02: 7/1/94 Chappaqua, Westchester Co., NY
89.03: 7/20/95 Lee Vining, Mono Co., CA
89.04: 6/25/88 Rock Creek Park, El Paso Co., CO
89.05: 7/19/98 Black Canyon, Okanogan Co., WA
89.06: 6/20/97 Mines Rd., Alameda Co., CA

91.01: 7/13/92 Mt. Zion, Jefferson Co., CO
91.02: 6/17/98 Descanso, San Diego Co., CA
91.03: 6/21/97 Mines Rd., Alameda Co., CA
91.04: 5/24/99 6 miles south of Globe, Gila Co., AZ
91.05: 5/28/99 McKittrick Canyon, Guadalupe Mountains NP, TX
91.06: 6/22/89 Ward Pound Ridge Reservation, Westchester Co., NY

93.01: 4/21/95 San Gabriel Canyon, Los Angeles Co., CA
93.01: inset. 6/27/91 Mt. Zion, Jefferson Co., CO
93.02: 7/3/81 north of Rose Peak, Greenlee Co., AZ. Photo by Jim Brock
93.03: 5/29/93 North Beach, San Francisco, CA. Photo by Bob Stewart
93.04: 7/22/95 Sonora Pass, Tuolumne Co., CA

93.05: 3/19/97 northwest of Goodsprings, Clark Co., NV. Photo by Jim Brock
93.06: 5/31/97 above Tinytown, Jefferson Co., CO
93.07: 5/1/98 Garden Canyon, Cochise Co., AZ
93.08: 5/1/98 Garden Canyon, Cochise Co., AZ

95.01: 5/1/98 Garden Canyon, Cochise Co., AZ
95.02: 7/7/91 Chappaqua, Westchester Co., NY
95.03: 5/10/98 Juan Tabo Rec. Area, Sandia Mtns., Bernallilo Co., NM
95.04: 5/30/99 Pine Canyon Trail, Big Bend NP, TX
95.05: 10/25/93 Hargill, Hidalgo Co., TX
95.06: Adult emerged 6/2/81 from caterpillar collected 4 miles e. of Sycamore Canyon, Santa Cruz Co., AZ. Photo by Steven J. Prchal, Sonoran Arthropod Studies Institute

97.01: 6/22/99 Bald Hill Rd., Humboldt Co., CA
97.01: inset. 6/18/99 Mount Ashland, Jackson Co., OR
97.02: 2/9/90 ex ova, Vernon, BC, Canada. Photo by Cris Guppy
97.02: inset. 6/29/97 Mines Rd., Alameda Co., CA
97.03: 2/28/98 Plum Canyon, Anza-Borrego SP, San Diego Co., CA
97.04: 3/27/96 Otay Mountain, San Diego Co., CA. Photo by Jack N. Levy
97.05: 7/1/99 Mount Lemmon, Pima Co., AZ
97.06: 7/22/95 Niagara Creek Rd., Tuolomne Co., CA

99.01: 6/17/98 Descanso, San Diego Co., CA
99.02: 6/19/98 Ridge Route, Los Angeles Co., CA
99.03: 3/27/94. Reecer Canyon, Ellensburg, Kittitas Co., WA. Photo by David Nunnallee
99.04: 6/23/99 Spikebuck Meadow, Humboldt Co., CA
99.05: 4/24/94 Larenim Park, Mineral Co., WV
99.06: 5/31/97 above Tinytown, Jefferson Co., CO
99.07: 4/8/98 Clark Mountain, San Bernardino Co., CA
99.08: 6/23/99 Spikebuck Meadow, Humboldt Co., CA

101.01: 5/3/98 California Gulch, Santa Cruz Co., AZ
101.02: 3/15/88 El Morro, Margarita Island, Venezuela
101.03: 3/21/93. San Jose Vista Hermosa, Oaxaca, Mexico
101.04: 11/18/98 Peñitas, Hidalgo Co., TX
101.05: 3/21/98 Bahia San Carlos, Sonora, Mexico. Photo by Jim Brock
101.06: 11/1/99 San Jose de Pimas, Sonora, Mexico. Photo by Priscilla Brodkin

103.01: 8/8/97 Jackson Slough, Sacramento Co., CA
103.02: 8/8/97 Jackson Slough, Sacramento Co., CA
103.03: 7/19/98 Black Canyon, Okanogan Co., WA
103.04: 7/8/97 Westridge Estates, Fort Collins, Larimer Co., CO
103.05: 9/13/93 Avalon, Santa Catalina Island, Los Angeles Co., CA
103.06: 12/17/99 south of Cd. Victoria, Tamps., Mexico

105.01: 10/19/99 Amistad Natl. Rec. Area, Val Verde Co., TX

105.02: 10/21/93 Roma, Starr Co., TX

105.03: Adult emerged June 1999, reared from an egg collected mid April, 1999, Landa Park, New Braunfels, Comal Co., TX. Photo by Jeff Slotten

105.04: March 1998 Tepoca, Sonora, Mexico. Photo by Jim Brock

105.05: 1/3/92. Rte. 134, Guerrero, Mexico

105.06: 2/23/98. Oahu, Hawaii

107.01: 9/3/97 Sierra Picachos, Monterrey, Nuevo Leon, Mexico

107.02: 6/17/97 Pozo, San Luis Obispo Co., CA

107.03: 8/11/89, Wilcox Playa, Cochise Co., AZ

107.04: 8/4/99 Marshall Gulch, Mt. Lemmon, Pima Co., AZ

107.05: 9/13/93 Avalon, Santa Catalina Island, Los Angeles Co., CA

107.06: 7/29/98 Mesa Verde NP, Montezuma Co., CO

107.07: 6/16/98 Descanso, San Diego Co., CA

107.08: 6/16/98 Descanso, San Diego Co., CA

107.09: 6/17/98 Descanso, San Diego Co., CA

107.10: 9/16/93 Morongo Valley, San Bernardino Co., CA

107.11: 9/23/98 Del Rio, Val Verde Co., TX

107.12: 9/23/98 Del Rio, Val Verde Co., TX

109.01: 6/23/99 Spikebuck Meadow, Humboldt Co., CA

109.02: 5/13/96 Reston, Fairfax Co., VA

109.03: 6/10/97 Apex Park, Jefferson Co., CO

109.04: 7/29/94 Blowing Rock, Watauga Co., NC

109.05: 7/6/97 Rabbit Ears Pass, Routt Co., CO

109.06: 6/24/99 Sayler, Trinity Co., CA

109.07: 3/19/94 In-Ko-Pah Gorge, Imperial Co., CA. Photo by Jack N. Levy

109.07: inset. 5/2/95 near Beatty, Nye Co., NV. Photo by Jim Brock

109.08: 12/13/99 south of Cd. Victoria, Tamps., Mexico

111.01: 7/1/99 Marshall Gulch, Mt. Lemmon, Pima Co., AZ

111.01: inset. 6/14/97 Tilden Park, Contra Costa Co., CA

111.02: 6/16/97 Burleigh Murray SP, San Mateo Co., CA

111.03: 4/20/94 Jamesburg, Middlesex Co., NJ

111.04: 6/10/97 Apex Park, Jefferson Co., CO

111.05: Same individual as 111.04

111.06: 2/27/98 Plum Canyon, Anza-Borrego SP, San Diego Co., CA

111.07: 2/27/98 Plum Canyon, Anza-Borrego SP, San Diego Co., CA

111.08: 2/28/98 Plum Canyon, Anza-Borrego SP, San Diego Co., CA

113.01: 8/7/97 Gaylor Lakes Trail, Yosemite NP, CA

113.02: 6/21/98 Carlisle Rd., Ventura Co., CA

113.03: 6/15/98 Descanso, San Diego Co., CA

113.04: 6/21/98 Carlisle Rd., Ventura Co., CA

113.05: 4/18/97 road to Gilroy Canyon, San Bernardino Co., CA. Photo by Jack N. Levy
113.06: 7/31/99 southwest of Eagar, Apache Co., AZ
113.07: 7/31/99 southwest of Eagar, Apache Co., AZ
113.08: 8/1/99 southwest of Eagar, Apache Co., AZ

115.01: 7/8/97 Apex Park, Jefferson Co., CO
115.02: 7/8/97 Apex Park, Jefferson Co., CO
115.03: 7/21/95 east of Sonora Pass, Mono Co., CA
115.04: 6/22/99 Bald Hill Rd, Humboldt Co., CA
115.05: 4/24/95 Bob's Gap, Los Angeles Co., CA
115.06: 6/22/99 Bald Hill Rd., Humboldt Co., CA
115.07: 9/19/93 Sentenac Canyon, Anza-Borrego SP, San Diego Co., CA
115.08: 6/22/99 Bald Hill Rd., Humboldt Co., CA

117.01: 8/10/99 Rockport, Weld Co., CO
117.02: same individual as 117.01
117.02: inset. 9/13/99 north of Paradise, Cochise Co., AZ. Photo by Jim Brock
117.03: 9/13/99 north of Paradise, Cochise Co., AZ. Photo by Jim Brock
117.04: 8/4/97 Esmeralda Co., NV
117.05: nr. Calneva, Lassen Co., CA. Photo by John Emmel
117.06: 7/29/98 Dove Creek, Dolores Co., CO
117.07: 7/29/98 Dove Creek, Dolores Co., CO
117.08: 7/29/98 Dove Creek, Dolores Co., CO

119.01: 6/1/97 southeast of Aurora, Arapahoe Co., CO
119.02: 7/2/97 Apex Park, Jefferson Co., CO
119.03: 4/28/95 Vogel Flat, Big Tujunga Canyon, Los Angeles Co., CA
119.04: 4/28/95 Vogel Flat, Big Tujunga Canyon, Los Angeles Co., CA
119.05: 3/1/98 Jacumba, San Diego Co., CA
119.06: 6/10/97 Apex Park, Jefferson Co., CO
119.07: 6/18/99 Mt. Ashland, Jackson Co., OR
119.08: 4/21/95 San Gabriel Canyon, Los Angeles Co., CA

121.01: 7/23/95 Sonora Pass, Tuolumne Co., CA
121.02: 6/1/97 southeast of Aurora, Arapahoe Co., CO
121.03: Mt. Pinos. Ventura Co., CA
121.03: inset. 7/17/97 Browning, Glacier Co., MT
121.04: 6/2/97 Elbert, Elbert Co., CO
121.04: inset. 6/18/98 Mt. Pinos, Ventura Co., CA
121.05: 6/16/99 northeast of Crescent City, Del Norte Co., CA
121.06: 7/22/92 Togwotee Pass, Teton Co., WY
121.06: inset. 7/22/98 Deer Park, Olympic NP, WA
121.07: 7/18/95 Crane Flat, Yosemite NP, CA
121.08: 6/21/99 northeast of Crescent City, Del Norte Co., CA

123.01: 7/19/98 Black Canyon, Okanogan Co., WA
123.02: 7/19/97 Polebridge, Flathead Co., MT
123.03: 7/19/97 Polebridge, Flathead Co., MT
123.04: 7/23/95 Niagara Creek Rd., Tuolomne Co., CA
123.04: inset. 7/19/98 Black Canyon, Okanogan Co., WA
123.05: 8/1/97 Sonora Pass, Tuolomne Co., CA
123.06: 6/2/97 Elbert, Elbert Co., CO
123.06: inset. 8/1/97 Sonora Pass, Tuolomne Co., CA
123.07: 6/2/97 Elbert, Elbert Co., CO
123.08: 6/10/97 Apex Park, Jefferson Co., CO

125.01: 6/20/98 Descanso, San Diego Co., CA
125.02: 4/21/95 San Gabriel Canyon, Los Angeles Co., CA
125.03: 7/19/95 Yosemite NP, CA
125.04: 5/7/98 south of Globe, Gila Co., AZ
125.05: 4/21/95 San Gabriel Canyon, Los Angeles Co., CA
125.06: 6/19/98 Ridge Route, Los Angeles Co., CA
125.07: 4/22/95 Santa Clarita Valley, Los Angeles Co., CA
125.08: 4/22/95 Santa Clarita Valley, Los Angeles Co., CA
125.09: 6/18/98 Mt. Pinos, Ventura Co., CA
125.10: 6/18/98 Mt. Pinos, Ventura Co., CA

127.01: 7/21/98 Hurricane Ridge, Olympic NP, WA
127.02: 8/7/97 road to Saddlebag Lake, Mono Co., CA
127.03: 7/18/95 Tamarack Flat, Yosemite NP, CA
127.04: 8/3/97 Tuolomne Meadows, Yosemite NP, CA
127.05: 7/31/99 Saddlebag Lake, Mono Co., CA. Posed photo by Jack N. Levy
127.06: 8/7/97 above Tioga Pass, Yosemite NP, CA
127.07: 8/6/97 Campito Mtn., Mono Co., CA
127.08: 8/6/97 Campito Mtn. Mono Co., CA

129.01: 8/4/96 San Pedro Riparian Area, Sierra Vista, AZ
129.02: 8/3/99 Box Canyon, Santa Cruz Co., AZ
129.03: 2/28/98 Plum Canyon, Anza-Borrego SP, San Diego Co., CA
129.04: 10/22/93 west of Roma, Starr Co., TX
129.05: 10/21/93 Roma, Starr Co., TX
129.06: 10/29/93 Santa Ana NWR, Hidalgo Co., TX
129.07: 10/19/93 Santa Ana NWR, Hidalgo Co., TX
129.08: 10/14/94 Mission, Hidalgo Co., TX

131.01: 8/2/96 Garden Canyon, Cochise Co., AZ
131.02: 8/2/96 Garden Canyon, Cochise Co., AZ
131.03: 4/30/98 Patagonia, Santa Cruz Co., AZ
131.04: 8/17/89 Madera Canyon, Santa Cruz Co., AZ
131.05: 8/15/89 Box Canyon, Pima Co., AZ

131.06: 8/7/86 Trinidad Mine, near Santa Rosa, Sonora, Mex. Photo by Jim Brock
131.07: 7/1/99 Mt. Lemmon. Pima Co., AZ
131.08: 6/27/91 Mt. Zion, Jefferson Co., CO
131.09: 5/29/99 Big Bend NP, TX
131.10: 5/29/99 Big Bend NP, TX

133.01: 9/12/93 Devil's Punchbowl, sw. of Palmdale, CA
133.02: 9/15/93 LA Crest Hwy., San Gabriel Mtns., CA
133.03: 4/23/95 Adelanto, San Bernardino Co., CA
133.04: 8/19/96 Patagonia, Santa Cruz Co., AZ
133.05: 8/9/96 Box Canyon, Pima Co., AZ
133.06: 9/26/98 Big Bend NP, TX
133.07: 8/3/96 San Pedro River, Sierra Vista, Cochise Co., AZ
133.08: 9/26/98 Chisos Basin, Big Bend NP, TX
133.09: 9/19/93 Sentenac Canyon, Anza-Borrego SP,CA
133.10: 8/22/98 Rt. 16, km 255, Sonora, Mexico. Photo by Jim Brock

135.01: 9/23/98 north of Del Rio, Val Verde Co., TX
135.02: 9/27/98 Chisos Basin, Big Bend NP, TX
135.03: 9/23/98 north of Del Rio, Val Verde Co., TX
135.04: 10/25/99 Santa An NWR, Hidalgo Co., TX
135.05: 5/7/98 south of Globe, Gila Co., AZ
135.06: 8/11/96 Canelo Hills Cienga, Santa Cruz Co., AZ
135.07: 10/26/98 Roma, Starr Co., TX
135.08: 10/24/94 Peñitas, Hidalgo Co., TX

137.01: 8/1/99 Campbell Blue River, Greenlee Co., AZ
137.02: same individual as 137.01
137.03: 7/24/97 West Glacier, Flathead Co., MT
137.03: inset. 6/13/95 Barry Co., MO
137.03: inset. 6/13/95 Barry Co., MO
137.04: 7/18/97 West Glacier, Flathead Co., MT
137.05: 8/2/97 east of Bridgeport, Mono Co., CA
137.06: 8/2/97 same individual as 137.05
137.07: 8/8/97 Eagle Creek Rd., Tuolomne Co., CA
137.08: 7/25/97 West Glacier, Flathead Co., MT

139.01: 6/11/95 Prairie SP, Barton Co., Missouri
139.02: same individual as 139.01
139.03: 8/5/98 Virginia Dale, Larimer Co., CO
139.04: 8/17/93 Fort Indiantown Gap, Lebanon Co., PA
139.05: 8/5/97 Kingston Canyon, Lander Co., NV
139.06: same individual as 139.03
139.07: 8/2/98 San Bernardino Mtns., San Bernardino Co., CA. Photo by Jack N. Levy
139.08: 6/7/97 San Bernardino Mtns., San Bernardino Co., CA. Photo by Jack N. Levy

141.01: 7/7/97 Westridge Estates, Fort Collins, Larimer Co., CO
141.01: top inset. Same individual
141.01: bottom inset. 7/7/97 Fort Collins, Larimer Co., CO
141.02: 8/5/98 Virginia Dale, Larimer Co., CO
141.03: 7/2/97 Apex Park, Jefferson Co., CO
141.03: inset. Same individual
141.04: 7/15/92 Rocky Mountain NP, CO
141.05: 7/5/97 Rabbit Ears Pass, Routt Co., CO
141.06: 7/25/97 West Glacier, Flathead Co., MT
141.07: 7/31/99 Campbell Blue River, Greenlee Co., AZ
141.08: same individual as 141.07

143.01: 7/25/95 Big Trees Park, Calaveras Co., CA
143.01: inset. 7/19/98 Black Canyon, Okanogan Co., WA
143.02: 7/22/95 Niagara Creek Rd., Tuolomne Co., CA
143.03: 6/19/99 Cecileville, Siskiyou Co., CA
143.04: 7/16/97 Rabbit Ears Pass, Routt Co., CO
143.05: 7/21/95 east of Devil's Gate Pass, Mono Co., CA
143.06: 7/19/98 Black Canyon, Okanogan Co., WA
143.07: 7/6/97 Rabbit Ears Pass, Routt Co., CO
143.08: 8/5/97 Kingston Canyon, Lander Co., NV

145.01: 6/6/97 south of Florence, Fremont Co., CO
145.02: 6/14/98 Mt. Lindo, Jefferson Co., CO
145.03: 7/13/92 Mt. Zion., Jefferson Co., CO
145.04: 6/10/97 Apex Park, Jefferson Co., CO
145.05: 6/19/99 Cecileville, Siskiyou Co., CA
145.06: 6/19/99 Cecileville, Siskiyou Co., CA
145.07: 6/14/97 Mt. Diablo summit, Contra Costa Co., CA
145.08: 4/26/95 Dictionary Hill, San Diego Co., CA

147.01: 7/5/97 Rabbit Ears Pass, Routt Co., CO
147.02: 7/18/97 Hungry Horse, Flathead Co., MT
147.03: 7/12/00 Snowbird, 11000 ft., Salt Lake Co., UT
147.04: 7/18/92 Sinks Canyon Loop Rd., near Lander, Fremont Co., WY
147.05: 7/24/95 Dorrington, Calveras Co., CA
147.06: 6/12/97 Boggs Mtn. SF, Lake Co., CA
147.07: 6/19/97 Chew's Ridge, Monterey Co., CA
147.08: 6/19/97 Chew's Ridge, Monterey Co., CA

149.01: 7/27/98 Mt. Uncompahgre, Hinsdale Co., CO
149.02: 7/27/98 Mt. Uncompahgre, Hinsdale Co., CO
149.03: 8/8/99 Elkhart Park, near Pinedale, Sublette Co., WY
149.04: 8/2/98 Pinedale, Sublette Co., WY
149.05: 8/8/97 Eagle Meadow Rd., Tuolomne Co., CA

149.06: same individual as 149.05
149.07: 7/30/99 Big Lake Rd., nr. Alpine, Apache Co., AZ
149.08: 7/20/00 Lamoille Canyon, 10,000 ft., Ruby Mtns., Elko Co.NV

151.01: 6/13/93 northeast of Errol, NH
151.02: 7/25/92 Beartooth Ridge, Park Co., WY
151.03: 7/19/97 southeast of Polebridge, Flathead Co., MT
151.04: 7/18/97 McGee Meadow, Glacier NP, MT
151.05: 6/25/90 Westchester Co., NY
151.06: 7/30/94 Roan Mountain, Carter Co., TN
151.07: 6/16/99 northeast of Crescent City, Del Norte Co., CA
151.08: same individual as 151.07

153.01: May 1981 Kalavella Bog, Carlton Co., MN. Photo by David H. Ahrenholz
153.02: 5/21/98 Glidden, WI. Photo by Ann B. Swengel
153.03: 6/4/97 above Fairplay, Park Co., CO
153.04: 6/4/97 above Fairplay, Park Co., CO
153.05: 7/26/97 Red Cloud Mtn., near Lake City, Hinsdale Co., CO
153.06: 7/26/98 Red Cloud Mtn., near Lake City, Hinsdale Co., CO
153.07: 7/22/92 Togwotee Pass, Teton Co., WY
153.08: 7/24/92 Beartooth Ridge, Park Co., WY

155.01: 8/4/98 Osborne Mtn., Sublette Co., WY
155.02: 8/4/98 Osborne Mtn., Sublette Co., WY
155.03: 7/22/97 Waterton Park, Alberta
155.04: 8/7/99 Vliate Lake, Sublette Co., WY
155.05: AMNH specimen.7/27/75 Plateau Mtn., Alberta
155.06: AMNH specimen. 7/22/75 Plateau Mtn., Alberta
155.07: AMNH specimen. 7/26/75 Plateau Mtn., Alberta
155.08: AMNH specimen. 7/22/75 Plateau Mtn., Alberta

157.01: 3/2/98 Anza-Borrego SP, San Diego Co., CA
157.02: 2/28/98 Anza-Borrego SP, San Diego Co., CA
157.03: 10/29/96 La Gloria, Starr Co., TX
157.04: 10/30/98 Weslaco, Hidalgo Co., TX
157.05: 9/18/93 Parker, Yuma Co., AZ
157.06: 7/29/99 Garden Canyon, Cochise Co., AZ
157.07: 5/14/98 Aguirre Springs Natl. Rec. Area, Dona Ana Co., NM
157.08: 5/14/98 Aguirre Springs Natl. Rec. Area, Dona Ana Co., NM

159.01: 9/3/98 Sierra Picachos, Nuevo Leon, Mexico
159.02: 1/4/92 Atoyac, Guerrero, Mexico
159.03: 9/3/99 La Estanzuela Park, Monterrey, Nuevo Leon, Mexico
159.04: same individual as 159.03
159.05: 10/31/96 Hargill, Hidalgo Co., TX

159.06: same individual as 159.05
159.07: 10/29/96 La Gloria, Starr Co., TX
159.08: 10/29/96 La Gloria, Starr Co., TX

161.01: 8/9/96 Box Canyon, Santa Cruz Co., AZ
161.02: 8/9/96 Patagonia, Santa Cruz Co., AZ
161.03: 8/6/96 Patagonia, Santa Cruz Co., AZ
161.04: 9/23/98 north of Del Rio, Val Verde Co., TX
161.05: 4/30/98 north of Sonoita, Santa Cruz Co., AZ
161.06: 7/15/92 Rocky Mountain NP, CO
161.07: 5/12/98 David Hill, Harding Co., NM
161.08: same individual as 161.07

163.01: 8/15/89 Box Canyon, Pima Co., AZ
163.02: 8/15/89 north of Del Rio, Val Verde Co., TX
163.03: 5/1/98 Garden Canyon, Cochise Co., AZ
163.04: 8/15/89 Box Canyon, Pima Co., AZ
163.05: 5/29/99 Chisos Basin, Big Bend NP, TX
163.06: 9/27/98 Chisos Basin, Big Bend NP, TX
163.07: 9/27/98 Chisos Basin, Big Bend NP, TX
163.08: 9/27/98 Chisos Basin, Big Bend NP, TX

165.01: 6/19/99 Cecileville, Siskiyou Co., CA
165.02: 6/12/97 R.L. Stevenson SP, Napa Co., CA
165.03: 4/9/98 Lucerne Valley, San Bernardino Co., CA
165.04: 4/9/98 Lucerne Valley, San Bernardino Co., CA
165.05: 4/30/98 north of Sonoita, Santa Cruz Co., AZ
165.06: 8/6/96 Grump Hill, Cochise Co., AZ
165.06: inset. 5/10/98 Sandia Mtns. Bernallilo Co., NM
165.07: 8/2/96 Garden Canyon, Cochise Co., AZ
165.08: 8/2/96 Garden Canyon, Cochise Co., AZ

167.01: 5/29/97 Apex Park, Jefferson Co., CO
167.02: 5/29/97 Apex Park, Jefferson Co., CO
167.03: 7/5/97 Rabbit Ears Pass, Routt Co., CO
167.04: 7/15/92 Rocky Mountain NP, CO
167.05: 6/30/96 Glacial Lakes SP, Pope Co., MN
167.06: same individual as 167.05
167.07: 8/4/98 above Green River Lakes, Sublette Co., WY
167.08: 8/4/98 above Green River Lakes, Sublette Co., WY
167.08: inset. 8/4/98 above Green River Lakes, Sublette Co., WY

169.01: 6/16/98 Descanso, San Diego Co., CA
169.02: same individual as 169.01
169.03: 4/5/98 Lucerne Valley, San Bernardino Co., CA

169.03: inset. 7/26/92 Gallatin, MT
169.04: 4/4/98 Lucerne Valley, San Bernardino Co., CA
169.05: 7/24/95 Dorrington, Calaveras Co., CA
169.06: 7/22/95 Niagara Creek Rd., Tuolomne Co., CA
169.06: inset. 7/5/97 Rabbit Ears Pass, Routt Co., CO
169.07: 7/22/95 Niagara Creek Rd., Tuolomne Co., CA
169.08: 7/23/95 Niagara Creek Rd., Tuolomne Co., CA

171.01: 4/27/95 Trabuco Canyon, Orange Co., CA
171.02: same individual as 171.01
171.03: 7/21/98 Hurricane Ridge, Olympic NP, WA
171.04: 6/16/97 Purisma Creek Preserve, San Mateo Co., CA
171.05: 7/31/99 Mexican Hay Lake, Apache Co., AZ
171.06: 8/4/98 Osborne Mtn., Sublette Co., WY
171.07: 5/25/99 west of Springerville, Apache Co., AZ
171.08: 7/22/95 Niagara Creek Rd., Tuolomne Co., CA

173.01: 7/22/92 Togwotee Pass, Teton Co., WY
173.02: 5/30/97 Apex Park, Jefferson Co., CO
173.03: 7/4/97 Above Fairplay, Park Co., CO
173.04: 4/3/98 Jacumba Mtn., San Diego Co., CA
173.05: 7/17/00 Mt. Baldy, Great Basin NP, NV
173.06: same individual as 173.05
173.07: 7/18/92 Wind River Mountains, Fremont Co., WY
173.08: 7/18/92 Wind River Mountains, Fremont Co., WY

175.01: 7/19/98 Black Canyon, Okanogan Co., WA
175.01: inset. 5/31/97 above Tinytown, Jefferson Co., CO
175.02: 6/10/97 Apex Park, Jefferson Co., CO
175.03: 8/8/97 Eagle Creek Rd. Tuolomne Co., CA
175.04: same individual as 175.03
175.05: 7/21/95 east of Sonora Pass, Mono Co., CA
175.06: same individual as 175.05
175.07: ex ova collected 5/26/84 Cecileville, Siskiyou Co., CA by Ken Hansen
175.08: ex ova collected 5/26/84 Cecileville, Siskiyou Co., CA by Ken Hansen

177.01: 5/4/98 Canelo Hills Cienega, Santa Cruz Co., AZ
177.02: 7/6/96 Troy Meadows, Morris Co., NJ
177.03: same individual as 177.01
177.04: 7/25/92 Wraith Falls, Yellowstone NP, WY
177.05: same individual as 177.04
177.06: 7/6/97 Rabbit Ears Pass, Routt Co., CO
177.07: 6/5/96 Jones Gap, Macon Co., NC
177.08: 6/28/96 McNair, Lake Co., MN

179.01: 6/12/97 Boggs Mountain SF, Lake Co., CA
179.02: 4/10/98 San Gabriel Canyon, Los Angeles Co., CA
179.03: 5/5/98 Garden Canyon, Cochise Co., AZ
179.04: 5/1/98 Garden Canyon, Cochise Co., AZ
179.05: 6/12/98 Tinytown, Jefferson Co., CO
179.06: 6/10/97 Apex Park, Jefferson Co., CO
179.07: 11/12/89 Falcon SP, Starr Co., TX
179.08: 10/25/95 Laguna Atascosa NWR, Cameron Co., TX

181.01: 9/23/98 Del Rio, Val Verde Co., TX
181.02: 8/17/96 McKinney, Collin Co., TX
181.03: 8/11/96 Canelo Hills Cienega, Santa Cruz Co., AZ
181.04: 8/11/96 Canelo Hills Cienega, Santa Cruz Co., AZ
181.05: 5/29/99 Chisos Basin, Big Bend NP, TX
181.06: 8/10/95 Barton Creek, Austin, Travis Co., TX
181.07: 9/4/97 Sierra Picachos, Nuevo Leon, Mexico
181.08: 5/28/00 Santa Ana NWR, Hidalgo Co., TX

183.01: 10/24/99 Roma, Starr Co., TX
183.02: 10/29/94 Morristown, Morris Co., NJ
183.03: 10/24/98 Santa Ana NWR, Hidalgo Co., TX
183.04: 9/25/98 Pine Canyon, Big Bend NP, TX
183.05: 8/22/92 Great Dismal Swamp NWR, Suffolk, VA
183.06: 7/12/95 Lunenburg, VT
183.07: 6/23/97 Burleigh Murray SP, San Mateo Co., CA
183.08: 6/23/97 Burleigh Murray SP, San Mateo Co., CA

185.01: 7/2/97 Apex Park, Jefferson Co., CO
185.02: 8/5/98 Virginia Dale, Larimer Co., CO
185.03: 7/23/91 Moose River Plains, Hamilton Co., NY
185.04: 7/26/91 Moose River Plains, Hamilton Co., NY
185.05: 6/12/95 Roaring River SP, Barry Co., MO
185.06: 7/12/95 Lunenburg, VT
185.07: 6/16/97 Burleigh Murray SP, San Mateo Co., CA
185.08: 6/16/97 Burleigh Murray SP, San Mateo Co., CA

187.01: 7/11/95 Gorham, NH
187.02: 7/19/98 Black Canyon, Okanogan Co., WA
187.03: 7/7/96 Troy Meadows, Morris Co., NJ
187.04: same individual as 187.03
187.05: 6/19/99 Ceciville, Siskiyou Co., CA
187.06: 6/19/99 Ceciville, Siskiyou Co., CA
187.07: 8/5/98 Virginia Dale, Larimer Co., CO
187.08: 7/20/95 Lee Vining, Mono Co., CA

189.01: 5/31/97 Mt. Falcon Park, Jefferson Co., CO
189.02: 6/10/97 Apex Park, Jefferson Co., CO
189.03: 8/7/96 Harshaw Creek, Santa Cruz Co., Az
189.04: 7/31/99 Campbell Blue River, Greenlee Co., AZ
189.05: 7/18/95 Crane Flat, Yosemite NP, CA
189.06: same individual as 189.05
189.07: 5/7/98 south of Globe, Gila Co., AZ
189.08: 3/2/98 Anza-Borrego SP, San Diego Co., CA

191.01: 9/26/98 Lost Mine Trail, Big Bend NP, TX
191.02: 6/16/98 Cuyamaca Lake, San Diego Co., CA
191.03: 11/19/98 El Canelo Ranch, Kenedy Co., TX
191.04: 5/3/98 California Gulch, Santa Cruz Co., AZ
191.05: 10/31/97 Santa Ana NWR, Hidalgo Co., TX
191.06: 10/17/99 Santa Ana NWR, Hidalgo Co., TX
191.07: 1/4/92 Atoyac, Guerrero, Mexico
191.08: 10/24/94 Peñitas, Hidalgo Co., TX
191.08: inset. 11/11/89 Bentsen-Rio Grande SP, Hidalgo Co., TX

193.01: 6/28/96 McNair, Lake Co., MN
193.02: 6/28/96 McNair, Lake Co., MN
193.03: 8/8/99 Elkhart Park, Pinedale, Sublette Co., WY
193.04: 6/10/98 Lewis Creek, Custer Co., CO
193.05: 7/23/95 Alpine Co., CA
193.06: 7/19/98 Black Canyon, Okanogan Co., WA
193.07: 6/20/98 Descanso, San Diego Co., CA
193.08: 6/19/99 Cecileville, Siskiyou Co., CA

195.01: 7/1/99 Marshall Gulch, Mt. Lemmon, Pima Co., AZ
195.02: 10/8/97 Garden Canyon, Cochise Co., AZ
195.03: 7/30/90 Kisco Swamp, Westchester Co., NY
195.04: 8/2/89 Cross River, Westchester Co., NY
195.05: 6/18/96 Brazos Bend SP, Fort Bend Co., TX
195.06: March 1994 Bill Williams NWR, AZ. Photo by S. Mark Nelson
195.07: 10/2/95 Tree Tops Park, Broward Co., FL
195.08: 10/21/93 west of Roma, Starr Co., TX

197.01: 12/12/99 Cd. Victoria, Tamps., Mexico
197.02: 12/15/99 Cd. Victoria, Tamps., Mexico
197.03: 2/9/99 Huatulco, Oaxaca, Mexico
197.04: 2/11/99 Huatulco, Oaxaca, Mexico
197.05: 10/25/98 La Lomita Mission, Hidalgo Co., TX
197.06: 10/26/99 Santa Ana NWR, Hidalgo Co., TX
197.07: 2/10/99 Candalaria Loxicha, Oaxaca, Mexico
197.08: 1-/24/93 Santa Ana NWR, Hidalgo Co., TX

199.01: 3/21/90 South Miami, Miami-Dade Co., FL
199.02: 3/21/90 South Miami, Miami-Dade Co., FL
199.03: 2/10/99 Candalaria Loxicha, Oaxaca, Mexico
199.04: same individual as 199.03
199.05: 10/22/94 Santa Ana NWR, Hidalgo Co., TX
199.06: 6/12/95 Roaring River SP, Barry Co., MO
199.07: 10/12/99 Chaparral WMA, Dimmit Co., TX
199.08: 5/29/99 Chisos Basin, Big Bend NP, TX

201.01: 5/13/98 Aguirre Springs Rec. Area, Dona Ana Co., NM
201.02: 7/8/97 Apex Park, Jefferson Co., CO
201.03: 4/29/98 Sabino Canyon, Tucson, Pima Co., AZ
201.04: 10/14/94 Roma, Starr Co., TX
201.05: 10/15/99 Landa Park, New Braunfels, Comal Co., TX
201.06: 11/26/98 Chisos Basin, Big Bend NP, TX
201.07: 10/3/99 Coronado Peak, Cochise Co., AZ
201.08: Same individual as 201.07

203.01: 6/30/94 Cross River, Westchester Co., NY
203.02: 7/17/95 Palo Alto, Santa Clara Co., CA
203.03: 8/5/97 Kingston Canyon, Lander Co., NV
203.04: 6/15/97 Mt. Diablo, Contra Costa Co., CA
203.05: 7/31/98 Rock Creek Park, El Paso Co., CO
203.06: 7/23/92 Wraith Falls, Yellowstone NP, WY
203.07: 7/28/98 Mesa Verde NP, CO
203.08: 7/31/99 Campbell Blue River, Greenlee Co., AZ

205.01: 6/7/97 southeast of Aurora, Elbert Co., CO
205.02: 6/1/97 southeast of Aurora, Arapahoe Co., CO
205.03: 10/9/97 Garden Canyon, Cochise Co., AZ
205.04: 6/30/96 Glacial Lakes SP, Pope Co., MN
205.05: 6/29/99 Barfoot Park, Cochise Co., AZ
205.06: 7/24/92 Clay Butte, Park Co., WY
205.07: 7/20/92 Brooks Lake Creek, Park Co., WY
205.08: 7/31/99 Mexican Hay Lake, Apache Co., AZ
205.09: 6/15/97 Mt. Diablo, Contra Costa Co., CA

207.01: 6/27/99 Saw Mill Canyon, Cochise Co., AZ
207.02: 6/26/99 Carr Canyon, Cochise Co., AZ
207.03: 7/2/96 Five Ridge Preserve, Plymouth Co., IA
207.04: 7/3/96 Homer, Dakota Co., NE
207.05: 10/25/99 Santa Ana NWR, Hidalgo Co., TX
207.06: 3/15/94 Kissimmee, FL
207.07: 8/2/96 Garden Canyon, Cochise Co., AZ
207.08: 5/15/98 Aguirre Springs Rec.Area, Dona Ana Co., NM

207.09: 10/15/99 Landa Park, New Braunfels, Comal Co., TX

209.01: 5/30/97 Apex Park, Jefferson Co., CO
209.02: 6/10/97 Apex Park, Jefferson Co., CO
209.03: 7/22/98 Deer Park, Olympia NP, WA
209.04: 7-17-98 Harts Pass, Okanogan Co., WA
209.05: 7/27/98 Mt. Uncompahgre, Hinsdale Co., CO
209.06: 7/24/92 Clay Butte, Park Co., WY
209.07: May, 1980 Calavella Bog,Carlton Co., MN. Photo by David H. Ahrenholz
209.08: June, 1980 Langlay River Preserve, McNair, Lake Co., MN. Photo by David H. Ahrenholz

211.01: 7/24/92 Clay Butte, Park Co., WY
211.02: 7/29/98 Mt. Uncompahgre, Hinsdale Co., CO
211.03: same individual as 211.02
211.04: 7/3/97 above Fairplay, Park Co., CO
211.05: 7/27/98 Mt. Uncompahgre, Hinsdale Co., CO
211.06: 7/22/97 Plateau Mtn., Alberta
211.07: 7/27/98 Mt. Uncompahgre, Hinsdale Co., CO
211.08: 7/3/97 above Fairplay, Park Co., CO

213.01: 7/19/98 Black Canyon, Okanogan Co., WA
213.02: 6/12/98 Mt. Lindo, Jefferson Co., CO
213.03: 7/4/97 above Fairplay, Park Co., CO
213.04: 8/7/97 above Tioga Pass, Yosemite NP, CA
213.05: 5/31/97 above Tinytown, Jefferson Co., CO
213.06: 6/3/97 Como, Park Co., CO
213.07: 8/3/98 Green River Lakes, Sublette Co., WY
213.08: same individual as 213.07

215.01: 5/28/99 McKittrick Canyon, Guadalupe Mtns. NP, TX
215.02: 1/7/96 El Rosario, Angangueo, Michoacan, Mexico
215.03: 7/30/90 Kisco Swamp, Westchester Co., NY
215.04: 10/17/99 Santa Ana NWR, Hidalgo Co., TX
215.05: 8/10/95 Barton Creek Park, Austin, Travis Co., TX
215.06: 6/28/99 Cave Creek Canyon, Cochise Co., AZ
215.07: 9/3/98 Sierra Picachos, Nuevo Leon, Mexico
215.08: 9/2/98 Sierra Picachos, Nuevo Leon., Mexico

217.01: 8/9/89 Cave Creek Canyon, Cochise Co., AZ
217.02: 8/8/89 Cave Creek Canyon, Cochise Co., AZ
217.03: 6/30/99 Marshall Gulch, Mt. Lemmon, Pima Co., AZ
217.04: 6/19/99 Cecileville, Siskiyou Co., CA
217.05: 6/1/98 Garden Canyon, Cochise Co., AZ

217.06: same individual as 217.05
217.07: 3/25/94 Stock Island, Monroe Co., FL
217.08: 10/31/96 north of Hargill, Hidalgo Co., TX

219.01: 5/31/99 Chisos Basin, Big Bend NP, TX
219.02: 8/10/95 Barton Creek Park, Travis Co., TX
219.03: 7/29/99 Carr Canyon, Cochise Co., AZ
219.04: 7/29/99 Garden Canyon, Cochise Co., AZ
219.05: 5/3/98 California Gulch, Santa Cruz Co., AZ
219.06: 1/20/96 Mismaloya, Jalisco, Mexico
219.07: 7/30/98 Alamo Canyon, Santa Cruz Co., AZ. Photo by Jim Brock
219.08: 1/22/96 south of Mismaloya, Jalisco, Mexico

221.01: 9/28/96 Savannah, GA
221.02: 5/22/94 Stock Island, Monroe Co., FL
221.03: 10/27/95 Santa Ana NWR, Hidalgo Co., TX
221.04: 12/6/99 Castellow Hammock, Miami-Dade Co., FL
221.05: 11/10/89 Santa Ana NWR, Hidalgo Co., TX
221.06: 11/11/89 Santa Ana NWR, Hidalgo Co., TX
221.07: 2/8/95 Mismaloya, Jalisco, Mexico

223.01: 8/15/89 Box Canyon, Pima Co., AZ
223.02: 5/31/99 Green Gulch, Big Bend NP, TX
223.03: 9/3/97 Sierra Picachos, Nuevo Leon, Mexico
223.04: 9/5/97 Chipinque Park, Monterrey, Nuevo Leon, Mexico
223.05: 9/1/99 Sierra Picachos, Nuevo Leon, Mexico
223.06: 8/15/98 Socorro Rivera, Chichuahua, Mexico. Photo by Jim Brock
223.07: 10/23/99 Santa Ana NWR, Hidalgo Co., TX
223.08: 9/3/97 Sierra Picachos, Nuevo Leon, Mexico

225.01: 6/13/90 Chappaqua, Westchester Co., NY
225.02: 10/21/93 La Joya, Starr Co., TX
225.03: 8/7/96 Harshaw Creek, Santa Cruz Co., AZ
225.04: same individual as 223.03
225.05: 7/29/99 Garden Canyon, Cochise Co., AZ
225.06: same individual as 223.04
225.07: 5/28/99 McKittrick Canyon, Guadalupe Mtns. NP, TX
225.08: 9/3/97 Sierra Picachos, Nuevo Leon, Mexico

227.01: 7/1/99 Mt. Lemmon, Pima Co., AZ
227.02: 8/1/99 Eager, Apache Co., AZ
227.03: 6/16/99 northeast of Crescent City, Del Norte Co., CA
227.04: same individual as 223.03
227.05: 7/21/95 east of Sonora Pass, Mono Co., CA

227.06: 7/19/95 Tuolomne Meadows, Yosemite NP, CA
227.07: 8/23/91 Gaineville, Alachua Co., FL
227.08: 3/17/94 Ocala NF, Marion Co., FL

229.01: 9/3/98 La Estanzuela Park, Monterrey, Nuevo Leon, Mexico
229.02: 8/8/89 Guadalupe Caonyon, Cochise Co., AZ
229.03: 4/28/98 "A" Mtn., Tucson, Pima Co., AZ
229.04: 10/15/94 Sabal Palms, Cameron Co., TX
229.05: 10/21/93 west of Roma, Starr Co., TX
229.06: 10/26/95 La Gloria, Starr Co., TX
229.07: 10/21/93 Roma Starr Co., TX
229.08: 8/19/97 Advana, Sorora, Mexico. Photo by Jim Brock

231.01: 6/10/98 Lewis Creek Trail, Custer Co., CO
231.01: inset. same individual as 231.01
231.02: 5/31/97 Tinytown, Jefferson Co., CO
231.03: same individual as 231.02
231.04: 6/18/99 Mt. Ashland, Jackson Co., OR
231.05: 6/20/99 Mt. Ashland, Jackson Co.,
231.06: OR 6/13/97 Lake Berryessa, Napa Co., CA
231.07: AMNH specimen. April. Paradise, AZ
231.08: AMNH specimen. Aug. Paradise, AZ

233.01: 5/5/98 Garden Canyon, Cochise Co., AZ
233.02: same individual as 231.01
233.02: inset. AMNH specimen. 8/19/69 Miller Canyon, Cochise Co., AZ
233.03: 5/22/92 Chappaqua, Westchester Co., NY
233.04: 4/25/98 Chatsworth, Ocean Co., NJ
233.05: 7/29/98 Mesa Verde NP, Montezuma Co., CO
233.06: 4/15/95 Busch, Carroll Co., AR
233.07: 7/29/98 Mesa Verde NP, Montezuma Co., CO
233.08: 7/29/98 7/29/8 Dove Creek, Dolores Co., CO

235.01: 8/9/89 Cave Creek Canyon, Cochise Co., AZ
235.02: 5/31/99 Chisos Basin, Big Bend NP, TX
235.03: 6/15/97 Mt. Diablo, Contra Costa Co., CA
235.04: 5/31/99 Chisos Basin, Big Bend NP, TX
235.05: 9/25/98 Pine Canyon trail, Big Bend NP, TX
235.06: 6/27/91 Mt. Zion, Jefferson Co., CO
235.07: 6/20/99 Mt. Ashland, Jackson Co., OR
235.08: 6/13/98 Mt. Lindo, Jefferson Co., CO

237.01: 5/11/96 Worthington SF, Warren Co., NJ
237.02: 7/15/92 Rocky Mountain NP, CO
237.03: 6/6/97 Lewis Creek Trail, Custer Co., CO

237.04: 5/7/98 south of Globe, Gila Co., AZ
237.05: 5/30/97 Apex Park, Jefferson Co., CA
237.06: 6/23/99 Spikebuck Meadow, Humboldt Co., CA
237.07: 8/1/99 Eagar, Apache Co., AZ
237.08: 6/20/98 Descanso, San Diego Co., CA
237.09: 5/29/92 Oakridge, Sussex Co., NJ
237.10: 7/11/96 Troy, Morris Co., NJ

239.01: 8/11/95 Texas Point NWR, Jefferson Co., TX
239.02: 8/9/97 Jackson Slough, Sacramento Co., CA
239.03: 3/1/98 west of Octotillo, Imperial Co., CA
239.04: 8/9/97 Jackson Slough, Sacramento Co., CA
239.05: 11/10/89 Santa Ana NWR, Hidalgo Co., TX
239.06: 3/25/94 Stock Island, Monroe Co., FL
239.07: 10/29/96 La Gloria, Starr Co., TX
239.08: 10-19-99 Amistad Natl. Rec. Area, Val Verde Co., TX

241.01: 7/4/97 above Fairplay, Park Co., CO
241.02: 7/3/97 above Fairplay, Park Co., CO
241.03: 6/22/97 Burleigh Murray SP, San Mateo Co., CA
241.04: 6/23/99 Spikebuck Meadow, Humboldt Co., CA
241.05: 6/3/97 Como, Park Co., CO
241.06: 6/3/97 Como, Park Co., CO
241.07: 8/8/97 Jackson Slough, Sacramento Co., CA
241.08: 8/8/97 Jackson Slough, Sacramento Co., CA

243.01: 9/12/93 Devil's Punchbowl, Los Angeles Co., CA
243.02: 6/19/98 Ridge Route, Los Angeles Co., CA
243.02: inset. 9/11/93 Devil's Punchbowl, Los Angeles Co., CA
243.03: 10/19/93 north of Hargill, Hidalgo Co., TX
243.04: 4/28/98 "A" Mountain, Tucson, Pima Co., AZ
243.05: 10/16/99 Santa Ana NWR, Hidalgo Co., TX
243.06: 10/24/94 Peñitas, Hidalgo Co., TX
243.07: 10/24/94 La Lomita Mission, Hidalgo Co., TX
243.08: 10/28/96 La Lomita Mission, Hidalgo Co., TX

245.01: AMNH specimen. 6/19/66 Tamps. Mexico. Collected by H.A. Freeman
245.02: 10/20/93 Sabal Palms, Cameron Co., TX
245.03: 11/15/89 Sabal Palms, Cameron Co., TX
245.04: 8/16/96 McKinney, Collin Co., TX
245.05: 5/14/98 Aguirre Springs Natl. Rec. Area, Dona Ana Co., NM
245.06: 8/9/97 Jackson Slough, Sacramento Co., CA
245.07: 8/8/97 Jackson Slough, Sacramento Co., CA
245.08: 6/17/00 Canyon Venado, 6 miles east of Clines Corners, Torrance Co., NM. Photo
by Steven J. Cary

247.01: 9/19/93 Sentenac Canyon, San Diego Co., CA
247.02: 10/4/99 Tucson, Pima Co., AZ
247.03: 8/3/96 San Pedro Riparian Area, Cochise Co., AZ
247.04: same individual as 247.03
247.05: 9/17/93 Parker, Yuma Co., AZ
247.06: 9/18/93 Parker, Yuma Co., AZ
247.07: 8/3/99 Box Canyon, Santa Cruz Co., AZ
247.08: 8/8/89 Guadalupe Canyon, Cochise Co., AZ

249.01: 5/18/99 Mt. Ashland, Jackson Co., OR
249.02: 8/3/98 Green River Lakes Trailhead, Sublette Co., WY
249.03: 6/25/88 Rock Creek Park, El Paso Co., CO
249.04: 6/26/91 Cherry Creek Park, Arapahoe Co., CO
249.05: 7/29/99 Carr Canyon-Comfort Springs, Cochise Co., AZ
249.06: 8/7/89 Carr Canyon-Comfort Springs, Cochise Co., AZ
249.07: 8/3/99 Peña Blanca Canyon, Santa Cruz Co., AZ
249.08: 8/3/99 Peña Blanca Canyon, Santa Cruz Co., AZ
249.09: 9/5/97 Chipinque Park, Monterrey, Nuevo Leon, Mexico
249.10: same individual as 249.09

251.01: 8/14/89 Patagonia Lake SP, Santa Cruz Co., AZ
251.02: same individual as 251.01
251.03: 7/2/96 Hole-in-the-Mountain Preserve, Lincoln Co., MN
251.04: 7/30/94 Roan Mtn., Carter Co., TN
251.05: 6/29/99 Portal, Cochise Co., AZ
251.06: 9/19/97 Sentenac Canyon, San Diego Co., CA
251.07: 9/30/96 Savannah, GA
251.08: 9/29/96 Savannah, GA
251.09: Photo by Jim Brock
251.10: AMNH specimen. 11/4/66 Morelos, Mexico

253.01: 9/23/98 north of Del Rio, Val Verde Co., TX
253.02: 10/25/95 Laguna Atascosa NWR, Cameron Co., TX
253.03: 6/27/91 Coal Creek Canyon, Jefferson Co., CO
253.04: 8/3/98 Green River Lakes Trailhead, Sublette Co., WY
253.04: inset. 7/2/92 Apex Park, Jefferson Co., CO
253.05: 7/20/93 Garden Canyon, Cochise Co., AZ. Photo by Jim Brock
253.06: 7/28/99 Garden Canyon, Cochise Co., AZ
253.07: 6/8/96 Morristown, Morris Co., NJ
253.08: 6/22/96 Cross River, Westchester Co., NY
253.09: 9/12/93 Palmdale, Los Angeles Co., CA
253.10: 9/12/93 Palmdale, Los Angeles Co., CA

255.01: 5/31/97 above Tinytown, Jefferson Co., CO
255.02: 5/31/97 above Tinytown, Jefferson Co., CO

255.03: 5/5/98 Garden Canyon, Cochise Co., AZ
255.04: 6/5/97 Royal Gorge overlook, Fremont Co., CO
255.05: 6/7/97 Royal Gorge overlook, Fremont Co., CO
255.06: 10/19/99 Amistad Natl. Rec. Area, Val Verde Co., TX
255.07: 6/1/97 southeast of Aurora, Arapahoe Co., CO
255.07: top inset. 8/3/99 west of Peña Blanca Canyon, Santa Cruz Co., AZ
255.07: bottom inset. 5/10/98 Sandia Mtns., Bernallilo Co., NM
255.08: 6/1/97 southeast of Aurora, Arapahoe Co., CO
255.09: 5/14/98 Aguirre Springs Natl. Rec Area, Dona Ana Co., NM
255.10: 10/9/97 Saw Mill Canyon, Cochise Co., AZ
255.11: 10/9/97 Saw Mill Canyon, Cochise Co., AZ
255.12: 10/9/97 Saw Mill Canyon, Cochise Co., AZ

257.01: 7/21/98 Hurricane Ridge, Olympic NP, WA
257.02: 7/21/98 Hurricane Ridge, Olympic NP, WA
257.03: 7/19/97 Polebridge, Flathead Co., MT
257.04: 7/19/97 southeast of Polebridge, Flathead Co., MT
257.05: 7/22/95 Niagara Creek Rd., Tuolomne Co., CA
257.06: 8/2/97 north of Bridgeport, Mono Co., CA
257.07: 8/15/94 Point Reyes Station, Marin Co., CA. Photo by Bob Stewart
257.08: 8/8/99 Elkhart Park, near Pinedale, Sublette Co., WY
257.09: 8/5/98 Virginia Dale, Larimer Co., CO
257.10: 7/22/80 above Saddlebag Lake, Mono Co., CA. Posed photo by Jack N. Levy
257.11: 6/19/99 Cecileville, Siskiyou Co., CA
257.12: 6/18/98 Mt. Pinos, Ventura Co., CA

259.01: 7/7/97 Westridge Estates, Fort Collins, Larimer Co., CO
259.02: 6/12/98 Mt. Lindo, Jefferson Co., CO
259.03: 6/7/97 Penrose, Fremont Co., CO
259.04: 9/20/93 south of Julian, San Diego Co., CA
259.05: 9/20/93 south of Julian, San Diego Co., CA
259.06: Sept. 96 Mt. Palomar, San Diego Co., CA. Photo by Jack N. Levy
259.07: 6/19/99 Cecileville, Siskiyou Co., CA
259.08: 6/15/97 Mt Diablo summit, Contra Costa Co., CA
259.09: 6/2/96 Saw Mill Mtns., Los Angeles Co., CA
259.10: 6/11/98 Fairplay, Park Co., CO
259.11: 6/26/88 San Antonio Mtn., Rio Arriba Co., NM. Photo by Steven J. Cary
259.12: same individual as 259.10

261.01: 7/7/97 Westridge Estates, Fort Collins, Larimer Co., CO
261.02: 7/8/97 Westridge Estates, Fort Collins, Larimer Co., CO
261.03: 7/2/96 Five Ridge Preserve, Plymouth Co., IA
261.04: 6/30/96 Glacial Lakes SP, Pope Co., MN
261.05: 6/30/96 Glacial Lakes SP, Pope Co., MN
261.06: 7/1/96 Glacial Lakes SP, Pope Co., MN

261.07: 8/17/94 Sheyenne National Grassland, ND. Photo by Ann B. Swengel
261.08: 8/17/94 Sheyenne National Grassland, ND. Photo by Ann B. Swengel
261.09: 9/24/95 Wellfleet, Barnstable Co., MA
261.10: 6/2/96 Sandhills Gamelands, Scotland Co., NC
261.11: 7/25/90 Lakehurst, Ocean Co., NJ
261.12: 8/26/91 Lake Delancey, Marion Co., FL
263.01: 9/16/93 Palm Springs, Riverside Co., CA
263.02: 11/16/89 Bentsen-Rio Grande SP, Hidalgo Co., TX
263.03: 9/11/93 Palmdale, Los Angeles Co., CA
263.04: 9/19/93 Anza-Borrego SP, San Diego Co., CA
263.05: 10/26/93 Bentsen-Rio Grande SP, Hidalgo Co., TX
263.06: 7/29/94 Blowing Rock, Watauga Co., NC
263.07: 9/13/93 Santa Catalina Island, Los Angeles Co., CA
263.08: 10/25/98 Peñitas, Hidalgo Co., TX
263.09: 6/14/97 Tilden Park, Contra Costa Co., CA
263.10: 9/13/93 Santa Catalina Island, Los Angeles Co., CA
263.11: 10/23/95 Roma, Starr Co., TX
263.12: 10/17/99 Santa Ana NWR, Hidalgo Co., TX

265.01: 7/4/97 above Fairplay, Park Co., CO
265.02: 7/3/97 above Fairplay, Park Co., CO
265.03: 7/23/92 Wraith Falls, Yellowstone NP, WY
265.04: 7/19/98 Black Canyon, Okanogan Co., WA
265.04: inset. 8/8/99 Pinedale, Sublette Co., WY
265.05: 8/8/99 Pinedale, Sublette Co., WY
265.06: 7/20/95 Lee Vining, Mono Co., CA
265.07: 7/7/97 Fossil Creek, Fort Collins, Larimer Co., CO
265.08: 7/2/97 Apex Park, Jefferson Co., CO
265.09: 7/20/97 east of Glacier NP, MT
265.10: 7/30/99 west of Alpine, Apache Co., AZ
265.11: 7/30/99 west of Alpine, Apache Co., AZ
265.12: 7/30/99 west of Alpine, Apache Co., AZ

267.01: 5/24/99 west of Springerville, Apache Co., AZ
267.02: 5/24/99 west of Springerville, Apache Co., AZ
267.03: 5/24/99 west of Springerville, Apache Co., AZ
267.04: 5/2/98 Sycamore Canyon, Santa Cruz Co., AZ
267.05: 4/19/93 Post Canyon, Santa Cruz Co., AZ. Photo by Jim Brock
267.06: 9/12/93 Palmdale, Los Angeles Co., CA
267.07: 7/26/95 Stockton, San Joaquin Co., CA
267.08: 9/12/93 Palmdale, Los Angles Co., CA
267.09: 9/16/93 Morongo Valley, San Bernardino Co., CA
267.10: 7/30/98 Russell Lakes WMA, Saguache Co., CO
267.11: 8/3/95 Saddlebag Lake, Mono Co., CA
267.12: 8/3/97 above Tioga Lake, Mono Co., CA

269.01: 7/22/97 Waterton Park, Alberta
269.01: inset. 7/30/99 west of Alpine, Apache Co., AZ
269.02: same individual as 269.01
269.03: 7/30/99 west of Alpine, Apache Co., AZ
269.04: 7/4/96 Minnesota Valley NWR, Scott Co., MN
269.05: 6/27/91 Mt. Zion Jefferson Co., CO
269.06: 6/6/96 Sandhills Gamelands, Scotland Co., NC
269.07: 6/16/99 northeast of Crescent City, Del Norte Co., CA
269.08: 6/20/99 northeast of Crescent City, Del Norte Co., CA
269.09: same individual as 269.07
269.10: 6/16/99 northeast of Crescent City, Del Norte Co., CA
269.11: 10/20/93 McAllen, Hidalgo Co., TX
269.12: 10/23/95 Peñitas, Hidalgo Co., TX

271.01: 7/7/97 Westridge Estates, Fort Collins, Larimer Co., CO
271.02: 7/8/97 Westridge Estates, Fort Collins, Larimer Co., CO
271.03: 6/9/95 north of Wagoner, Wagoner Co., OK
271.04: 7/8/97 Apex Park, Jefferson Co., CO
271.05: 7/8/97 Apex Park, Jefferson Co., CO
271.06: 7/9/95 Kitchewan Preserve, Westchester Co., NY
271.07: 6/29/89 Lakehurst, Ocean Co., NJ
271.08: 6/29/89 Lakehurst, Ocean Co., NJ
271.09: 6/28/95 Lakehurst, Ocean Co., NJ
271.10: 7/2/97 Apex Park, Jefferson Co., CO
271.11: same individual as 271.10
271.12: 6/27/91 Mt. Zion, Jefferson Co., CO

273.01: 9/15/93 San Gabriel Mtns., Los Angeles Co., CA
273.01: inset. 9/15/93 San Gabriel Mtns., Los Angeles Co., CA
273.02: 9/15/93 San Gabriel Mtns., Los Angeles Co., CA
273.03: 9/15/93 San Gabriel Mtns., Low Angeles Co., CA
273.04: 7/16/95 Skyline Dr., Palo Alto, Santa Clara Co., CA
273.04: inset. 6/16/98 Descanso, San Diego Co., CA
273.05: 6/24/99 Sayler, Trinity Co., CA
273.06: 6/15/97 Mt. Diablo, Contra Costa Co., CA
273.07: 8/4/97 Big Smoky Valley, Nye Co., NV
273.08: 8/4/97 Big Smoky Valley, Nye Co., NV
273.09: 8/4/97 Big Smoky Valley, Nye Co., NV
273.10: 7/30/99 west of Alpine, Apache Co., AZ
273.11: 7/30/98 La Veta Pass, Huerfano Co., CO
273.12: 8/5/96 Carr Canyon-Comfort Springs, Cochise Co., AZ

275.01: 6/8/96 Morristown, Morris Co., NJ
275.02: 5/20/90 Chappaqua, Westchester Co., NY
275.03: 6/4/96 Jones Gap, Macon Co., NC

275.04: 7/8/99 Apex Park, Jefferson Co., CO
275.05: 7/8/97 Fort Collins, Larmier Co., CO
275.06: 8/5/96 Carr Canyon-Comfort Springs, Cochise Co., AZ
275.07: 6/22/97 Burleigh Murray SP, San Mateo Co., CA
275.08: 4/29/95 Dalton Canyon, Los Angeles Co., CA
275.09: 5/29/95 Dalton Canyon, Los Angeles Co., CA
275.10: 6/8/96 Morristown, Morris Co., NJ
275.11: 8/5/96 Carr Canyon-Comfort Springs, Cochise Co., AZ
275.12: 10/15/99 Landa Park, New Braunfels, Comal Co., TX

277.01: 6/6/97 Lewis Creek Trail, Custer Co., CO
277.02: 6/6/97 Lewis Creek Trail, Custer Co., CO
277.03: 5/13/98 Aguirre Springs Natl. Rec. Area, Dona Ana Co., NM
277.04: 5/15/98 Aguirre Springs Natl. Rec. Area, Dona Ana Co., NM
277.05: 7/29/99 Garden Canyon, Cochise Co., AZ
277.06: 8/2/96 Garden Canyon, Cochise Co., AZ
277.07: 5/25/99 Garden Canyon, Cochise Co., AZ
277.08: 5/26/99 Garden Canyon, Cochise Co., AZ

279.01: 10/9/97 Garden Canyon, Cochise Co., AZ
279.02: same individual as 279.01
279.03: 5/26/99 Garden Canyon, Cochise Co., AZ
279.04: 5/26/99 Garden Canyon, Cochise Co., AZ
279.05: 5/3/98 California Gulch, Santa Cruz Co., AZ
279.06: 5/3/98 California Gulch, Santa Cruz Co., AZ
279.07: 8/9/96 Box Canyon, Santa Cruz Co., AZ
279.08: 9/4/97 Sierra Picachos, Nuevo Leon, Mexico

281.01: 5/13/98 Aguirre Springs Natl. Rec. Area, Dona Ana Co.NM
281.02: same individual as 281.01
281.03: 5/12/98 Mills Canyon, Harding Co., NM
281.03: inset. 6/28/99 Portal, Cochise Co., AZ
281.04: 7/29/99 Garden Canyon, Cochise Co., AZ
281.05: 6/30/99 Marshall Gulch, Mt. Lemmon, Pima Co., AZ
281.06: 7/28/99 Garden Canyon, Cochise Co., AZ
281.07: 7/29/99 Garden Canyon, Cochise Co., AZ
281.08: 7/28/99 Garden Canyon, Cochise Co., AZ

283.01: 8/2/96 Garden Canyon, Cochise Co., AZ
283.02: 7/29/99 Garden Canyon, Cochise Co., AZ
283.03: 8/31/96 Southwestern Research Station, Cochise Co., AZ. Photo by Jim Brock
283.04: 8/2/99 Patagonia, Santa Cruz Co., AZ
283.05: 8/8/96 Sycamore Canyon, Santa Cruz Co., AZ
283.06: 8/8/96 Sycamore Canyon, Santa Cruz Co., AZ

283.07: 7/27/99 Peña Blanca Lake, Santa Cruz Co., AZ
283.08: 7/27/99 Peña Blanca Canyon, Santa Cruz Co., AZ

285.01: 6/12/98 Tinytown, Jefferson Co., CO
285.02: 7/5/97 Rabbit Ears Pass, Routt Co., CO
285.03: 2/27/00 Santa Ana NWR, Hidalgo Co., TX
285.04: 9/3/98 Sierra Picachos, Nuevo Leon, Mexico
285.05: 6/15/98 Montezuma, San Miguel Co., NM. Photo by Jane Ruffin
285.06: 6/15/98 Montezuma, San Miguel Co., NM. Photo by Jane Ruffin
285.07: 6/27/99 Carr Canyon-Comfort Springs, Cochise Co., AZ
285.08: 6/29/99 Barfoot Park, Cochise Co., AZ

287.01: 8/15/96 Duck Creek Park, Dallas Co., TX
287.02: 9/2/99 Sierra Picachos, Nuevo Leon, Mexico
287.03: 8/7/89 Lower Carr Canyon, Cochise Co., AZ
287.04: 7/28/99 Lower Carr Canyon, Cochise Co., AZ
287.05: 6/5/97 Penrose, Fremont Co., CO
287.06: 6/5/97 Penrose, Fremont Co., CO
287.07: 6/6/97 south of Florence, Fremont Co., CO
287.08: 6/7/97 Penrose, Fremont Co., CO

289.01: 8/8/97 Jackson Slough, Sacramento Co., CA
289.02: 8/8/97 Jackson Slough, Sacramento Co., CA
289.03: 9/9/79 Upper Newport Beach, Orange Co., CA. Photo by Philip Nordin
289.04: 10/15/99 New Braunfels, Comal Co., TX
289.05: 4/29/98 "A" Mtn., Tucson, Pima Co., AZ
289.06: 10/17/99 Santa Ana NWR, Hidalgo Co., TX
289.07: 10/25/98 Mission, Hidalgo Co., TX

291.01: 3/19/94 Gainesville, Alachua Co., FL
291.02: April, 1983 Kelbaker Rd., San Bernardino Co., CA. Photo by John Hafernik
291.03: 6/5/97 Penrose, Fremont Co., CO
291.04: 6/10/98 Penrose, Fremont Co., CO
291.05: adult emerged 8/2/99 from a pupa found west of Peña Blanca Lake, Santa Cruz
Co., AZ. Photo by Jim Brock
291.06: AMNH specimen. 9/9/61 west of Cameron, AZ
291.07: 10/12/97 Molino Basin, Pima Co., AZ
291.08: 10/4/99 Molino Basin, Pima Co., AZ

293.01: 10/10/97 mouth of Garden Canyon, Cochise Co., AZ
293.02: 9/19/93 Sentenac Canyon, San Diego Co., CA
293.03: 10/10/97 upper Garden Canyon, Cochise Co., AZ
293.04: 9/68 southwest of San Manuel, AZ. Photo by E.S. Ross
293.05: 10/20/99 Amistad Natl. Rec. Area, Val Verde Co., TX

293.06: 10/20/99 Amistad Natl. Rec. Area, Val Verde Co., TX
293.07: 10/19/99 Amistad Natl. Rec. Area, Val Verde Co., TX
293.08: AMNH specimen. 9/16/59 Del Rio, Val Verde Co., TX. Collected by H.A. Freeman
293.08: inset. Same individual as 293.08

295.01: 1/27/98 Hawaii, HI
295.02: 1/27/98 Hawaii, HI
295.03: 7/8/76 Volcano, HI. Photo by W.R. Mull
295.04: 7/8/76 Volcano, HI. Photo by W.R. Mull
295.05: 1/3/92 Guerrero, Mexico
295.06: 1/28/98 Bird Park, Hawaii Volcanoes NP, HI
295.07: 1/28/98 Bird Park, Hawaii Volcanoes NP, HI
295.08: 1/27/98 Ookala, Hawaii, HI
295.09: 1/27/98 Ookala, Hawaii, HI

Foodplant Scientific Names

Acacias (*Acacia*) (Leguminosae)
Acanthus family (Acanthaceae)
Adelias (*Adelia*) (Euphorbiaceae)
Agaves (*Agave*) (Agavaceae)
Alfalfa (*Medicago sativa*) (Leguminosae)
Alkali-mallows (*Sida*) (Malvaceae)
Anise (*Foeniculum vulgare*) (Umbelliferae)
Arctic willow (*Salix arctica*) (Salicaceae)
Ashes (*Fraxinus*) (Oleaceae)
Aspens (*Populus*) (Salicaceae)
Aster family (Compositae)
Balloon-vine (*Cardiospermum*) (Sapindaceae)
Bamboo muhly (*Muhlenbergia dumosa*) (Poaceae)
Barbados cherry (*Malpighia glabra*) (Malpighiaceae)
Beach aster (*Corethrogyne filaginifolia*) (Compositae)
Bearberry (*Arctostyphylos uva-ursi*) (Ericaceae)
Beardtongues (*Penstemon*) (Scrophulariaceae)
Beggar-ticks (*Desmodium*) (Leguminosae)
Bentgrasses (*Agrostis*) (Poaceae)
Bermuda grass (*Cynodon dactylon*) (Poaceae)
Big bluestem (*Andropogon gerardi*) (Poaceae)
Bindweed (*Convolvulus arvensis*) (Convolvulaceae)
Birches (*Betula*) (Betulaceae)
Bird's-foot trefoils (*Lotus*) (Leguminosae)

Bitter brush (*Purshia tridentata*) (Rosaceae)
Bleeding hearts (*Dicentra*) (Fumariaceae)
Blueberries (*Vaccinium*) (Ericaceae)
Blue grama grass (*Bouteloua gracilis*) (Poaceae)
Bluegrass (*Poa*) (Poaceae)
Bluestem grasses (*Andropogon*) (Poaceae)
Broad dock (*Rumex obtusifolius*) (Polygonaceae)
Buckwheats (*Eriogonum*) (Polygonaceae)
Bulb panic-grass (*Panicum bulbbosum*) (Poaceae)
Bullgrass (*Muhlenbergia emersleyi*) (Poaceae)
California buckwheat (*Eriogonum fasciculata*) (Polygonaceae)
Cannas (*Canna*) (Cannaceae)
Canyon dudleya (*Dudleya cymosa*) (Crassulaceae)
Canyon oak (*Quercus chrysolepis*) (Fagaceae)
Cassias (*Cassia*) (Leguminosae)
Ceanothus (*Ceanothus*) (Rhamnaceae)
Cherries (*Prunus*) (Rosaceae)
Chinese houses (*Collinsia*) (Scrophulariaceae)
Chinquapin (*Castanopsis*) (Fagaceae)
Chuperosa (*Beloperone californica*) (Acanthaceae)
Cinquefoils (*Potentilla*) (Rosaceae)
Citrus family (Rutaceae)
Clematis (*Clematis*) (Ranunculaceae)

Cliff rose (*Cowania mexicana*) (Roasaceae)

Clovers (*Trifolium*) (Leguminosae)

Common beardgrass (*Bothriochloa barbinodis*) (Poaceae)

Cottonwoods (*Populus*) (Salicaceae)

Crabgrass (*Digitaria*) (Poaceae)

Crown vetch (*Coronilla varia*) (Leguminosae)

Crucifers (Cruciferae)

Curled dock (*Rumex crispus*) (Polygonaceae)

Currants (*Ribes*) (Grossulariaceae)

Deerweed (*Lotus scoparius*) (Leguminosae)

Desert agave (*Agave deserti*) (Agavaceae)

Desert aster (*Machaeranthera tortifolia*) (Compositae)

Desert hackberry (*Celtis pallida*) (Ulmaceae)

Desert scrub oak (*Quercus turbinella*) (Fagaceae)

Desert sunflower (*Viguiera deltoides* var. *parishii*) (Compositae)

Docks (*Rumex*) (Polygonaceae)

Dwarf bilberry (*Vaccinium caespitosum*) (Ericaceae)

Dwarf mistletoes (*Arceuthobium*) (Viscaceae)

Elm family (Ulmaceae)

Elongated buckwheat (*Eriogonum elongatum*) (Polygonaceae)

Emory oak (*Quercus emoryi*) (Fagaceae)

Englemann's spruce (*Pinus engelmannii*) (Pinaceae)

False indigo (*Amorpha californica*) (Leguminosae)

Fern acacia (*Acacia angustissima*) (Leguminosae)

Figs (*Ficus*) (Moraceae)

Flat-topped white aster (*Aster umbellatus*) (Compositae)

Flax (*Linum*) (Linaceae)

Fleabanes (*Erigeron*) (Compositae)

Fogfruits (*Lippia*) (Verbenaceae)

Gambel's oak (*Quercus gambelii*) (Fagaceae)

Giant cedar (*Thuja plicata*) (Cupressaceae)

Giant reed (*Phragmites australis*) (Poaceae)

Golden banners (*Thermopsis*) (Leguminosae)

Gooseberries (*Ribes*) (Grossulariaceae)

Gray oak (*Quercus grisea*) (Fagaceae)

Gumbo-limbo (*Bursera simaruba*) (Burseraceae)

Hackberries (*Celtis*) (Ulmaceae)

Hairy tubetongue (*Siphonoglossa pilosella*) (Acanthaceae)

Heath family (Ericaceae)

Honey mesquite(*Prosopis glandulosa*) (Leguminosae)

Hops (*Humulus*) (Moraceae)

Horkelias (*Horkelia*) (Rosacea)

Horsenettles (*Solanum*) (Solanaceae)

Incense cedar (*Calocedrus decurrens*) (Cupressaceae)

Indian paintbrushes (*Castilleja*) (Scrophulariaceae)

James' buckwheat (*Eriogonum jamesii*) (Polygonaceae)

Junipers (*Juniperus*) (Cupressaceae)

Kidneywoods (*Eysenardtia*) (Leguminosae)

Knotweed family (Polygonaceae)

Knotweeds (*Polygonum*) (Polygonaceae)

Koa (*Acacia koa*) (Leguminosae)

Lambsquarters (*Chenopodium*) (Chenopodiaceae)

Lecheguilla (*Agave lecheguilla*) (Agavaceae)

Legumes (Leguminosae)

Lignum vitae (*Guaiacum*) (Zygophyllaceae)

Lime prickly-ash (*Zanthoxylum fagara*)

Locusts (*Robinia*) (Leguminosae)

Lomatiums (*Lomatium*) (Umbelliferae)

Loose buckwheat (*Eriogonum effusum*) (Polygonaceae)

Lotuses (*Lotus*) (Leguminosae)
Louseworts (*Pedicularis*) (Scrophulari-
aceae)
Lupines (*Lupinus*) (Leguminosae)
Mallow family (Malvaceae)
Mallows (*Malva*) (Malvaceae)
Mamaki (*Pipturus albidus*) (Urticaceae)
Marifolium buckwheat (*Eriogonum
marifolium*) (Polygonaceae)
Mesquites (*Prosopis*) (Leguminosae)
Milkweeds (*Asclepias*) (Asclepiadaceae)
Milkweed vines (*Sarcostemma*) (Ascle-
piadaceae)
Mistflowers (*Eupatorium*) (Composi-
tae)
Mistletoes (*Phoradendron*) (Loran-
thaceae)
Monkeyflowers (*Mimulus*) (Scrophu-
lariaceae)
Mountain avens (*Dryas octopetala*)
(Rosaceae)
Mountain heather (*Cassiope merten-
siana*) (Ericaceae)
Mountain mahogany (*Cercocarpus mon-
tanus*) (Rosaceae)
Naked buckwheat (*Eriogonum nudum*)
(Polygonaceae)
Nettles (*Urtica*) (Urticaceae)
Noseburns (*Tragia*) (Euphorbiaceae)
Oaks (*Quercus*) (Fagaceae)
Obtuse panic-grass (*Panicum obtusum*)
(Poaceae)
Panic-grasses (*Panicum*) (Poaceae)
Palmer's agave (*Agave palmeri*)
(Agavaceae)
Parry's agave (*Agave parryi*)
(Agavaceae)
Parsley family (Umbelliferae)
Passionvines (*Passiflora*) (Passiflo-
raceae)
Pea family (Leguminosae)
Pearly everlastings (*Anaphalis*) (Com-
positae)
Pigweeds (*Amaranthus*) (Amaran-
thaceae)
Pines (*Pinus*) (Pinaceae)

Pipevines (*Aristolochia*) (Aristoloci-
aceae)
Ponderosa pine (*Pinus ponderosa*)
(Pinaceae)
Poplars (*Populus*) (Salicaceae)
Prairie violet (*Viola pedatifida*) (Vio-
laceae)
Privas (*Priva*) (Verbenaceae)
Punctured bract (*Oxytheca perfoliata*)
(Polygonaceae)
Purple top (*Tridens flavus*) (Poaceae)
Rabbitbrush (*Chrysothamnus*) (Com-
positae)
Racemose buckwheat (*Eriogonum race-
mosum*) (Polygonaceae)
Ratanys (*Kramerias*) (Krameriaceae)
Rattleweeds (*Astragalus*) (Legumi-
nosae)
Redberry (*Rhamnus crocea*) (Rham-
naceae)
Redbud (*Cercis canadensis*) (Lehgumi-
nosae)
Rock cresses (*Arabis*) (Cruciferae)
Rock-primroses (*Androsace*) (Primu-
laceae)
Ruellias (*Ruellia*) (Acanthaceae)
Saltbushes (*Atriplex*) (Chenopodi-
aceae)
Saltgrasses (*Distichlis spicata* and *D. stric-
ta*) (Poaceae)
Sargent cypress (*Cupressus sargentii*)
(Cupressaceae)
Sassafras (*Sassafras albidum*) (Lau-
raceae)
Screwbean mesquite (*Prosopis pub-
sescens*) (Leguminosae)
Sedges (*Carex*) (Cyperaceae)
Seepwillow (*Baccharis glutinosa*) (Com-
positae)
Shaggy tuft (*Stendandrium barbatum*)
(Acanthaceae)
Shindagger (*Agave schottii*) (Agavaceae)
Shooting-stars (*Dodecatheon*) (Primu-
laceae)
Side-oats grama (*Bouteloua
curtipendula*) (Poaceae)

Silverleafs (*Leucophyllum*) (Scrophulariaceae)
Silver-leaved lotus (*Lotus argophyllus*) (Leguminosae)
Snapdragons (*Antirrhinum*) (Scrophulariaceae)
Snowberries (*Symphoricarpus*) (Caprifoliaceae)
Snow willow (*Salix nivalis*) (Salicaceae)
Sorrels (*Oxyria*) (Polygonaceae)
Southwestern bernardia (*Bernardia myricifolia*) (Euphorbiaceae)
Spicebush (*Lindera benzoin*) (Lauraceae)
Spotted saxifrage (*Saxifraga bronchialis*) (Saxifragaceae)
Stonecrops (*Sedum*) (Crassulaceae)
Sulphur buckwheat (*Eriogonum umbellatum*) (Polygonaceae)
Sunflowers (*Helianthus*) (Compositae)
Sweetbush (*Bebbia juncea*) (Compositae)
Tecate cypress (*Cupressus forbesii*) (Cupressaceae)
Texas beargrass (*Nolina texana*) (Agavaceae)
Texas ebony (*Pithecellobium ebano*) (Leguminosae)
Texas persimmon (*Diospyros texana*) (Ebenaceae)
Thistles (*Cirsium*) (Compositae)

Timothy (*Phleum pratense*) (Poaceae)
Toothworts (*Dentaria*) (Cruciferae)
Tulip tree (*Liriodendron*) (Magnoliaceae)
Turpentine-broom (*Thamnosma montana*) (Rutaceae)
Twinberry honeysuckle (*Lonicera involucrata*) (Caprifoliaceae)
Utah agave (*Agave utahensis*) (Agavaceae)
Vetches (*Vicia*) (Leguminosae)
Violets (*Viola*) (Violaceae)
Water dock (*Rumex orbiculatus*) (Polygonaceae)
Western soapberry (*Sapindus drummondii*) (Sapindaceae)
Wheatgrasses (*Agropyron*) (Poaceae)
Wild cherries (*Prunus*) (Rosaceae)
Wild indigo (*Baptisia tinctoria*) (Leguminosae)
Wild pansy (*Viola pedunculata*) (Violaceae)
Wild parsnips (*Lomatium*) (Umbelliferae)
Wild plums (*Prunus*) (Rosaceae)
Wild tarragon (*Artemisia dracunculoides*) (Compositae)
Willows (*Salix*) (Salicaceae)
Wintergreens (*Gaultheria*) (Ericaceae)
Wright's buckwheat (*Eriogonum wrightii*) (Polygonaceae)
Yuccas (*Yucca*) (Agavaceae)

Organizations Concerned with Butterflies

The North American Butterfly Association (NABA) promotes public enjoyment, awareness, and conservation of butterflies and all aspects of recreational, nonconsumptive butterflying, including field identification, butterfly gardening, and photography. NABA publishes a full-color magazine, *American Butterflies*; a newsletter, *Butterfly Gardening News*; has chapters throughout North America; and runs the annual NABA Fourth of July Butterfly Counts. These one-day counts, held mainly in June and July (centered on the Fourth of July period), are growing rapidly. Currently almost 400 counts are conducted each year, at sites across North America. They are a fun-filled way to help monitor butterfly populations, to learn about butterfly identification, and to meet other butterfliers.

NABA
4 Delaware Rd.
Morristown, NJ 07960
Web site: http://www.naba.org

The Lepidopterists' Society is an international organization devoted to the scientific study of all lepidoptera. The Society publishes the *Journal of the Lepidopterists' Society* as well as the *News of the Lepidopterists Society*.

Lepidopterists' Society
1608 Presidio Way
Roseville, CA 95661
Web site: http://www.furman.edu

The Xerces Society is an international organization dedicated to the global protection of habitats for all invertebrates, including butterflies. The Society publishes *Wings*.

Xerces Society
4828 Southeast Hawthorne Blvd
Portland, OR 97215

The Nature Conservancy buys land to preserve natural diversity and owns more than 1,300 preserves —the largest private system of nature sanctuaries in the world.

The Nature Conservancy
1815 Lynn St.
Arlington, VA 22209
Web site: http://www.tnc.org

Glossary

ANTENNAL CLUB The thickened end of the antenna. Variable Checkerspot, page 171, photo 2, usually has luminous golden antennal clubs.

APEX The tip of the wing. California Sister, page 193, photo 8, has a large orange spot at the FW apex.

APICAL Referring to the area at the tip of the wing.

BASAL Referring to the area near the base of the wing, adjacent to the body. Great Purple Hairstreak, page 85, photo 1, has red basal spots.

BORDER A band of color along a wing margin. Red Admiral, page 189, photo 2, has a red-orange HW border.

CELL The central area of the wing, bounded on all sides by veins. Common Buckeye, page 191, photo 2, has two orange bars in each FW cell.

CELL-END BAR A bar of color along the vein bounding the outer edge of the cell, contrasting with the ground color of the wing. Gray Marble, page 57, photo 10, has a small, black FW cell-end bar; 'Desert' Pearly Marble, page 57, photo 4, has a very thick, black FW cell-end bar. Soapberry Hairstreak, page 87, photo 1, has a white HW cell-end bar.

COSTAL MARGIN (COSTA) The leading edge of the FW. Gold-costa Skipper, page 219, photos 3 and 4, has a gold-colored costal margin.

CROWN The top of the head. Gray Hairstreak, page 103, photos 2 and 4, has an orange-red crown.

DISK The central area of the wing, including, but larger than, the cell. Red-disked Alpine, page 209, photo 7, has a reddish-brown FW disk.

DISTAL Away from the body.

DORSAL Toward the back. The dorsal wing surface is the upper surface.

FOREWINGS (FWs) The leading pair of wings. Sara Orangetip, page 59, photos 2–9, has bright orange patches on its FWs but no orange on the HWs.

FRINGES Scales that stick out from the edges of the wing membranes. Funereal Duskywing, page 235, photos 4 and 5, has a white HW fringe.

FRONS The area in the front of the head between the eyes.

GROUND COLOR The basic or background color of the wing.

HINDWINGS (HWs) The rear pair of wings. Red Rim, page 197, photos 1 and 2, has pink or red bands on its HWs but not its FWs.

HYALINE Glassy and translucent.

LEADING MARGIN The margin of the HW that is on top as the butterfly sits upright. Female Taxiles Skipper, page 275, photo 11, has a partly white HW leading margin.

MARGIN Any of the wing edges, but usually referring to the outer margin.

MARGINAL LINES, BANDS, or SPOTS A series of lines, bands, or spots along the outer margin. Coral Hairstreak, page 87, photo 2, has red HW marginal spots.

MEDIAN About one-half of the way out the wing, passing the distal end of the cell. Red Admiral, page 189, photo 2, has a red-orange median band on the FW above. Giant Swallowtail, page 45, photo 7, has, on the HW below, a black median band enclosing some blue and red spots.

OUTER MARGIN The wing edge farthest from the body, it is more or less perpendicular to the ground as the butterfly sits upright. Ruddy Copper, page 81, photo 2, has a thin black line along the outer margins of the FWs and HWs.

POSTMEDIAN The wing regions farther from the body than (distal to) the median region. Silver-banded Hairstreak, page 95, photo 5, has a white postmedian line on its HW.

POSTMEDIAN BAND A series of spots or lines in the postmedian region of the wing, either darker or paler than the ground color. Dusky-blue Groundstreak, page 101, photo 4, has a postmedian band that is partially red.

STIGMA A structure, usually black and visible, on the FWs of most grass-skippers, formed by specialized scales. Male Sachem, page 263, photo 9, has a prominent black stigma in the center of the FW.

SUBAPICAL Referring to the region just before the tip of the wing. Golden Banded-Skipper, page 223, photo 2, in addition to having a striking golden-yellow band in the middle of the FW, has a small subapical white patch on the FW.

SUBMARGINAL Referring to the region just before the area at the outside edge of the wing. Carolina Satyr, page 207, photo 5, has submarginal eyespots on the HW below.

VENTRAL Toward the belly. The ventral wing surface is the lower wing surface.

VEINS A series of visibly raised structural elements on the wings which serve as wing struts. The branching pattern of the veins is important in lepidopteran systematics. Monarch, page 215, photos 2 and 4, has the veins covered with black scales.

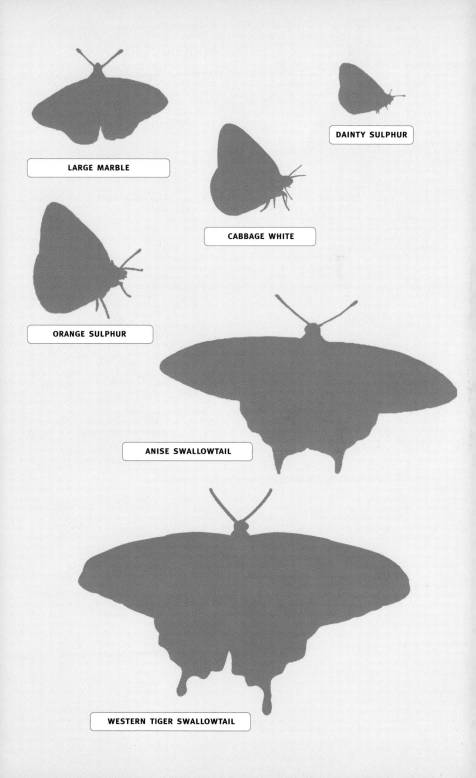

LARGE MARBLE

DAINTY SULPHUR

CABBAGE WHITE

ORANGE SULPHUR

ANISE SWALLOWTAIL

WESTERN TIGER SWALLOWTAIL

AMERICAN SNOUT

FATAL METALMARK

COMMON RINGLET

COMMON WOOD-NYMPH

MONARCH

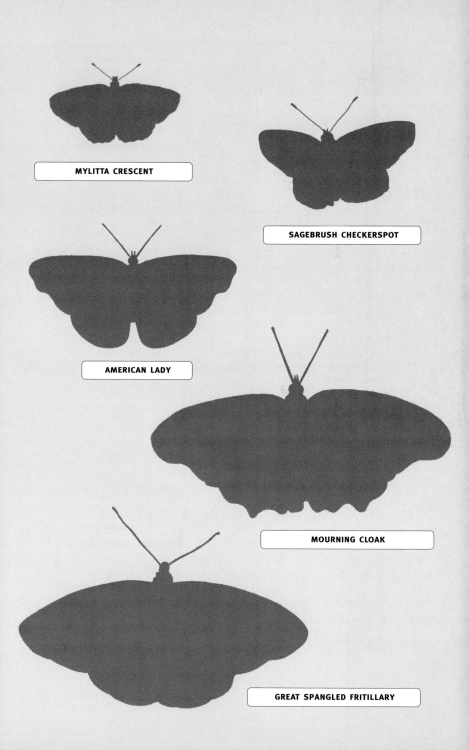

MYLITTA CRESCENT

SAGEBRUSH CHECKERSPOT

AMERICAN LADY

MOURNING CLOAK

GREAT SPANGLED FRITILLARY

PURPLISH COPPER

SPRING AZURE

BOISDUVAL'S BLUE

BRAMBLE HAIRSTREAK

CALIFORNIA HAIRSTREAK

GRAY HAIRSTREAK

BLUE COPPER

COLORADO HAIRSTREAK

COMMON BRANDED SKIPPER

COMMON SOOTYWING

SILVER-SPOTTED SKIPPER

NORTHERN CLOUDYWING

Bibliography

Acorn, J. 1993. *The Butterflies of Alberta*. Edmonton: Lone Pine Publishing.

Austin, G.T. 1985. "Lowland Riparian Butterflies of the Great Basin and Associated Areas." *J. Res. Lep.* 24:117–131.

Austin, G.T. 1986. "Nevada Butterflies, Preliminary checklist and distribution." *J. Lep. Soc.* 39(2):95–118.

Austin, G.T. 1987. "Nevada Populations of *Polites sabuleti* and the Descriptions of Three New Subspecies. *Bull. Allyn Mus.* 109:1–24.

Austin, G.T. 1992. "*Ceryonis pegala* in the Great Basin: New Subspecies and Biogeography." *Bull. Allyn Museum* 135:1–59.

Austin, G.T. 1998. "Definitive Destination: Spring Mountains, Nevada." *American Butterflies*, Winter: 4–11.

Austin, G.T. "Definitive Destination: Great Basins NP, Nevada." (in prep).

Austin, G.T. and Austin, A.T. 1980 (1981). "Butterflies of Clark County Nevada." *J. Res. on the Lep.* 19:163.

Austin, G.T. and Smith, M.J. 1999. Revision of the *Thessalia leanira* complex. In Emmel, T.C., ed., *Systematics of Western North American Butterflies*. Gainesville, Florida: Mariposa Press.

Bird, C.D., et.al. 1995. *Alberta Butterflies*. Edmonton: The Provincial Mus. of Alberta

Bailowitz, R.A. and Brock, J.P. 1991. *Butterflies of Southeastern Arizona*. Tucson: Sonoran Arthropod Studies, Inc.

Bailowitz, R.A. and Upson, S. 1998. *Fort Huachuca, Arizona Butterfly List*. Sierra Vista, AZ: Dept. of the Army,.

Brock, J. 1993. "Definitive Destination: Garden Canyon, Huachuca Mountains, Arizona." *American Butterflies*, Aug. 4–10.

Brock, J. 1996. *Checklist of Butterflies and Skippers of Southeastern Arizona*. Tucson: privately printed.

Brock, J. 1999. "Definitive Destination: The White Mountains of Arizona." *American Butterflies*, Winter: 4–15.

Brown, F.M., Eff, D., and Rotger, B. 1957. *Colorado Butterflies*. Denver: Denver Mus. Nat. Hist.

Brown, J.W., Real, H.G., and Faulkner, D.K. *Butterflies of Baja California*. Beverly Hills, Cal.: Lep. Res. Foundantion.

Burns, J.M. 1964. *Evolution of Skipper Butterflies in the Genus Erynnis.* Univ. Cal. Publ. Ent. 37:1–216.

Cary, S.J. 1994. "Gray Ranch: Fire and Butterflies in Southwestern New Mexico." *Holarctic Lep.* 1:65–68.

Cary, S.J. 1996. "Definitive Destination: Sitting Bull Falls, Guadalupe Mountains, New Mexico." *American Butterflies,* Summer: 4–13.

Cary, S. J. and Holland, R. 1992. "New Mexico Butterflies: Checklist, Distribution and Conservation." *J. Res. Lep.* 31:57–82.

Cary, S.J. and Stanford, Ray E. 1995. "A new subspecies of *Ochlodes yuma* with notes on life history and historical biogeography." *Bull. Allyn Mus.* 140:1–7.

Christensen, J.R. 1981. *A Field Guide to the Butterflies of the Pacific Northwest.* Moscow, Idaho: University Press of Idaho.

Comstock, J.A. 1927. *Butterflies of California.* Privately published: Los Angeles.

Davenport, K. 1983. "Geographic Distribution and Checklist of the Butterflies of Kern County, California." *J. Lep. Soc.* 37:46–69.

Dornfeld. 1980. *The Butterflies of Oregon.* Forest Grove, Ore.: Timber Press.

Durden. 1982. "Butterflies of the Austin, Texas Vicinity." *J. Lep. Soc.* 36:1–17.

Elrod, M.J. 1906. *The Butterflies of Montana.* University of Montana Bulletin No. 30. Biological Series No. 10:1–174

Ely, C.A., Schwilling, M.D. and Rolfs, M.E. 1986. *An Annotated List of the Butterflies of Kansas.* Fort Hays Studies; Third Series (Science) No. 7. Hays, Kansas: Fort Hays Studies Committee.

Emmel, T.C., ed. 1999. *Systematics of Western North American Butterflies.* Gainesville: Mariposa Press.

Emmel, T.C. and Emmel, J.F. 1973. *The Butterflies of Southern California.* Natural History Museum of Los Angeles County. Science Series 26:1–148.

Emmel, T.C., Minno, M.C. and Drummond, B.A. 1992. *Florissant Butterflies: A Guide to the Fossil and Present-day Species of Central Colorado.*

Ferris, C.D. 1971. *An Annotated Checklist of the Rhopalocera (Butterflies) of Wyoming.* University of Wyoming, Laramie, Agricultural Experiment Station. Science Monograph 23:1–75.

Ferris, C.D. 1993. "Reassessment of the *Colias alexandra* Group, the Legume-Feeding Species, and Preliminary Cladistic Analysis of the North American *Colias.*" *Bull.Allyn Mus.* 138:1–91.

Ferris, C.D. 1989. "A New Species of *Colias* from Utah." *Bull. Allyn Mus.* 128:1–11.

Ferris, C.D. and Brown, F., eds. 1981. *Butterflies of the Rocky Mountain States.* Norman: University of Oklahoma Press.

Fleishman, E., Austin, G.T., and Murphy, D.D. "Natural History and Biogeography of the Butterflies of the Toiyabe Range, Nevada." *Holarctic Lep.* 4:1–18.

Gaskin, D.E. 1999. "Butterflies of the Upper Frio-Sabinal Region, Central Texas, and Distribution of Faunal Elements Across the Edwards Plateau. J. Lep. Soc. 52:229–261.

Garth, J.S. 1944. "Butterflies of the Organ Pipe Cactus National Monument, Arizona." *Ent. News* 55:120–121.

Garth, J.S. 1950. *Butterflies of Grand Canyon National Park.* Grand Canyon National History Assn., Bulletin 11:1–52.

Garth, J.S. and Tilden, J.W. 1963. "Yosemite Butterflies." *J. Res. on Lep.* 2:1–96.

Garth, J.S. and Tilden, J.W. 1986. *California Butterflies.* Berkeley: U. Cal. Press.

Geiger, H. and Shapiro, A.M. 1986. "Electrophorectic evidence for speciation within the nominal species." *Anthocharis sara* Lucas (Pieridae). *J. Res. Lep.* 25:15–24.

Gill, R. and Gill. E. 1997. *Butterflies of Prescott and the Central Arizona Highlands: Provisional Checklist.* Prescott: Privately printed.

Glassberg. J. 1999. *Butterflies through Binoculars: The East.* New York: Oxford University Press.

Grimble, D.G., Beckwith, R.C., and Hammond, P.C. 1992. "A Survey of the Lepidoptera Fauna from the Blue Mountain of Eastern Oregon." *J. Res. Lep.* 31:83–102.

Gunder, J.D. 1930. "The Butterflies of Los Angeles County, California." *Bulletin of the Southern California Academy of Sciences* 29:1–59.

Hafernik, J.E. 1995. "Butterflies by the Bay: Winners and Losers in San Francisco's Urban Jungle." *American Butterflies,* Fall: 4–11.

Hardesty, R.L. and Groothuis, D.R. 1993. "Butterflies of the Laramie Mountains, Wyoming." *J. Res. Lep.* 32:107–123.

Hartjes, G.J. 1980. *Checklist of the Butterflies of Nevada.* Carson City: Nevada State Museum.

Herlan, P.J. 1962. *A List of the Butterflies of the Carson Range, Nevada.* Carson City: Nevada State Museum.

Hinchliff, J. 1994. *An Atlas of Oregon Butterflies.* Corvallis: Oregon State University Bookstore.

Hinchliff, J. 1996. *An Atlas of Washington Butterflies.* Corvallis: Oregon State University Bookstore.

Hinchliff, J. 1984. "Butterflies of Two Northwest New Mexico Mountains." *J.Lep.Soc.* 38:220–234.

Hinchliff, J. 1995. "Distribution of selected *Anthocharis, Euchloe, and Pontia* in New Mexico, Texas, Chihuahua and Sonora." *J. Lep. Soc.* 49:119–135.

Holland, R. 1974. "Butterflies of Six Central New Mexico Mountains, with Notes on *Callophrys (Sandia) macfarlandi.*" *J. Lep. Soc.* 28:38–52.

Holland, R. and Carey, S.J. 1996. "Butterflies of the Jemez Mountains of Northern New Mexico." *J. Lep. Soc.* 50:61–79.

Hooper, R.R. 1973. *Butterflies of Saskatchewan.* Regina: Museum of Nat. Hist.

Hooper, R.R. 1986. "Revised Checklist of Saskatchewan Butterflies." *Blue Jay* 44:154–163.

Howe, W.H. 1975. *The Butterflies of North America.* Garden City, NY.: Doubleday and Co.

Johnson, K. 1972 (1973). "The butterflies of Nebraska." *J. Res on the Lep.* 11:1–64.

Jones, J.R.J.L. 1951. "An Annotated Check-list of the Macrolepidoptera of British Columbia." *Ent. Soc. British Columbia, Occasional Papers,* 1:1–148.

Karges, J. 1994. *Checklist of Butterflies of Tarrant County*. Fort Worth, Texas: Privately printed.

Kendall, R.O. and McGuire, W.W. 1984. "Some New and Rare Records of Lepidoptera Found in Texas." *Bull. Allyn Mus.* 86:1–50.

Klassen, P.; Westwood, A.R. Preston, W.B., and McKillop, W.B. 1989. *The Butterflies of Manitoba*. Winnipeg: Manitoba Museum of Man and Nature.

Kohler, S. 1980. "Checklist of Montana Butterflies." *J. Lep. Soc.* 34:1–19.

Layberry, R.A., Hall, P.W., and Lafontaine, J.D. 1998. *The Butterflies of Canada*. Toronto: University of Toronto Press.

Leighton, B.V. 1946. "The Butterflies of Washington." *University of Washington Publications in Biology* 9:47–53.

Levy, J.N. 1998. "Definitive Destination: Anza–Borrego Desert State Park, California." *American Butterflies*, Spring:4–15.

Llorente-Bousquets, J.E.; Oñate-Ocaña, L; Luis-Martínez, A.; Vargas-Fernández, I. 1997. *Papilionidae y Pieridae de México: Distribución Geográfica E Ilustración*. Universidad Nacional Autónoma de México. México D.F.

MacNeill, C.D. 1964. *The Skippers of the Genus Hesperia in Western North America, with Special Reference to California*. University Cal. Publications in Ent.: 35.

Marrone, G.M. 1994. "Checklist of South Dakota Butterflies." *J. Lep. Soc.* 48:228–247.

Mattoni, R. 1988 (1989). "The *Euphilotes battoides* Complex: Recognition of a Species and Description of a New Subspecies." J. Res. Lep. 27:173–185.

Mattoni, R. 1990. *Butterflies of Greater Los Angeles*. Beverly Hills: Lepidoptera Res. Foundation, Inc.

Miller, S. 1985. "Butterflies of the California Channel Islands." *J. Res. Lep.* 23:282–296.

Mori, J. and Coyle, R. 1996. "Definitive Destination: Sonora Pass and Dardanelles, California." *American Butterflies*, Summer: 12–19.

Neck, R. 1996. *A Field Guide to Butterflies of Texas*. Houston: Gulf Publishing.

Neill, W.A. and Hepburn, D.J. 1976. *Butterflies Afield in the Pacific Northwest*. Seattle: Pacific Search.

Nelson, J. 1979. "A Preliminary Checklist of the Skippers and Butterflies of Oklahoma." *Proceedings of the Oklahoma Academy of Sciences* 59:41–46.

Opler, P.A. and Langston, R.L. 1968. "A Distributional Analysis of the Butterflies of Contra Costa County, California." *J Lep. Soc.* 22:89–107.

Orsak, L. J. 1977. *The Butterflies of Orange County, California*. Irvine: University of Cal.

Parmesan, C. 1995. "Traversing the Checkerboard of *Euphydryas* Identification." *American Butterflies*, Winter: 12–22.

Puckering, D.L. and Post, R.L. 1960. *Butterflies of North Dakota*. Dept. of Agricultural Ent., North Dakota Agricultural College.

Pyle, R.M. 1974. *Watching Washington Butterflies*. Trailside Series. Seattle Audubon Soc.

Pyle, R.M. 1981. *The Audubon Society Field Guide to North American Butterflies*. New York: Chanticleer Press.

Rosche, R.C. 1986. *Nebraska Butterfly Distribution Maps*. Chadron, Neb: Published by the author.

Royer, R.A. 1988. *Butterflies of North Dakota*. Science Monograph No. 1. Minto, N.D.: Minto State University.

Shapiro, A.M. 1975. "The Butterfly Fauna of the Sacramento Valley, California." *J. Res. on the Lep*. 13:73–82, 115–222, 137–148.

Shapiro, A.M. 1986. "Montane Insular Butterfly Geography: Fauna of Ball Mountain, Siskiyou County, California." *Great Basin Naturalist* 46:336–347.

Shapiro, A.M., Palm, C.A. and Wcislo, K.L. 1979 (1981) "The Ecology and Biogeography of the Butterflies of the Trinity Alps and Mount Eddy, Northern California." *J. Res. on the Lep*. 18:69–152.

Sims, S.R. and Shapiro, A.M. 1983. "Seasonal Phenology of *Battus philenor* in California." *J. Lep. Soc*. 37:281–288.

Smith, M. J. and Brock, J.P. 1988. "A Review of the *Thessalia leanira* Complex in the Southwestern United States with a Description of Two New Subspecies of *Thessalia fulvia*." *Bull. Allyn Mus*. 118:1–21.

Sourakov, A. 1995. "Systematics, Evolutionary Biology and Population Genetics of the *Cercyonis pegala* group." *Holarctic Lep*. 2:1–20.

Sperling, F. 1996. "'Black' Swallowtails of North America: Zelicaon, Machaon, and Zen Koan." *American Butterflies*, Spring:10–17.

Stanford, R.E. and Opler, P.A. 1993. *Atlas of Western USA Butterflies, Including Adjacent parts of Canada and Mexico*. Fort Collins: Privately published.

Steiner, J. 1988. *Butterflies of the San Francisco Bay Region. A County Species List*. San Francisco Bay Wildlife Society. Publication No. 1.

Sutton, , P.L. and Sutton, C. 1999. *How to Spot Butterflies*. Boston: Houghton-Mifflin.

Threatful, D.L. 1989. "A list of the butterflies and skippers of Mount Revelstoke and Glacier National Parks, British Columbia, Canada. *J. Res. Lep*. 27:213–221.

Tidwell, K.B. and Callaghan, C.J. 1972. "A Checklist of Utah Butterflies and Skippers." *Mid. Cont. Lep. Ser*. 4(51):1–16.

Tilden, J.W. 1965. *Butterflies of the San Francisco Bay Region*. Berkeley: University of Cal. Press.

Tilden, J.W. and Huntzinger, David H. 1977. "The Butterflies of Crater Lake National Park, Oregon." *J. of Res. on the Lep*. 16:176–192.

Tilden, J.W. and Smith, A.C. 1986. *A Field Guide to Western Butterflies*. Boston: Houghton-Mifflin.

Toliver, M.E. and Holland, R. 1977. *Distribution of Butterflies in New Mexico*. Albuquerque: Privately published by the authors.

Tyler, H.A. 1975. *The Swallowtail Butterflies of North America*. Happy Camp, Cal.: Naturegraph Publishers.

Underhill, J.E. and Harcombe, A. 1970. "Moths and Butterflies of Manning Park, British Columbia." *Parks Branch* 1:1–9.

Warren, A. 1995. "Definitive Destination: Apex Park, Front Range, Colorado." *American Butterflies*, Spring: 4–11.

Warren, A. 1998. "Greater Fritillaries—Lesser Frustration: A Guide to the Species at Rabbit Ears Pass." *American Butterflies,* Spring: 16–27.

Wauer, R. 1999. "Butterfly Checklist—Big Bend National Park, Texas." Victoria, Texas: Privately printed draft.

Wright, D. 1995. "The American Azures: Our Blue Heaven." *American Butterflies,* Spring: 20–30.

Index

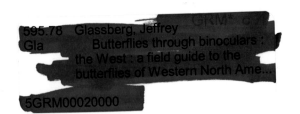